1984

University of St. Francis
GEN 001.642 S851
Sebesta, Robert W.
VAX 11 :

W9-ADR-874

VAX 11

Structured
Assembly
Language
Programming

The Benjamin/Cummings Series in Computing and Information Sciences

G. Booch
Software Engineering with Ada (1983)

H. L. Capron, B. K. Williams
Computers and Data Processing, Second Edition (1984)

D. M. Etter
Structured FORTRAN 77 for Engineers and Scientists (1983)

D. M. Etter
Problem Solving with Structured Fortran 77 (1984)

P. Linz
Programming Concepts and Problem Solving: An Introduction to Computer Science Using PASCAL (1983)

W. Savitch
Pascal Programming: An Introduction to Computer Science (1984)

R. Sebesta
Structured Assembly Language Programming for the VAX II (1984)

R. Sebesta
Structured Assembly Language Programming for the PDP-11 (1984)

M. Sobell
A Practical Guide to UNIX (1984)

M. Sobell
A Practical Guide to XENIX (1984)

VAX 11

Structured
Assembly
Language
Programming

Robert W. Sebesta
University of Colorado
at Colorado Springs

LIBRARY
College of St. Francis
JOLIET, ILL.

The Benjamin/Cummings Publishing Company

Menlo Park, California · Reading, Massachusetts
London · Amsterdam · Don Mills, Ontario · Sydney

To Joanne

Sponsoring Editor: Alan Apt
Production Coordinator: Susan Harrington
Copyeditor: Polly Koch
Cover and Chapter Opener Designer: Gary Head
Artist: John Foster

VAX 11 is a registered trademark of the Digital Equipment Corporation.

Copyright © 1984 by The Benjamin/Cummings Publishing Company, Inc.

All rights reserved. No part of this publication may be reproduced, stored in a
retrieval system, or transmitted, in any form or by any means, electronic,
mechanical, photocopying, recording, or otherwise, without the prior written
permission of the publisher. Printed in the United States of America. Published
simultaneously in Canada.

Library of Congress Cataloging in Publication Data
Sebesta, Robert W.
    VAX 11: structured assembly language programming.
    Includes index.
    1. VAX-11 (Computer)—Programming.   2. Assembler language (Computer
program language)   3. Structured programming.   I. Title.
QA76.8.V37S4   1984   001.64′2   83-14316
ISBN 0-8053-7001-3

    BCDEFGHIJ-DO -8987654

The Benjamin/Cummings Publishing Company, Inc.
2727 Sand Hill Road
Menlo Park, California 94025

001.643
8851

16-22-84 Gulrelia $ 25,23

Preface

Why VAX Assembly Language? : : : : : : : : : : : : : : : :

The VAX series of superminicomputers is particularly suited to the study of assembly language. First, the VAX architecture represents that of many other computers. The VAX instruction set includes many of the features of the instruction sets of earlier computers, such as the PDP-11 and IBM 360. The assembly language of any of these would be easy to learn for VAX assembly programmers.

The second advantage of studying VAX assembly language lies in the complexity of the VAX architecture. The VAX has a rich set of instructions and addressing modes that make programming it in assembly language far easier than on simpler computers. The obvious price is the increased difficulty in learning the assembly language. However, the orthogonality of the VAX instruction set goes a long way toward balancing the increase in complexity with a measure of simplicity. For example, indexing can be learned as a programming concept and then used to specify nearly any operand on nearly any instruction.

Features of the Book :

Structured Assembly Language Programming for the VAX 11 has been designed to be one of the most readable and useful books available for the classroom, and is the most comprehensive book yet available for professional reference.

Structured Programming

Structured programming is stressed throughout the book. The program design method of creating pseudocode solutions and then translating the pseudocode to assembly language is described in detail and used in all

112, 446

example programs. This method, which is clearly a top-down approach, yields far more readable programs that sacrifice very little in efficiency.

Complete Program Examples

Nearly all example programs are stand-alone systems. Macroinstructions for terminal input and output of three integer types and character strings are used for nearly all example program input and output. Appendix D is a listing of the input/output package we use. It includes a macro for dumping registers and memory.

Student Aids

Every chapter has a summary, lists of new terms and new instructions, and a problem set. Nearly all of the problem sets have both programming and nonprogramming exercises.

Instructional Software

Both the TOYCOM simulator and VAX input/output package are available on magnetic tape for a minimal fee. Those interested should contact the author at the University of Colorado at Colorado Springs (College of Engineering) or their local Benjamin/Cummings Representative.

VAX/VMS Debugger

An entire chapter is devoted to the VAX/VMS Debugger. That chapter describes the most useful debugger commands and includes the complete text of a debugging session.

Complete Instruction Coverage

We have included a description of all of the user-accessible VAX instructions. (Instructors who feel that the entire instruction set cannot be effectively covered in a course can choose sections according to their tastes.)

RMS

The book has a complete chapter on RMS, the VMS subsystem that the VAX high-level languages use for input and output.

Using the Book in the Classroom : : : : : : : : : : : : : : :

This book is intended for the standard course on assembly language programming, described in the ACM 1978 Curriculum Recommendations as

CS 3. We assume that the reader has had at least one course in high-level language programming.

The first chapter describes the architecture and assembly language of a model computer named TOYCOM. TOYCOM is a decimal machine with a dozen instructions, a 100 word memory, and a single accumulator register. As was mentioned earlier, interactive simulation of TOYCOM is available so that students can write and debug TOYCOM assembly language programs. Chapter 1 is meant to provide a somewhat simple introduction to machine organization and assembly language. For more advanced or knowledgable classes—or if it is more desirable for students to get right to the VAX—this chapter can be left out with very little impact on the rest of the course using this book.

Chapter 2 covers the required material on binary and hexadecimal numbers, the addition and subtraction operations on binary and hexadecimal numbers, number base conversions, and twos complement notation. This chapter can obviously be skipped for classes that have already had this material.

The meat of the book is in Chapters 3–11, in which we discuss in depth the VAX architecture and instructions, coding control structures, the VMS debugger, indexing, indirect addressing, character manipulation, subprograms, and macros . . . in short, the main substance of VAX assembly language programming. Chapters 12–15 complete the discussion of the VAX instruction set and the RMS input/output system.

Acknowledgments :

Textbooks are created over a long period of time by a large number of people. Many of those people deserve mention here.

Ken Klingenstein and his fine staff at the computer center of the University of Colorado at Colorado Springs provided generous amounts of disk space and computer time for editing and text formatting, lots of printer ribbons, and good advice. The manuscript was reviewed by Theodore Bashkow of Columbia University, M. Faiman of the University of Illinois, George Rice of De Anza College, Arthur Gill of the University of California at Berkeley, Henry Leitner of Harvard University (Aiken Computation Laboratory), and Robert Muller of Boston University. All contributed to the quality of this book. Special thanks go to Richie L. Lary for his technical review. Richie was one of the designers of the VAX instruction set, and his advice added immensely to the accuracy, completeness, and quality of this work.

The students of my 1982 Fall assembly language course at UCCS deserve special recognition for their perseverence. They had to wade through an early draft of the book, dodging both typographical and other kinds of errors, to learn to program the VAX. Many (though not all) of their comments were both correct and constructive.

John Noon and Alan Apt of Benjamin/Cummings encouraged and advised me throughout the project, and Susan Harrington, the book's production coordinator, deserves thanks for her extensive work on the project, especially as the contact between me and the compositor. Jim Kraushaar deserves recognition on two counts: He was responsible for several of the key concepts in Chapter 1, and he was instrumental in getting me started in the business of writing textbooks.

Finally, I thank my wife Joanne for her patience during my endless hours of composing and editing at my terminal.

Robert Sebesta
Colorado Springs, Colorado

Brief Contents

Complete Contents

1

A SIMPLE
COMPUTER

The goal of this text is to take the reader from his or her basic skills of programming in a high-level language to a detailed knowledge of VAX series machine organization and assembly language. In particular, our goal is to give the student a high level of assembly language programming skill.

It is reasonable to ask why anyone should invest the considerable time and effort necessary to learn to program a computer in assembly language, especially when virtually all computers are sold with reasonably good system software, nearly always including compilers or interpreters for modern, well-structured, high-level languages.

The answer is as follows. First, although most system software is written in high-level languages, programming is still done in assembly language in a number of computer applications. The lowest level input/output drivers, along with a varied collection of other modules, are often written in assembly language because writing them requires direct access to machine capabilities. Such software is often written in special-purpose languages that are oriented to a particular machine. To use such languages effectively requires the kind of experience you receive from studying the assembly language of that machine.

The innermost loops of numerical analysis programs that do large numbers of arithmetic operations are sometimes written, for optimum efficiency, in assembly language. There are also many *real-time applications*, or applications that require very fast responses to external stimuli and precisely timed processes, that can only be done in assembly language.

The second reason to study assembly language is that it leads the student to a knowledge and understanding of machine organization that is otherwise very difficult to attain. This fundamental awareness of how computers work provides the basis for becoming better programmers in high-level languages.

The VAX-11 superminicomputers are very modern, incorporating and enhancing most of the positive features of previous generations of computer architecture. (In this book we will refer to one of the VAX-11 series simply as a VAX.) They are therefore highly complex machines. The VAX assembly language is, accordingly, also quite complicated. Because of this complexity, we will first discuss basic machine organization and assembly language programming on a very simple computer model. Our simplified computer, named TOYCOM (an acronym for *toy computer*), exists only as a simulation program written in a high-level language. However, you can still learn a great deal about the nature of computer operation and assembly-level programming by studying TOYCOM.

1.1   The Overall Structure of TOYCOM : : : : : : : : :

TOYCOM was invented solely as a pedagogic tool. It has no other purpose. To start with a real, contemporary computer like the VAX and end up with TOYCOM requires that we discard the vast majority of inconvenient details and complications. TOYCOM, however, retains most of the flavor, some of the power, and much of the ability to frustrate its users to be found in its more complex relatives.

To begin our discussion of TOYCOM, consider its system diagram, shown in Figure 1.1.

TOYCOM consists of memory, input, *central processing unit* (CPU), and output. In Figure 1.1, the solid lines indicate data transfer and the dashed lines control signals. The CPU contains the *instruction register* (IR), the *program counter* (PC), and the *accumulator register* (ACC). Registers are special high-speed memory locations, or storage cells. They are the same size as the memory storage cells, which are discussed below. The ACC is an operand source and a result destination for many of TOYCOM's instructions. It is, in a real sense, where most things happen. The IR and the PC are more difficult to explain, so we will allow them to remain enigmas for now.

TOYCOM's memory consists of a sequence of storage cells called words. Each word can store a signed four-digit decimal number. Therefore, the range of values that TOYCOM can store is -9999 to $+9999$. Because decimal points cannot be stored, fractional numbers cannot be stored. If TOYCOM were a real machine, this would be a severe restriction and would render it unsalable. But TOYCOM is neither real nor for sale. TOYCOM's memory can store 100 words, addressed by the integers 0, 1, . . . , 99.

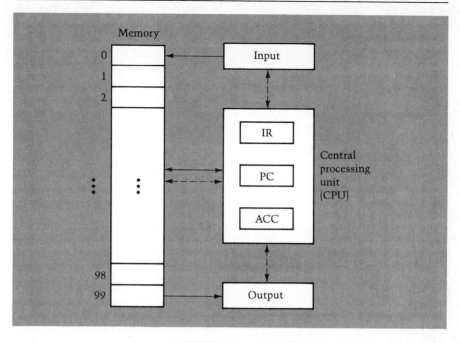

Figure 1.1 TOYCOM system diagram

The input and output components of TOYCOM are actually combined into one device, a terminal. The input is via a keyboard, and the output can be via either a video display or a printer.

1.2 *Machine Language Instructions* : : : : : : : : : : :

It may seem surprising, but the repertoire of instructions that computers understand is a relatively small set of fairly simple operations. Most high-level programming language statements are too complex to be executed directly by a computer, so programs written in high-level languages must be translated to machine language before they can be executed.

Machine instructions nearly always consist of two logically separate parts: the *operation code*, usually abbreviated as "op code," and the *operand* (or operands). The op code is nothing more than a numeric name that identifies the instruction. The operand often refers to one or more memory addresses. In the simplest sense, the op code tells the machine what to do, and the operand tells it what to do it to.

Although TOYCOM is far less complex than contemporary computers, its instructions are quite similar in structure. But because it was designed to be simple, TOYCOM's instruction set is unusually small, and its instructions are all quite simple.

1.3   The Stored Program Concept : : : : : : : : : : : : :

Before looking at TOYCOM's instructions, we need to see how it and other computers handle programs. TOYCOM is a *stored program* computer, as are most digital computers: It can execute only instructions that are in its memory. A typical procedure for a stored program computer is to read an entire program into its memory and then start executing its instructions. The alternative is for the computer to read a single instruction from an input device, execute that instruction, and then repeat the read/execute sequence until it encounters a STOP instruction. One compelling reason to use the stored program procedure is that machines can execute instructions much faster than input devices can provide them. It takes far less time to fetch a word from memory than from an input device, so it is natural to put a program into memory for execution. Another good reason for storing programs in memory is the problem of handling the instruction loops that occur in nearly all programs. If instructions were executed one at a time as they were brought into the machine, loops would have to be fed in once for each trip through the loop. One primitive machine of the early 1950s, called the programmable card punch, actually used this cumbersome procedure. If the instructions are stored in memory, however, loops are no problem at all. The machine just needs a mechanism for executing instructions that are not sequential.

While the stored program concept is the basis for all digital computers, it is also the cause of a fairly common programming problem in certain programming languages. Because instructions and data are stored in the same memory and the machine cannot differentiate between the two, programs can operate on themselves. That is, if a machine can do an operation that changes a memory location containing a data value, it can do the same operation to a location containing an instruction. This is a useful and powerful capability, but a dangerous one: Programs may change themselves when the programs' author did not intend them to! This accidental modification or destruction of instructions was once a major cause of programming errors. While most early machine languages required the use of *self-modifying programs,* the practice was later discouraged by those who sought to improve programming practices. Many contemporary programming languages such as Pascal have safeguards against such problems. Lower-level languages, such as the VAX assembly language, often do not. However, they do provide capabilities so that intentional code modification is unnecessary.

1.4   The TOYCOM Instruction Set : : : : : : : : : : : : :

The op codes in TOYCOM instructions are all two-digit decimal numbers stored in the first two digits of memory words. The operands of TOYCOM's instructions are nearly always memory addresses, which are also two-digit decimal numbers. TOYCOM uses the last two digits for the operand addresses. In general, then, instructions appear as AABB, where AA is an op code and BB is the memory address operand.

While a program in a high-level language consists of a list of statements, a TOYCOM machine language program is a list of four-digit decimal numbers. Because TOYCOM is a stored program computer, it cannot determine whether a given word is an instruction or a data value. Any word that is encountered during execution is considered an instruction. The sequence control functions of the machine and the machine code determine which words are encountered during execution.

We need some means of getting data in and out of TOYCOM. The IN instruction, op code 07, causes TOYCOM to print or display a question mark on the terminal and then wait for the user to type a number. After the number is typed and the carriage return pressed, TOYCOM places the number in its memory at the address specified in the instruction's operand. For example, the instruction 0742 would cause TOYCOM to get a number from the keyboard and place it at memory location 42. Note that the action of placing a value in a memory location, whether by an IN instruction or some other means, always destroys the former value in that location.

The OUT instruction, op code 08, prints or displays a number from memory in the format "OUTPUT = number." For example, if memory location 22 contained the value 427, the instruction

    0822

would print

    OUTPUT= 427

Notice that neither of the input/output instructions affects the ACC. Also, printing the contents of a location does not affect that location.

The other two move instructions move data between the ACC and memory. The LOAD instruction, op code 01, moves a copy of a number from a specified memory location to the ACC. The LOAD action does not affect the memory location from which the value is gotten. A copy of that value is moved.

The STORE instruction, op code 02, does the opposite of the LOAD instruction. It moves a copy of the contents of the ACC to a specified memory location. Once again, the source location—in this case, the ACC—is not affected. Examples of the LOAD and STORE operations are shown in Figure 1.2.

The TOYCOM arithmetic instructions are simple and very similar to one another. They all use the ACC as the implied location of the first operand. The second operand is always the specified memory location. The result of the operation is always placed in the ACC, destroying the first operand. As an example, consider the following ADD instruction (the ADD instruction's op code is 03):

    0327

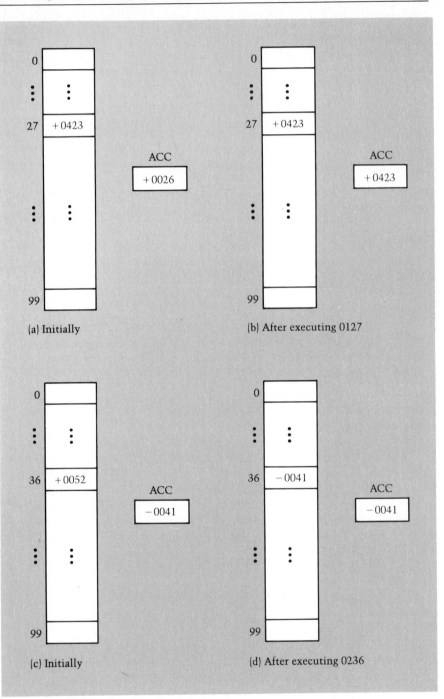

Figure 1.2 Examples of LOAD and STORE operations

This instruction adds the contents of location 27 to the ACC. In a high-level language, the operation can be written:

ACC := ACC + C(27)

In this case, and throughout this book, the notation C(address) indicates the contents of that location. Thus, C(27) means the contents of location 27.

The other arithmetic instructions operate in exactly the same manner. Their op codes are 04 for SUBTRACT, 05 for MULTIPLY, and 06 for DIVIDE. TOYCOM's STOP instruction, with an op code of 0, is somewhat peculiar in that it requires no operand; it can be written as 0000, or simply as 0. There are several other TOYCOM instructions, but we will delay explaining them until after we have written a simple program using the instructions already discussed.

The first problem we will solve with a TOYCOM machine language program is that of adding two numbers.

· ·

Example 1.1

: Problem Statement

In: Two numbers.
Out: The sum of the input.

There are two separate tasks in creating a program that solves a problem. First, an algorithmic solution must be created. Then, that algorithm must be translated to the language to be used on the computer. Although it is often tempting to solve the problem directly in the programming language, it is good to keep these as separate tasks.

This algorithmic solution to the problem is best developed and stated in a sort of structured English called a *pseudocode*. Pseudocodes consist of a combination of control statements, often borrowed from some contemporary high-level language, and noncontrol statements in an abbreviated form of English. They are never implemented on real computers; their sole purpose is to express solutions to programming problems in a somewhat simplified form. Because we do not need the pseudocode control statements for Example 1.1, we will discuss them later in the book.

:· Pseudocode Solution

Get input (two integers)
Compute SUM
Print SUM
End-of-program

The simplicity of our pseudocode solution reflects the simplicity of the problem, but this almost trivial example still shows the flavor and style of noncontrol statements.

It may appear that the TOYCOM machine language program can be written easily with the instruction set already described, which is actually only part of TOYCOM's repertoire. The "get" and "print" statements are simply IN and OUT instructions, respectively. The "compute" operation also looks as though it could be handled with what we have. One somewhat subtle operation will be the assignment of storage locations to variables used in a program; we will have to decide which machine memory location will be associated with which variable in the pseudocode. In this case, the pseudocode does not even specify the identifiers, or names, of the required variables for input data. We will name these two variables FIRST and SECOND. The only other required variable, for the sum, will be named SUM, as it was in the pseudocode.

TOYCOM programs are placed in memory, starting at address 0, where execution always begins. In the absence of any instructions beyond those we have discussed, instructions are executed sequentially, so that the second instruction to be executed is at address 1, and so forth until a STOP instruction is encountered.

Suppose we assign the variables' locations in the high end of memory (the area with the highest numbered addresses), so that they will be as far as possible from the instructions. For this problem, we will let FIRST be assigned to location 99, SECOND to location 98, and SUM to location 97. Note that the machine need not know the variable names the pseudocode uses. Helpful as they are for humans, TOYCOM has no use for them in a machine language program.

We are now ready to tackle the actual coding of the Example 1.1 program.

The first two instructions of the program will be input instructions, which correspond to the first line of the pseudocode.

```
0799
0798
```

These instructions move the first input number into location 99 and the second into location 98.

The next step is to translate into machine language the pseudocode line "compute SUM." The arithmetic operations in such common expressions are often binary—that is, involving two operands. Further, both of the operands are in memory. If we compare this situation with the arithmetic instructions in TOYCOM, we see that the primary difference lies in the source of the first operand. The machine instructions always require that the first operand be in the ACC. Therefore, we must first get the value from FIRST into the ACC. After the addition operation, the only required action that remains is to put the result back into memory at location SUM. This operation is essential in any language. Our instructions, then, are:

```
0199
0398
0297
```

This sequence of three instructions is typical of all assignments that involve only one arithmetic operation.

The remaining operations in the program are the printing of the input and the result, followed by the STOP instruction. The following is the complete TOYCOM *machine language* program, with comments attached to each instruction to explain its purpose.

:: *TOYCOM Machine Code Solution*

Memory Address	Instruction	Comments
0	0799	Read the first input into FIRST
1	0798	Read the next input into SECOND
2	0199	Load FIRST into the ACC
3	0398	Add SECOND to the ACC
4	0297	Store the ACC at SUM
5	0899	Output FIRST
6	0898	Output SECOND
7	0897	Output SUM
8	0000	STOP

We have numbered the instructions of the program to show their addresses in memory.

. . . .

1.5 Machine Operation: The Fetch-Execute Cycle

We can now take a closer look at TOYCOM's execution of programs, and explain the purposes of the PC and the IR in the process.

TOYCOM, like other computers, executes programs cyclically. Each *fetch–execute cycle* consists of two basic steps, instruction fetch and instruction execution, although each step actually includes a number of secondary tasks. The PC is used to point to the memory location of the next instruction to be executed.

During the fetch step of a cycle, the machine gets the address of the next instruction from the PC. That particular instruction is then moved from memory to the IR in the CPU. Immediately after the instruction is fetched, the PC is incremented. The execution step of a cycle is the actual execution of the instruction in the IR.

We explained earlier that TOYCOM programs are always stored beginning at memory location 0. Therefore, the initial value of the PC must be zero. As long as the program has no loops or other decisions, the PC simply steps through the program, with the machine busily fetching and executing instructions, until a STOP instruction is found.

1.6   Decision-Making with TOYCOM   : : : : : : : : : :

Most programming languages include statements that allow the computer to decide between two choices of statement or statement group to execute next. Even our pseudocode includes the *selection construct*. This is accomplished in machine language by allowing the machine to change the value of the PC conditionally. Different machines allow different sorts of conditions to be tested.

TOYCOM, as might be expected, tests only the simplest conditions: whether the value in the ACC is greater than zero or whether it is equal to zero. Instructions that change the PC are generally called "branch" or "jump" instructions. In TOYCOM, we have the BRANCH GREATER-THAN-ZERO (op code 10) and the BRANCH ZERO (op code 11).

The BRANCH GREATER-THAN-ZERO instruction causes the CPU to move the instruction's operand from the IR into the PC if the ACC is greater than zero. The BRANCH ZERO does the same, but only if the current value of the ACC is zero.

If the tested condition is not met at the time a *conditional branch* instruction is executed, the instruction has no effect whatever, and the next instruction to be executed comes from the next location in memory. For example, suppose the following instruction was at location 14 of memory.

      1042

When the instruction was executed, it would test the ACC. If the ACC was greater than zero, TOYCOM would move 42 from the IR into the PC, so that the next instruction to be executed would come from location 42. If, on the other hand, the ACC's value was either zero or negative, the instruction would do nothing at all, and the next instruction would come from location 15.

Although it is possible to write programs in well-structured high-level languages without using unconditional branches, all machine languages require *unconditional branches* because of their lack of sufficiently powerful control instructions. TOYCOM has an unconditional branch instruction, called BRANCH, with an op code of 09. It causes TOYCOM to move its operand from the IR to the PC, regardless of the value in the ACC, or, for that matter, any other location.

We now have seen all of TOYCOM's instructions, which are summarized below:

Op Code	Meaning
00	Stop
01	Load (ACC <- memory)
02	Store (ACC -> memory)
03	Add
04	Subtract
05	Multiply
06	Divide
07	In
08	Out
09	Branch
10	Branch greater-than-zero
11	Branch zero

We will now complete our discussion of pseudocode.

There are three fundamental control structures in which all programs can be expressed: sequence, selection, and pretest logical loop. Our pseudocode embodies these in the forms shown below:

Sequence	*Selection*
| ```
statement-1
statement-2
  •
  •
  •
statement-n
``` | ```
IF condition
    THEN statement(s)
    [ELSE statement(s)]
ENDIF
``` |

Pretest Logical Loop

```
WHILE condition DO
    statement(s)
END-DO
```

If you have written programs in Pascal, these forms should be familiar except for the closing keywords on the IF and WHILE constructs, ENDIF and END-DO. These are used to show the ends of these structures clearly. The square brackets around the ELSE clause indicate that it is optional. One other difference between our IF and WHILE and those of Pascal is that no BEGINs are included.

A pseudocode description of TOYCOM's operation is as follows:

Initialize PC to zero
Fetch an instruction into the IR
Increment PC
WHILE the op code in the IR <> 0 DO
    Execute the instruction in the IR
    Fetch an instruction into the IR
    Increment PC
END-DO
End-of-program

The pseudocode shows how the PC is incremented during each cycle. (Note that <> denotes "not equal to.")

We are now equipped to write a program that requires decision-making. The following is a simple example using branching.

. . . .

Example 1.2

⋮   *Problem Statement*

    In: Two numbers.
    Out: The larger of the input numbers.

⋮•   *Pseudocode Solution*

Get input (two integers, named FIRST & SECOND)
IF FIRST > SECOND
    THEN print FIRST
    ELSE print SECOND
ENDIF
End-of-program

The first step in writing this program in machine language is to assign storage locations to the variables used in the pseudocode. Let FIRST be at 99 and SECOND be at 98, as in the last example.

The first part of the program is straightforward: 0799, 0798, as in Example 1.1. It is the IF construct that creates our first problem. What machine code can we use for this condition?

Note that if the THEN clause instructions are to precede the ELSE clause instructions, which is surely the most natural order, we must use a conditional branch to get around the THEN clause. To do this, we must invert the logic of the condition before the conditional branch. In this case, we must branch IF FIRST <= SECOND to the ELSE clause and then follow the conditional branch with the THEN clause instructions.

But how do we code the conditional FIRST < = SECOND? The central problem is that the pseudocode allows conditions in IF constructs that compare two unrestricted expressions, while TOYCOM machine language allows only two comparisons, both of which have a second quantity of zero. We can compare one value with zero, and that's all.

In this problem, we must compare two memory locations using the less-than-or-equal-to comparator (< =). We must algebraically manipulate the inequality in the IF statement to get zero on the left side. The machine code must compute the resulting right side in the ACC and then use the BRANCH GREATER-THAN-ZERO and BRANCH ZERO instructions. The question, or inequality, in *logical inverse* form, that we need to code is FIRST < = SECOND. Subtracting FIRST from both sides yields 0 < = SECOND – FIRST. So the machine code must compute the quantity SECOND – FIRST in the ACC.

The THEN clause code that follows the conditional branch instruction associated with a pseudocode IF must always have an unconditional branch to avoid the ELSE clause code.

:: *TOYCOM Machine Code Solution*

Memory Address	Instruction	Comment
0	0799	Input FIRST
1	0798	Input SECOND
2	0198	Load SECOND in the ACC
3	0499	Subtract FIRST from the ACC
4	1008	Branch to print SECOND if ACC > 0
5	1108	Branch to print SECOND if ACC = 0
6	0899	Then print FIRST
7	0909	And branch to the STOP
8	0898	Else print SECOND
9	0000	And STOP

The instructions at locations 2 and 3 get the quantity SECOND – FIRST into the ACC. Then the BRANCH GREATER-THAN-ZERO at 4 puts 08 into the PC if the ACC is greater than zero (which would mean that SECOND is greater than FIRST). If the ACC is greater than zero, the next instruction is the one in location 8, which prints SECOND. If the BRANCH GREATER-THAN-ZERO fails, then the PC is incremented by one, and the next instruction is the one in location 5, which tests the ACC for zero. If the ACC is zero, 08 is placed in the PC, so that in this case SECOND is also printed. If the BRANCH ZERO instruction fails, the

PC is incremented by one, which causes FIRST to be printed. In either case, the larger of the two numbers is printed, which is the objective of this problem solution. Note that while the two conditional branch instructions are needed here, a single test for greater-than-or-equal-to is possible in many other languages. Furthermore, when the two input values are equal, either value could be printed, so the second conditional branch is unnecessary. This is, however, an oversight in the pseudocode, because it specifies to print FIRST only if FIRST > SECOND.

We will present a more thorough discussion of coding conditions in Section 1.9.

1.7   The Disadvantages of Machine Language Programming

Although we need to understand something of machine language to understand assembly language, computers have rarely been programmed in machine language since the earliest days of computer history.

First, it is very difficult for human readers to peruse a list of numbers and attach significance to them. There are enough problems in programming without using such a cryptic method of expression. Moreover, in real machines, the problem of readability is much worse than it is in TOYCOM. Although TOYCOM uses decimal (base ten) numbers of relatively short length to designate instructions, most real machines use larger instructions, which are rarely stored in decimal. Most are actually stored in binary (base two), but are represented in either octal (base eight) or hexadecimal (base 16) in output. In either case, machine language programs for real computers are far more difficult to read than those for TOYCOM, which are bad enough.

Second, branch instructions in machine language must use actual machine addresses as operands. In Example 1.2, there was a conditional branch to an output instruction at location 7. You can easily imagine a five-page program with a dozen or more branch instructions. Suppose that you add an instruction near the beginning of the program. All the branch destinations are now wrong, since the addresses of all of the instructions are larger by one. Similarly, deleting one or more instructions in a machine language program requires modification of all branch instructions that refer to locations after the change. Your experience with high-level language programming should have made you aware of the large number of changes required in debugging programs—changes that make programming in machine language highly impractical.

1.8 TOYCOM Assembly Language : : : : : : : : : : : :

The two disadvantages of machine language programming just described were the primary motivation for the invention in the early 1950s of a class of languages at a slightly higher level than machine languages, called assembly languages.

Assembly languages use nonnumeric op codes, called mnemonics, and symbolic addresses. Furthermore, symbolic labels can be attached to instructions, which can then be used as operands on branch instructions. Meaningful names can thus be used for op codes, instruction addresses, and data operands. In addition, a number of other features have been added that make programming easier.

1.8.1 Translators

We stated before that machines understand only their own machine languages. For each language in which programs are written by humans, the machine must have either a translation program to convert programs from that language into the machine's language or an interpretive program for that language.

Programs in high-level languages are not always translated into machine code. When they are, the translation program is called a *compiler*. Sometimes, however, programs in high-level languages are either translated into some new, intermediate-level language, or, occasionally, not translated at all. These systems are called interpretive and pure interpretive systems, respectively. In either system, programs are interpreted, which means that instead of translating the whole program at once, the machine determines the meaning of one statement at a time, and then carries out the required operations. This interpretive technique can be used with either the original program or a translation of it in an intermediate-level language. In either case, the decoded version is not kept, so that if a statement is in a loop, it is decoded every time it is executed. The program that decodes and causes the subsequent execution of instructions is called an *interpreter* or *pure interpreter*. Interpretive systems execute programs more slowly than compiled systems, because they require repetitive statement translations. Interpretive systems may be used instead of compilers, which generate machine code, because they are easier to create and take much less memory space. It is also relatively easy for interpretive systems to provide useful debugging information when programs encounter error conditions.

In the case of assembly language, the translator is called an *assembler*. Every computer has its own machine language, and nearly all have an assembler program available that allows users to write programs in the assembly language of the machine. The user then submits his or her assembly language program to the assembler program, which translates it to machine code. The machine code is then executed. Because assembly languages are primarily symbolic forms of machine languages, every machine with a different machine language has a different assembly language—and because the purpose of assembly languages is to provide symbolic op codes and addresses, programming in assembly language is sometimes called symbolic coding. We will discuss the assembler for the VAX in Chapter 3.

The operations of compilers, interpreters, pure interpreters, and assemblers are shown in Figure 1.3.

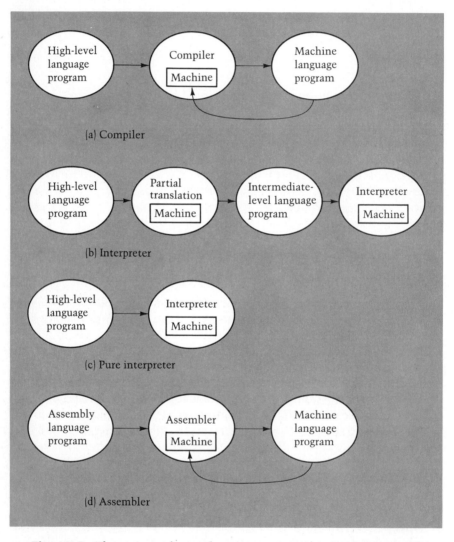

Figure 1.3 The actions of compilers, interpreters, pure interpreters, and assemblers

1.8.2 Actual Instructions

Let's take a look at TOYCOM assembly language. TOYCOM's mnemonic op codes are shown below.

Numeric Op Code	Mnemonic Code	Name
00	STOP	Stop
01	LD	Load
02	STO	Store
03	ADD	Add
04	SUB	Subtract
05	MPY	Multiply
06	DIV	Divide
07	IN	Input
08	OUT	Output
09	B	Branch
10	BGTR	Branch greater-than-zero
11	BZ	Branch zero

To simplify our discussion of TOYCOM assembly language, we have given it the name TOYCODE. All of the instructions shown above are *actual instructions*, which are translated directly into machine code instructions by the TOYCOM assembler.

1.8.3 Assembler Directives

In addition to the TOYCODE instructions associated with the TOYCOM machine language, listed in Section 1.8.2, TOYCODE has two instructions called *directives*. The main purpose of directives in assembly languages is to convey information to the assembler program. Directives are not translated into machine code. They do not end up in the machine language program that the translator constructs. Most assembly languages have a substantial number of directives, many of which are used to carry out storage allocation tasks for the programmer. The purpose of one of TOYCODE's directives, DC, an acronym for *define constant*, is exactly that.

The machine language programs we wrote earlier in this chapter required that we assign memory addresses to variable names in the pseudocode. In TOYCODE, because we are allowed to use pseudocode variable names to refer to memory addresses in the program, we must tell the TOYCODE assembler the names we are using in the program. To associate names and addresses, we place the variable name as a label on the DC directive that allocates the storage location. The assembler then takes care of the details of recording the association. Labels are attached to TOYCODE instructions by following them immediately by colons. The DC directive also allows—in fact requires—the programmer to have the assembler place an initial value into the location, at assembly time (during the assembly process). If the initial value of a variable does not matter, you can simply use a zero operand.

The general form of the DC directive is:

Label: DC   Constant

For example:

```
SUM:   DC    0
TIME:  DC    100
```

These two allocate two words of memory, associate the names SUM and TIME with them, and initialize SUM's value to zero and TIME's to 100.

TOYCODE's other directive, REM, is a very simple one. It allows the programmer to give TOYCODE statements for the sole purpose of documentation (often called comments). REM is an acronym for *rem*ark. The general form of the REM directive is as follows:

REM   anything

"Anything" can be any string of characters. The entire REM directive is ignored by TOYCOM, except when it is showing a listing of the program. Programmers are encouraged to use REM directives to explain, in clear English, what it is their programs are doing. The next example will demonstrate.

1.8.4   A TOYCODE Program

Now, finally, we are ready to write our first TOYCODE program. Let us use the Example 1.2 program as our first example. The TOYCODE program for Example 1.2 is shown below, along with the machine language program:

Machine
Code   *TOYCODE*

```
             REM    PROGRAM TO PRINT THE LARGER OF
             REM    TWO INPUT NUMBERS
             REM    READ THE TWO INPUT VALUES
0799         IN       FIRST
0798         IN       SECOND
             REM    DECIDE WHICH IS LARGER BY
             REM    COMPUTING THE DIFFERENCE
0198         LD       SECOND
0499         SUB      FIRST
             REM    IF THE DIFFERENCE IS >= 0
             REM    BRANCH TO PRINT SECOND (IT'S LARGER)
1008         BGTR     ELSE
1108         BZ       ELSE
             REM    THE FIRST IS LARGER
0899         OUT      FIRST
0909         B        FINISH
             REM    ELSE THE SECOND IS LARGER
0898   ELSE:    OUT      SECOND
0000   FINISH:  STOP
       FIRST:   DC       0
       SECOND:  DC       0
```

The most striking aspect of the TOYCODE program is its readability, even without its documentation via remarks. Although it is much less readable than a high-level language version, this (or any other program in assembly language) can be said to be much more readable than its machine language version. Even so, TOYCODE is readable only in comparison with machine code.

1.9   Translating Pseudocode to TOYCODE : : : : : :

One way to improve both the accuracy and readability of TOYCODE programs is to translate pseudocode programs directly into TOYCODE. Writing assembly language programs as strict translations from pseudocode imposes a high degree of structure on those programs; moreover, using the pseudocode in the assembly language as documentation makes the assembly language programs much more readable.

1.9.1   The WHILE Construct

The general technique for translating WHILE statements to TOYCODE is shown below.

Pseudocode	*TOYCODE Format*
WHILE condition DO	Loop-label
	Evaluate the inverse of the condition
	Branch if true to loop-end-label
while-body	TOYCODE for while-body
	Branch to loop-label
END-DO	Loop-end-label

You may have noticed one peculiarity in our general translation form for the WHILE statement: the evaluation of the inverse of the condition. This is much like our TOYCODE solution for Example 1.2, except that in Example 1.2 the condition was part of a selection construct. The WHILE statement causes the execution of its while-body statements when its condition is true. Therefore, we want to branch around those statements when the condition is false. Because TOYCOM does not have BRANCH-ON-FALSE instructions, we must invert the condition before the conditional branch instruction.

The following example should help the reader understand the process. It is a program segment that reads, counts, and adds numbers to a SUM while a COUNTER remains less than a variable named HEADER. (Note that it assumes that SUM has been initialized to zero.)

. . . .

Example 1.3: *Translation of a Pseudocode WHILE Construct to TOYCODE*

Pseudocode

WHILE counter < header DO
   Get a number
   Add the number to the sum
   Increment counter
END-DO

TOYCODE

```
      REM   WHILE COUNTER < HEADER DO
LOOP:    LD       COUNTER
         SUB      HEADER
         BZ       LOOPEND
         BGTR     LOOPEND
      REM         GET A NUMBER
         IN       NUMBER
      REM         ADD THE NUMBER TO THE SUM
         LD       SUM
         ADD      NUMBER
         STO      SUM
      REM         INCREMENT THE COUNTER
         LD       COUNTER
         ADD      ONE
         STO      COUNTER
         B        LOOP
      REM   END-DO
LOOPEND: ...
            .
            .
            .
ONE:     DC       1
```

The first two lines of TOYCODE after the first REM are the inverted condition evaluation process. The BGTR and BZ are the conditional branches out of the WHILE. The next seven lines of code correspond to the WHILE body statements, followed by the branch back to the beginning of the WHILE loop. The LOOPEND label will be on the first TOYCODE instruction following the WHILE loop, whatever that may be. This is indicated by the three periods following LOOPEND. The constant 1 that is needed to increment COUNTER is built with the DC directive labeled ONE.

The inverses of all of the comparison operators are shown below.

Operator	Inverse
=	<>
>	<=
<	>=
>=	<
<=	>
<>	=

1.9.2   The IF Construct

In the translation of pseudocode IF statements to TOYCODE, the IF pseudocode statement can appear in two forms, either with or without the ELSE clause. In the following example, we will show the form of the IF statement with an ELSE clause. The other form is identical, except, of course, that it does not have an ELSE clause. An IF statement is used with an ELSE clause when it is selecting one of two different code sequences. It is used without the ELSE clause to choose or bypass a single code sequence.

The following is the general technique for translating the IF statement to TOYCODE.

Pseudocode	*TOYCODE Format*
IF condition	Evaluate the inverse of the condition
THEN then-clause	Branch if true to else-label TOYCODE for then-clause Branch to end-if-label
ELSE else-clause	Else-label TOYCODE for else-clause
ENDIF	End-if-label

In the case of an IF statement without an ELSE clause, the conditional branch would be to the end-if-label instead of to the else-label, which in that case would not exist. (Note that we must evaluate the inverse of the condition, exactly as we did with the WHILE statement.)

The following is an example of a complete IF statement translation. In this case, we add two to TOTAL if SCORE is greater than BREAK, and add three to TOTAL otherwise.

. . . .

Example 1.4:   ***Translation of a Pseudocode IF Construct to Toycode***

Pseudocode	TOYCODE
| IF SCORE > BREAK | ```
REM   IF SCORE > BREAK
   LD BREAK
   SUB SCORE
   BGTR ELSE
   BZ ELSE
``` |
| THEN add 2 to TOTAL | ```
REM      THEN ADD 2 TO TOTAL
   LD TOTAL
   ADD TWO
   STO TOTAL
   B ENDIF
``` |
| ELSE add 3 to TOTAL | ```
REM       ELSE ADD 3 TO TOTAL
ELSE:  LD TOTAL
   ADD THREE
   STO TOTAL
REM   ENDIF
``` |
| ENDIF | ```
ENDIF:  ...
``` |

This example demonstrates the great difference in clarity and code length between pseudocode and TOYCODE—a difference typical of that between assembly languages and high-level languages.

1.10   Examples of TOYCODE Programs : : : : : : : : :

The following problem accepts input in *trailer value form* and calculates the percentage of data that is positive. "Trailer value data form" means that the list of data is followed by a peculiar value that does not appear in the list. This peculiar data value is used to indicate to the program that no more data are to be processed.

. . . .

Example 1.5

: Problem Statement

> *In:*   A list of more than one nonzero numbers, followed by zero.
> *Out:* The percentage of input numbers greater than zero.

:• *Pseudocode Solution*

You should be able to solve this problem in pseudocode without difficulty.

```
Initialize TOTAL-DATA and POSITIVE-DATA to zeros
Get a NUMBER
WHILE NUMBER <> 0 DO
    Increment TOTAL-DATA
    IF NUMBER is positive
        THEN increment POSITIVE-DATA
    ENDIF
    Get the next NUMBER
END-DO
Compute percentage of data that are positive
Print percentage
End-of-program
```

:: *TOYCODE Solution*

```
10    REM   THE % OF INPUT DATA THAT ARE POSITIVE
20    REM   IN: A LIST OF NONZERO NUMBERS FOLLOWED
25    REM        BY ZERO
30    REM   OUT: % OF INPUT DATA THAT ARE POSITIVE
40    REM
50    REM   GET THE FIRST NUMBER
60      IN NUMBER
70    REM   WHILE NUMBER <> 0 DO
80    LOOP:   LD NUMBER
90      BZ LOOPEND
100   REM   INCREMENT TOTAL-DATA
110      LD TOTAL
120      ADD ONE
130      STO TOTAL
140   REM   IF NUMBER IS POSITIVE
150      LD ZERO
160      SUB NUMBER
170      BGTR ENDIF
180      BZ ENDIF
190   REM        THEN INCREMENT POSITIVE-DATA
200      LD POSITIVES
210      ADD ONE
220      STO POSITIVES
230   REM   ENDIF
```

```
240   REM   GET THE NEXT NUMBER
250 ENDIF:   IN NUMBER
260   REM   END-DO
270      B LOOP
280   REM   COMPUTE PERCENTAGE OF DATA THAT ARE
285   REM   POSITIVE
290 LOOPEND:   LD POSITIVES
300      MPY HUNDRED
310      DIV TOTAL
320      STO PERCENT
330   REM   PRINT THE PERCENTAGE
340      OUT PERCENT
350      STOP
360   REM   END-OF-PROGRAM
370   REM   STORAGE ALLOCATION
380 NUMBER:   DC 0
390 TOTAL:   DC 0
400 ONE:   DC 1
410 POSITIVES:   DC 0
420 HUNDRED:   DC 100
430 PERCENT:   DC 0
440 ZERO:   DC 0
```

. . . .

A number of features of this program are worthy of explanation. First, the documentation is almost exclusively the pseudocode statements— one of the great advantages of using pseudocode over flowcharts, for the preliminary work can become a permanent part of the implemented program. This is true regardless of the target language, or language in which the program will be written and run, but it is especially true when the target language is a low-level one, such as an assembly language. As was mentioned previously, then, pseudocode provides a powerful, structured, and readable tool for algorithm development, as well as the documentation for the implemented program. We have included line numbers in this program and the next because they would be required if you were to run it with the TOYCOM simulator. (TOYCODE programs can be assembled and run with the TOYCOM simulator. The details of how to use the simulator are explained in Appendix A.)

Note also the computation required to get the logical inverse of the IF condition. The condition is that the number is positive, and the inverse is that the number is negative or zero. Because we do not have a BRANCH-ON-NEGATIVE instruction in TOYCODE, we must invert the sign of NUMBER by subtracting it from zero. Then, all that is required are the

112,446

LIBRARY
College of St. Francis
JOLIET, ILL.

BGTR and BZ instructions. The logical inverse of the WHILE condition is easier in this case, because the inverse of <> is simply =. Just the BZ is required. Computing the inverse of conditions is not really difficult, although it requires a little practice.

One final point: The computation of the final result of this problem, the percentage of positive data, must be done in the order stated. That is, you could not use the following sequence:

```
LD POSITIVES
DIV TOTAL
MPY HUNDRED
```

While this sequence appears to be perfectly correct mathematically, the result will be incorrect. It is correct mathematically only if real arithmetic is used instead of integer arithmetic. With integer arithmetic, the result of nearly all such division operations will be numbers less than one, all of which will be truncated to zero by integer arithmetic. Therefore, the only possible nonzero result will occur when POSITIVES = TOTAL or when 100% is the correct answer. Because TOYCOM uses only integer arithmetic, the sequence used in the program is mandatory to produce a correct result consistently. This is an important point to remember, not only in TOYCOM, but in any computer system that uses integer arithmetic either exclusively, as does TOYCOM, or optionally, as do most programming languages.

. . . .

Example 1.6

: Problem Statement

> *In:*   A header value, LENGTH, followed by LENGTH-numbers.
> *Out:* The position of the smallest number in the input list.

This problem is essentially to find the smallest of a group of numbers. The program, however, is being asked to print not the smallest number, but the position of the smallest number. Consequently, it must keep track of the smallest number as well as its position. Note that the input to this problem is in *header value form*, which is, in a sense, like the opposite of trailer value form.

:• Pseudocode Solution

Get LIST-LENGTH
Initialize SMALLEST by reading first value
Initialize DATA-COUNTER to one
Initialize SMALLEST-POSITION to one

LIBRARY
College of St. Francis
JOLIET, ILL.

WHILE DATA-COUNTER < LIST-LENGTH DO
    Get a new VALUE
    Increment DATA-COUNTER
    IF VALUE < SMALLEST
        THEN
            Replace SMALLEST with VALUE
            Replace SMALLEST-POSITION with DATA-COUNTER
    ENDIF
END-DO
Print SMALLEST-POSITION
End-of-program

The pseudocode ought to be self-explanatory. Note that we have assumed that LIST-LENGTH is greater than zero—not always a safe assumption, but when the input is from a terminal it is not overly risky.

:: *TOYCODE Solution*

```
 10   REM   THE POSITION OF THE SMALLEST NUMBER
 20   REM   IN:  A NUMBER LENGTH, FOLLOWED BY
 25   REM        LENGTH-NUMBERS
 30   REM   OUT:  POSITION OF THE SMALLEST INPUT
 35   REM         NUMBER
 40   REM
 50   REM   GET LIST-LENGTH
 60      IN LENGTH
 70   REM   READ THE FIRST VALUE AS SMALLEST
 80      IN SMALLEST
 90   REM   INITIALIZE DATA-COUNTER AND POSITION
100      LD ONE
110      STO COUNTER
120      STO POSITION
130   REM   WHILE DATA-COUNTER < LIST-LENGTH DO
140 LOOP:  LD COUNTER
150      SUB LENGTH
160      BGTR LOOPEND
170      BZ LOOPEND
180   REM    GET A NEW VALUE
190      IN VALUE
200   REM    INCREMENT DATA-COUNTER
210      LD COUNTER
220      ADD ONE
230      STO COUNTER
```

Continued

```
240  REM      IF NEW VALUE < SMALLEST
250      LD VALUE
260      SUB SMALLEST
270      BGTR ENDIF
280      BZ ENDIF
290  REM      THEN
300  REM          REPLACE SMALLEST WITH NEW VALUE
310      LD VALUE
320      STO SMALLEST
330  REM          REPLACE SMALLEST-POSITION WITH
335  REM          DATA-COUNTER
340      LD COUNTER
350      STO POSITION
360  REM      ENDIF
370 ENDIF:   B LOOP
380  REM   END-DO
390  REM   PRINT SMALLEST-POSITION
400 LOOPEND:   OUT POSITION
410      STOP
420  REM   END-OF-PROGRAM
430  REM   STORAGE ALLOCATION
440 LENGTH:   DC 0
450 SMALLEST:   DC 0
460 COUNTER:   DC 0
470 ONE:   DC 1
480 VALUE:   DC 0
490 POSITION:   DC 0
```

. . . .

We have now seen two complete examples of problems, solved in pseudocode and in TOYCODE. The reader who fully understands both examples has indeed taken a significant step in learning about assembly-level programming. Remember, TOYCOM is realistic in its basic structure and operation, but unrealistically simple. In Chapter 3, we will make use of much of this knowledge to introduce you to a very real assembly language, VAX-11 Macro assembly language.

Chapter Summary :

1. Assembly language is still the language of choice for some problems, and it is the best way to gain a solid understanding of how a computer operates. Because real assembly languages are very complex, we have used a simplified machine and its assembly language as a model for study.

2. TOYCOM has 12 actual instructions. Its memory has 100 four-digit signed decimal memory locations, addressed as 0-99. Its CPU contains three registers: the ACC for operands and results, the IR for instruction decoding, and the PC for instruction sequence control.

3. Pseudocode is a program development language that includes the essential control statements for selection and pretest loops along with abbreviated English to describe other processes. It provides not only a development tool, but a documentation device for assembly language programs.

4. The stored program concept refers to the process of executing programs only after they have been loaded into memory. Instructions and data in memory are indistinguishable to the computer.

5. Computers execute their instructions in a simple cycle. The fetch part of the cycle moves an instruction from memory into the IR; the execute part performs the indicated operation.

6. Machine language suffers from two fundamental problems: Its op codes and operand addresses are difficult for human beings to comprehend because they consist entirely of numbers, and its branch destinations are absolute machine addresses, which greatly complicates program modifications.

7. The assembly language of TOYCOM, TOYCODE, has two directives, DC and REM, in addition to symbolic op codes for TOYCOM's 12 machine instructions.

8. Pseudocode control statements can be translated to TOYCODE in standard ways. The control statements impose a structure on the essentially unstructured TOYCODE.

New Terms

Accumulator

Actual instructions

Assembler

Central processing unit

Compiler

Conditional branch

Directives

Fetch-execute cycle

Header value form

Instruction register

Interpreter

Logical inverse

Machine language

Operand

Operation code

Pretest logical loop

Program counter

Pseudocode

Pure interpreter

Real-time applications

Selection construct

Self-modifying program

Stored program concept

Trailer value form

Unconditional branch

Chapter 1 Problem Set :

1. What are the two main advantages of assembly language over machine language?

2. Rearrange the following conditions so that all the variables are on the left-hand side of the relational operator (=, <, and so on).

    a. N + 1 < SUM
    b. N + 2 = TOT
    c. C < = NVALUES
    d. SMALL < VALUE
    e. SUMPOS > = TOTAL − 47

3. Provide the inverse of the conditions in Problem 2 and then rearrange them so that all variables are on the left side of the relational operator.

Write pseudocode solutions to the following problems, translate the pseudocode to TOYCODE, and test the resulting programs thoroughly.

4. *In:* A number LENGTH, followed by LENGTH-integers.
    Out: The sum of the positive numbers in the input.

5. *In:* A list of negative numbers followed by zero.
    Out: The number of times the number − 3 appears in the input.

6. *In:* A list of nonzero numbers followed by zero.
    Out: The average of the input data.

7. *In:* A number LENGTH, followed by LENGTH-numbers.
   Out: The percentage of the input data that are positive.

8. *In:* A number LENGTH followed by a list of LENGTH-ages of employees of a company.
   Out: The number of employees who are older than 39.

9. *In:* Three integers.
   Out: The three input numbers with the largest first and the smallest last.

10. *In:* Several groups, each consisting of three positive integers, followed by − 1. Each integer represents the length of one side of a triangle. The largest integer is always first in the group.
    Out: Indicate which groups are right triangles. Right triangles have the property that the length of the longest side squared equals the sum of each of the other two squared lengths.

11. *In:* The input is identical to the last problem, except that the largest integer in each group may be first, second, or third.
    Out: The same as in Problem 10.

12. *In:* A number LENGTH followed by LENGTH-pairs of numbers. Each pair of numbers has the number of wins and the number of losses for one season for a baseball pitcher.
    Out: *a.* The lifetime percentage of wins of the pitcher.
    b. The number of years his percentage of wins was over 50%.

13. *In:* A positive integer less than eight.
    Out: The factorial function of the input, which is defined as follows.

    $$factorial(N) = N \cdot factorial(N - 1)$$

    $$factorial(0) = factorial(1) = 1$$

14. *In:* A positive integer less than 20, named TOTAL.
    Out: The first TOTAL Fibonacci sequence numbers, defined as follows. The first three numbers in the sequence are 1, 1, and 2, and each of the others is found by adding the previous two numbers in the sequence.

2

NONDECIMAL NUMBERS AND ARITHMETIC

The number base of the decimal system undoubtedly evolved because we have ten digits on our two hands. Unfortunately, computers do not have fingers, and their number system depends on characteristics of the devices from which their memories are constructed. Because the most inexpensive means of building memories is to use bistate devices, all contemporary computers use the *binary* system, or base two.

High-level languages consistently and automatically convert all input from decimal to binary and all of their output from binary to decimal, so that programmers using high-level languages need not be familiar with binary numbers. Assembly-level languages, however, do not allow that luxury. In addition to binary, assembly language programmers must be familiar with other number bases that are *binary-compatible*. When exact memory contents must be output, they are usually gathered into a different number base before they are printed by the computer. Binary-compatible systems have bases that are powers of two, allowing orderly and straightforward conversions between the two bases. In most cases, the other base is *hexadecimal*, or base 16, although octal, or base eight, is sometimes used. In this chapter we will discuss binary and hexadecimal numbers, addition and subtraction of these numbers, and algorithms for converting numbers from decimal, binary, and hexadecimal bases to any of the other bases. Be assured that you will need the skills this chapter explains!

2.1 Positional Number Systems : : : : : : : : : : : : : :

The decimal-based number system is a *positional number system:* The position of a symbol in a number representation is essential in expressing the value of the number. To see clearly the positional aspects of numbers, it is instructive to write a number down in polynomial form. Although you probably do not consciously think of it this way, numbers in a positional number system are valued by considering the value of a polynomial whose coefficients are the symbols in the number. For example, the number 342 in decimal can be thought of as being the following polynomial.

$$(3 \cdot 10^2) + (4 \cdot 10^1) + (2 \cdot 10^0)$$

or

$$(3 \cdot 100) + (4 \cdot 10) + (2 \cdot 1)$$

Not all of the number systems that various civilizations have used have been positional. The most famous example is the Roman numeral system. In it, different symbols are used for the different powers, and their positions do not determine the value being represented (although their ordering is significant). For example, X means ten no matter where it appears in a string of symbols that represents a number. Nonpositional number systems are inconvenient for people and unusable for computers (except as programming assignments to convert numbers between Roman numerals and the system we use). But the binary and hexadecimal numbers that we will use in this chapter are positional, so they are highly related to the numbers with which you are familiar. Working with them should, therefore, be a relatively easy task if you continually relate what you learn to your knowledge of decimal numbers.

2.2 Binary and Hexadecimal Numbers : : : : : : : : : :

The value of a number base is also the number of symbols required to represent values in that number base. The decimal system is base ten and uses ten symbols, from 0–9. Because the binary system is base two, it uses just two symbols. While any two symbols would suffice, it is most natural to use the first two symbols from the decimal system, 0 and 1. Binary numbers, then, are strings of one or more symbols from the set {0, 1}. The binary system is positional; the position of a particular symbol in the string helps determine the value of the number being represented. For example, the binary number 1011 can be written in the polynomial form:

$$(1 \cdot 2^3) + (0 \cdot 2^2) + (1 \cdot 2^1) + (1 \cdot 2^0)$$

or simply

$$(1 \cdot 8) + (0 \cdot 4) + (1 \cdot 2) + (1 \cdot 1)$$

which is 11 in decimal.

Counting in decimal amounts to listing all of the decimal symbols, 0–9, and then adding a second position to the left, giving it a value of one, and reusing the ten symbols in the right symbol position. The pattern is repeated as long as necessary. The binary system works identically, except that the recycling is much more frequent because there are only two symbols rather than ten. The following shows the numbers involved in counting from 0–20 in both decimal and binary.

Decimal	Binary
0	0
1	1
2	10
3	11
4	100
5	101
6	110
7	111
8	1000
9	1001
10	1010
11	1011
12	1100
13	1101
14	1110
15	1111
16	10000
17	10001
18	10010
19	10011
20	10100

Often, we must see the individual binary symbols, or bits (binary dig*its*), in the machine code and data of a machine language program. However, binary numbers are often too lengthy and cumbersome for people to comprehend, so computers usually express binary values in some binary-compatible number base. In the early days of computing, the binary-compatible base that was most often used was octal, or base eight. However, when the IBM 360 line of computers was introduced in the early 1960s, the use of hexadecimal, or base 16, became widespread. The IBM 360's memory and character representation uses an eight-bit byte, or unit of memory, for its op codes and its character codings and as the basic addressable unit of memory. One of the main reasons for using eight bits rather than six is that the six-bit form allows for just 64 different characters, and the upper and lower case letters alone require 52 of these. Because the new bytes were eight bits long, and octal symbols represent exactly three binary bits each (the decimal values of 0–7, or 000–111 in binary), octal was not compatible with the new system. (Eight is not evenly divisible by three.) The next larger number base that is compatible with binary, hexadecimal, is perfectly compatible with eight-bit bytes because a hexadecimal symbol represents four bits. Two hexadecimal symbols can be used to represent eight bits of binary data. Because most of the computers that have been developed since the IBM 360 have used eight-bit bytes, the hexadecimal system has become dominant in assembly-level programming. (Note: we will use the usual abbreviation, hex, for the word hexadecimal in the remainder of this book.)

Hex numbers require 16 different symbols. For number bases smaller than our familiar base ten, we simply use the familiar symbols from that base. However, for hex we need six more symbols. While any six symbols could be used, it is best to use a set of six symbols that have a meaning that is somehow compatible with their use as numeric symbols. The choice was simple: the first six alphabetic symbols. In addition to being very familiar, the alphabetic order of A,..., F makes them seem quite natural as part of the ascending numeric order of the hex values. Consequently, the symbols that are used for hex numbers are: 0, 1,..., 9, A, B, C, D, E, F. You may think that numbers built from these symbols look strange, but think how much stranger they would appear if we used Greek alphabetic symbols, or some other equally unfamiliar symbols.

Counting in hex proceeds exactly as in decimal and binary. To count from 0, you simply enumerate all of the symbols, and then begin a new symbol position to the left of the current position. The following are the decimal numbers from 0–20, along with their equivalent representations in hex and binary.

Decimal	Binary	Hexadecimal
0	0	0
1	1	1
2	10	2
3	11	3
4	100	4
5	101	5
6	110	6
7	111	7
8	1000	8
9	1001	9
10	1010	A
11	1011	B
12	1100	C
13	1101	D
14	1110	E
15	1111	F
16	10000	10
17	10001	11
18	10010	12
19	10011	13
20	10100	14

Notice that when the hex count changed from one symbol to two, from F to 10, the binary count changed from four symbols to five. This is rudimentary evidence of the relationship between binary and hex. A hex symbol is precisely equivalent to a four-bit string in its power to express numeric values.

2.3   Addition and Subtraction : : : : : : : : : : : : : : : : :

2.3.1 Addition

How are the addition and subtraction operations done in the binary and hex systems? Actually, the operations are exactly the same regardless of the number base being used, so learning them in binary and hex is not a difficult task.

The following is an algorithm for adding two numbers that works for any base. (We will discuss an algorithm for converting binary numbers to decimal numbers in Section 2.4.)

Initialize a vertical pointer to point at the rightmost symbols in the two numbers

WHILE the pointer points to any symbols DO
    Add the symbols being pointed to by the pointer (possibly includ-
      ing a carry of 1)
    IF the sum is >= the base
      THEN
          Write the rightmost symbol of the sum below the added
            symbols
          Write a 1 above the next column of symbols to the left
      ELSE
          Write the sum below the two added symbols
    ENDIF
    Move the pointer left one symbol
END-DO
End-of-program

Let's try this algorithm on two decimal numbers, 127 and 13. Each execution of the WHILE-loop is shown as a step below:

Step:	1	2	3	4
	↓	↓	↓	↓
		1	1	1
	127	127	127	127
	13	13	13	13
	0	40	140	

Now let's try the algorithm on two binary numbers, 1001 and 101:

Step:	1	2	3	4	5
	↓	↓	↓	↓	↓
		1	1	1	1
	1001	1001	1001	1001	1001
	101	101	101	101	101
	0	10	110	1110	

Note that the sum of the binary numbers one and one is 10 in binary, which is equal to the base and thus produces a "carry" to the next position. Perhaps we should check the accuracy of the answer. The decimal values of 1001, 101, and 1110 are:

$$1 \cdot 8 + 0 \cdot 4 + 0 \cdot 2 + 1 \cdot 1 = 9 \text{ (decimal)}$$
$$1 \cdot 4 + 0 \cdot 2 + 1 \cdot 1 \qquad\quad = 5 \text{ (decimal)}$$
$$1 \cdot 8 + 1 \cdot 4 + 1 \cdot 2 + 0 \cdot 1 = 14 \text{ (decimal)}$$

It worked! Now we can try another example:

Step:	1	2	3	4
	↓	↓	↓	↓
		1	11	111
	10111	10111	10111	10111
	1011	1011	1011	1011
		0	10	010

5	6	7
↓	↓	↓
1111	11111	11111
10111	10111	10111
1011	1011	1011
0010	00010	100010

In this case, 10111 is equal to 23 in decimal, 1011 is equal to 11 in decimal, and 100010 is equal to 34 in decimal, so our algorithm worked again.

Now we will try the addition algorithm on the two hex numbers, 70B and 16:

Step:	1	2	3	4
	↓	↓	↓	↓
		1	1	1
	70B	70B	70B	70B
	16	16	16	16
		1	21	721

This task is clearly more complex than adding binary numbers. While we would add two or even three ones to get 10 or 11 in binary, it is easier than adding two hex symbols. B + 6 is 11 in hex, but it takes more thought than 1 + 1 in binary. In fact, it is better to convert the two hex symbols mentally to decimal and then add the converted values in decimal. For example, for B + 6, we would add 11 + 6 to get 17 (in decimal). Because 17 is greater than the base of 16, we subtract 16 to get the result of one with a carry of one. Note that the conversions required in this process are for just the hex symbols A, . . . , F, which are 10–15 in decimal. With a little practice, this process should be easy.

Before going on, let's check to see if the answer is correct in our first hex addition:

$$70B\,(hex) = 7 \cdot 256 + 11 \qquad = 1792 + 11 \qquad = 1803\,(decimal)$$

$$16\,(hex) = 1 \cdot 16 + 6 \qquad = \qquad\qquad\qquad 22\,(decimal)$$

$$721\,(hex) = 7 \cdot 256 + 2 \cdot 16 + 1 = 1792 + 32 + 1 = 1825\,(decimal)$$

As another example, let's add 1A7F and 535:

Step:	1	2	3	4	5
	↓	↓	↓	↓	↓
		1	1	1	1
	1A7F	1A7F	1A7F	1A7F	1A7F
	535	535	535	535	535
		4	B4	FB4	1FB4

The answer is correct: 1A7F, 535, and 1FB4 in hex are 6783, 1333, and 8116 in decimal, and 6783 + 1333 = 8116.

We urge you to do the addition exercises at the end of this chapter to become familiar with addition in these three number bases.

2.3.2 Subtraction

You already know how to subtract in decimal form. As in addition, to subtract in other number bases you must simply apply what you know to operands that are not decimal.

An algorithm for subtraction of one number from another follows. It assumes, as the algorithm for addition did, that you can do the single symbol variety of the operation.

Initialize a vertical pointer to point at the rightmost symbols of the
    two numbers
WHILE the pointer points at any symbols DO
    IF the lower symbol is < = the upper symbol
        THEN
            Subtract the lower symbol from the upper symbol
            Write the difference below the lower symbol
        ELSE
            Borrow one from the symbol to the left of the upper symbol
            Add the base to the upper symbol
            Subtract the lower symbol from the upper symbol
            Write the difference below the lower symbol
    ENDIF
    Move the pointer left one symbol
END-DO
End-of-algorithm

The only difficulty with this algorithm, which works on numbers of any base, is that it ignores borrowing, which, as any elementary school child can testify, is the most difficult to master. Because you are comfortable with borrowing in decimal, we will discuss it in that context.

Borrowing from a symbol greater than zero is simple; you subtract 1 and then add the base to the symbol for which you are borrowing. When the symbol from which you must borrow has a value of zero, you search left until a nonzero symbol appears. You then borrow 1 from it and replace each 0 you passed in the search with the last symbol in the number base (9 in base ten, 1 in base two, and F in base 16). Then you add the base to the value of the symbol for which you were borrowing.

Let's try the algorithm on decimal values first. The subtraction of 53 from 424 is shown below:

Step: 1   2   3   4

         ↓   ↓   ↓   ↓
        424   424   3(12)4   3(12)4
      __53__   __53__   __53__   __53__
                    1   71   371

Note that the notation (12) means that 12 is the value of the symbol for which you borrowed.

Now, let's try the subtraction algorithm on binary operands. The following shows the subtraction of 101 from 1011 in binary:

Step: 1   2   3   4

         ↓   ↓   ↓   ↓
       1011   1011   1011   (2)11
      _101_ _101_ _101_   _101_
                0   10   110

We used the same notation as in the decimal example to indicate the value of the symbol to which a borrow has been made. That is, the value appears in decimal base, in parentheses, although it should still occupy just one position.

In the following example, we subtract 11 from 10001 in binary:

Step: 1   2   3   4   5

          ↓   ↓   ↓   ↓   ↓
        10001   10001   11(2)1   11(2)1   11(2)1
       __11__   __11__   __11__   __11__   __11__
                   0   10   110   1110

The operation for subtracting hex numbers is exactly the same, although it looks a little more peculiar than decimal. Our first example is to subtract A4 from 29B:

Step: 1   2   3   4

       ↓   ↓   ↓   ↓

  29B 29B 1(25)B   1(25)B
   A4   A4   A4   A4
             7   F7   1F7

As with addition of hex numbers, it is best to convert the operand symbol pairs mentally before the subtraction operation between symbols. In the above example, we do a decimal subtraction of 4 from 11, rather than a hex subtraction of 4 from B. In the case of the second pair of symbols, the symbol is actually two decimal symbols, 25, after borrowing. Once again, it is much easier to convert the 19 in hex to 25 in decimal, subtract 10 from 25 in decimal, and then convert the result of 15 to hex (F). It may seem strange to have both decimal and hex symbols in the first string after borrowing, but as long as they are parenthesized, they should be acceptable.

Let's look at just one more example of hex subtraction:

Step: 1   2   3   4

      ↓   ↓   ↓   ↓

  1001 FF(17) FF(17)   FF(17)
    52   52   52   52
               F   AF   FAF

A check gives the following results:

  1001 (hex) = 4096 + 1   = 4097 (decimal)

    52 (hex) =   80 + 2   =   82 (decimal)

 FAF (hex) = 3840 + 160 + 15 = 4015 (decimal)

Once again, you'll quickly become proficient with practice, so you are urged to try out a few of the subtraction exercises at the end of this chapter.

2.4 *Conversions Between Number Bases* : : : : : : :

Your next task is to learn to do conversions of numbers in one base to numbers in another base. In general, the job involves a substantial amount of simple arithmetic—and if people were especially proficient at arithmetic, the computer age would have been delayed for decades. Careful attention to detail is the watchword in doing number base conversions.

2.4.1   Conversion to Decimal Numbers

The pseudocode below is a general algorithm for converting numbers of any other base to decimal-based numbers. Note that all of the arithmetic is done in decimal, so this is a relatively easy task.

Initialize a vertical pointer to the leftmost symbol in the number
Initialize RESULT to the value of the pointed-to symbol
Move the pointer to the right by one symbol
WHILE the pointer points to a symbol DO
    Multiply RESULT by the base of the number (in decimal)
    Add the decimal value of the pointed-to symbol to the RESULT
    Move the pointer to the right by one symbol
END-DO
End-of-algorithm

Our first example of using the conversion-to-decimal algorithm is shown below, with the conversion of the binary number 10110 to decimal.

$$
\begin{array}{c}
\downarrow \\
10110
\end{array}
\qquad
\begin{array}{r}
\text{Result:} \quad 1 \\
\times 2 \\
\hline
2 \\
+0 \\
\hline
2
\end{array}
$$

$$
\begin{array}{c}
\downarrow \\
10110
\end{array}
\qquad
\begin{array}{r}
\times 2 \\
\hline
4 \\
+1 \\
\hline
5
\end{array}
$$

$$
\begin{array}{c}
\downarrow \\
10110
\end{array}
\qquad
\begin{array}{r}
\times 2 \\
\hline
10 \\
+1 \\
\hline
11
\end{array}
$$

$$
\begin{array}{c}
\downarrow \\
10110
\end{array}
\qquad
\begin{array}{r}
\times 2 \\
\hline
22 \\
+0 \\
\hline
22
\end{array}
$$

$$
\begin{array}{c}
\downarrow \\
10110
\end{array}
$$

Now let's try the conversion algorithm on the hex number 3F7:

$$\downarrow$$
3F7 Result:
$$
\begin{array}{r}
3 \\
\times\,16 \\
\hline
48 \\
+\,15 \\
\hline
63 \\
\end{array}
$$

$$\downarrow$$
3F7
$$
\begin{array}{r}
\times\,16 \\
\hline
1008 \\
+\,7 \\
\hline
1015 \\
\end{array}
$$

$$\downarrow$$
3F7

2.4.2 Conversion Between Binary and Hex Numbers

To convert from binary to hex, you must either be familiar with the hex values of all of the different four-bit binary numbers, or else have a table of those values (the values are listed below).

Binary	Hex	Binary	Hex
0000	0	1000	8
0001	1	1001	9
0010	2	1010	A
0011	3	1011	B
0100	4	1100	C
0101	5	1101	D
0110	6	1110	E
0111	7	1111	F

The process is as follows. Divide the binary symbols into four-bit groups, starting on the right end of the binary number. If the leftmost group has fewer than four symbols, add 0s to the left end to make a total of four. Now, look up each four-bit group in the table and write down the equivalent symbols in hex. Those symbols represent the hex value of the binary number. For example, with the binary number 10111100111, the four-bit groups are 0101, 1110, and 0111. The hex equivalent is 5E7.

The conversion of hex numbers to binary numbers is the inverse of this process. We simply convert each hex symbol to its binary equivalent and write down the resulting four-bit binary numbers. Once again, you can use the table if you are unfamiliar with the four-bit binary numbers that are equivalent to the hex symbols. For example, the hex number 3F7A has as its four-bit binary equivalents 0011, 1111, 0111, and 1010. The equivalent binary number is 0011111101111010.

2.4.3   Conversion to Nondecimal Numbers

What about the conversion of decimal numbers to their equivalents in nondecimal bases? This is a much more lengthy and error-prone process. It is the inverse of the process of converting nondecimal numbers to decimal numbers. Because that process used multiplication by the base from which we converted, this process requires division by the target base.

The following pseudocode describes a process for converting decimal numbers to numbers of any other base.

Set DIVIDEND to the decimal number
WHILE DIVIDEND > 0 DO
    Divide DIVIDEND by the target base
    Replace DIVIDEND by the quotient
    Place the remainder (in the target base) in LIST
END-DO
Print the symbols in LIST in reverse order
End-of-algorithm

Note that LIST is some storage device, such as an array.

We can now try the conversion algorithm to convert the decimal numbers 79 and then 64 to binary. Note that you must be careful not to stop too soon at the end.

```
2|79
2|39      Remainder = 1
2|19      Remainder = 1
 2|9      Remainder = 1
 2|4      Remainder = 1
 2|2      Remainder = 0
 2|1      Remainder = 0
  0       Remainder = 1
Result: 1001111
```

```
2|64
2|32      Remainder = 0
2|16      Remainder = 0
 2|8      Remainder = 0
 2|4      Remainder = 0
 2|2      Remainder = 0
 2|1      Remainder = 0
  0       Remainder = 1
```
Result: 1000000

Let's use the same algorithm to convert the decimal number 1471 to hex:

```
16|1471
  16|91      Remainder = F
   16|5      Remainder = B
    0        Remainder = 5
```
Result: 5BF

The obvious problem here is that most of us need time, paper and pencil, and a certain amount of good luck to get the right answer when we divide by 16. Consequently, it's better to convert to binary first or else use a decimal-to-hex conversion table to do these conversions. We have included such a table in Appendix B.

Because assembly language programmers must often make number base conversions, some calculators now convert numbers between decimal, hex, octal, and binary bases.

2.5   *Twos Complement Notation* : : : : : : : : : : : : : :

Integer data values are represented in a computer's memory as binary numbers. If a particular data type of a computer consists of two-byte (16-bit) integers, that data type can simply use 16 bits of memory for each variable of its type.

The only question is how negative values are to be stored in that 16-bit "word." One way is to reserve one of the bits for the sign, and let the rest of the "word" be used to represent the magnitude of the number. This is called the *sign-magnitude method*, and is the method people use for keeping written decimal numbers on paper.

Computers, however, are more efficient when they use a different notation to represent negative integers. Some early computers and a few contemporary computers use what is called *ones complement notation*. Ones complement notation uses the *bitwise complement* of a binary number to represent the negative of that value. The bitwise complement is computed by changing each bit to the opposite value (all 1s become 0s, and all 0s become 1s). If the range of possible values in a binary number is restricted to magnitudes that can be stored in one less bit than the size of the data type, this method is feasible. For example, if the data type was eight bits, or a single byte, the range of magnitudes would be the values that can be stored in a seven-bit binary value. In such a system, the numbers 5 and − 5 would be represented by:

        5 : 00000101
      − 5 : 11111010

The difficulty with the ones complement system is that it allows two different representations of 0:

        0 : 00000000
      − 0 : 11111111

Because additional circuitry is required to detect zero, most contemporary computers use a slightly different notation that bypasses this problem: *twos complement* notation. Twos complement notation adds one to the bitwise complement notation for negative number representation. For example, − 5 is represented in twos complement notation by:

5:	00000101
Ones complement:	11111010
Add 1:	+1
Twos complement:	11111011

In twos complement notation, the inverse is found in exactly the same way as was the complement: To discover the magnitude and sign of a twos complement negative number, you complement it bitwise and add 1. To determine the value of the binary representation -5, we do the following:

Twos complement:	11111011
Bitwise complement:	00000100
Add 1:	+1
Magnitude:	00000101

We use the same process to find the value of any twos complement integer. If the top (leftmost) bit is clear (0), the number represented is positive, and we just need to convert it to decimal. However, if the top bit is set (1), the number represented is negative, and we must take its twos complement, convert the result to decimal, and add a negative sign. Consider the following example:

Given binary number:	11011010
Bitwise complement:	00100101
Add 1:	00100110
Magnitude:	38
Value:	− 38

The designers of early computers, who worked hard to minimize the circuitry of their machines, realized that subtraction could be done by simply negating the second operand and adding. Because bitwise complemention circuitry is very simple, they built subtract circuitry from simple complement circuitry along with the add circuits. The advantage of twos complement notation for negative numbers is entirely the machine's; it may confuse beginning assembly language programmers, but it saves circuitry.

Consider the following example, which subtracts 10 (in decimal) from 54 (in decimal) in an eight-bit machine.

    00110110 (54 in decimal)
 − 00001010 (10 in decimal)

Twos complement of the second value is 11110110.

    00110110
 + 11110110
   100101100

But because we assumed eight-bit locations, we will lose the leftmost bit of the result. The correct result, then, is 00101100, or 44 in decimal.

Remember, any integer binary value from a register or memory location that has its leftmost bit set must be twos complemented and then base converted to determine its decimal value. Because many of the values from the VAX's registers and memory will be in hex, you will have to determine whether an integer value is positive or negative by examining its highest order hex symbol. Note that all hex symbols greater than 7 have the leftmost bit set. Any value that has one of these hex symbols in its highest order position is negative and is stored in twos complement notation.

Chapter Summary :

1. You have used positional number systems in most arithmetic experience you have had. All of the numbers in Chapter 2 use that system.

2. Addition and subtraction can be defined in pseudocode, and the algorithms are independent of the base of the numbers being added or subtracted.

3. Base conversions of numbers are somewhat tedious, except for those between compatible bases, such as binary and hex. Unfortunately, decimal is not compatible with either of these two useful bases.

4. Twos complement notation is used by most contemporary computers to store negative integers because it simplifies subtraction.

New Terms

Binary   Ones complement
Binary-compatible   Positional number systems
Bitwise complement   Sign-magnitude method
Hexadecimal   Twos complement

Chapter 2 Problem Set :

1. Perform the following operations.

   a.   101010   b.   10111   c.   10000   d.   1010
         + 1100   + 110   + 1100   + 11111

   e.   110011   f.   100100   g.   11100   h.   1100
         − 111   − 101   − 11   − 1001

2. Perform the following operations.

   a.   1FB3   b.   ABC   c.   1C9   d.   4F01
        + 133   + 393   + F18   + FFF

   e.   200A   f.   44FE   g.   107A   h.   77AA
        − 14   − F01   − 52C   − 856

3. Convert the following binary numbers to decimal. Note that these numbers are not in twos complement notation.

   a. 1010   b. 11111   c. 10000   d. 1011110

4. Convert the following decimal numbers to eight bit twos complement binary numbers.

   a. 47   b. −32   c. 63   d. −100   e. 129

5. Convert the following binary numbers to hex. Note that these numbers are not in twos complement notation.

   a.   1010101010   b.   11001101010   c.   1010010101001

   d.   10101111100   e.   111111110   f.   110111100011

6. Convert the following hex numbers to binary.

   a. 14FB   b. 23AA   c. 10BB   d. FF18

7. Convert the following decimal numbers to hex.

   a. 4512   b. 2489   c. 9431   d. 285

8. Convert the following hex numbers to decimal.

    a. 1FB7   *b.* 6AC   *c.* C1F3   *d.* 37AC3

9. Convert the following binary numbers to decimal. These numbers are to be considered eight-bit numbers with negative values represented in twos complement notation.

    a. 00010111   *b.* 11101001   *c.* 11111111

    d. 11110000   *e.* 10101010   *f.* 01010101

    g. 10000000   *h.* 10000001   *i.* 01111111

3

INTRODUCTION TO VAX ARCHITECTURE AND ASSEMBLY LANGUAGE

In contrast to the ten executable instructions of TOYCOM, a standard VAX has over 255 executable instructions, as well as many nonexecutable assembler directives supported by Digital Equipment Corporation's assembler. Instead of 100 single-sized words of memory, a VAX can have millions of memory locations in several different sizes. Instead of one accumulator register, the VAX has 16 registers, most of which can be used either as source operands or destinations, or in a wide variety of ways to form source or result operand addresses. In short, mastering the VAX assembly language is vastly more difficult than learning TOYCODE.

The Digital Equipment Corporation (DEC) system software for its VAX series of computers runs under the operating system, which is called VMS (virtual memory system). Included in the system software is the assembler program for Macro. In the remainder of the book, the directives we will describe are those defined by DEC.

DEC calls the VAX assembly language VAX-11 Macro to differentiate it from Macro, the assembly language for its PDP-11 series minicomputers. We will, however, usually refer to it as Macro.

3.1 Introduction to VAX Architecture : : : : : : : : : :

The organization of the VAX-11/780 is shown in Figure 3.1. Later VAX models use a different method to connect memory and peripherals, as is explained below. However, the rest of the figure describes all VAX computers.

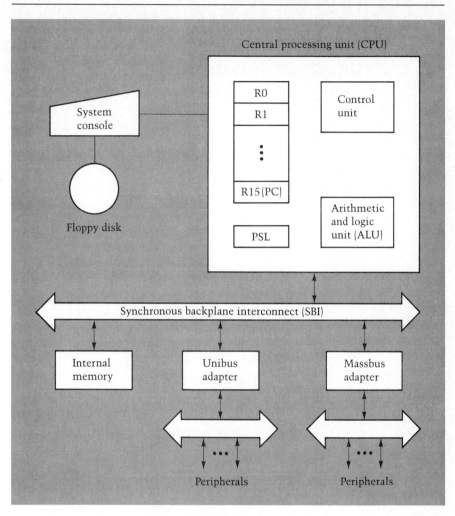

Figure 3.1 VAX organization

The console is a terminal used during system software initialization, modifications, and system parameter changes. The attached floppy disk is an inexpensive memory device used to load system software. The synchronous backplane interconnect (SBI) is the connector between the VAX CPU and its internal memory and all external devices (except the console). A *backplane* is a sequence of sockets into which printed circuit boards can be plugged. Note that the SBI is a device used in the VAX-11/780 systems, but not necessarily in later VAX systems.

The VAX was designed to be a machine to which DEC PDP-11 users could migrate. The VAX can be connected to all peripheral devices (disks, magnetic tape drives, printers, and so on) through bus connections that are common to PDP-11 machines. (A *bus* is a set of wires into which several cable connectors can be plugged. The three-wire 110 volt cable in your living room, with its multiple outlets, can be considered a bus.)

The internal memory of the VAX is arranged as a sequence of bytes. Each byte is addressable and consists of a string of eight binary digits, or bits. The bits in a byte are numbered from 0–7, counting from right to left.

The structure of the internal memory of the VAX is shown below.

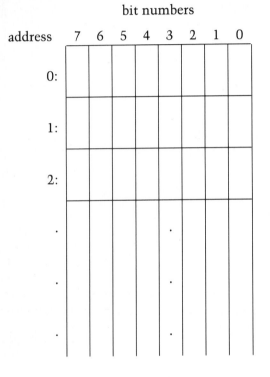

All of the VAX data types, except one, are made up of one or more bytes. There are four different integer data types: BYTE, WORD (two adjacent bytes), LONGWORD (four adjacent bytes), and QUADWORD (eight adjacent bytes). We will discuss some of the instructions involving LONG-WORD integers in this chapter. The other integer data types and the instructions that deal with them will be discussed in Chapter 6. All integer data types use twos complement notation to store negative values. We defined twos complement notation in Chapter 2.

The address space of a computer is the range of all possible memory addresses. TOYCOM has a 100-word address space. Its instructions contain two decimal digits to address memory locations.

Memory addresses in the VAX architecture, in contrast, are LONG-WORDs and are four bytes long, so the address space of the VAX is a 32-bit number. Because the maximum size of a 32-bit number is 4,294,967,295, that number plus 1 (for 0) is the size of the VAX address space—an enormous number.

Terms referring to computer memory sizes were invented for the purpose. Because addresses are nearly always specified with binary numbers, most memories come in sizes that are powers of two in length. One exception is the (non-VAX) decimal-based computers, which are a small minority. Because of its proximity to 1000, the tenth power of two (1024 in decimal) is called K, an abbreviation for kilo. A 16K byte—or 16 *kilobyte*, or simply 16KB—memory has 16 · 1024, or 16,384, bytes. Because of its proximity to the number one million, the twentieth power of two (1,048,576 in decimal) is called M, an abbreviation for mega. A 16M byte—or 16 *megabyte*, or 16MB—memory has 16,777,216 bytes. Because of its proximity to the number one billion, the thirtieth power of two (1,073,741,824 in decimal) is called G, an abbreviation for giga. A 4G byte—or four *gigabyte*, or 4GB—memory has 4,294,967,296 bytes.

We may have misled you concerning the relationship between memory space and actual memory size. The fact that a machine has a 4GB address space does not imply that it has four gigabytes of memory. In fact, most current VAX systems are limited to 8MB of memory. A typical VAX system has 2MB–4MB of actual memory. Moreover, the user does not have access to all 4GB of the VAX memory space. Half of it is reserved for system software, mainly the VMS operating system.

In some older or smaller machines, the hardware regarded as illegal any addresses within the address space but beyond the installed actual memory. In many larger machines, including the VAX, however, a technique known as "virtual memory" is used to make the system appear as if all its memory space is filled with real memory, regardless of the amount of actual memory. The name VAX (virtual *address* extended) indicates that the VAX is indeed a virtual memory computer. Virtual memory is a complex topic, and it is not essential to understand it to learn Macro. We will therefore not discuss it in detail in this book. However, all of our references to memory addresses will be to virtual addresses.

The VAX CPU contains the control logic that governs instruction fetching and execution. It also contains the arithmetic and logic unit *(ALU)* that includes the circuitry of the actual instructions. Also included in the CPU is a collection of registers, some accessible to the users, and some used exclusively by the CPU. As was stated earlier, there are 16 32-bit user-accessible registers in a VAX CPU. Twelve of these, named R0–R11, are almost completely general purpose (we'll explain the restrictions in Chapter 9). While the R0–R11 registers can be used for the same purposes as the ACC in TOYCOM, they can also be used in complex ways to form operand addresses, as we will discuss in Chapters 7 and 8. The other four VAX registers can be used only by programmers who understand their special uses by the system. For now, we'll just give you the names of the four registers; explanations will follow in later chapters. The register R12, or AP (argument pointer), and R13, or FP (frame pointer), are used by the subprogram linkage mechanisms of VAX. The register R14, or SP (stack pointer), is used to point to the top of an area of memory used for a data structure called a stack. The register R15, or PC, is the program counter for the VAX. It is used in much the same way the PC of TOYCOM was used, to control the sequence of instruction execution. Rather than moving in increments that are instruction lengths, as in TOYCOM, the VAX PC moves by operand-length increments. For example, in an instruction with a single operand, the PC contains the address of that operand while the op code is being decoded, or analyzed. While the operand address is being determined, the PC contains the address of the next instruction.

The VAX CPU also includes a 32-bit register, the "processor status longword" *(PSL)*. Its upper, or second, 16 bits contain privileged processor information not writeable by user programs. The lower 16 bits of the PSL are called the program status word *(PSW)*. It contains information about the current status of the executing program. We will discuss how the PSW is used in flow control operations in Chapter 4.

3.2   *LONGWORD Integer Instructions* : : : : : : : : : :

In this section we discuss a small group of VAX assembly instructions that perform data moves and arithmetic on four byte integers, or LONGWORDs.

3.2.1   *Symbols and Storage Allocation*

Symbols serve the same purpose in Macro as they do in TOYCODE, although there are also other more varied uses. Symbols are strings of characters built from alphabetic characters, decimal digits, and underlines (__). They can have up to 31 characters, but cannot begin with a digit. Dollar signs and periods are also legal characters, but they should not be used, because they are used in systems programs.

The rules of good programming dictate that symbols must be connotative—that is, imply what they symbolize. The underline character can be used to build meaningful multiword names. For example, SUM__OF NEGATIVES, MALE__TOTAL, and TOTAL__DEBT are legal Macro symbols. (Note that, although both uppercase and lowercase alphabetic characters can be used in Macro programs, the assembler converts all lowercase characters to uppercase).

Macro instructions can be categorized, like TOYCODE instructions, as executable or nonexecutable. Executable instructions are eventually translated into machine language instructions. Nonexecutable instructions (directives) are messages to the assembler, or translator. They do not result in any machine code. In a sense, of course, the assembler directives are executable, because the assembler "executes" them. Directives are easily distinguishable from the executable instructions, because their names all begin with periods. Executable instructions all begin with alphabetics.

The format of Macro assembly instructions is similar to that of TOY-CODE instructions. Labels, which are usually optional, precede op codes, which are followed by operands and comments. As was the case with TOYCODE, the differentiation between labels and op codes is simplified for the assembler because all labels must be terminated by a colon (:). Furthermore, comments must be separated from operands by semicolons (;). The general instruction format is shown below.

[label:] op code operand(s) [; comment]

Note that whatever is enclosed by the square brackets is optional. Also, note that comments can (and should) appear on separate lines: Comments should be associated with small blocks of code rather than individual instructions. Also, rarely is there sufficient space for an adequate comment on a line with an instruction. Labels can, and often do, appear on otherwise blank lines. In these cases, the address value of the label is that of the next allocated byte.

Instructions can be continued on consecutive lines if each line to be continued ends with a minus sign (−). Breaking a symbol across a line boundary, however, is illegal. Blank lines always terminate continuations. (Note that instructions should rarely be continued: It is hardly ever necessary, and continued instructions are harder to read.)

There are two directives for allocating storage for LONGWORD integer data. .LONG allocates at least one longword of storage and provides an initial value for each allocated location. The general form of the instruction is:

[label:] .LONG constant-list

Although the constant list can employ expressions for specifying constants, at this point we will assume that it is simply a list of decimal values, each of which may be followed by a repetition factor in square brackets. For example, consider

```
HEIGHT:   .LONG   47
```

This instruction allocates one longword with an initial value of 47, and associates the symbol HEIGHT with that address. The instruction

```
LIST:   .LONG   36,24,36
```

allocates three longwords initialized to the values 36, 24, and 36, and associates the symbol LIST with the address of the first.

We will restrict repetition factors, for now, to positive integers enclosed in square brackets. For example,

```
TABLE:   .LONG   20[10], 6, 10[5]
```

allocates 16 longwords, ten with the initial value of 20, one with the initial value six, and five with the initial value ten.

The .BLKL directive is used to allocate one or more longwords with initial values of zero. The general form of the .BLKL is:

[label:] .BLKL count

The count is the number of longwords to be allocated and initialized to zero. For example,

```
SCORES:   .BLKL  5
```

allocates five longwords of storage, initializes each to zero, and associates the symbol SCORES with the address of the first. We will discuss later how certain kinds of expressions can be used to specify the count operands.

All multi-byte integers are stored in memory byte-backwards. For example, the hex value 12345678 would be stored in memory as:

78
56
34
12

Although byte-backwardness may seem confusing, it adds a great deal of flexibility. Consider a register or LONGWORD location that contains a value less than 100 in decimal. It is sometimes convenient to use such values as BYTE operands. Because the values are stored byte-backwards, the address of that LONGWORD location or register as a BYTE type will result in using the first byte. The first byte is the lowest order byte, so the correct value is used (the value of the last byte would be zero). If the bytes of a longword were stored in the same order in which they are written, the highest order byte would be first, which in many cases would not be useful.

3.2.2   *Simple Machine Instruction Formats*

We will use two simple forms of operands on the Macro instructions we introduce in this chapter. They are symbols, which are defined by .BLKL or .LONG directives, and registers, which we will use less frequently.

First, we must know how the machine's instructions specify the addresses for these two forms of operands. Recall that TOYCOM machine instructions all have the same, simple format, two digits of op code and two digits of operand address. As you may have expected, there are many different instruction formats for the VAX.

The general machine language format of all VAX instructions is:

op spec n ... op spec 2   op spec 1   op code

The first byte of most VAX instructions is the complete op code. (Some VAX options include instructions with two-byte op codes, although we will discuss them only briefly.)

The "op spec" fields are operand specifiers. The op code and operands are ordered backwards, as are all VAX instructions written as horizontal collections of bytes, because bytes are numbered right to left within instructions. Because many operands are multiple-byte, they are stored byte-backwards like LONGWORD values. If they are written backwards, they appear in correct order. Fortunately, the VAX assembly language allows us to specify the instructions in their "natural" order.

Operand specifiers can appear in a large number of different forms, reflecting the wide diversity of VAX addressing modes. Operands in assembly instructions that are in registers are addressed directly with the register names, such as R7. The operand specifier of a machine language instruction that specifies a register operand also includes a *mode code*. The mode code specifies to the machine how the register is to be used to indicate an operand. When the register is used simply as the place for the operand, the mode code is 5. The mode code is placed in the left "nibble" (four bits, or one-half byte) of the first byte of the operand specifier, while the rightmost nibble specifies the register number. This works out perfectly, because one of the 16 VAX registers can be specified by binary numbers that fit exactly into this nibble. The format of an instruction with just one register operand is:

```
    1        0
 ┌─────┬───┬─────────┐
 │ 5 │reg│ op code  │
 └─────┴───┴─────────┘
```

The numbers above the box are the byte numbers, in byte-backwards order.

There are also instructions including two or three register operands. Their formats are:

```
     2        1        0
 ┌─────┬───┬─────┬───┬─────────┐
 │ 5 │reg│ 5 │reg│ op code  │
 └─────┴───┴─────┴───┴─────────┘
```

```
     3        2        1        0
 ┌─────┬───┬─────┬───┬─────┬───┬─────────┐
 │ 5 │reg│ 5 │reg│ 5 │reg│ op code  │
 └─────┴───┴─────┴───┴─────┴───┴─────────┘
```

The second operand-addressing technique we will discuss is that used to address all simple operands of Macro instructions. All TOYCODE operands are symbolic. But rather than placing all 32 bits of the address in the machine language instruction, the VAX uses a relative addressing method called *PC-relative*.

Suppose an instruction specifies the symbol SUM as an operand, and SUM is the only operand of that instruction. The distance in bytes between the next instruction's address and the address value of SUM is computed by the assembler at assembly time. This distance is then placed in the instruction, along with one additional code byte to indicate that the PC, or R15, is to be used as a base address in computing the operand address and to indicate the size of the distance value, or *displacement*. For example, consider the following.

Address (Hex)	Instruction
0160	op code SUM
0164	.
.	.
.	.
.	
0180	SUM: .LONG 0

The distance between the address following the first instruction and the address of SUM is 1C in hex. This is the *offset* value, which is placed in the machine language instruction as the operand.

The displacement, or offset, is added to the value of the PC at run time to compute the operand address. Because the PC will contain the next instruction's address when the SUM operand is gotten, the sum of the value in the PC and the displacement is the correct operand address. In our example, 1C is added to 164 to produce 180, which is the correct address of SUM. (We will discuss PC-relative addressing again in Section 3.3.2.)

The actual memory address referred to by an operand is called its *effective address*. The machine instruction format for a PC-relative single operand instruction is:

```
 · · ·    2        1        0

 · · ·  displ. │ X ┊ F │ op code
```

X is a hex digit that indicates the size of the displacement; hex A means BYTE, hex C means WORD, and hex E means LONGWORD. The displacement is a twos complement integer.

The system uses this complicated scheme to address operands in order to save memory. The PC-relative technique can address any operand with an address within about 127 bytes of the instruction by using just a two-byte machine code operand. A WORD displacement can be used to address operands between 127 and 32,767 bytes. A PC-relative BYTE displacement is two bytes shorter than a whole address operand, and a WORD displacement is one byte shorter.

Suppose the symbol SUM has been assigned the address 429 (hex), and that a four-byte instruction at location 312 (hex) specifies SUM as its only operand. The PC-relative address of the machine code version of that operand would be:

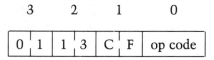

3   2   1   0

| 0 | 1 | 1 | 3 | C | F | op code |

In this case, the displacement is a word with a value of 113 (hex), the difference between 429 and 316 (316 is the address of the instruction following the one in which SUM is being addressed). The C in the second byte indicates the length of the displacement. The displacement itself appears to be in proper order because it is written backwards.

The instructions described in this chapter have one, two, or three operands, each of which can be either a register or a PC-relative symbol. The machine instruction formats can be any combination of the two operand addressing formats we have discussed.

3.2.3   *Data Move Instructions*

TOYCOM has just two data move instructions. One moves data from its register to memory (STO), and the other moves data from memory to its register (LD). The VAX has a collection of registers, but unlike some multiregister machines, the VAX uses the same op code for all of the registers' data moves. The general form of the Macro *move* LONGWORD (MOVL) instruction is:

MOVL source-operand, destination-operand

Either or both of the operands can be registers or symbols representing memory locations (or, as you will see later, many other memory-addressing expressions). Some examples of legal MOVL instructions are:

```
MOVL  R0 , R5
MOVL  R3 , SUM
MOVL  COUNT , R10
MOVL  COUNT , SUM
```

The first example moves the contents of R0 to R5, the second moves the contents of R3 to memory location SUM, the third moves the longword at the memory location COUNT to R10, and the fourth moves the longword at memory location COUNT to memory location SUM. Both SUM and COUNT are assumed to have been associated with memory locations by either .BLKL or .LONG directives. As in TOYCOM LD and STO, MOVL always destroys the destination operand, but does not affect the source operand.

3.2.4   Arithmetic Instructions

In this section we will explain the VAX instructions for performing integer arithmetic on LONGWORD data.

The *clear* LONGWORD (CLRL) instruction has no TOYCOM counterpart. It simply sets the value of a LONGWORD location to zero. Because it affects just one location, it has just one operand, either a register or a memory location. Some examples are:

```
CLRL R3
CLRL SUM
```

Two other VAX instructions without TOYCOM equivalents are the *inc*rement LONGWORD and *dec*rement LONGWORD instructions, INCL and DECL, respectively. INCL adds 1 to its operand, and DECL subtracts 1 from its operand. Because both operations are often needed, the VAX, along with most contemporary machines, implements them in a single instruction. Some examples follow.

```
INCL R3
DECL COUNT
```

The first example adds 1 to R3 and the second subtracts 1 from memory location COUNT.

All of TOYCOM's arithmetic instructions have one explicit operand and one implicit operand. The VAX has instructions for the usual four arithmetic operations that can have two operands, either or both of which can be registers or memory locations. When two operands are specified, one both stores one of the operands and acts as a destination for the result. In the case of TOYCOM, that dual purpose operand is always the ACC. In VAX instructions with two operands, the second has the dual purpose.

In addition to the four two-operand LONGWORD arithmetic instructions, the VAX has four three-operand instructions, for which the two source operands are specified along with a destination location. Neither source operand is affected. The VAX LONGWORD addition instructions are named ADDL2 and ADDL3, specifying two and three addresses, respectively. The general forms of these instructions are:

ADDL2 operand-1, operand-2-destination
ADDL3 operand-1, operand-2, destination

For example,

```
ADDL2 VALUE,SUM
ADDL3 MALES, FEMALES, PEOPLE
ADDL2 R3, TOTAL
```

In the first example, the longword at memory location VALUE is added to the contents of memory location SUM, and the result is placed in SUM, destroying its previous value. In the second example, the longword at memory location MALES is added to the longword at memory location FEMALES, and the result is placed at memory location PEOPLE. Neither location MALES nor FEMALES is affected, although location PEOPLE is changed. In the third example, the contents of R3 are added to the longword at location TOTAL, and the result is placed back at TOTAL, destroying its previous value.

The instructions for subtraction, multiplication, and division are very similar to the addition instructions. SUBL2 and SUBL3 are the two- and three-operand subtraction instructions, respectively, the general forms of which are:

SUBL2 subtrahend, minuend-destination
SUBL3 subtrahend, minuend, destination

The *subtrahend* is the quantity that is subtracted. The *minuend* is the quantity from which the subtrahend is subtracted. In the two-operand instruction, the minuend is destroyed because it becomes the destination for the result, or difference. In the three-operand instruction, both the subtrahend and minuend are preserved. For example:

```
SUBL3 POSITIVES, INTEGERS, NEGATIVES
```

computes the number of NEGATIVES by subtracting the POSITIVES from the INTEGERS.

The multiply instructions are MULL2 and MULL3, the general forms of which are:

MULL2 multiplier, multiplicand-destination
MULL3 multiplier, multiplicand, destination

In both cases, the second operand, the *multiplicand,* is multiplied by the first operand, the *multiplier.* In MULL2, the multiplicand location receives the product, or result. In MULL3, the product is placed in the third operand location.

The general forms of the LONGWORD division instructions (DIVL2 and DIVL3) are:

DIVL2 divisor, dividend-destination
DIVL3 divisor, dividend, destination

In both cases, the second operand, the *dividend*, is divided by the first operand, the *divisor*. In the case of DIVL2, the dividend operand is destroyed to become the destination of the quotient, or result. In the case of DIVL3, both the divisor and the dividend are preserved because the quotient is placed in the third operand. Neither of these instructions provides the remainder from the division operation.

3.2.5   An Example Program Segment

We now have sufficient instructions to write a program segment (not a complete program, because we cannot yet do input and output, nor do we know what other directives are required).

The following code computes the sum and average of three exam scores. It first allocates the required storage, including a location for a constant three, and then later computes the required values.

```
EXAM1:      .BLKL   1
EXAM2:      .BLKL   1
EXAM3:      .BLKL   1
SUM:        .BLKL   1
AVERAGE:    .BLKL   1
THREE:      .LONG   3

          .
          .
          .

          ADDL3   EXAM1, EXAM2, SUM
          ADDL2   EXAM3, SUM
          DIVL3   THREE, SUM, AVERAGE
```

This small segment of code gives the first real evidence of the power of VAX Macro code, especially compared to TOYCODE. Note that we used memory locations for all data, although it is far more efficient in terms of the machine itself to use registers when they are available. We use memory locations because it is impossible to use meaningful names for program variables, which allows increased programmer efficiency, when those variables are in registers on the VAX. If the program were to be written for maximum machine efficiency, we would sacrifice some readability and use registers wherever possible. However, there is another argument for using memory locations instead of registers: On small programs, efficiency is not an issue, and on large programs, most of the registers are used for other purposes, as you will discover in later chapters.

3.2.6   Constant Operands

There is a much easier way to create and use constants like the three we just discussed. The VAX assembler provides two techniques for using constant operands, *immediate mode* and *literal mode*. The choice between the two can be made by the programmer or the assembler. In most cases, we will leave the decision up to the assembler, which will always choose the mode that requires the smallest space. The general format of a two-operand Macro instruction that uses a constant operand is:

op code   #constant, operand-2

The constant operand is seldom the last, because that operand is usually the destination of the operation result. When the the assembler chooses the immediate mode, the machine language instruction format would be as is shown in the following example with the instruction MOVL #9999,R3.

6		5		4		3		2		1		0	
5	3	0	0	0	0	2	7	0	F	8	F	D	0

This instruction format deserves further investigation, especially because similar formats are used in many other addressing modes. First, the instruction appears in reverse order, as it always will. While the order may seem confusing, note that the constant operand (270F in hex) is now actually in correct order, as was the case with PC-relative address displacements. If the instruction were written left to right, that constant would be backwards by bytes. The second byte of the instruction is the operand specifier byte. The left nibble (8) indicates that the operand is immediate. The right nibble (F) indicates that register 15 (F in hex), or PC, is used to address that operand. The size of the constant in this case is LONGWORD, which was chosen by the assembler because the op code specifies LONGWORD operands. The last byte (leftmost) indicates that the second operand is a register (the 5 mode), and that the specified register is R3. The hex value D0 in byte 0 is the machine op code for MOVL.

The literal mode is used with small constant operands. Consider the machine code for MOVL #5, R2.

2		1		0	
5	2	0	5	D	0

The *literal operand* occupies just one byte (the second) of the instruction. In fact, literal mode can be used only with integer operands 0–63. All larger constant operands use immediate mode. Literal mode is four bytes shorter than immediate mode when the op code specifies LONGWORD operands, and is chosen by the assembler, when possible, to save those three bytes.

In the literal addressing mode, bits 6 and 7 within the byte are always zero. The two zero bits specify literal mode, and the other six bits specify the constant value. Either immediate or literal mode can be specified by a Macro operand, by means we will discuss in Chapter 15. For now, we will simply let the assembler choose the more efficient one.

3.2.7 Input and Output

Assembly languages usually do not provide straightforward ways to do simple input and output. We have all been spoiled by the powerful input and output statements provided by higher-level languages. However, even getting an integer value from a register or memory location to the terminal involves a number of messy steps. The value must first be converted from binary twos complement notation to decimal, then the decimal version must be coded in the character code used by the terminal (usually ASCII), and then the string of ASCII characters that represents the value must be transmitted to the terminal.

To keep from getting hopelessly bogged down in complexity at this stage, we will use some small language extensions to do simple terminal input and output. These instructions are called macros (not to be confused with the language name Macro), and they look like a cross between actual instructions and higher-level language statements. We will discuss the creation and use of macros in Chapter 11.

INIT__IO is a macro without operands. It must appear in every program that uses our other macros for terminal input and output, to prepare the terminal to act as both an input and an output device. INIT__IO must appear before any of the other input and output macros.

The macro PRINT__L displays (or prints) the values of LONGWORD integers at the terminal. One to seven parameters can appear on a PRINT__L instruction. The first parameter must be a literal string, delimited by apostrophes. It must be preceded by a circumflex (^), for reasons we will discuss later. The other parameters, when present, can be symbols or register names, or more complex expressions. PRINT__L allows printing of just a literal, or a literal followed by up to six values. Note that the literal can contain any printable character except @ and '.

The macro READ__L accepts integer values from the terminal keyboard and places them in memory locations as LONGWORD integers. It prints a question mark as a prompt for the data it is to read. It can read from one to six integers into its one to six operands. The values can be separated by either commas or blanks. If fewer values are keyed in than the number of operands in the list, the ignored operands are set to zero. If more data values are keyed in than there are operands, the extra values are ignored. Signed values must have their signs immediately to the left of their most significant digits.

The general forms of the PRINT__L and READ__L are:

PRINT__L ^literal[, arg1[,arg2[,arg3[,arg4[,arg5[,arg6]]]]]]
READ__L arg1[,arg2[,arg3[,arg4[,arg5[,arg6]]]]]

Both READ__L and PRINT__L destroy R0 and R1.

Examples of the input and output macro instructions will appear in the example program in Section 3.3.

3.3 *Running VAX Macro Programs* : : : : : : : : : : : :

We have now explained a few instructions for directing simple manipulations on LONGWORD integers, as well as how to create storage for such values with the directives .BLKL and .LONG. A few more assembler directives are needed to complete a program module.

3.3.1 *Required Assembler Directives*

The .PSECT (*program sect*ion) directive provides a wide variety of capabilities, most having to do with sharing, separating, and write-protecting sections of Macro programs. We will discuss just one of the possible parameters in this chapter.

The general form of .PSECT is:

.PSECT program-section-name, [, parameter-list]

The program-section-name symbol is used mainly for collecting and sharing code. For example, if two separate sections of a program begin with a .PSECT with the same program-section-name, the assembler catenates (collects) them together. We mention the program-section-name only because it is a necessary part of .PSECT. The name is inconsequential at this point.

The one .PSECT parameter that we need now is a keyword to specify the alignment for the code in a program section. An alignment specified by the keyword WORD, for example, forces the assembler to begin allocating memory for the code or data (whichever is first) for the section on a memory address that is divisible by two (for the two bytes of a WORD). The only reason we need to set this parameter now is that the sections of data that describe the file and record information for doing the simple input and output in our package are required to begin on divisible-by-four memory addresses. The alignment boundary keywords are BYTE for one, WORD for two, LONG for four, QUAD for eight, and PAGE for 512. The default is BYTE, which actually does nothing—all addresses are divisible by one! Because of our input/output package, you must include in programs a .PSECT directive with the keyword parameter LONG, and it must appear before the INIT_IO instruction. We will explain in Chapter 14 why this is required. Were it not for our input/output package, the .PSECT directive would not be absolutely necessary in every Macro program.

The only other reason for specifying an alignment is execution efficiency. VAX programs execute faster if the data locations are aligned on boundaries equal to their size in bytes. Because we are dealing with all LONGWORD data for now, this is another reason to specify LONG as the alignment keyword. Then, if your .PSECT directive precedes your data declarations immediately, all of the LONGWORD data locations that follow it will begin on LONGWORD boundaries. Alignment can also be specified with another directive, .ALIGN. However, .ALIGN cannot specify a boundary larger than the last alignment set by a .PSECT. Therefore, if no .PSECT is found in a program, alignment defaults to BYTE, and the .ALIGN directive is ineffective.

All Macro programs must contain the directive .ENTRY. The general form of this directive is:

.ENTRY symbol, 0

The first operand of the .ENTRY directive is a symbol with an address value set to the address of the next executable instruction after .ENTRY, which then becomes the first executable instruction of the program. The symbol on the .ENTRY directive never appears as a label in the program. The second operand of .ENTRY is used in Macro subprograms, but because we are discussing only main programs at this point, we do not need a nonzero value for it here. Incidentally, you can assemble a program that does not contain an .ENTRY directive, but you could never execute the resulting machine code; it does not have an entry address and therefore cannot be executed.

Every Macro program must have the .END directive as its last instruction. In addition to indicating the end of a program, .END again specifies the transfer address, or address where execution is to begin. The general form of the .END directive is:

.END [symbol]

The symbol, when present, matches the first operand on the .ENTRY directive. The symbol is not always used (it is not used in subprograms, for example), but for now, we will include the symbolic transfer address on all .END directives.

One final feature required in all Macro programs is the code to set the termination condition and get back to the operating system. To indicate normal termination and get back to the system, we use the system service macro $EXIT__S, which has no parameters.

Let's use these ingredients to build a small program. (We have not yet explained any facilities for control flow in a Macro program, so our example must by necessity be somewhat dull.)

· ·

Example 3.1

: *Problem Statement*

    In: Three integers (named FIRST, SECOND, and THIRD).
    Out: *a.* The sum of the input data.
           b. The average of the input data.
           c. FUN1 = 17 · FIRST / SECOND − THIRD
           d. FUN2 = THIRD · THIRD + SECOND / 3 + 1

:• *Pseudocode Solution*

Get input (FIRST, SECOND, and THIRD)
Compute sum and average
Compute FUN1 = 17 · FIRST / SECOND − THIRD
Compute FUN2 = THIRD · THIRD + SECOND / 3 + 1
Print sum, average, FUN1, FUN2
End-of-program

Now we can write our first complete Macro program.

:: *Macro Solution*

```
; SOME INTEGER ARITHMETIC
;
; ALLOCATE MEMORY TO VARIABLES
;
        .PSECT   EXAMPLE, LONG
FIRST:      .BLKL          1 ; THE FIRST INPUT VALUE
SECOND:     .BLKL          1 ; THE SECOND INPUT VALUE
THIRD:      .BLKL          1 ; THE THIRD INPUT VALUE
SUM:        .BLKL          1 ; THE SUM OF THE INPUT
                             ; VALUES
AVERAGE:    .BLKL          1 ; THE AVERAGE OF THE INPUT
                             ; VALUES
FUN1:       .BLKL          1 ; THE VALUE OF FUNCTION 1
FUN2:       .BLKL          1 ; THE VALUE OF FUNCTION 2
        .ENTRY   EXAMPLE_3_1, 0
        INIT_IO
;
; GET INPUT
;
        READ_L   FIRST, SECOND, THIRD
;
; COMPUTE SUM AND AVERAGE
;
        ADDL3    FIRST, SECOND, SUM
        ADDL2    THIRD, SUM
        DIVL3    #3, SUM, AVERAGE
;
```

Continued

```
; COMPUTE FUN1 = 17 * FIRST / SECOND - THIRD
;
      MULL3    #17, FIRST, R1
      DIVL2    SECOND, R2
      SUBL3    THIRD, R1, FUN1
;
; COMPUTE FUN2 = THIRD * THIRD + SECOND / 3 + 1
;
      MULL3    THIRD, THIRD, R1
      DIVL3    #3, SECOND, R2
      ADDL3    R1, R2, FUN2
      INCL     FUN2
;
; PRINT SUM, AVERAGE, FUN1, FUN2
;
      PRINT_L   ^'SUM, AVERAGE =', SUM, AVERAGE
      PRINT_L   ^'FUN1, FUN2 =', FUN1, FUN2
;
; END-OF-PROGRAM
;
      $EXIT_S
      .END     EXAMPLE_3_1
```

. . . .

The operand ordering for the arithmetic instructions may seem a bit awkward at first, but be assured that you will quickly become comfortable with it.

We now describe the operating system commands that are needed to run Macro programs on a VAX computer that uses the VMS operating system. This interface with the operating system is necessary in all programming, although users do not always discern it.

3.3.2   *Program Creation, Assembly, Linking, and Execution*

Program file creation, assuming terminal access (as we do throughout this book), is done with the aid of a text editor. The standard file extension for VAX assembly programs is .MAR; all program-storage filenames must have that extension.

The first step of running a Macro program is assembly. This is accomplished by the following operating system command:

   $ MACRO [/qualifiers] filename

Most of the optional qualifiers are accessible via assembler directives within the program and will be described as needed later in this book. They include directives for getting various kinds of cross-references and listings as well as for setting options for debugging. In those instances when the assembly process succeeds, a VAX object program file named *filename.OBJ* is created to save it.

The next step in the sequence is the *link operation*, which builds a complete object module called an executable *image*. The object, or machine language, version of your program is combined with whatever system modules, or programs, are used to form this image and is written to another file named *filename.EXE*. The link operation is initiated by the following command:

    $ LINK filename

Note that the file extension is not required if .OBJ is the extension of the filename.

Errors in this linking process—for example, a misspelled program name—may prevent the creation of the .EXE file. Once the assembly and linking processes are accomplished without error, the image in the .EXE file is executed by the following command:

    $ RUN filename

Once again, the extension is not required; .EXE is assumed.

To avoid always having to type in the three-command sequence to assemble, link, and execute a Macro program, you can build a command file. A command file is a file of desired commands. To permit the command file to be used for any Macro program, we will have it prompt the user with an INQUIRE command for the name of the file where the desired Macro program is stored.

When an assembly or linking error occurs, you will want to terminate the command sequence. The VMS operating system provides an error-trapping command, ON ERROR, to deal with that situation. This command is incorporated into the command file program as shown below:

```
$ INQUIRE P1 "PLEASE ENTER FILENAME"
$ MACRO 'P1'
$ ON ERROR THEN EXIT
$ LINK 'P1'
$ ON ERROR THEN EXIT
$ ASSIGN/USER SYS$COMMAND SYS$INPUT
$ RUN 'P1'
```

Once you have placed this sequence in a file named MAC.COM, you can execute it by typing @MAC. Note that the command filename must have the extension .COM, although the MAC part of the name can be any legal filename.

The purpose of the ASSIGN command in this file is to set the system default input file, SYS$INPUT, to the terminal. Any program run with this command file will get its input data from the terminal. Depending on how you store our input and output package in your VAX system, you may have to modify the command file slightly to allow your program access to the package. We will explain in Chapter 14 how the command file can be changed to accept data from elsewhere.

When running and debugging programs, you will usually be working with program listings. While most programming work can be done with a full screen video terminal, a hardcopy listing is essential. A simple listing of the source program file will usually be sufficient. For some debugging purposes, however, and to learn the form of the VAX machine code, you will sometimes need the listing that contains the machine code and the machine addresses of the instructions and data.

This listing can be requested from the assembler by including the option /LIST in the MACRO command. For example,

```
$ MACRO/LIST PGM1
```

assembles the program in file PGM1.MAR, creates an object program in file PGM1.OBJ, and a listing in file PGM1.LIS. The .LIS file can be either printed to produce a hardcopy listing or read at a video terminal. If you need only a partial listing of your program—for example, the part you are currently working on—you can use the .SHOW and .NOSHOW directives within your Macro program. .NOSHOW turns the listing off and .SHOW turns it back on. Some optional parameters that can also be used with these directives will be explained in Chapter 11. On pages 72–73 is a listing of the macro solution to Example 3.1.

The first two lines of the listing indicate the name of the program, the default name .MAIN. (In Chapter 4 we will explain how this name can be set to whatever we like.) Also included are the times of the assembly and listing file creation and the full name of the file containing the source program.

The right half of the listing is the source program with line numbers attached. To the left of the line numbers is the generated column of code addresses. These are all four-digit hex values. Note that the addresses increase from one instruction to the next by the size of the upper instruction. To the left of the addresses is the actual machine code generated by the assembler. It is also in hex, written right to left. The first byte left of an address is always the op code. Following that, right to left, are the hex values for the operands or operand addresses.

Note that all of the .BLKL directives have the addresses of the next location shown as their values. This is misleading, since they are actually set to zero. The .LONG directive, as it should, shows its operand as its value. No code is shown for most of the directives and the input and output macro instructions. Note, however, that some of them take a substantial amount of memory. Consider, for example, the INIT__IO macro instruction.

All of the PC-relative address values in this listing use WORD displacement, since the symbols are all too far away for BYTE displacement and too near to need LONG displacement. These are also all negative, since the data are all before the instructions.

A closer look at one of these values, the first operand on the first ADDL3, should be instructive. The hex machine language version of the PC-relative address is FD94CF. It is, of course, byte-backwards, but since the WORD integer is also backwards, it appears in the correct order. The CF byte specifies a WORD displacement PC-relative mode operand. The FD94 is the negative WORD displacement. To determine its magnitude, we will convert it to binary and take its twos complement as is shown below:

FD94 (hex) = 1111 1101 1001 0100 (binary)
Twos complement = 0000 0010 0110 1100
Hex magnitude = 26C

The address of the operand, FIRST, is 0. Now we can see clearly that the PC is pointing at the next operand when the effective address of an operand is evaluated, since 26C (hex) is the address of the second operand mode byte.

The listing we showed for the Macro solution to Example 3.1 is not the entire file that the MACRO/LIST command creates. The assembler also lists a very large symbol table, most of which is of no value to us at this time. Moreover, the symbols in the Macro program are embedded among a huge number of symbols that are involved in the input and output macros package. So while it is sometimes valuable to see your own symbols in the table, you may have to search through the whole table to find them.

You should print the whole listing file at least once to see what it looks like and to see how to find your program symbols. When getting a hardcopy of a program listing, though, if you do not need the symbol table, you can use the editor to discard everything in the file after your .END directive.

One last note concerning assembler listings. While the assembler always creates machine language programs and listings as if they started at address 0, programs are never actually executed there on the VAX. Instead, machine language programs are loaded at some address beyond the first 200 bytes, which are reserved for system use. Since the addresses in VAX programs are all relative, the code does not need to be modified to be loaded at an address other than 0. The result of loading programs at addresses other than 0 is that the code addresses of assembler listings will be different from those of the code as it is actually executed. This is shown in Section 3.4.

:: *Macro Solution to Example 3.1*

.MAIN.

```
21-NOV-1982  12:00:20   VAX-11 Macro V03-00 Page 1
21-NOV-1982  11:58:27   DRA1:[RSEBESTA]EX31.MAR;3

                 0000    1 ; SOME INTEGER ARITHMETIC
                 0000    2 ;
                 0000    3 ; ALLOCATE MEMORY TO VARIABLES
                 0000    4 ;
        00000000         5         .PSECT EXAMPLE, LONG
        00000004 0000    6 FIRST:  .BLKL  1 ; FIRST INPUT VALUE
        00000008 0004    7 SECOND: .BLKL  1 ; SECOND INPUT VALUE
        0000000C 0008    8 THIRD:  .BLKL  1 ; THIRD INPUT VALUE
        00000000 000C    9 SUM:    .LONG  0 ; SUM OF THE INPUT
        00000014 0010   10 AVERAGE: .BLKL  1 ; AVERAGE OF INPUT
        00000018 0014   11 FUN1:   .BLKL  1 ; VALUE OF FUNCTION 1
        0000001C 0018   12 FUN2:   .BLKL  1 ; VALUE OF FUNCTION 2
             0000 001C  13         .ENTRY EXAMPLE_3_1, 0
                  001E  14         INIT_IO
                  0251  15 ;
                  0251  16 ; GET INPUT
                  0251  17 ;
                  0251  18         READ_L FIRST, SECOND, THIRD
                  0268  19 ;
                  0268  20 ; COMPUTE SUM AND AVERAGE
                  0268  21 ;
                  0268  22         ADDL3  FIRST, SECOND, SUM

FD9A CF  FD95 CF  FD94 CF  C1
```

```
0272 23  FD93 CF FD92 CF       C0      ADDL2   THIRD, SUM
0279 24  FD8F CF FD8E CF 03    C7      DIVL3   #3, SUM, AVERAGE
0281 25                                ;
0281 26                                ; COMPUTE FUN1
0281 27                                ;
0281 28  51   FD7A CF 11       C5      MULL3   #17, FIRST, R1
0287 29  51   FD79 CF          C6      DIVL2   SECOND, R1
028C 30  FD80 CF 51 FD78 CF    C3      SUBL3   THIRD, R1, FUN1
0294 31                                ;
0294 32                                ; COMPUTE FUN2
0294 33                                ;
0294 34  51   FD6D CF FD70 CF  C5      MULL3   THIRD, THIRD, R1
029C 35  52   FD63 CF 03       C7      DIVL3   #3, SECOND, R2
02A2 36  FD70 CF 52 51         C1      ADDL3   R1, R2, FUN2
02A8 37  FD6C CF               D6      INCL    FUN2
02AC 38                                ;
02AC 39                                ; PRINT SUM, AVERAGE FUN1, FUN2
02AC 40                                ;
02AC 41                                PRINT_L 'SUM,AVERAGE=',SUM,AVERAGE
02D9 42                                PRINT_L 'FUN1,FUN2=',FUN1,FUN2
0304 43                                ;
0304 44                                ; END-OF-PROGRAM
0304 45                                ;
0304 46                                $EXIT_S
030D 47                                .END    EXAMPLE_3_1
```

3.4   *Runtime Errors* :

One of the most valuable applications of the assembler listing is as an aid
in finding the Macro instructions that cause *runtime errors*. Recall that
runtime is the time during which the machine language program is being
executed. Runtime errors, therefore, are errors that occur during this time.
They are the result of either syntactic errors that were not caught by the
assembler or logic errors in the algorithm. A large number of different
runtime errors can cause your program to stop its execution prematurely,
but the method of finding the offending instruction is the same for most
of them.

To illustrate the process, we will create a common runtime error in
the program of Example 3.1. Removal of the literal operator (#) from the
first operand of the first MULL3 instruction causes the assembler, and
thus the VAX, to assume that we want to access location 17 in memory
rather than use the value 17 as an operand. Since location 17 is reserved
for system use, it is protected from our program; when our program attempts
the access, we get an *access violation* runtime error. Here is how the
system responds to this error when we run it with our command file,
MAC.COM:

```
$ @MAC
PLEASE ENTER FILENAME: EX31
?4 6 8
%SYSTEM-F-ACCVIO, access violation, reason
    mask=00, virtual address=00000011,
                        PC=00000DFD, PSL=03C00000
%TRACE-F-TRACEBACK, symbolic stack dump follows
module name     routine name      line
  .MAIN           EXAMPLE

    rel PC          abs  PC
    00000281        00000DFD
 $
```

Much of this is not useful in our simple example program. However,
we do get the message that we have created a runtime error of access
violation. The error was caused during execution of the program named
.MAIN., which is the default name for all of our programs for now. (Later
we will see how to specify module names.) The routine name was EXAM-
PLE, as we specified on the .PSECT directive. The virtual address of the
violation—that is, the address in the VAX's virtual address space that we
attempted to access—is 11 in hex, or 17 in decimal, which is the first
operand's value in the MULL3 instruction after we deleted the #.

The "rel PC" entry is most important, since it gives the value of the
PC relative to the beginning of our program, where the error occurred

(281). Note that both the "abs PC" (absolute PC) and the PC value given in the second line of the error information have the same value, DFD. This is the actual address in memory of the offending instruction, but since our assembler listing has just relative addresses, it is of little value. If we look back at the assembler listing for this program, we see that 281 is the hex address of the MULL3 instruction that caused the error.

3.5 *The Assembly Process* : : : : : : : : : : : : : : : : : :

Assembly language programs can be translated to machine code during a single *assembler pass,* or reading. The assembler considers the program as a single string of characters to be read left to right. In a Macro program, most lines cause the assembler to allocate storage. For example, the .BLKL directive causes the allocation of at least four bytes of memory.

All executable instructions cause the allocation of sufficient memory for their machine code versions. To effect these allocations, the assembler maintains a pointer, or address variable with the address of the next available location, in the memory address area where the machine language program is being built. While the actual machine language program is written to a disk file, the assembler must build it as if it were going directly into memory, assigning addresses to instructions and labels accordingly.

The address pointer is usually called the location counter *(LC)*. The LC moves along through the address values where the machine language program is to be placed as the assembler determines the size required by the next instruction or operand. The LC is also used by the assembler in its computation of the offsets required by PC-relative operands. Although it is rarely useful, the value of the LC can be specified in Macro instruction operands by a period (.), as we will see in Chapter 6.

One of the fundamental tasks of every assembler is to construct and maintain a *symbol table*. The symbol table consists of an entry for each symbol in the program being assembled and each symbol's program address value. Since programs are usually assembled as if they were going to be placed in memory at location 0 for execution, the address values in the symbol table are offsets from the program beginning.

During assembly, the LC at the beginning of an instruction or directive corresponds to the PC at execution time. Therefore, the symbol table values for the symbols in a program are the same as those found in the assembler listing of the program. For example, in Example 3.1, the symbol table value for FUN2 is 18 (hex); for FIRST, 0.

Symbol table values for labels are easy for the assembler to determine since the LC has exactly the right value at the time a label is encountered. However, consider the problem of forward references—uses of symbols as operands occurring before the symbols have been defined. Nearly all of the operands in TOYCODE programs fall into this category since the data area appears after the instructions.

Consider the following:

```
LD  COUNT
        .
        .
        .
COUNT:    DC        0
```

When a single-pass assembler encounters the LD instruction, it needs to know the address value of COUNT. If it has not been used in any earlier instruction, COUNT may not appear in the symbol table, in which case the assembler must place it there and indicate in the address value entry that it has not yet been defined. While the assembler still needs to build the machine language version of the LD instruction, this obviously cannot be completed until an instruction or directive with the label COUNT is found.

Because of the forward reference problem and some other inconveniences of single-pass assembly, many assemblers use two passes to translate assembly language programs. In an interactive environment, the source file (the file containing the assembly language program) is read twice, start to finish, during the assembly process. In a batch system, in which programs are submitted as card decks, a deck is read and immediately written to a disk file, then for the second pass, the disk file is read as in an interactive system.

Following are the primary tasks of the two passes of a two-pass assembler. Some of these steps involve a great number of details, but the overall process should be reasonably clear after you study the procedure.

PASS 1:
    Initialize the LC and the symbol table length to zeros
    FOR each instruction of the source program DO
        IF the instruction has a label
        THEN place the label in the symbol table with the value of
            the LC (if it's already there, signal an error—multiply
            defined symbol)
        ENDIF
        Increment LC by the size of the op code
    END-FOR
    FOR each operand DO
        Determine the length of the operand and increment the LC
            by that amount
    END-FOR

PASS 2:
> Initialize the LC to zero
> FOR each instruction in the source program DO
> > Determine the machine code op code for the Macro op code and place it in the machine language program
> > Increment the LC by the size of the op code
> > FOR each operand DO
> > > Compute the machine language for the operand and place it in the machine language program
> > > Increment the LC by the size of the operand
> > END-FOR
> > IF a listing file was requested
> > > THEN
> > > > Convert the machine language instruction to printable form
> > > > Write the printable form of the machine code, along with the source instruction to the list file
> > ENDIF
> END-FOR

Chapter Summary :

1. In this chapter we have weaned you from TOYCOM and launched you into the puppy-chow stage of the VAX assembly language, Macro.

2. The VAX has a four gigabyte virtual address space, half for the users and half for the system.

3. Although there are 16 32-bit registers, only the first 12 are really general purpose.

4. User-defined symbols are strings of 31 or fewer alphanumeric and underline characters. These cannot begin with a numeric.

5. The .BLKL directive allocates one or more longwords of memory and initializes them to zero.

6. The .LONG directive allocates one or more longwords of memory and initializes them to the specified values.

7. The two most basic addressing modes are register and PC-relative. PC-relative addressed operands use the position of the instruction plus an offset to compute an effective operand address.

8. MOVL moves a longword from one place to another, where the places can be either memory or registers.

9. The instructions for the four basic arithmetic operations for LONGWORD data can have either two or three operands. When two are used, the second is both a source and a destination. The operands, both sources and destinations, can be either registers or memory locations.

10. Three more arithmetic instructions are available: INCL adds 1 to the operand, DECL subtracts 1 from the operand, and CLRL clears the operand to 0.

11. Constant operands can be written simply as the operands if they are preceded by #. They are placed in machine code in two different ways: immediate mode and literal mode. They can be used only as source operands.

12. Input and output of LONGWORD data is done through the macro instructions INIT__IO, READ__L, and PRINT__L.

13. Macro programs require the directives .ENTRY and .END, along with a call to the system routine $EXIT__S to properly terminate. Furthermore, because of our input and output macro package, all programs require the .PSECT directive when the LONG keyword parameter is specified.

14. Running a program can be done in three stages using the system commands MACRO to assemble the program, LINK to build the executable image, and RUN to execute the image.

15. A highly informative program listing file can be requested from the assembler.

16. Assemblers often use two passes over the source program to translate it to machine code although it can be done in a single pass. The primary database involved in the assembly process is the symbol table.

17. The Macro instruction that caused a runtime error can be found by looking up the address given in the error message in the assembler listing of the program.

New Instructions

ADDL2	DECL	INCL	MULL2	SUBL2
ADDL3	DIVL2	MOVL	MULL3	SUBL3
CLRL	DIVL3			

New Directives

.BLKL   .END   .ENTRY   .LONG   .PSECT

Input and Output Macros and System Routines

$EXIT_S   INIT_IO   PRINT_L   READ_L

New Terms

Address space
ALU
Assembler pass
Backplane
Bus
Byte-backwards
Displacement
Dividend
Divisor
Effective address
Gigabyte
Image
Immediate mode
Kilobyte
LC
Link operation

Literal mode
Literal operand
Megabyte
Minuend
Mode code
Multiplicand
Multiplier
Offset
PC-relative
PSL
PSW
Runtime error
Subtrahend
Symbol table
Transfer address

Chapter 3 Problem Set :

1. Define address space.

2. What are the other names of R12 through R15?

3. Which half of the PSL does the PSW occupy?

4. What is a connotative symbol?

5. What are the differences in effect between the .LONG and the .BLKL directives?

6. Why are longwords stored backwards in memory?

7. How does PC-relative addressing work?

8. Describe the operands for a DIVL3 instruction.

9. What is the difference between literal mode and immediate mode?

10. What is the primary task of the first pass of a two-pass assembler?

11. Given the following Macro data declarations, translate the two Macro instructions below to machine code. Note that the hex op codes for MOVL and ADDL3 are D0 and C1, respectively.

address (hex)

```
254           COUNT:   .LONG   0
258           VALUE:   .LONG   1
25C           SUM:     .BLKL   1
                          .
                          .
                          .
454                    MOVL    R3, VALUE
459                    ADDL3   COUNT, R5, SUM
```

12. Rework Problem 11 with the instructions at addresses 268 and 26C, respectively.

13. Rework Problem 11 with the instructions at addresses 20F1D and 20F24, respectively.

Write and debug structured Macro programs for the following simple problems. Use memory locations for all variables in Problems 14, 15, and 17.

14. *In:* Two integers.
    Out: The sum, difference, quotient (first divided by second), and product of the two numbers.

15. *In:* Four integers (named FIRST, SECOND, THIRD, and FOURTH).
    Out: **a.** Sum of all input.
           b. FUN1 = FIRST · SECOND − (THIRD / FOURTH).
           c. FUN2 = (FIRST · FIRST − 1) / (SECOND − 17).

16. Repeat Problem 15 using registers in place of all memory locations.

17. *In:* Two integers (named FIRST and SECOND).
    Out: **a.** The third power of FIRST divided by SECOND.
           b. The fourth power of FIRST divided by the square of SECOND.
           c. The fifth power of FIRST divided by the cube of SECOND.

Note: Assume that the input values are sufficiently small so that you needn't worry about results getting too large.

18. Repeat Problem 17 using registers in place of all memory locations.

19. *In:* Three integers, V0, ACCEL, and TIME.

  Out: The distance traveled by an object that uniformly accelerates at ACCEL meters per second per second, starting at V0 meters per second, in TIME seconds. Use the formula:

$$\text{distance} = \text{V0} \cdot \text{TIME} + (\text{ACCEL} \cdot (\text{TIME}^2) / 2)$$

20. *In:* Three integers, LENGTH, WIDTH, and HEIGHT.

  Out: The surface area of a box with the input dimensions.

21. *In:* Five integers, COEF1, COEF2, COEF3, COEF4, and X.

  Out: The value of the following polynomial:

$$\text{COEF1} + (\text{COEF2} \cdot \text{X}) + (\text{COEF3} \cdot (\text{X}^2)) + (\text{COEF4} \cdot (\text{X}^3))$$

Note: Write this program for maximum efficiency, minimizing arithmetic and using registers whenever possible.

22. *In:* Three pairs of integers, named (X1, Y1), (X2, Y2), and (X3, Y3), where each pair represents the horizontal and vertical positions, respectively, of a point on a grid.

  Out: The area of the triangle formed by the three points, as given by the formula:

$$\begin{aligned}\text{AREA} = ((\text{X1} \cdot \text{Y2}) &- (\text{X2} \cdot \text{Y1}) + (\text{X2} \cdot \text{Y3}) - (\text{X3} \cdot \text{Y2}) \\ &+ (\text{X3} \cdot \text{Y1}) - (\text{X1} \cdot \text{Y3})) / 2\end{aligned}$$

4

LOOPS AND
SELECTION
STRUCTURES

The power of the digital computer lies in its capability of choosing, at runtime, among alternate instructions or instruction paths in a program. This capability leads immediately to a facility for forming loops of instructions.

Recall from Chapter 1 that all algorithms can be expressed in three fundamental structures: sequence, selection, and pretest loop. The program solution to Example 3.1 shows the sequence structure. The IF construct of languages such as Pascal and PL/1 represents the selection structure. The WHILE statement of ALGOL and Pascal represents the pretest loop structure.

Once you learn how to use the selection and pretest loop structures in Macro, you will be able to write useful and readable programs with the language. This chapter discusses the VAX mechanisms for building loops and selection structures and includes instructions for testing and comparing the values of registers and memory locations, for conditionally branching, and for building counter-controlled loops.

4.1 Conditional and Unconditional Branch Instructions :

Conditional branching in the TOYCOM architecture involves testing for zero and greater-than-zero values of the ACC register. That is an adequate, though restrictive, technique for a machine that has only one general register. The VAX, however, has 16 registers. Rather than use separate branch instructions to test each of these registers, you could simply add a second operand to specify the place being tested. Another solution is to have the arithmetic, move, and certain other instructions always set certain indicators in one accessible location to indicate information about the results of these operations. Branch instructions, then, could simply test those *indicator bits* and branch or not branch accordingly. The actual branching is done in exactly the same way on the VAX as it is in TOYCOM; that is, the register containing the address of the next instruction is altered. On both machines, that register is called the PC, although on the VAX it is referred to as register F in machine code.

Recall from Chapter 3 that the PSW is the right half of the PSL. The PSW contains the status indicator bits that allow conditional branching. *Setting an indicator* means the bit is given the value of one; *clearing an indicator* means the bit is given the value of zero.

Bit 0 of the PSW, named C, is the carry indicator. It is used internally to facilitate branching and directly for multi-word arithmetic. Bit 1, or V, is the overflow indicator. It is used to indicate that a result cannot be represented correctly in the designated destination location.

Bit 2, or Z, is the zero indicator. A value of one (showing the bit is set) indicates that the last instruction executed produced a zero-valued result. Bit 3, or N, is the negative indicator. It is set when an instruction produces a negative result.

Bits 5, 6, and 7 are *trap bits*. When a trap bit is set for a particular error, the VAX hardware causes a termination of execution when that kind of error is detected. When the trap bit is cleared, that particular kind of error is ignored.

The only relevant trap bit at this point is integer overflow or bit 6. When this bit is set, integer overflows cause the program to stop execution. We will show you how to set and clear trap bits in Chapter 5 and explain overflows in Chapter 6.

The first four bits of the PSW (C, V, Z, and N) are used by the conditional branch instructions individually or in pairs. We will cover the following conditional branch instructions in this chapter:

Mnemonics	Description	Bit Condition
BEQL	Branch on equal	Z = 1
BNEQ	Branch on not equal	Z = 0
BGTR	Branch on greater than	N = 0 and Z = 0
BLSS	Branch on less than	N = 1
BGEQ	Branch on greater than or equal to	N = 0
BLEQ	Branch on less than or equal to	N = 1 or Z = 1

These mnemonics and descriptions may seem somewhat disconnected from the conditions being tested; for example, what has "branch-on-equal" to do with the last instruction having produced a zero-valued result? This will become clear when we introduce the most common techniques for affecting the indicator bits.

The arithmetic and move instructions we covered in Chapter 3 all set the Z and N bits. For example, if the following sequence were executed, the BEQL instruction would succeed—that is, the branch would be taken—since the SUBL2 instruction would cause the Z bit to be set:

```
MOVL  #3, R2
SUBL2 #3, R2
BEQL  LOOP
```

Note that the names of the conditional branch instructions seem to indicate that two operands are being or have been compared, while the arithmetic instructions do not perform direct comparisons. The subtract instruction does the sort of thing a comparison requires, but it also produces a result, which must be placed somewhere. Furthermore, the subtract instruction does the opposite of what is connoted by the conditional branch instruction mnemonics. For example,

```
SUBL2 A, B
BGTR  OUT
```

branches to OUT if B > A—not A < B, which BGTR seems to indicate. This problem occurs because the subtract instruction has its operands in the reverse of the order with which we are most familiar. SUBL2 A, B means B − A. So when a comparison is required, a different instruction, called *compare LONGWORD* (CMPL), should be used.

The general form of the VAX compare instruction for LONGWORD integers is:

CMPL source1, source2

CMPL subtracts the second operand from the first and affects the N, Z, and C indicators according to the difference. The actual result of the compare operation—the difference—is discarded, and neither operand is altered.

The subtraction is done in the normal order we all learned in school and not in the form described in Chapter 3 (that is, the SUBL2 and SUBL3 instructions). The designers of the VAX did not do this just to keep us on our toes; actually, good reasons exist for having two different orderings. Input operands on all instructions appear at the left end of the operand lists, and result-address operands appear at the right end. Therefore, the subtract instruction uses the first operand for the subtrahend, but in the case of CMPL, since both operands are input operands, it makes sense to order them naturally.

It is sometimes convenient to affect the N and Z bits according to a single longword. This can be done with the *test* LONGWORD (TSTL) instruction, the general form of which is:

TSTL source

The TSTL instruction clears the V and C indicators and affects the N and Z indicators according to whether the value of the LONGWORD operand is negative (N is set and Z is cleared) or zero (Z is set and N is cleared), respectively. Note that TSTL is identical to a CMPL instruction whose second operand is zero. However, the TSTL is a shorter instruction. In a sense, using TSTL on a longword is similar to loading a value into the ACC in TOYCOM—it enables a conditional branch depending on that value.

Another instruction, the unconditional branch instruction, corresponds to the B mnemonic in TOYCODE. Macro has three unconditional branch instructions, which are of different sizes; for now, we will explain only the two most simple instructions.

The general form of these two unconditional branch instructions is:

BRx destination-address

The two varieties of this instruction are BRB and BRW. Each uses the PC as a base address for its target, or the place to which it is to branch.

BRB uses a BYTE offset from the PC, which requires its target to be within 127 bytes. Since this is a severe restriction, we do not recommend using BRB unless you are under extreme memory limitations. Even if the target is within 127 bytes when the program is written, later program additions between the branch instruction and its target can cause the instruction to be in error.

BRW uses a WORD (two-byte) offset from the PC to address its target. This allows the target to be anywhere within 32,767 bytes of the PC, which is adequate for nearly all program situations.

Both BRB and BRW are very compact instructions, since neither uses a mode byte. The length of BRB is two bytes; BRW, three.

The machine code for the conditional branch instructions is only two bytes: the op code and a BYTE displacement. The displacement is added to the updated PC to get the target address. The PC points to the first byte of the next instruction when the BYTE displacement is added. Both BRB and BRW also operate this way. While this form of instruction is indeed compact, it also causes some difficulties. Since it uses only a BYTE displacement, the destination must be within 127 bytes of the end of the instruction or 126 bytes of its beginning. This is sometimes not enough. In these cases we must use a conditional branch on the inverse condition to branch around a BRW instruction. For example, if we need to branch to label LOOP when Z is set, we would use:

```
BNEQ AROUND
BRW  LOOP
AROUND:
```

We will now proceed to our discussion of the pretest loop structure in Macro.

4.2   *Pretest Loops* :

In Chapter 1 we presented a standard method of constructing a TOYCODE pretest loop from a given pseudocode pretest loop. We will now do the same for Macro. With Macro's greater expressive power, this should be a much simpler task.

The pseudocode pretest loop and the general translation scheme to express it in Macro are:

Pseudocode	*Macro*
WHILE condition DO	LOOP:
·	Code to evaluate the condition
·	Branch if false to LOOPEND
·	·
END-DO	·
	·
	BRW to LOOP
	LOOPEND:

The following are two examples of pseudocode WHILE loops and their equivalent Macro translations. Note the similarities and differences between these translations and those from pseudocode to TOYCODE. The overall structure is the same: two labels, one at the top and one at the bottom, and an unconditional branch from just before the bottom label to the loop top. The differences lie in the use of the CMPL instruction and the variety of available conditional branch instructions in Macro, which highly simplify the test portion of the loop structure.

Pseudocode	*Macro*	
WHILE IN__DATA >= 100 DO	LOOP1:	
	CMPL	IN_DATA, #100
	BLSS	LOOPEND1
Add IN__DATA to SUM	ADDL2	IN_DATA, SUM
Get IN__DATA	READ_L	IN__DATA
END-DO	BRW	LOOP1
	LOOPEND1:	
WHILE COUNT <= 10 DO	LOOP2:	
	CMPL	COUNT, #10
	BGTR	LOOPEND2
Add COUNT to SUM	ADDL2	COUNT, SUM
Increment COUNT	INCL	COUNT
END-DO	BRW	LOOP2
	LOOPEND2:	

If a WHILE condition contains one or more arithmetic expressions, we must first write the code to evaluate the expressions, and then place those values either in registers or in memory locations. The CMPL instruction is used with those result locations as operands. Consider the following example:

```
WHILE (2 * VALUE) < (SUM / COUNT) DO
    .
    .
    .
END-DO

LOOP:
    MULL3 #2, VALUE, R1
    DIVL3 COUNT, SUM, R2
    CMPL R1, R2
    BGEQ LOOPEND
    .
    .
    .
    BRW LOOP
LOOPEND:
```

Note that we use registers for the temporary values in the WHILE translation. The values being stored in this case cannot be given connotative names, so there is no reason not to use registers for them.

We are now ready to deal with a complete example.

. . . .

Example 4.1

:   Problem Statement

In: A list of nonzero integers from the terminal, followed by a zero.
Out: The sum and average of the input data.

Since this is a very simple example, we will present the pseudocode version of the solution without explanation.

:•   Pseudocode Solution

Initialize SUM and COUNT to zero
Get a VALUE
WHILE VALUE <> 0 DO
    Add VALUE to SUM
    Increment COUNT
    Get a VALUE
END-DO
Compute AVERAGE
Print SUM, AVERAGE
End-of-program

The Macro version of this pseudocode is also quite simple but still new to you, so study it carefully.

::   Macro Solution

```
; SUM AND AVERAGE OF A LIST OF INTEGERS
; IN: A LIST OF NONZERO INTEGERS, FOLLOWED BY ZERO
; OUT: THE SUM AND AVERAGE OF THE INPUT DATA
;
        .PSECT EXAMPLE, LONG
SUM:            .BLKL    1    ; SUM OF INPUT DATA
AVERAGE:        .BLKL    1    ; AVERAGE OF INPUT DATA
COUNT:          .BLKL    1    ; COUNTER FOR INPUT DATA
VALUE:          .BLKL    1    ; AN INPUT VALUE
        .ENTRY EXAMPLE_4_1, 0
        INIT_IO
;
; INITIALIZE SUM AND COUNT TO ZERO
;
```

```
        CLRL    SUM
        CLRL    COUNT
;
; GET A VALUE
;
        READ_L  VALUE
;
; WHILE VALUE <> 0 DO
;
LOOP:
        TSTL    VALUE
        BEQL    LOOPEND
;
;       ADD VALUE TO SUM
;
        ADDL2   VALUE, SUM
;
;       INCREMENT COUNT
;
        INCL    COUNT
;
;       GET A VALUE
;
        READ_L  VALUE
        BRW     LOOP
;
; END-DO
; COMPUTE AVERAGE
;
LOOPEND:
        DIVL3   COUNT, SUM, AVERAGE
;
; PRINT SUM, AVERAGE
;
        PRINT_L  ^'SUM, AVERAGE =', SUM, AVERAGE
        $EXIT_S
;
; END-OF-PROGRAM
;
        .END    EXAMPLE_4_1
```

. . . .

Note that we initialized both SUM and COUNT at execution time with CLRL instructions rather than just using .LONG directives to set them to zero at assembly time. This is a good habit to develop, because occasions may arise when programs are reexecuted without being reloaded. Under these circumstances, the programs would not execute correctly if initialization had been done at assembly time.

While our general rule is that all pseudocode statements should be carried over into the Macro version, we will make some exceptions to this rule in subsequent examples. For instance, we will always forgo writing the end-of-program statement into our Macro programs. Also, we will not explain our PRINT__L and READ__L statements with pseudocode, as these instances of documentation are superfluous.

4.3   *Selection Structures* :

The selection structure in Macro is also similar to, but much simpler than, the TOYCODE version. The general scheme for translating a complete pseudocode IF statement is:

Pseudocode   Macro

IF condition	Code to evaluate the condition
THEN	Branch if false to ELSE
.	.
.	.
.	.
ELSE	BRW to ENDIF
.	ELSE:
.	.
.	.
ENDIF	.
	ENDIF:

Two examples of IF construct translations follow:

Pseudocode

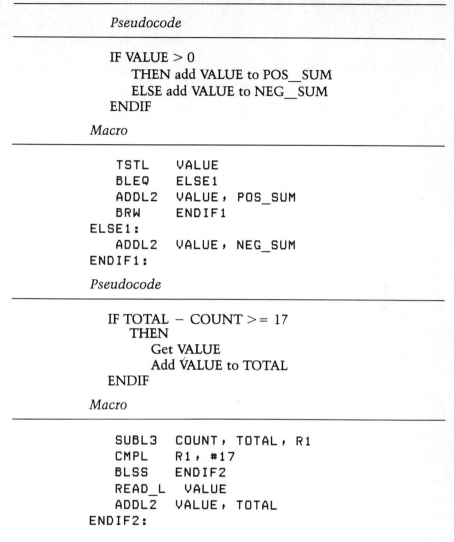

```
IF VALUE > 0
    THEN add VALUE to POS__SUM
    ELSE add VALUE to NEG__SUM
ENDIF
```

Macro

```
    TSTL    VALUE
    BLEQ    ELSE1
    ADDL2   VALUE, POS_SUM
    BRW     ENDIF1
ELSE1:
    ADDL2   VALUE, NEG_SUM
ENDIF1:
```

Pseudocode

```
IF TOTAL - COUNT >= 17
    THEN
        Get VALUE
        Add VALUE to TOTAL
ENDIF
```

Macro

```
    SUBL3   COUNT, TOTAL, R1
    CMPL    R1, #17
    BLSS    ENDIF2
    READ_L  VALUE
    ADDL2   VALUE, TOTAL
ENDIF2:
```

We are now ready to examine another example. Once again, we will use a very simple numerical exercise, as we want to concentrate on the form of the program, not the solution to the problem.

. . . .

Example 4.2

:   *Problem Statement*

In: A list of positive integers representing exam grades, followed
by a negative integer.

Out: **a.** The percentage of passing grades ($>= 60$).
  b. The number of A grades ($>= 90$).

:•   *Pseudocode Solution*

```
Initialize NUM__PASS, NUM__A, and TOTAL to zero
Get a GRADE
WHILE GRADE > 0 DO
    Increment TOTAL
    IF GRADE >= 60
        THEN increment NUM__PASS
    ENDIF
    IF GRADE >= 90
        THEN increment NUM__A
    ENDIF
    Get a GRADE
END-DO
Compute % of passing grades
Print % of passing grades and NUM__A
End-of-program
```

Note that we used separate IF structures for the two conditionals in this program. Although this is slightly less efficient than nesting the second inside the first by placing it in the THEN clause, we prefer this structure. Nested IF structures are difficult to read, especially when nested to a depth greater than two. This doesn't mean we will never nest IF structures, nor does it mean we are dogmatic about this particular program. Either form would be acceptable in this case.

As you study the following Macro translation of the pseudocode solution, remember that Macro programs should be written as translations of—not as start-from-scratch, less-structured lists of—Macro instructions.

:: *Macro Solution*

```
; GRADING PROGRAM
; IN:   A LIST OF POSITIVE INTEGER GRADES, FOLLOWED BY
;        A NEGATIVE INTEGER.
; OUT:  (A) THE PERCENTAGE OF PASSING GRADES ( >= 60).
;       (B) THE NUMBER OF A GRADES ( >= 90).
;
        .PSECT  EXAMPLE, LONG
GRADE:          .BLKL   1  ; INPUT GRADE
NUM_A:          .BLKL   1  ; NUMBER OF A GRADES
TOTAL:          .BLKL   1  ; TOTAL NUMBER OF GRADES
NUM_PASS:       .BLKL   1  ; NUMBER OF PASSING GRADES
PERCENT_PASS:   .BLKL   1  ; PERCENTAGE OF GRADES
;                              THAT ARE PASSING
        .ENTRY  EXAMPLE_4_2,0
        INIT_IO
;
; INITIALIZE NUM_A, TOTAL, & NUM_PASS TO ZERO
;
        CLRL    NUM_A
        CLRL    TOTAL
        CLRL    NUM_PASS
        READ_L  GRADE
;
; WHILE GRADE > 0 DO
;
LOOP:
        TSTL    GRADE
        BLEQ    LOOP_END
;
;       INCREMENT TOTAL
;
        INCL    TOTAL
;
;       IF GRADE >= 60
;         THEN INCREMENT NUM_PASS
;
        CMPL    GRADE, #60
        BLSS    IS_IT_A
        INCL    NUM_PASS
;
```

Continued

```
;         ENDIF
;         IF GRADE >= 90
;            THEN INCREMENT NUM_A
;
IS_IT_A:
        CMPL     GRADE, #90
        BLSS     NOT_A
        INCL     NUM_A
;
;         ENDIF
;
NOT_A:
        READ_L   GRADE
        BRW      LOOP
;
; END-DO
; COMPUTE % OF PASSING GRADES
;
LOOP_END:
        MULL3    #100, NUM_PASS, R1
        DIVL3    TOTAL, R1, PERCENT_PASS
        PRINT_L  ^'% OF CLASS WHO PASSED:', PERCENT_PASS
        PRINT_L  ^'NUMBER OF A GRADES :', NUM_A
        $EXIT_S
        .END     EXAMPLE_4_2
```

. . . .

Note that again we have avoided using registers for data and results. In later chapters this will become even more necessary, as we will need the registers for a variety of memory addressing schemes (for example, dealing with data structures). Recall that, although registers are faster, we often prefer memory locations because they can be given connotative names, whereas registers cannot.

4.4   *Counter-Controlled Loops* : : : : : : : : : : : : : : : : :

Another control structure that is very common in algorithms for computers is the *counter-controlled loop*. This control structure is not really essential, since it can be simulated with a WHILE structure. However, as the VAX instruction repertoire provides a somewhat convenient method for implementing counter-controlled loops, we will include them here.

The simplest counter-controlled loop is the Pascal FOR statement, which has the following two forms:

1. FOR index : = initial-value TO terminal-value DO statement(s)

2. FOR index : = initial-value DOWNTO terminal-value DO statement(s)

In the first form, the index is set to the initial-value and then compared with the terminal-value. If it is less than or equal to the terminal-value, the statement or statements are executed. Control is returned to the FOR statement, and the index is then incremented by one and again compared to the terminal-value. If it is less than or equal to the terminal-value, the statement or statements are again executed. This process is repeated until the index becomes greater than the terminal-value. In the second form, a similar process takes place, but the index is repeatedly decremented until it becomes less than the terminal-value.

In both cases, FOR is a *pretest counter-controlled loop* construct. Recall that pretest means that the test for completion is done at the top, rather than at the bottom, of the loop. Placing the completion test at the top of the loop prevents the execution of the statement or statements when the index is initially greater than the terminal-value. Versions of FORTRAN that came before FORTRAN 77 used a *posttest counter-controlled loop*, but Pascal, FORTRAN 77, and most other languages with counter-controlled loops use the pretest form. We will henceforth include the FOR statement in our pseudocode. However, we will use the statement closing bracket END-FOR instead of the BEGIN/END brackets that are used in Pascal.

The FOR construct has four logically separate parts: the initialization of the index, the test and conditional branch, the increment, and the loop branch or the branch back to the top of the loop.

In pseudocode, we could write these four parts of the FOR-TO construct as:

```
        Initialize index to initial-value
        IF index < = terminal-value
            THEN go to LOOP
            ELSE go to LOOPEND
        ENDIF
LOOP:
        Execute loop statement(s)
        Increment index
        IF index < = terminal-value
            THEN go to LOOP
        ENDIF
LOOPEND:
```

This pseudocode is unlike any we have used in that it is unstructured. While it faithfully models the action of the Pascal FOR-TO statement, note that it repeats the test and conditional branch. Our purpose in duplicating this code was to show how it can be naturally implemented using the following VAX instruction.

The VAX instruction set includes an instruction that does both the index increment operation and the conditional branch to the loop statement or statements. This instruction is the ACBL, for *a*dd, *c*ompare, and *b*ranch LONGWORD. The general form of the ACBL instruction is:

ACBL limit, stepsize, index, address

The limit and stepsize can be constants, registers, or memory locations. When implementing the FOR-TO construct, the stepsize will always be 1, whereas it will always be −1 for the FOR-DOWNTO construct. The index can be a register or a memory location.

The exact actions of the ACBL can be described by the following pseudocode:

```
Add stepsize to index
IF stepsize >= 0
    THEN IF index <= limit
            THEN branch
         ENDIF
    ELSE IF index >= limit
            THEN branch
         ENDIF
ENDIF
```

Note that ACBL, which is far more complex than any of the instructions previously described, represents a class of instructions not usually found on small computers, nor on computers of any size built before 1963.

Because the ACBL instruction was obviously designed for posttest loops (it includes the increment operation), we must place it at the end of the loop. To implement the more common pretest loop, we will have to build in a second test at the top of the loop for the initial-value of the index. The ACBL instruction then can be used for all increments and subsequent tests.

The following shows the two forms of the Pascal FOR statement in Macro:

```
FOR INDEX1 := INITIAL1 TO LIMIT1 DO
    statement(s)
END-FOR
```

```
        MOVL    INITIAL1, INDEX1
        CMPL    INDEX1, LIMIT1
        BLEQ    LOOP1
        BRW     LOOPEND1
LOOP1:
        code for statement(s)
        ACBL    LIMIT1, #1, INDEX1, LOOP1
LOOPEND1:
```

```
FOR INDEX2 := INITIAL2 DOWNTO LIMIT2 DO
    statement(s)
END-FOR
```

```
        MOVL    INITIAL2, INDEX2
        CMPL    INDEX2, LIMIT2
        BGEQ    LOOP2
        BRW     LOOPEND2
LOOP2:
        code for statement(s)
        ACBL    LIMIT2, #-1, INDEX2, LOOP2
LOOPEND2:
```

Note the two differences between the code for the FOR-TO construct and the code for the FOR-DOWNTO construct. First, the conditional branch is BLEQ for FOR-TO and BGEQ for FOR-DOWNTO. Second, the stepsize on the ACBL is 1 for FOR-TO and -1 for FOR-DOWNTO.

In both forms of the FOR statement, when the initial-value and terminal-value of the FOR variable are constants, the compare, conditional branch, and unconditional branch instructions, as well as the last label, are unnecessary.

Examples of Pascal FOR statements and their Macro equivalents are shown below:

Pseudocode

FOR COUNT : = 1 TO 15 DO
   SUM : = SUM + COUNT
END-FOR

Macro

```
      MOVL      #1, COUNT
LOOP1:
      ADDL2     COUNT, SUM
      ACBL      #15, #1, COUNT, LOOP1
```

Pseudocode

FOR INDEX : = 100 DOWNTO 1 DO
   SUMSQ: = SUMSQ + INDEX*INDEX
END-FOR

Macro

```
      MOVL      #100, INDEX
LOOP2:
      MULL3     INDEX, INDEX, R1
      ADDL2     R1, SUMSQ
      ACBL   #1, #-1, INDEX, LOOP2
```

We are now ready for another example program. You should already know how to find the largest and smallest values in a list of numbers, so we will forgo explaining the process for the following problem and simply list the pseudocode solution.

. . . .

Example 4.3

⦂ Problem Statement

> *In:* An integer, LENGTH, followed by LENGTH-integers.
> *Out:* **a.** The maximum value in the input data.
> **b.** The minimum value in the input data.

⦂ Pseudocode Solution

```
Get LENGTH
IF LENGTH > 0 THEN
    Get VALUE
    Initialize MAX and MIN to VALUE
    FOR COUNT := 2 to LENGTH DO
        Get VALUE
        IF VALUE > MAX
            THEN set MAX to VALUE
        ENDIF
        IF VALUE < MIN
            THEN set MIN to VALUE
        ENDIF
    END-FOR
    Print results
    ELSE print error message—no data
ENDIF
End-of-program
```

The Macro version of this pseudocode is a straightforward application of the translation techniques discussed in this chapter.

:: *Macro Solution*

```
; MAXIMUM AND MINIMUM OF A LIST OF INTEGERS
; IN:  A HEADER-VALUE LIST OF INTEGERS
; OUT: THE LARGEST AND THE SMALLEST OF THE INPUT
;
        .PSECT  EXAMPLE, LONG
LENGTH: .BLKL 1  ; THE NUMBER OF INPUT INTEGERS
VALUE:  .BLKL 1  ; INPUT DATA VALUE
MAX:    .BLKL 1  ; LARGEST INPUT VALUE
MIN:    .BLKL 1  ; SMALLEST INPUT VALUE
COUNT:  .BLKL 1  ; COUNTER FOR INPUT DATA
        .ENTRY  EXAMPLE_4_3, 0
        INIT_IO
        READ_L  LENGTH
;
; IF LENGTH > 0 THEN
;
        TSTL    LENGTH
        BGTR    START
        BRW     ERROR
START:
        READ_L  VALUE
;
;    INITIALIZE MAX AND MIN TO THE VALUE
;
        MOVL    VALUE, MAX
        MOVL    VALUE, MIN
;
;    FOR COUNT := 2 TO LENGTH DO
;
        MOVL    #2, COUNT
        CMPL    COUNT, LENGTH
        BLEQ    LOOP
        BRW     LOOPEND
LOOP:
        READ_L  VALUE
;
;       IF VALUE > MAX
;           THEN SET MAX TO VALUE
;
```

```
        CMPL      VALUE, MAX
        BLEQ      ENDIF1
        MOVL      VALUE, MAX
;
;          ENDIF
;          IF VALUE < MIN
;             THEN SET MIN TO VALUE
;
ENDIF1:
        CMPL      VALUE, MIN
        BGEQ      ENDIF2
        MOVL      VALUE, MIN
;
;          ENDIF
;
ENDIF2:
        ACBL      LENGTH, #1, COUNT, LOOP
;
;       END-FOR
;
LOOPEND:
        PRINT_L   ^'MAXIMUM & MINIMUM =', MAX, MIN
        BRW       ENDIF3
;
;       ELSE PRINT ERROR MESSAGE--NO DATA
;
ERROR:
        PRINT_L   ^'*** ERROR--NO DATA'
;
; ENDIF
;
ENDIF3:
        $EXIT_S
        .END      EXAMPLE_4_3
```

4.5   More Loop Instructions : : : : : : : : : : : : : : : : : :

AOB (for *add* *one* and *branch*) and SOB (for *subtract* *one* and *branch*) do not add anything to the power of Macro, but they do provide more efficient ways of forming certain counter-controlled loops. These instructions should be used, where applicable, in place of the FOR loops built from the ACBL instruction.

The general forms of the AOB and SOB instructions are:

AOBLSS limit, index, address
AOBLEQ limit, index, address
SOBGTR index, address
SOBGEQ index, address

The AOBLEQ instruction performs the same operation as ACBL with a stepsize of 1: It increments the index and branches as long as the index stays less than or equal to the limit. The AOBLSS instruction also performs this operation except that the comparison with the index is strictly for less than, rather than less than or equal to, the limit.

The SOBGTR instruction decrements the index and branches as long as the index remains greater than zero. The SOBGEQ instruction performs the same function except that the comparison is for greater than or equal to, rather than just greater than, zero.

Although we could have used the AOBLEQ instruction for our translation of FOR-TO constructs, we still would have had to use ACBL for the FOR-DOWNTO construct, because the SOB instructions are slightly less general than the AOB instructions. To keep it simple, we chose to use ACBL for both. In the remainder of the book, however, we will use the slightly more efficient AOB instructions whenever possible.

4.6   More Assembler Directives : : : : : : : : : : : : : :

The directive .TITLE is used to name the object module created from the assembly of a Macro program. This name bears no relationship to the name of the file where the object module is stored (*filename.OBJ*). If a .TITLE directive is not present in a Macro program, the module is assigned the name .MAIN.

The primary reason to name an object module using .TITLE is to identify it in the linker load map, in the trace caused by runtime errors, and for use in the debugger facilities of the VMS discussed in Chapter 5.

The general form of the .TITLE directive is:

.TITLE module-name

The module name can be a string of one to 31 characters. Any excess characters are truncated.

The .SUBTITLE directive (abbreviated as .SBTTL) is used to name sections of Macro programs. Any program that is over two pages in length should be broken into logical units by .SUBTITLE. The general form of .SUBTITLE is:

.SUBTITLE   comment-string

The comment string, which can have up to 40 characters, is printed on the second line of each page of the program listing. It is also entered into the table of contents section that precedes the program listing in the listing file, along with the page number and line sequence number where the .SUBTITLE directive occurred.

You sometimes will wish to begin a portion of the program listing on a new page, particularly when the code begins a new logical unit. This can be accomplished with the .PAGE directive, which has no parameters.

Many more directives are available in Macro, some of which will be covered in later chapters. Complete explanations of all of the Macro directives can be found in the VAX-11 Macro Language Reference Manual.

Chapter Summary :

1. Branching in the VAX is similar to branching in TOYCOM, except that the C, V, Z, and N indicators of the PSW are used to determine whether a branch succeeds.

2. The CMPL instruction simplifies the comparison of two LONGWORD quantities. The TSTL instruction allows the testing of the value of a single register or longword in memory.

3. The BRW and BRB instructions are unconditional branches that correspond to the TOYCODE B instruction.

4. General translation techniques are used to implement in Macro the pseudocode WHILE loops, IF-THEN-ELSE selections, and FOR-TO and FOR-DOWNTO counter-controlled loops.

5. The ACBL instruction, while designed for posttest loops, can be used to implement Pascal pretest FOR loops. It increments a given index, compares it to a given limit, and conditionally branches, depending on the comparison.

6. The SOB and AOB instructions provide slightly faster execution for some of the simpler loops normally implemented using ACBL.

7. Other assembler directives include .TITLE, which is used to label object modules; .SUBTITLE, which is used to put listing headings on sections of code; and .PAGE, which ejects the current page of the listing.

New Instructions

ACBL	BEQL	BLEQ	BRB	SOBGEQ
AOBLEQ	BGEQ	BLSS	BRW	SOBGTR
AOBLSS	BGTR	BNEQ	CMPL	TSTL

New Directives

.PAGE   .SUBTITLE (or .SBTTL)   .TITLE

New Terms

Clearing an indicator   Pretest counter-controlled loops
Indicator bits   Setting an indicator
Posttest counter-controlled loops   Trap bits

Chapter 4 Problem Set :

1. Describe the first four bits of the PSW.

2. What is the length in bytes of a BRW instruction?

3. What is the disadvantage of posttest counter-controlled loops?

4. Explain all of the differences between .TITLE and .SUBTITLE.

5. What are the differences between SOBGTR and ACBL?

Write Macro translations of the following pseudocode constructs:

6. IF SUM · 3 > SUPERSUM
       THEN print AVERAGE
    ENDIF

7. IF KOUNT < = LENGTH
       THEN
           Add NEXT to SUM
           Increment KOUNT
       ELSE
           Set RESULT to SUM
           Set KOUNT to zero
    ENDIF

8. IF FIRST < SECOND
       THEN IF FIRST < THIRD
               THEN print FIRST
               ELSE print THIRD
           ENDIF
       ELSE IF SECOND < THIRD
               THEN print SECOND
               ELSE print THIRD
           ENDIF
    ENDIF

9. WHILE IN_DATA > 0 DO
       Set SUM to IN_DATA · IN_DATA / 2
       Get IN_DATA
    END-DO

10. WHILE KOUNT < LENGTH DO
  Increment KOUNT
  IF VALUE < MAX
    THEN add VALUE to TOTAL
  ENDIF
  Get VALUE
  END-DO

11. FOR KOUNT := 1 TO 100 DO
  Get VALUE
  Add VALUE to SUM
  END-FOR

12. FOR INDEX := TOTAL DOWNTO 10 DO
  IF INDEX > 100
    THEN add INDEX to TOP_SUM
    ELSE add INDEX to BOT_SUM
  ENDIF
  Print INDEX
  END-FOR

Write and debug Macro programs for the following problems. Be sure to design your programs by first writing a pseudocode solution, ensuring the pseudocode is correct, and then directly translating the pseudocode to Macro.

13. *In:* A list of positive integers, followed by a negative integer.
  Out: The largest and smallest values in the input.

14. *In:* A list of nonzero integers followed by zero.
  Out: *a.* The sum of the squares of the input data.
    b. The percentage of the data that are positive.

15. *In:* An integer, LENGTH, followed by LENGTH-integers.
  Out: *a.* The average of the input.
    b. The square of the sum of the positive values of the input.

16. *In:* An integer.
  Out: *a.* If the input is even, the tenth power of the input.
    b. If the input is odd, the eighth power of the input.

17. *In:* Ten integers.
  Out: For each input value:
    a. If the value is > 100, its square.
    b. If the value is < 0, its cube.
    c. If the value is > 0 but < 50, the fourth power of the value.
    d. Print "NOT APPLICABLE" for all other values.

18.   *In:*   A number, LENGTH, followed by LENGTH-pairs of integers. The first number in each pair has a value of one, two, or three, and indicates that the second number in the pair is a value associated with a list number of one, two, or three, respectively.

   Out: For each list, the sum of the squares of its values.

19.   *In:*   A list of positive integers, followed by − 1.

   Out: *a.* The percentages of input integers that are in the range:
   (1) 0–50
   (2) 51–74
   (3) 75–100
   b. If any input value is greater than 100, have an error message printed, but allow execution to continue.

20.   *In:*   A single integer, LAST.

   Out: The sum, by repeated addition, of the integers between and including 1 and LAST.

21.   *In:*   A number, LENGTH, followed by LENGTH-integers.

   Out: *a.* The number of times the value 27 occurs.
   b. The average of all input data that are > 100.
   c. The message "ALL DATA OK" if no input value is outside the range 0–1000.

22.   *In:*   Three pairs of integers, where each pair represents the lower and upper bounds of the values for the dimensions of a box. The first pair is for length, the second for width, and the third for depth.

   Out: *a.* The volumes of all possible boxes with dimensions in the given ranges, in steps of one.
   b. If the box volume for any combination of dimensions exceeds 1000, have an error message printed but allow execution to continue.

23.   *In:*   A list of positive integers followed by − 1.

   Out: The largest and second largest values in the input.

5

USING THE
VAX/VMS
DEBUGGER

This chapter discusses the VAX/VMS debugging facility, a powerful and indispensable aid to the Macro programmer that enables speedy investigations and convenient monitoring of program execution.

5.1 What Is a Debugger? :

If your programming experience has been largely with high-level languages, you probably have had no occasion to use a debugging system. However, debugging systems for high-level languages are starting to become available.

Since assembly language programmers deal with very small portions of data and rather simple instructions, they need special assistance in eliminating program errors. A debugger provides that assistance. Although we, of course, can use the same tools commonly used in debugging high-level language programs, such as instructions to display a multitude of intermediate results, the VMS debugger provides much more powerful assistance.

The debugger is an attractive tool because it allows complete runtime control of program execution. For example, we can execute single instructions, or we can temporarily stop the program at any desired location and then restart it at our command. While execution is suspended, we can poke around in memory or the registers, determining current values or even changing those values, before continuing. To allow such symbolic access to storage locations, both the assembler and the linker must be instructed to retain the symbol table that is normally discarded by execution time.

5.2   Breakpoints, Tracepoints, and Watchpoints : : :

You will have a number of commands available when working on a program whose execution is controlled by the debugger. To assist debugging, three kinds of points, or markers, can be set at addresses in a Macro program. These points signify that the locations at which they are set have significance to the debugger during program execution.

5.2.1   Breakpoints

Breakpoints are used to tell the debugger to suspend execution when the program reaches the addresses at which they are set; that is, when the PC equals the value of the address at which a breakpoint is set, execution is suspended. A breakpoint must be set while in the debugger, using the SET BREAK command. The general form of this command is:

SET BREAK [/AFTER:n] address [DO (command(s))]

If you ignore the bracketed or optional parts, this command simply sets a breakpoint at the indicated address, usually a label on an instruction. Execution under the debugger will halt just before that instruction is executed.

The "/AFTER:n" option allows you to set the breakpoint to take effect when the program reaches that address the nth time during execution and every time after that; the first $n - 1$ times are ignored. This is very useful when an area of code operates correctly for a while and then goes bad. You do not need to halt execution during the correct circuits through the code.

The "DO (command(s))" option allows you to instruct the debugger to execute a list of debugger commands when it reaches the breakpoint. We will discuss the commands you would place in the DO list in Section 5.5.2.

Although you may carefully plan, thoughtfully write, and thoroughly document your program, execution time errors can still occur. Sometimes arithmetic is the cause of the problem; for example, your program may request that a value be divided by zero. Other times your code may generate invalid addresses, causing the system to stop execution and display an error message. These are places where it would be valuable to have breakpoints; the debugger can place those breakpoints for you. The following command causes the system to treat execution exceptions as breakpoints, giving control to the user rather than aborting the program and giving control back to VMS:

SET EXCEPTION BREAK

After working on a program with the debugger for a while, you may forget where you have placed the breakpoints in the code. To find out where all of the current breakpoints are, you can use the command:

SHOW BREAK

When the usefulness of a particular breakpoint has ended, but you wish to continue the debugging session, you can remove that breakpoint with the following command:

CANCEL BREAK address

To cancel only the breakpoint that stops execution when an error occurs, you use the command:

CANCEL EXCEPTION BREAK

If you wish to remove all breakpoints from a program, you use the following command:

CANCEL BREAK/ALL

You will have a better understanding of the use of breakpoints after we discuss in Section 5.4 the commands you will use to determine the values of memory locations and registers while execution is suspended.

5.2.2 Tracepoints

It often occurs that, although the code is there, whatever it is supposed to do never seemed to happen. To find out whether the program ever reached that particular code, you can use the debugger to set a *tracepoint*. A tracepoint, when reached during execution while under control of the debugger, causes the debugger to print a message indicating that the point has been reached before continuing execution.

The command to set tracepoints is similar to the command for setting breakpoints. Its general form is:

SET TRACE address

The address is any address within your program. As an example, consider the following:

```
SET TRACE IN_LOOP
```

When the address value of IN__LOOP is reached during debugger execution, the following is printed (or displayed):

```
trace at IN_LOOP
```

Branch instructions, subprogram call instructions, or both can be traced using tracepoints. Because we have not yet explained Macro subprograms, we will limit our discussion to branch-tracing. To trace all branch instructions, use the following command:

SET TRACE/BRANCH

Placing a tracepoint where a breakpoint has already been set cancels the breakpoint; only the tracepoint remains. To find out where all of your tracepoints are, use the command:

SHOW TRACE

To cancel particular tracepoints, give the CANCEL command the specific address operands or the qualifier BRANCH. To cancel all tracepoints, the following form can be used:

CANCEL TRACE/ALL

For example, suppose we have an IF-THEN-ELSE construct that seems to operate incorrectly. To discover which clause, ELSE or THEN, is reached each time the IF is encountered, we can place a label on the THEN clause and set tracepoints on both that label and the label already on the ELSE clause. The following example demonstrates this.

. . . .

Example 5.1

: *Using Tracepoints*

```
; IF VALUE > 0 THEN
;
        TSTL        VALUE
        BLEQ        ELSE
;
;       INCREMENT COUNT
;
THEN:
        INCL        COUNT
        BRW         ENDIF
;
;   ELSE DECREMENT COUNT
;
ELSE:
        DECL        COUNT
;
; ENDIF
;
ENDIF:
```

. . . .

After these tracepoints are set, the debugger commands

```
SET TRACE THEN
SET TRACE ELSE
```

will cause the debugger to indicate which path is chosen each time the selection is executed.

5.2.3 Watchpoints

Tracepoints allow you to monitor any memory location in your program's executable code. Sometimes, however, it is a data location that mysteriously changes to an absurd value, obviously without your intending it. It helps to solve such mysteries if you can stop program execution at the time the value is altered and investigate the cause. The debugger provides this capability with *watchpoints*.

Watchpoints can be set at almost any data location in your program. The command to set a watchpoint is as follows:

SET WATCH address

Fetching values from data locations with attached watchpoints does not cause any action. When storing values in a data location, however, you receive some very pertinent information from the debugger. Suppose you have set a watchpoint at the address of the data location labeled SUM. When a new value, say 27, is stored into SUM, the following is printed or displayed:

```
write to .MAIN.\SUM at PC .MAIN.\LOOP+6
old value = 00000000
new value = 0000001B
```

This means that the instruction at address LOOP + 6 of your module named .MAIN. has stored the value 1B (hex for decimal 27) into location SUM whose value at that time was 0. Section 5.5.1 will show you how to get decimal instead of hex values. Note that .MAIN. is the default name for the object module; if you have specified a name with a .TITLE directive, it will be used in place of .MAIN.

After these three lines are printed, execution is suspended at the address of the instruction following the instruction that changed SUM, address LOOP + 6. Section 5.3 will explain how to restart the program.

A regrettable weakness of the current version (3.0) of the VAX/VMS debugger is that it cannot watch registers. Because the memory write-protect mechanism of the VAX is used to implement watchpoints, registers were necessarily excluded.

To find out where you have set the watchpoints in your program, use the command:

SHOW WATCH

To cancel a particular watchpoint, use the command:

CANCEL WATCH address

To cancel all watchpoints in your program, use the command:

CANCEL WATCH/ALL

If you should ever wish to cancel all three kinds of points set in your program, you can use the CANCEL ALL command. This command also sets the debugger parameters back to their original default values. (This is significant only if you have changed the default values as described in Section 5.5.1.)

5.3   Running Programs with the Debugger : : : : : : :

Three commands cause execution of program code under the control of the debugger: GO, STEP, and CALL.

Note that these commands are significant only when a program has been assembled and linked with options set for the debugger before execution. Section 5.5 will explain the syntax of these options.

To cause the debugger to start (or restart) execution and to continue until a breakpoint, watchpoint, or program completion suspends that execution, use the GO command. Its general form is as follows:

GO [address]

The address option allows you to choose a particular address where you want execution to begin. If you do not take this option, execution will begin at the current value of the PC (just after the last position executed) or at the transfer address of your program if you are beginning a debugging session. Since addressing in the debugger is symbolic by default, you can easily begin or restart execution at any program label.

The output of the GO command is a single line indicating the symbolic address where execution began, as shown below:

```
DBG>GO LOOP
start at .MAIN.\LOOP
```

"DBG>" is the debugger prompt. If the address given on the GO command is the name on an .ENTRY directive, the message is:

```
routine start at .MAIN.\program-name
```

When you wish to execute only a few instructions so you can closely monitor what is happening, use the STEP command. Its general form is as follows:

STEP {/qualifier} [n]

Note that we use braces to identify items that can appear zero or more times. Therefore, the STEP command can have either no qualifiers or a succession of them, all beginning with a slash. Qualifiers that can be attached to STEP are INTO, which means that the stepping should include steps into subprograms, and SYSTEM, which means that the stepping should include instructions inside system subprograms. If these options are not set, STEP goes directly from a subprogram call to the following instruction, totally ignoring the subprogram. Note that SYSTEM has no effect if INTO is not also set.

Two other qualifiers can be attached to a STEP command: OVER, which is the opposite of INTO, and NOSYSTEM, which is the opposite of SYSTEM. Both of these are the system default values. We are allowed to request them because a command exists that can reset any system default during a debugging session. We will explain how to use this command in Section 5.5.1.

The optional value *n* that can be attached to the STEP command is the number of instructions that you want executed before a halt is forced. If left out of the command, *n* defaults to one.

When the STEP command is given, the debugger displays two lines. The first is the symbolic address at which execution was started. The second gives the symbolic address at which execution was suspended, as well as a disassembled version of the instruction at that address, which will be executed next. The following example demonstrates this.

. . . .

Example 5.2: The STEP Command

```
DBG>STEP
start at .MAIN.\OUT
stepped to .MAIN.\OUT+08: DIVL3   #0A,W.MAIN.\POZ_KNT,R1
```

. . . .

The instruction executed by the STEP command was at address OUT and was eight bytes in length. The next instruction is DIVL3 whose operands are a literal 10 (A in hex), the memory location POZ_KNT, and R1. The W^ indicates that the operand is addressed with WORD-offset PC-relative mode.

A third method of executing code under the control of the debugger, for when the code to be executed is a subprogram, uses the CALL command. We will explain the CALL command after we have introduced you to Macro subprograms in Chapter 10.

5.4   EXAMINE and DEPOSIT Commands : : : : : : :

We have described how to set monitoring points in code and data. This section will show how you can use the opportunities provided by the temporary halt of execution to poke about in memory and the registers to find out what has been going on.

To display the contents of memory locations or registers, use the EXAMINE command. Its general form is:

EXAMINE {/qualifier} [address [:address]] {, address [:address]}

We will discuss the qualifiers of the EXAMINE command later in this section. The rest of the command parameters are used for specifying the addresses of the locations you want to examine. You can look at a single LONGWORD location, a span of longwords, or a list of locations or location spans. A span is specified by supplying two addresses separated by a colon.

The output of the EXAMINE command shows the module name, the symbolic name of the location, with an offset if necessary, and the hex value of that location. For example, consider the following. (The default radix of all output from the debugger is in hex, although this can be reset.)

. . . .

Example 5.3: The EXAMINE Command

```
DBG>EXAMINE KOUNT
.MAIN.\KOUNT:    00000042

DBG>EXAMINE KOUNT:KOUNT+4
.MAIN.\KOUNT:    00000042
.MAIN.\KOUNT+4:    00000244

DBG>EXAMINE
.MAIN.\KOUNT+8:    00000006
```

. . . .

The last output in this example shows what happens if you do not include a parameter on an EXAMINE command; the longword following the last displayed longword is displayed. Register names, perfectly valid parameters for the EXAMINE command, are shown in their natural order; that is, if you ask to examine the span of R4:R8, you will see those five registers.

The one qualifier for the EXAMINE command that we will discuss here is INSTRUCTION; all of the other options are set to reasonable values by default. Section 5.5.1 will explain how to change these default values, both for individual commands and for all future commands in a debugging session. The EXAMINE/INSTRUCTION command disassembles the instruction or instructions at the address or addresses specified in the parameter list.

Disassembly means that the machine language instruction or instructions are translated back to symbolic form: The Macro op code and the symbols from the Macro program are used in place of the machine language operands. This can be very helpful for determining the cause of runtime errors. The form of the output produced by EXAMINE/INSTRUCTION is shown in the following example, which disassembles and displays two instructions.

. . . .

Example 5.4: EXAMINE with the INSTRUCTION Qualifier

```
DBG> EXAMINE/INSTRUCTION ENDIF
EX_5_5\ENDIF:    ACBL    #0A,#01,W^EX_5_5\COUNT,EX_5_5\LOOP
DBG> EXAMINE/INSTRUCTION
EX_5_5\ENDIF+08:    DIVL3    #0A,W^EX_5_5\SUM,W^EX_5_\AVERAGE
```

In the first, an ACBL instruction is displayed with the following operands: a constant 10 (A in hex), a constant one, COUNT, and the branch address of LOOP. The next instruction is displayed by leaving the parameter blank in a second EXAMINE/INSTRUCTION. It shows a DIVL3 instruction with a constant 10 (A in hex), SUM, and AVERAGE as the operands.

Although doing so is somewhat hazardous, you can use the DEPOSIT command to change the values of registers and memory locations while the debugger has halted program execution. This command's general form is:

DEPOSIT {/qualifiers} address = expression {, expression}

The qualifiers can be overlooked for now. The parameter allows you to place a value or list of values into memory locations and registers starting at the specified address. For example,

```
DBG>DEPOSIT KOUNT = 0
```

places the value of zero into the longword at location KOUNT. The following example,

```
DBG>DEPOSIT KOUNT = 0, 42, 133
```

places the values of zero in KOUNT, 42 (hex) in KOUNT + 4, and 133 (hex) in KOUNT + 8.

You can examine and deposit values to registers as if they were memory locations. However, the names R12 through R15 cannot be used and must be replaced with FP, AP, SP, and PC, respectively.

The PSL can be examined; its bottom half, the PSW, can be the destination of a DEPOSIT command as well. When the PSL is examined upon initial entry to the debugger, the following is displayed:

```
PSL: CMP TP FPD IS CURMOD PRVMOD IPL DV FU IV T N Z V C
       0   0   0   0   USER    USER   00  0  0  0  0 0 0 0 0
```

Although the left half contains privileged data for examination only, the right half, the PSW, is user-writable: We can deposit a new value to it. However, because the top (left) half of the PSL is not changeable, we must add a type qualifier on the DEPOSIT command to force the deposited value into the bottom half. The type qualifiers BYTE, WORD, and LONG determine the size of the value to be deposited.

For example, to set the trap bit for integer overflow, we could use the following command:

```
DBG>DEPOSIT/WORD PSL = 20
```

This assumes that the mode is hex, the default value; 20 (hex) has a 1 in bit 5, and 0s elsewhere. This command will cause the program to intercept integer overflow conditions, suspend execution, and display a message that an arithmetic trap has occurred. WORD is the type qualifier.

The type qualifier of the DEPOSIT command to the PSL must be WORD or BYTE. If the default of LONG is used, the command will attempt to change the privileged (left) end of the PSL, which is illegal. We will explain the use of type qualifiers more fully in Chapter 6.

Use of the DEPOSIT command requires self-restraint. It is easy to believe, after finding a program bug through the debugger and changing the value of some location to fix the bug, that you have fixed the program. To really fix the program, you must exit the debugger, change the source version of the program with an editor, and then reassemble and retest the program. Try to remember that changes with the DEPOSIT command are merely quick-and-dirty checks of ideas. When they work, you must go back and change the source version to effect a real correction.

5.5   *Getting Into and Out of the Debugger* : : : : : : :

This section explains how to get into and out of the debugger, how to set certain debugger default values, and how to use the breakpoint DO options.

The debugger's value is greatly enhanced by its ability to reference memory locations symbolically. If we had to refer to program variables and code symbols by their machine addresses during debugging, the lack of readability would discourage its use. To avoid that problem, we make the assembler symbol table available to the debugger by adding the parameter ENABLE = DEBUG to the MACRO assembly command. This parameter also places execution under the control of the debugger when the RUN command is used. The following command saves the symbol table for the debugger:

$ MACRO/ENABLE = DEBUG filename

We will see in Chapter 10 the importance of symbols from other routines that the linker brings together with our code. To provide access to such global symbols, we must include the qualifier DEBUG on the LINK command as shown below:

$ LINK/DEBUG filename

After you have enabled the DEBUG option on the MACRO command, the RUN command produces a message that you are running under the control of the debugger and shows the current version number of the debugger. It also provides the name of the language of your program and the name of the module you will be debugging. You are then presented with the debugger prompt: DBG>. You can type in any of the debugger commands after the prompt.

To exit the debugger, use any of the following commands. EXIT and control/Z both get you out of the debugger, but you cannot restart debugging without beginning an entirely new session. Control/C and control/Y also get you out of the debugger, but these commands allow you to restart your debugging session with all points and parameter settings intact. You restart the session using either the CONTINUE or the DEBUG command.

5.5.1 *Changing Parameter Default Values*

Several times in this chapter we have stated that certain debugger parameters have default values. This section explains how to change these parameters.

The default mode is hex. The *mode parameter* controls the radix of all debugger input (from DEPOSIT) and output (from EXAMINE and WATCH). To set the mode to some new radix, use the following command:

SET MODE mode-keyword

The mode keywords are DECIMAL, HEXADECIMAL, and OCTAL. (The OCTAL keyword is an option for those users of PDP-8 and PDP-11 minicomputers who have become so comfortable with octal that they refuse to adjust their thinking to hex.)

To find out the current mode setting, use the SHOW MODE command. The mode can be changed for individual commands by attaching the mode keyword to the command as a qualifier. For example, when the mode parameter is set to HEXADECIMAL, you can find out the decimal value of R5 with the following command:

EXAMINE/DECIMAL R5

The *type parameter* controls the data type of debugger input and output. In Section 5.4, we showed how to change the type parameter for the DEPOSIT command when it is used to deposit to the PSL. In Chapter 6, after you have learned more about the other integer sizes, we will give a more detailed description of setting the type parameter.

In our discussion of the STEP command, we mentioned that its qualifiers can be used to reset the debugger parameters INTO, OVER, SYSTEM, and NOSYSTEM. The defaults are OVER and NOSYSTEM. They can be changed for all future STEP commands (in that debugging session) by using the following form of the SET command:

SET STEP parameter {, parameter}

To find out the current STEP parameter settings, use the command SHOW STEP.

5.5.2 *Breakpoint DO Options*

Recall that DO and an attached list of commands can be placed at any breakpoint. Consider the following example:

```
SET BREAK LOOP DO(EXAMINE/DECIMAL R2; GO)
```

This command sets a breakpoint at address LOOP and specifies that R2 is to be output at that time in decimal. It then indicates that execution is to continue without delay. The commands in the list are separated by semicolons, and the list may be of any length. Commands are continued in the usual way, by placing a minus sign at the ends of all continued lines.

When you find yourself working with the debugger on a particularly nasty bug, you will quickly tire of typing out the full names of the commands and keywords. Therefore, you are allowed to abbreviate. The abbreviations that follow are acceptable to the VMS debugger:

Command or Keyword	*Abbreviation*
BREAK	B
DEPOSIT	D
DECIMAL	DEC
EXAMINE	E
GO	G
INSTRUCTION	I
STEP	S
SET	SE
SHOW	SH
TRACE	T
WATCH	W

The VMS policy on command abbreviations is that if the first letter will differentiate a command from all others, it is all that is required; however, when more than one command starts with a particular letter, more letters must be added.

5.6   An Example Debugging Session : : : : : : : : : : : :

This section will show an example of a debugging session that solves some rather simple problems with a small program. Parts of this example were used previously to illustrate the STEP and EXAMINE/INSTRUCTION commands.

. . . .

Example 5.5

:   *Macro Example for Debugging*

```
; A DEBUGGING SESSION
;  IN:   TEN INTEGERS
; OUT: (A)  THE AVERAGE
;      (B)  THE % OF DATA THAT ARE > 0
;
        .TITLE   EX_5_5
        .PSECT   EXAMPLE, LONG
NUMBER:          .BLKL   1   ; INPUT VALUES
SUM:             .BLKL   1   ; SUM OF INPUT VALUES
AVERAGE:         .BLKL   1   ; AVERAGE OF INPUT DATA
PERCENT_POS:     .BLKL   1   ; % OF INPUT DATA THAT
;                              ARE POSITIVE
COUNT:           .BLKL   1   ; COUNTER FOR INPUT
;                              DATA
POZ_KNT:         .BLKL   1   ; COUNTER FOR POSITIVE
;                              INPUT DATA
        .ENTRY   EXAMPLE_5_5, 0
        INIT_IO
        CLRL     SUM
        CLRL     COUNT
        CLRL     POZ_KNT
;
; FOR COUNT := 1 TO 10 DO
;
        MOVL     #1, COUNT
```

Continued

```
LOOP:
        READ_L   NUMBER
;
;       ADD NUMBER TO SUM
;
        ADDL2    NUMBER, SUM
;
;       IF NUMBER > 0
;
        TSTL     NUMBER
        BLEQ     ENDIF
;
;           THEN INCREMENT POSITIVE COUNTER
        INCL     POZ_KNT
;
;       ENDIF
;
ENDIF:
        ACBL     #10, #1, COUNT, LOOP
;
; END-FOR
; COMPUTE AVERAGE & % > 0
;
        DIVL3    SUM, #10, AVERAGE
        DIVL3    POZ_KNT, #10, R1
        MULL3    #100, R1, PERCENT_POS
        PRINT_L  ^'AVERAGE=', AVERAGE
        PRINT_L  ^'PERCENT POSITIVE=', PERCENT_POS
        $EXIT_S
        .END
```

. . . .

Example 5.5 was typed into the file named EX55.MAR. Using a command file named MACD.COM to run it, we now will use the debugger to correct the errors we have carefully placed in the code. The following is a listing of our debugging session. We have intermingled comments with the terminal transcript.

:: *Macro Debugging Listing*

```
$ @MACD
PLEASE ENTER FILENAME:   EX55


        VAX-11 DEBUG Version 3.0-5

%DEBUG-I-INITIAL, language is MACRO,
     module set to 'EX_5_5'
DBG>GO
routine start at EX_5_5\EXAMPLE_5_5
?-4
?16
?5
?-3
?-2
?20
?-1
?-5
?6
?18
AVERAGE = +00000000000
PERCENT POSITIVE = +00000000200
%DEBUG-I-EXITSTATUS,
     is '%SYSTEM-S-NORMAL successful completion'
DBG>^Z
```

We obviously have some problems. According to our calculations, the average should be five, and the percentage of data that are positive should be 50. The first step is to find out some intermediate results by setting a breakpoint just after the loop that computes the sum and the count of the positive values and then examining these locations when the breakpoint is reached. To do this we must add an auxiliary label at that position so we can attach the breakpoint: We will use CHECK. After putting CHECK on the first DIVL3 instruction, we run the program again.

```
$ @MACD
PLEASE ENTER FILENAME: EX55


        VAX-11 DEBUG Version 3.0-5

%DEBUG-I-INITIAL, language is MACRO,
     module set to EX_5_5
DBG>SET BREAK CHECK
```

Continued

```
DBG>GO
routine start at EX_5_5\EXAMPLE_5_5
?-4
?16
?5
?-3
?-2
?20
?-1
?-5
?6
?18
break at EX_5_5\CHECK
DBG>EXAMINE/DECIMAL SUM, POZ_KNT
EX_5_5\SUM:    50
EX_5_5\POZ_KNT:    5
```

Note that these numbers are correct. Therefore, the code in the loop is correct, at least on these data. Our next move is to step through the next instruction, DIVL3 SUM, #10, AVERAGE, which should calculate the average. Since we know the value of SUM, this should produce the correct value for AVERAGE, which is five.

```
DBG>STEP
start at EX_5_5\CHECK
stepped to EX_5_5\CHECK+08:
    DIVL3 W^EX_5_5\POZ_KNT,#0A,R1
DBG>E/DEC AVERAGE
EX_5_5\AVERAGE:   0
```

How can the average be zero? Doesn't DIVL3 know how to divide? Yes, it does, but we had the operands out of order, a common beginner's mistake. The divisor must be first. The next DIVL3 has the same error. So let's get out of the debugger and fix the program by reordering these operands.

```
DBG>^Z
$ ED/EDT EX55.MAR
    1 ; A DEBUGGING SESSION
*'DIVL3
   48            DIVL3    SUM, #10, AVERAGE
*S/SUM, #10/#10, SUM
   48            DIVL3    #10, SUM, AVERAGE
1 substitution
```

```
*  (carriage  return)
   49                DIVL3   POZ_KNT, #10, R1
*S/POZ_KNT, #10/#10, POZ_KNT
   49                DIVL3   #10, POZ_KNT, R1
1 substitution
*EX
SYS$USERDEVICE:[UCCS.RWSEBESTA]EX55.MAR;2 54 lines
```

Hopeful and naive, we assume that the program is now correct and run it without breakpoints.

```
$ @MACD
PLEASE ENTER FILENAME:   EX55


        VAX-11 DEBUG Version 3.0-5


%DEBUG-I-INITIAL, language is MACRO,
     module set to 'EX_5_5'
DBG>G
routine start at EX_5_5\EXAMPLE_5_5
?-4
?16
?5
?-3
?-2
?20
?-1
?-5
?6
?18
AVERAGE = +00000000005
PERCENT POSITIVE = +00000000000
%DEBUG-I-EXITSTATUS, is '%SYSTEM-S-NORMAL,
     normal successful completion'
DBG>^Z
```

More problems! Now we have the correct average, but the percentage of data that are positive is zero instead of 50. We set our breakpoint again to step through the crucial code.

```
$ R EX55
```

Continued

```
             VAX-11 DEBUG Version 3.0-5

%DEBUG-I-INITIAL, language is MACRO,
     module set to 'EX_5_5'
DBG>SET BREAK CHECK
DBG>GO
routine start at EX_5_5\EXAMPLE_5_5
?-4
?16
?5
?-3
?-2
?20
?-1
?-5
?6
?18
break at EX_5_5\CHECK
DBG>S
start at EX_5_5\CHECK
stepped to EX_5_5\CHECK+08:
     DIVL3  #0A,W^EX_5_5\POZ_KNT,R1
```

We now look at POZ__KNT to make sure it still has the correct value
(five).

```
DBG>E POZ_KNT
EX_5_5\POZ_KNT:   00000005
```

It does. So let's step once more and then look at R1.

```
DBG>S
start at EX_5_5\CHECK+08
stepped to EX_5_5\CHECK+0E:
     MULL3 #00000064,R1,W^EX_5_5\PERCENT_POS
DBG>E R1
R1:   00000000
```

Seeing the value of zero for R1 reminds us that we are doing integer
division. Therefore, dividing 10 into five produces zero. To fix this problem, we must reorder our operations to compute the percentage: multiplying POZ__KNT by 100 first and then dividing the result by 10.

```
DBG>^Z
$ ED/EDT EX55.MAR
     1   ; A DEBUGGING SESSION
```

```
*'MULL3
   50    MULL3    #100, R1, PERCENT_POS
*-
   49    DIVL3    #10, POZ_KNT, R1
*R
1 line deleted
         MULL3    #100, POZ_KNT, R1
         DIVL3    #10, R1, PERCENT_POS
^Z
   50    MULL3    #100, R1, PERCENT_POS
*D
1 line deleted
   51    PRINT_L    ^'AVERAGE =', AVERAGE
*EX
SYS$USERDEVICE:[UCCS.RWSEBESTA]EX55.MAR;3 54 lines
```

Now, we will try the program again.

```
$ @MACD
PLEASE ENTER FILENAME:  EX55


        VAX-11 DEBUG Version 3.0-5

%DEBUG-I-INITIAL, language is MACRO,
     module set to 'EX_5_5'
DBG>GO
routine start at EX_5_5\EXAMPLE_5_5
?-4
?16
?5
?-3
?-2
?20
?-1
?-5
?6
?18
AVERAGE = +00000000005
PERCENT POSITIVE = +00000000050
%DEBUG-I-EXITSTATUS, is '%SYSTEM-S-NORMAL,
     normal successful completion
DBG>^Z
```

Finally, we have the correct results.

5.7   The DUMP Instruction : : : : : : : : : : : : : : : : :

Another tool that can sometimes be useful in debugging programs is the DUMP instruction, which is part of our input/output package. The DUMP instruction produces a snapshot of the registers and a specified area of the executing program. DUMP can be used to find inadvertent modifications of code or data areas. It can be placed in the same locations as any other executable instruction. The form of the DUMP instruction is:

DUMP   starting-address, ending-address

where the two addresses are specified by any VAX addressing mode.

The memory locations that are printed by DUMP appear in lines that contain eight longwords each. The 32 bytes on each line appear in right-to-left order, with the address of the first byte shown on the right end of the line. The starting address is in the first printed longword, and the ending address is somewhere in the last printed line.

Rather than show you an example of the output of the DUMP instruction, we invite you to try a DUMP in your last program.

Chapter Summary :

1.   The VAX/VMS debugger is a very powerful tool for studying and debugging Macro programs.

2.   Breakpoints are markers attached to instruction addresses that, when reached during program execution, cause execution to be suspended.

3.   Tracepoints are markers attached to instruction addresses that, when reached during execution, cause a message to be printed (or displayed); execution then continues.

4.   Watchpoints are markers attached to data addresses. When a data location with an attached watchpoint is changed, the old and new values, as well as the address of the instruction that caused the change, are displayed (or printed).

5.   Breakpoints, tracepoints, and watchpoints are set by the SET command, destroyed by the CANCEL command, and listed by the SHOW command.

6.   Execution under the debugger is started by the STEP or GO command.

7.   The EXAMINE command is used to look at memory locations or registers when execution has been stopped. The DEPOSIT command can be used to place values in memory locations or registers when execution has been halted.

8. To use the debugger you must enable it in the MACRO and LINK commands.

9. The mode, type, and STEP parameters can be reset from their default values with the SET command.

New Commands

CALL	DEPOSIT	SET
CANCEL	EXAMINE	SHOW
CONTINUE	EXIT	STEP
DEBUG	GO	

New Terms

Breakpoint	Tracepoint
Disassembly	Type parameter
Mode parameter	Watchpoint

Chapter 5 Problem Set :

1. Explain the use of the DO option of the SET BREAK command.

2. What purpose does the AFTER option of the SET BREAK command serve?

3. What is the difference between the GO and STEP commands?

4. Describe all of the qualifiers of the STEP command.

5. Why must the DEPOSIT command be used with care?

6. What happens when an EXAMINE command has no parameters?

7. Why must a type qualifier be used in a DEPOSIT command to the PSL?

8. What is the purpose of the VMS DEBUG command?

9. What is the difference between exiting the debugger with control/C and exiting it with EXIT?

10. Type the Macro solution to Example 4.2 into your VAX system. Then add the auxiliary labels NEWMAX and NEWMIN on the MOVL VALUE, MAX and MOVL VALUE, MIN instructions, respectively. Set tracepoints at NEWMAX and NEWMIN. Set a watchpoint at COUNT and a breakpoint at LOOPEND. Now run the program under the debugger with the following data: 6, 5, 3, 7, 2, 6, 1.

When COUNT is changed for the sixth time (to six), step through the remainder of the program, one instruction at a time, carefully observing the form of the disassembled instructions and using the EXAMINE command to view the PSL after each CMPL instruction.

Then, clear all program points, set a breakpoint at NEWMAX, and rerun the program with the same data. Each time the breakpoint is reached, examine MIN, MAX, and COUNT. At the first break, also examine the three instructions starting at ENDIF1.

11. Place a DUMP instruction in the Example 4.2 program just before the $EXIT__S instruction, using GRADE and LOOP__END + 20 as the parameters. Then get an assembler listing of the program and run it. Carefully compare the machine code of the listing with that shown in the DUMP output.

6

INTEGERS OF DIFFERENT SIZES

The VAX can deal with integers in a variety of sizes. To avoid confusing you, until now we have limited our discussion of the instructions for dealing with integers to those that deal with longwords. The VAX, however, has many more instructions for the other integer data types. This chapter discusses the nonLONGWORD integer data types and the VAX instructions for manipulating values for these data types, as well as non-decimal constants and the use of the overflow indicator. Although this chapter presents an apparent barrage of new instructions and directives, most of these new instructions are just new versions of old friends.

6.1 The Other Integer Data Types : : : : : : : : : : : :

LONGWORD integers are the natural choice for the VAX because its registers are that size. However, often you will wish to store integer values in locations of other sizes: For example, you may need a large array of integers, but every value to be stored in the array is small enough to fit into two bytes. Being able to store two-byte, or WORD, values saves half of the storage that would be required if LONGWORD values were used. Less often, you may need to store integers larger than the LONGWORD locations; for example, it may be convenient to move blocks of storage around in chunks that are larger than longwords. Several situations will arise in Chapters 9, 10, and 11 that require the use of nonLONGWORD integers. Therefore, good reasons exist for including in the VAX architecture the means to deal with integers both larger and smaller than longwords.

In all of the instructions for dealing with the various integer sizes, a single letter of the op code indicates the operand size. As we stated in Chapter 3, the four integer data types are BYTE, WORD, LONGWORD, and QUADWORD, whose sizes are one, two, four, and eight bytes, respectively. In both executable instructions and directives, the code letters are B for BYTE, W for WORD, L for LONGWORD, and Q for QUADWORD.

6.1.1   Directives for nonLONGWORD Integers

The smallest integer data type in the VAX is BYTE. The .BLKB directive is used to allocate one or more bytes of storage for one or more BYTE integers and to initialize them to zero. The .BYTE directive is used to allocate BYTE locations and to initialize them to any desired value.

.BLKW is the directive for allocating blocks of WORD integers, and .WORD is the directive for allocating their locations and initializing them to any desired value.

Blocks of QUADWORD integers can be allocated using the .BLKQ directive, and QUADWORD locations can be allocated with the .QUAD directive. Unlike BYTE, WORD, and LONGWORD integers, the VAX has few instructions for QUADWORD integers.

Following are a few examples showing how to use these directives.

. . . .

Example 6.1: Allocation Directives for nonLONGWORD Integers

```
BIG_NUMBS:      .BLKQ     25
LITTLE_ONES:    .BLKB     35
SUM_W:          .WORD     427
KOUNT:          .BYTE     42
BIG_VALUE:      .QUAD     1000000000000000
```

. . . .

BIG__NUMBS is the address of the first of 25 QUADWORD integers, each set to zero; this line allocates 200 bytes of storage. LITTLE__ONES is the address of the first of 35 BYTE integers, each initialized to zero. SUM__W is the address of a WORD integer with an initial value of 427. KOUNT is a BYTE integer with an initial value of 42. BIG__VALUE is a QUADWORD integer with an initial value of one quadrillion, or 10 to the 15th power.

6.1.2   Move and Arithmetic Instructions for nonLONGWORD Integers

Many of the instructions for dealing with integers on the VAX use the same form with a different code letter for each of the integer types. This is the case with the *clear* instruction, CLRx. CLRL clears a longword to zero, CLRB clears a byte to zero, CLRW clears a word to zero, and CLRQ clears a quadword to zero. CLRQ is sometimes used to clear two adjacent longwords, four adjacent words, or eight adjacent bytes. For example, the CLRQ instruction in the following sets both SUM and COUNT to zero.

```
SUM:    .BLKL       1
COUNT:  .BLKL       1
          .
          .
          .
        CLRQ        SUM
```

Note that when CLRx is used with a register operand and x is either B or W, the rest of the register remains undisturbed. For example, if the contents of R4 is 12345678 in hex, and we execute

```
CLRW    R4
```

the resulting value in R4 would be 12340000.

Like CLRx, MOVx is an instruction with a variable letter code for each of the four integer types. MOVB moves a byte, MOVW moves a word, and MOVQ moves a quadword. Once again, the QUADWORD version is useful for moving a number of smaller, adjacent integers. For example, if LIST is the address of the first of four WORD integer locations, the instruction

```
MOVQ    LIST, R6
```

moves the longword at LIST to R6, and the longword at LIST + 4 to R7.

Again as with CLRx, specifying a register as the destination of a MOVB or MOVW instruction does not affect the higher order portions of the register. For example, if the hex contents of R4 is 3F56B831, the hex contents of the BYTE location VALUE is 7F, and the following instruction is executed,

```
MOVB    VALUE, R4
```

the resulting value of R4 would be 3F56B87F. (Don't forget that multibyte values are always written backwards.) If you want a BYTE or WORD integer to completely replace the former contents of a register, use one of the size conversion instructions discussed in Section 6.1.3.

On the other hand, using a register as the source of an instruction that deals with BYTE or WORD types involves only the first byte or first word, respectively. For example,

```
MOVB    R4, VALUE
```

takes only the first or lowest order byte of R4 and moves it to VALUE.

In general, the op codes in the instructions determine the size of the operands, regardless of the particular operands that are used. For example,

```
MOVW    FIRST, SECOND
```

moves a word from address FIRST to address SECOND, regardless of how FIRST and SECOND are associated with their memory addresses. FIRST may be the label of a .BLKB directive, and SECOND may be the label of a .QUAD directive, but two bytes still would be the amount of data that is moved.

This same principle applies to registers. The size of a register has nothing to do with the size of the area that is affected by an instruction. As we saw earlier, a MOVB instruction with a register operand deals only with the lowest order byte of that register. A MOVQ instruction that specifies a register operand is really specifying a register pair. For example,

```
MOVQ    R4, AREA
```

moves the contents of both R4 and R5 to the memory location AREA.

MNEGx is a new move instruction. It moves an integer the same way MOVx does, but the sign of the moved value is changed in transit. Therefore,

```
MNEGL   SUM, SUM
```

changes the longword at SUM to the negative of whatever value it previously contained. MNEGx can also be used to negate the contents of one location and then place them in a different location. The MNEGx instruction has versions for BYTE, WORD, and LONGWORD integers, but not for QUADWORD integers.

The ten arithmetic instructions, INCx, DECx, ADDx2, ADDx3, SUBx2, SUBx3, DIVx2, DIVx3, MULx2, and MULx3 all have versions for BYTE, WORD, and LONGWORD integers; again, none of these are implemented for QUADWORD integers. As with the move instructions that have BYTE or WORD operands but use registers as destinations, the arithmetic instructions leave the extra portions of the registers undisturbed. For example, the instruction

```
SUBB2   PART, R7
```

subtracts the byte at PART from the lower-order byte of R7 and places the result in that lower-order byte, leaving the three higher-order bytes of R7 as they were.

Two additional arithmetic instructions that are useful for dealing with integers are EDIV and EMUL.

EDIV (extended *div*ide) is used to divide LONGWORD integers into quadwords. It has four operands: The first is the LONGWORD divisor, the second is the QUADWORD dividend, the third is a LONGWORD location for the quotient, and the fourth is a LONGWORD location for the remainder. For example,

```
EDIV    KOUNT, SUM, RATIO, REMAIN
```

divides the longword KOUNT into the quadword SUM, and places the quotient into the longword RATIO and the remainder into the longword REMAIN.

EMUL (extended *mul*tiply) also has four operands. The first is the LONGWORD multiplier, the second is the LONGWORD multiplicand, the third is a LONGWORD addend, and the fourth is the QUADWORD location for the double-length result of the multiplication. The addend is sign-extended to a quadword and added to the result after the multiplication is complete. *Sign-extended conversion* means that the integer is enlarged to the required size by placing copies of the sign bit in the higher-order bit positions. This process preserves the sign of the value.

The addend operand allows even larger integers to be multiplied conveniently. Recall that long multiplication by hand requires lots of multiplications by relatively small operands before adding with the results together.

As an example of EMUL, consider the following:

```
EMUL    QUANTITY, VALUE, #0, ITEM_VALUE
```

This instruction multiplies the longword in QUANTITY times the longword in VALUE, adds zero to the result, and then places the resulting quadword into memory at location ITEM_VALUE. Since we were multiplying two single longwords, we used a zero for the addend.

The EDIV instruction is especially useful when it directly follows an EMUL instruction. For example, to compute the quantity FIRST · SECOND / THIRD, where all three integers are longwords, you could use the following code.

· ·

Example 6.2: EMUL–EDIV Chains

```
EMUL    FIRST, SECOND, #0, TEMP_QUAD
EDIV    THIRD, TEMP_QUAD, QUO, REM
```

· ·

In programs where space efficiency is important, it is a good idea to use BYTE or WORD locations for flags and counters. In these roles, we need the ability to compare and test such locations. The test and compare instructions of the VAX have versions for BYTE and WORD data types. TSTB tests a byte, TSTW tests a word, and both set the indicator bits of the PSW to allow conditional branches based on the testing. CMPB and CMPW compare pairs of bytes and words, respectively. Both behave exactly like the CMPL instruction we have been using.

We have constructed our counter-controlled loops using longwords as the index variables, initial-values, and limits. In most cases, however, the number of loop iterations is reasonably small—nearly always in the range of a word (-32768 to $+32767$) and frequently in the range of a byte (-128 to $+127$). Bytes or words can be used for loops by using the ACBB or ACBW instructions. ACBB uses bytes for the limit, increment, and index operands, and ACBW uses words for the limit, increment, and index operands. Both operate exactly like the ACBL instruction. As an example of an ACBW instruction, consider the following example.

. . . .

Example 6.3: Using ACBW

```
        INDEX:    .BLKW     1
                    ◆
                    ◆
                    ◆
;
; FOR  INDEX  :=  1  TO  100  DO
;
        MOVW      #1, INDEX
LOOP:
          ◆
          ◆
          ◆
        ACBW      #100, #1, INDEX, LOOP
;
; END-FOR
;
```

. . . .

This example uses words for the index, initial, and limit values in a translation of the FOR construct. The initial- and terminal-value sizes for the constants are determined by the assembler from the context (in this case, the op code).

We do not recommend the use of ACBB unless you are absolutely certain that the loop will never need an index smaller than -128 or larger than 127. Even if this restriction is met at the time you write the program it may not remain true in some later modification.

6.1.3   Size Conversion Instructions

Now that we have four different integer sizes available as operands, we will often find ourselves needing to mix operands of different integer types. Consequently, we will often need to convert an integer to an equivalent integer of another size.

Usually, this will involve converting integer values to equal integer values of different sizes. When larger integers are converted to smaller integers, the higher-order bits are simply truncated. If the truncated bits are not all 0s for positive values or all 1s for negative values, the overflow indicator bit is set to indicate that part of the value has been lost. Section 6.6 explains how the overflow bit can be tested.

To convert a smaller integer to a larger integer, the smaller is sign-extended to the larger size. The CVT*xx* (*convert*) instructions are used for the sign-extended size conversions. The specific op codes are shown below:

Op Code	Description
CVTBW	Converts a byte to a word
CVTBL	Coverts a byte to a longword
CVTLB	Converts a longword to a byte
CVTLW	Converts a longword to a word
CVTWB	Converts a word to a byte
CVTWL	Converts a word to a longword

If we want to move a smaller integer into a larger location, but want the upper-order bits to be set to zero instead of using the correct sign bits (0s when positive, 1s when negative), we use *zero-extended conversion*. Zero-extended conversions are done by the MOVZ*xx* instructions. MOVZBL moves a byte to a LONGWORD location, putting zeros in the upper 24 bit positions; MOVZBW moves a byte to a WORD location, putting zeros in the upper eight positions; and MOVZWL moves a word to a LONG-WORD location, placing zeros in the upper 16 positions. These instructions are used for unsigned values. Chapter 15 will discuss operations on unsigned data in greater detail.

As an example of sign-extended and zero-extended conversions, consider the following examples.

. . . .

Example 6.4: Converting Integers to Other Sizes

```
MOVB    #-5, PLACE
MOVZBL  PLACE, R1
CVTBL   PLACE, R2
```

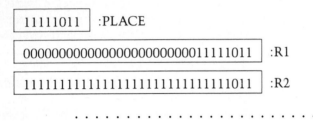

. . . .

Placing the labels on the right end to indicate that the address of the labeled location is actually the address of the lowest order byte is most important on multi-byte locations.

6.1.4   The Debugger and nonLONGWORD Integers

The type parameter of the debugger defaults to LONGWORD. This means that all DEPOSIT and EXAMINE commands use LONGWORD integers as the values or locations being deposited and locations being examined. This is clearly inappropriate when the values or locations being deposited or examined are not four bytes long. The type parameter of the debugger can be changed to BYTE, WORD, or LONGWORD, by using the SET TYPE command and the keywords BYTE, WORD, or LONG, respectively.

The type parameter can be set temporarily for individual DEPOSIT and EXAMINE commands by attaching a type qualifier to the command. The type qualifiers are the same as the keywords in the SET TYPE command: BYTE, WORD, and LONG. LONG would be used only if the default type had been changed previously to BYTE or WORD. For example,

```
EXAMINE/BYTE    SUM
```

would print just one byte from address SUM.

Since the type parameter cannot be set to deal with quadwords, they must be handled as sequences of two longwords.

6.1.5   Input and Output of nonLONGWORD Integers

To get a particular integer data type in or out of the machine, we have provided different versions of the READ and PRINT instructions. The names of these instructions are READ_B, READ_W, PRINT_B, and PRINT_W. Since few instructions deal with quadwords and their need is infrequent, we did not build input/output instructions for them.

6.2   *Operand Expressions* :

Until now we have been dealing with the simplest of operands: literals, registers, and symbols. Macro also allows rather complex expressions as operands (the operands we have been using are also called expressions).

Operand expressions are categorized as relocatable, absolute, and external.

Relocatable operand expressions are those whose address values are fixed relative to the start of the program. Regardless of where the program is loaded into memory, relocatable addresses are always a fixed distance from the beginning of the program. All of the symbolic address operands we have been using are relocatable.

Absolute operand expressions are those having values that are fixed locations in memory. They are specified by *assembly-time constants.* Two examples of such expressions are numeric constants and the difference between two relocatable symbols, for example, A − B. Absolute operand expressions are rarely used, and we will not discuss them further in this book.

External operand expressions are those containing one or more symbols that are not defined in the *current module,* or the module currently being assembled. Their values cannot be determined by the assembler and must be inserted into the machine language program by the program LINK. Although we will not be using externally defined symbols until later in the book, all of your programs have contained external operand expressions indirectly: The input/output instructions are externally defined and use symbols that are externally defined.

Operands can be specified with restricted arithmetic expressions. The terms of these operand expressions can be symbols, numbers, and the symbol for the LC, which is a period (.).

Recall that the LC is the assembly-time equivalent of the PC. It always contains the address of the next available byte in the program's address range relative to the beginning of the program. The assembler initializes the LC to zero at the beginning of each module. At the time of operand evaluation during the assembly process, the LC is set to the address of the first byte of the operand. Note also that the LC is considered a relocatable symbol except within program modules that use absolute addressing, which are rare.

The usual four arithmetic operators, +, −, *, and /, can appear in operand expressions. (All arithmetic uses longwords, because the final value of an address expression must be a longword.) Unary + and − operators are also allowed. Note that these operators are executed at assembly time, not runtime. Do not fall into the trap of thinking that values of memory locations can be modified by these operators. Memory locations can be modified only at runtime by executable instructions. Operators in operand expressions are used to calculate address values for operands at assembly time.

The following example illustrates these two kinds of arithmetic.

· ·

Example 6.5: Operand Arithmetic versus Runtime Arithmetic

```
MOVL    COUNT + 1, RESULT
ADDL3   #1, COUNT, RESULT
```

· ·

In the first case, the longword at COUNT + 1 is moved to RESULT. In the second, the longword at COUNT is incremented, and the result is placed in memory at RESULT.

In addition to the arithmetic operators, shift and logical operators can be used, although their use is far less valuable. The operator & indicates bitwise AND; the operator ! indicates bitwise inclusive OR; and the operator \ indicates bitwise exclusive OR. (Bitwise logical operations are discussed in Chapter 13.) The operator @ indicates a shift of its first operand by the number of bits of the second operand. For example, the expression

```
1 @ 3
```

indicates a binary one, shifted left by three bits to specify the value 1000 in binary, or eight in decimal. If the second operand is negative, the shift is to the right and the sign bit is extended.

All of the binary operators that can appear in operand expressions have equal precedence, unlike the arithmetic expressions of most high-level programming languages. To indicate *subexpressions* in operand expressions, pointed brackets rather than parentheses are used as shown below:

```
<SYMBOL1 1> * 17
```

The most common operand expression consists of a relocatable symbol and a positive or negative constant offset. For example, to access the byte just after the byte at location VALUE, which happens to be unlabeled, VALUE + 1 is used.

Operand expressions must contain symbols that have already been defined when they are used as the count operands of the .BLKx directives, as repetition factors on .BYTE, .WORD, .LONG, and .QUAD directives, and in some other directives not yet discussed. When we do discuss them, we will point out this restriction.

Note that using operand expressions other than these simple constant offset expressions is rare. To use more complex expressions requires the utmost care, because they invite errors. Therefore, we will rarely use complicated address operand expressions and urge you to avoid them.

6.3   Constants of Nondecimal Bases : : : : : : : : : : :

Until now we have used only decimal integers as constants. Because you may wish to specify constants in other bases, this capability is a part of Macro. A unary operator, consisting of the circumflex character (ˆ) and a letter, is used to indicate the desired base of a string of digits. For example, ˆB1010 is a binary constant, ˆO732 is an octal constant, and ˆXF3B is a hexadecimal constant. Because these operators can also be applied to sub-expressions, you may wish to use the unary operator ˆD to indicate that a decimal constant is embedded in an expression of a different base.

The following are examples of legal constants and address expressions.

· ·

Example 6.6: Nondecimal Constants

```
ˆB10110011
ˆX<F3 - 1A + ˆD12>
COUNT + ˆO37
```

· ·

The unary operator ˆC is used to form the ones complement of its operand. For example,

```
VALUE:  .BYTE ˆC15
```

produces the ones complement of 15 (in decimal), which is F0 in hex.

We will introduce several other unary operators for constants in Chapters 10 and 12.

6.4   Direct Assignment Statements : : : : : : : : : : : :

The *direct assignment* statement is a mechanism that allows you to use symbolic address constants. These constants aid readability, allow you through an expression to compute an operand value once and then repeatedly use it, and finally provide a method of changing a parametric value in just one spot while in effect changing the parameter in many locations.

The form of the direct assignment is:

symbol = expression

The symbol is placed in the symbol table, with the value of the expression as its address value. The expression cannot contain undefined symbols. The following are examples of direct assignment statements.

. . . .

Example 6.7: Direct Assignment Statements

```
TAB_LEN  =  100
TABLE:    .BLKQ    TAB_LEN

VALUE  =  ^XFEB / ^O713 + 17
MOVL      #VALUE, FACTOR
```

. . . .

The symbols defined by direct assignment are used primarily for naming assembly-time constants, which are sometimes constant-valued expressions. They are used in the same way named constants are used in high-level languages, such as Pascal. For example, consider a program that uses a number of different arrays, all of the same length. Suppose a specification change for such a program requires that all of these arrays be lengthened by some number. If the lengths of those arrays are all set by a named constant, the change can be made by changing a single line, the direct assignment. If actual constants are used for the lengths of the arrays, it would be easy to miss one of them in the directives that allocate their storage. This would cause an error when the program is executed and the missed array is filled beyond its declared length.

The LC can be modified by using it as the symbol in a direct assignment statement. For example,

```
. = . + 10
```

allocates ten bytes of storage. Although this is seldom a desirable method of storage allocation, it can be useful for defining some kinds of data structures.

6.5   An Example Program   :

The following rather contrived program demonstrates some of the facilities of Macro discussed in this chapter. Because we were unable to invent a realistic problem that would require so many of the features we wanted to display, the program is somewhat artificial.

. . . .

Example 6.8

:   *Problem Statement*

    In: Three small integers in the range of -100 to $+100$.
    Out: **a.** The sum of the input, as a word.
            b. The product of the squares of the input, as a quadword.
            c. The result of (b) divided by 6B3B1 (hex).

Note that part (b) of the output cannot be printed with our input/output instructions. Although we could use the debugger to see the actual values, we will know if the program worked by the result of (c), which is a printable longword. For this example we will not use pseudocode to develop a solution.

:• *Macro Solution*

```
; ARITHMETIC ON VARIOUS SIZES OF INTEGERS
;
        .PSECT  EXAMPLE, LONG
IN_DATA:        .BLKB   3   ; INPUT VALUES
IN_W:           .BLKW   1   ; WORD VERSION OF AN
                            ; INPUT VALUE
SUM_W:          .BLKW   1   ; SUM OF THE WORD
                            ; VERSIONS OF INPUT
PROD_Q          .BLKQ   1   ; PRODUCT OF THE
                            ; SQUARES OF THE INPUT
QUOTIENT_L:     .BLKL   1   ; QUOTIENT OF
                            ; PROD_Q AND 6B3B1
REMAIN_L:       .BLKL   1   ; REMAINDER FROM
                            ; COMPUTATION OF
                            ; QUOTIENT_L
;
        .ENTRY  EX_6_8, 0
        INIT_IO
        CLRW    SUM_W
        READ_B  IN_DATA, IN_DATA+1, IN_DATA+2
;
; COMPUTE THE SUM OF THE DATA
;
        CVTBW   IN_DATA, IN_W
        ADDW2   IN_W, SUM_W
        CVTBW   IN_DATA+1, IN_W
        ADDW2   IN_W, SUM_W
        CVTBW   IN_DATA+2, IN_W
        ADDW2   IN_W, SUM_W
        PRINT_W ^'SUM=', SUM_W
;
```

Continued

```
; COMPUTE PRODUCT OF THE SQUARES OF THE DATA
;
        CVTBL   IN_DATA, R1
        MULL2   R1, R1
        CVTBL   IN_DATA+1, R2
        MULL2   R2, R2
        EMUL    R1, R2, #0, PROD_Q
        CVTBL   IN_DATA+2, R1
        MULL2   R1, R1
        EMUL    R1, PROD_Q, #0, PROD_Q
;
; DIVIDE THE PRODUCT OF SQUARES BY 6B3B1 (HEX)
;
        EDIV    #^X6B3B1, PROD_Q,-
                QUOTIENT_L, REMAIN_L
        PRINT_L ^'QUOTIENT=', QUOTIENT_L
        PRINT_L ^'REMAINDER=', REMAIN_L
        $EXIT_S
        .END    EX_6_8
```

. . . .

Note that in computing the product of the squares of the data, we use the result from the EMUL instruction that computes the product of the squares. This action is feasible only because we are certain that the square of any input value will fit into a longword $((100 \cdot 100) = 10{,}000 < 2^{32})$. The higher-order longword of PROD__Q is always cleared by the first EMUL.

The results of running EX__6__8 are as follows:

```
?75 80 90
SUM= +000000000245
QUOTIENT= +00000663908
REMAINDER= +00000319964
```

The actual result for the product of the squares of the three input values 75, 80, and 90 is 291,600,000,000,000. The decimal value of the divisor is 439,216, so the quotient and remainder are indeed correct.

Although artificial, this example does demonstrate the use of a few of the instructions introduced in this chapter. Later chapters will incorporate nonLONGWORD integers wherever appropriate.

6.6 The Overflow and Carry Indicators : : : : : : : : :

We described the overflow and carry indicators in Chapter 3. This section explains the circumstances under which they are set and how they can be used. While many instructions in the VAX repertoire change the overflow and carry indicators, the arithmetic instructions are of primary interest to us at this point.

The overflow indicator is used to signal that the result of an arithmetic operation cannot be stored correctly in the designated destination. The result that is placed in the destination is wrong because the upper-order bits that will not fit have been truncated.

The carry bit is used primarily for unsigned operands, for example in multi-precision arithmetic. For example, to add two quadwords together, you must do two consecutive LONGWORD adds. The first of these operations is considered unsigned, and a carry from it can be included in the second add. We will thoroughly explain this process in Chapter 15. For now, we will deal only with the overflow bit.

All of the regular integer instructions for adding, subtracting, multiplying, and dividing affect the overflow indicator. It is cleared if the result fits in the destination and set if the result is too large to be placed in the destination. To determine the value of the overflow indicator, the VAX provides two conditional branch instructions. The BVC (*branch on overflow clear*) instruction succeeds (that is, it branches) when the overflow bit is zero. The BVS (*branch on overflow set*) instruction succeeds when the overflow bit is one.

Therefore, if you want to halt processing when a particular arithmetic operation produces an overflow, you can follow it with a BVS to some label for error processing (producing an error message, for example). The following example shows a typical situation.

. . . .

Example 6.9: Detecting Overflow

```
        .
        .
        .
        ADDL2    VALUE, SUM
        BVS      ERROR
        .
        .
        .
ERROR:  PRINT_L    ^'ERROR - OVERFLOW IN "SUM"'
        .
        .
        .
```

. . . .

EMUL can produce an overflow condition only if its addend is a non-zero integer, because its destination is large enough to hold the result of multiplying any two longwords together.

EDIV, along with all of the DIVxx instructions, sets the overflow indicator in two situations: when the quotient is too large and when the divisor is zero.

Note that ACBx also affects the overflow indicator. If the condition is not tested or trapped, the lower-order bits of the correct result are used in the test against the limit. Recall that *trapped* means that the hardware detects the condition and halts execution at that time. Rather than testing the overflow indicator after every arithmetic operation, integer overflows should be trapped by setting the integer overflow trap bit. Trap bits can be set in the debugger as discussed in Chapter 5, and also by bit setting instructions, as discussed in Chapter 15.

When the overflow indicator is tested for a particular operation, we sometimes need to conditionally branch out of the code sequence for that operation. Since we insist on using pseudocode as both the development tool and the documentation of our programs, we need a new pseudocode structure to handle these kinds of error interruptions. We will use the pseudocode EXIT statement for this purpose. Wherever EXIT is placed, it causes control to leave the innermost block or loop in which it is embedded, as shown in the following example.

. . . .

Example 6.10: Pseudocode EXIT

```
FOR INDEX := 1 TO LENGTH DO
   .
   .
   .

   IF condition THEN EXIT
   .
   .
   .

END-FOR
```

. . . .

This procedure causes control to be transferred to the first statement after END-FOR.

The Macro code for EXIT is simply the conditional branch to the label just after END-FOR in the case of a FOR loop. If EXIT were placed in a WHILE loop, the branch would be to a label just after END-DO.

Note that the best way to deal with overflow, besides checking for it with the methods we just described, is to make an effort to avoid overflow by desk testing some of the data extremes to discover potential problems before a program is run the first time.

Chapter Summary :

1. In addition to LONGWORD integers, the VAX has instructions to deal with BYTE, WORD, and QUADWORD integers.

2. .BLKB, .BLKW, and .BLKQ are directives to allocate blocks of BYTE, WORD, and QUADWORD locations, respectively.

3. Quadwords are represented in registers by pairs of sequentially numbered registers.

4. .BYTE, .WORD, and .QUAD are directives to allocate BYTE, WORD, and QUADWORD locations, respectively, and to initialize them to non-zero values.

5. CLRB, CLRW, and CLRQ are instructions that clear BYTE, WORD, and QUADWORD types, respectively, to zero.

6. MOVB, MOVW, and MOVQ move BYTE, WORD, and QUAD-WORD integers, respectively. When MOVB and MOVW use registers as destinations, the upper three bytes and upper two bytes, respectively, are unaffected. MNEGB, MNEGW, and MNEGL move negated bytes, words, and longwords, respectively.

7. INCx, DECx, ADDx2, ADDx3, SUBx2, SUBx3, DIVx2, DIVx3, MULx2, and MULx3 are instructions for arithmetic on bytes, words, and longwords. In the x position, B always indicates BYTE, W always indicates WORD, and L always indicates LONGWORD.

8. EMUL is a LONGWORD multiply instruction that saves the whole QUADWORD result. It also has an operand for adding in the LONGWORD result of an earlier operation.

9. EDIV divides a longword into a quadword, yielding both a LONG-WORD quotient and the LONGWORD remainder.

10. The CVTxx instructions provide arithmetic conversions between all combinations of BYTE, WORD, and LONGWORD integers.

11. MOVZxx instructions provide zero-extended, rather than sign-extended, conversions from bytes to words (MOVZBW), bytes to long-words (MOVZBL), and words to longwords (MOVZWL).

12. TSTB and TSTW are the test instructions for bytes and words, respectively. CMPB and CMPW are the compare instructions for bytes and words, respectively.

13. ACBB and ACBW are the add, compare, and branch instructions that use bytes and words, respectively, as the index locations.

14. Operands can be specified by complicated expressions, consisting of arithmetic, logical, and shift operators; subexpressions delimited by pointed brackets; symbols; and constants.

15. Expressions can also be used to specify the operands of the .BLKx directives and the repetition factors for the .BYTE, .LONG, .WORD, and .QUAD directives, as long as the symbols in those expressions have been previously defined.

16. Binary, octal, decimal, and hexadecimal constants can be specified by the unary operators ˆB, ˆO, ˆD, and ˆX, respectively.

17. The complement of an operand expression can be produced with the ˆC unary operator.

18. The value of any operand expression, except one containing a register name, can be assigned to a symbol with the direct assignment statement.

19. The overflow indicator is affected by most of the arithmetic instructions and can be tested with the conditional branch instructions, BVS and BVC.

20. The pseudocode EXIT is used to break out of loop structures in response to error conditions.

New Instructions

ACBB	CLRW	DECW	MNEGL	MULB3
ACBW	CMPB	DIVB2	MNEGW	MULW2
ADDB2	CMPW	DIVB3	MOVB	MULW3
ADDB3	CVTBL	DIVW2	MOVQ	SUBB2
ADDW2	CVTBW	DIVW3	MOVW	SUBB3
ADDW3	CVTLB	EDIV	MOVZBL	SUBW2
BVC	CVTLW	EMUL	MOVZBW	SUBW3
BVS	CVTWB	INCB	MOVZWL	TSTB
CLRB	CVTWL	INCW	MULB2	TSTW
CLRQ	DECB	MNEGB		

New Directives

.BLKB	.BLKW	.QUAD
.BLKQ	.BYTE	.WORD

Unary Operators for Operand Expressions

ˆB   ˆC   ˆD   ˆO   ˆX

New Input/Output Instructions

PRINT_B   READ_B
PRINT_W   READ_W

New Terms

Assembly-time constant	Sign-extended conversion
Current module	Subexpressions
Direct assignment	Zero-extended conversion
Operand expressions	

Chapter 6 Problem Set :

1. What justification is there for integer data types that are smaller than longwords?

2. What justification is there for integer data types that are larger than longwords?

3. What happens to the upper half of a register when a WORD integer is moved to it with MOVW?

4. What byte of a register is moved when it is used as the source of a MOVB instruction?

5. What problem can arise when using ACBB?

6. What is the difference between CVTBL and MOVZBL?

7. Explain clearly the difference between the following two instructions:

```
MOVL    IN_DATA - 4, OUT
SUBL3   #4, IN_DATA, OUT
```

8. Explain the difference between the overflow and carry indicators.

Write and debug structured Macro programs for the following problems:

9. *In:* An integer, LENGTH, followed by LENGTH-integers, all in the range of −1000 to +1000. LENGTH will be <= 20000.
   Out: **a.** The sum of the squares of the input data.
   b. The square of the sum of the input data.

Note: Use words for the input data, a longword for (a), and a quadword for (b). Use a word as the loop control counter. Test for overflow after all multiply and add instructions. When overflow occurs, an error message must be printed and execution halted. Use the EXIT construct.

10.   *In:*   A list of positive integers, followed by a negative integer. All of the positive input will be in the range of 0–100.

   Out: **a.** The sum of the input data, as a word.

   b. The sum of the cubes of the input data, as a longword.

Note: Input data must be read as BYTE integers.

11.   *In:*   An integer, LENGTH, followed by LENGTH-integers. LENGTH will be <= 120. All of the input values will be in the range of − 10000 to + 10000.

   Out: **a.** The average of input values that are negative, as a word.

   b. The average of the input values that are positive, as a word.

Notes:

   a.   *Zero-valued input is to be ignored.*

   b.   *The counters for the positive and negative input data are to be bytes.*

   c.   *Use a byte as your loop control counter.*

   d.   *Test for overflow after all additions. When overflow is detected, an error message is to be printed and execution halted. Use the EXIT construct.*

12.   *In:*   An integer.

   Out: **a.** The highest power of the integer that does not cause overflow in a longword.

   b. The lowest power (negative) of the integer that does not cause overflow in a longword (by becoming too large in absolute value).

13.   *In:*   A number, LENGTH, followed by LENGTH-integers.

   Out: For each input value:

   a. If the value is > − 10 and < 10, convert it to a BYTE integer and compute and print its square, as a BYTE integer.

   b. If the value is > − 100 but <= − 10, or < 100 but >= 10, convert it to a WORD integer and compute and print its square, as a WORD integer.

   c. If the value is <= − 100 or >= 100, print an error message and continue.

14.   *In:*   A single integer in the range of 10–100.
     Out: All prime numbers that are > 10 but less than or equal to the input value, by repeated division (using the remainder).

15.   *In:*   Two integers, X1 and Y1.
     Out: The value of the following formula, up to but not including the terms after the last that can be computed without overflow:

$$((X1^3) / (Y1^2)) + (142 \cdot (X1^4) / (Y1^3)) + (1526 \cdot (X1^5) / (Y1^3)) + (293 \cdot (X1^6) / (Y1^4))$$

Note: You must use the EMUL–EDIV chains where possible to avoid overflow as long as you can.

16.   *In:*   An integer in the range of 100,000–1,000,000.
     Out: **a.** Four WORD integers, each containing one byte of the LONGWORD input, gotten by sign-extended conversion.
             b. Same as (a) except by zero-extended conversion.

17.   *In:*   An integer in the range of 1,000,000,000–2,000,000,000.
     Out: Each of the ten digits of the input value, as a byte, in a column.

18.   *In:*   Four integers in the range of 0–100.
     Out: A longword, whose four BYTE parts are actually the input values.

7

ARRAYS AND INDEXING

This chapter introduces indexing, one of the methods of implementing arrays in Macro. The concept of indexing is relatively simple, and Macro uses a straightforward method of implementation.

7.1 The Need for Arrays :::::::::::::::::::::

Most of the more interesting or valuable programs contain arrays. Innumerable data processing tasks, normally handled by computers, must use arrays; for example, sorting lists of numbers, strings, or data records all require at least one array. Any task that involves a list of related data values that must be accessed more than once requires some method of array handling.

Every general purpose high-level programming language, from FORTRAN to BASIC to COBOL to Ada, includes array handling techniques. We will take a brief look at how Pascal handles single-dimensioned arrays.

Suppose a Pascal program requires storage for a list of 100 integer values. The program would inform the Pascal compiler it needs such storage using the following nonexecutable declarative statement:

```
LIST : ARRAY [1..100] OF INTEGER;
```

This statement first tells the compiler that LIST is the identifier that will be used as the *base array address* for that block of storage. Second, it informs the compiler that the legal range of subscripts, or address varia-

bles, is 1–100, which indicates that the compiler must allocate 100 locations for the block. The final keyword, INTEGER, identifies the data type
of the locations in the block. The structure of the array is as follows:

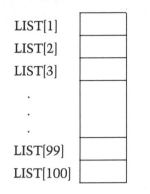

LIST[1]	
LIST[2]	
LIST[3]	
.	
.	
.	
LIST[99]	
LIST[100]	

The storage block for the array is in contiguous memory; that is, LIST[2]
is just before LIST[3], LIST[49] is just before LIST[50], and so on, not just
logically but also physically.

Within the Pascal program, the elements of LIST are referred to using
a two-part address indicator. The first part, the identifier LIST, is static:
It remains the same for all elements of the array. The second part, the
subscript, can be an integer constant, an integer variable, or any arithmetic
expression that evaluates to an integer value in the range of 1–100. For
example, if the subscript INDEX is an integer variable whose current
value is 12,

LIST[10] is the name of the 10th element
LIST[INDEX] is the name of the 12th element
LIST[(2 · INDEX) − 1] is the name of the 23rd element

The following Pascal code computes the sum of the elements of the
LIST array, assuming that SUM and INDEX are declared integers and that
all 100 elements of the array have legitimate integer values.

. . . .

Example 7.1: Summing an Array in Pascal

```
SUM := 0;
FOR INDEX := 1 TO 100 DO
        SUM := SUM + LIST[INDEX];
```

7.2   The Concept of Indexing :::::::::::::::::

Because as assembly language programmers we deal with the machine at a much lower level than a Pascal programmer, we must investigate array handling more deeply to understand how such addressing is implemented in machine code.

In an array whose smallest subscript is B, whose beginning address is BASE, and whose elements have length L, the address of the element whose subscript is INDEX is given by:

BASE + (INDEX − B) · L

Using LONGWORD integers, as are used in VAX Pascal, and a smallest subscript of one, this becomes

BASE + (INDEX − 1) · 4

as is shown below:

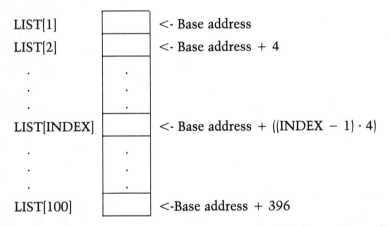

```
LIST[1]                        <- Base address
LIST[2]                        <- Base address + 4
  .              .
  .              .
  .              .
LIST[INDEX]                    <- Base address + ((INDEX − 1) · 4)
  .              .
  .              .
  .              .
LIST[100]                      <-Base address + 396
```

Computers built in the early 1950s used very cumbersome methods to implement this kind of addressing. The operand addresses of an instruction dealing with array elements had to be modified during program execution by other instructions to permit each use of such an instruction to address a different element of the array. In the middle to late 1950s, however, a new mechanism made array addressing much easier.

Unless the subscript is a constant, the address indicated by each array reference instruction cannot be precomputed at the time a program is translated to machine code; there has to be code to compute it at runtime. To make this frequently used code efficient, indexing was used to implement part of the address computation in hardware. Therefore, the concept of *indexing* is to use hardware to hasten the computation of array access addresses. Effective address computation in array referencing instructions requires that the base address of the array be added to an offset, or displacement, at runtime. Indexing provides a hardware operation in the address computation to perform this addition.

Machine code that implements indexing must have some means of storing both parts of the address: the static base array address and the dynamic subscript value or offset. The base array address is usually stored like other addressing modes. Indexing then uses a register to store the offset. Many early computers used special registers for indexing, as do many smaller computers today, but starting with the IBM 360 series in 1963, most larger computers allow any of their general purpose registers to be used.

7.3 *Indexing on the VAX* :

The VAX architecture allows its general purpose registers to be used for indexing. The only VAX register that cannot be used is the PC.

Although nearly all of the VAX addressing modes can be used to form the base array address, we have only studied a few such modes, so it may appear that very few are legal. For now, only the PC-relative mode will be useful; register and literal modes cannot sensibly be used for indexing.

Many computers allow only a subset of their instructions or even just certain operands of those instructions to use indexing. One of the most useful and distinguishing features of the VAX architecture, however, is its *instruction set orthogonality*. This means that almost any addressing mode can be used for almost any operand on almost any instruction. We qualify this statement primarily because situations will arise where a particular addressing mode is not applicable; for example, the operand of a BGEQ instruction cannot gainfully employ indexing.

Section 7.2 stated that indexing includes hardware for the addition of the base array address and the offset value indicated by the subscript. The VAX takes indexing one step farther: It also provides hardware for the equivalent of the multiplication operation to compute the correct offset. Because the factor used in this computation depends only on the type of the operand, which can be determined from the op code, this is not a difficult task. Nevertheless, this implicit multiplication by the operand size is rare among computers. The result is that Macro indexing appears very much like subscripting in high-level languages. We will further explain the VAX indexing operation in Section 7.3.2 after we have explained the Macro syntax of indexing.

7.3.1 *Macro Indexing Syntax*

Allocating the storage for an array in Macro is a simple task using the .BLKx directive. To allocate the 100 integer locations for our Pascal example, we would use:

```
LIST:    .BLKL   100
```

Recall that this also initializes those 100 longwords to zero.

To indicate that indexing is to be used in the address computation of an operand, we would attach the register name, enclosed in square brackets, just like a subscript in Pascal. In the following example, the first operand's address is computed by adding the contents of R6, multiplied by the number of bytes in each LIST element (four), to the address value of the symbol LIST:

```
ADDL2    LIST[R6], SUM
```

The effective address of an operand is its actual machine address. Using this same indexing example, the computation of the effective address of the first operand is shown in Figure 7.1.

One primary difference between Pascal and Macro when specifying the subscript INDEX of LIST is that in Macro the value of INDEX must be moved to a register before it can be used, because only a register can appear between the square brackets. Since the value of INDEX can remain in the register throughout the execution of an instruction loop that deals with LIST, this is not a disadvantage. To make our example array reference in Macro refer to the same array element as the following Pascal statement

```
SUM := SUM + LIST[INDEX]
```

the array LIST must have a lower bound of zero.

In Pascal, while INDEX moves by one each time through the loop to add the elements of the array, the compiler arranges for the address indicating LIST[INDEX] to increase by the required offset. The VAX architecture also takes care of this slight complication. The context of the operand that uses indexing, usually the op code, indicates the size of the addressed operand. This size indicates the factor that must be multiplied times the value of the index register to get the proper offset value. In our example instruction, this factor is four because ADDL2 deals with four-byte longwords. If the op code had been ADDW2, the factor would have been two.

The machine language format for the indexed addressing mode is a mode byte that has the code 4 in the left nibble and the register number in the right nibble. Folowing the mode byte for the index register is the operand specifier for the base array address operand expression. For our example, the machine instruction would appear as follows:

```
  5   4   3   2   1   0
| 83 | AF | 8F | AF | 46 | C0 |
```

Bytes 1, 2, and 3 specify the first operand address, LIST[R6]. The first byte, 46, specifies R6 as an index register, which will be used to modify the address of the following specifier, 8F AF. The AF specifies a PC-relative BYTE-offset address, as explained in Chapter 3, with 8F, or − 113 (decimal) as the offset value. This means that the operand address is the value of

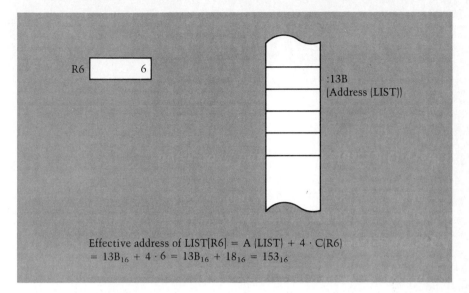

R6 [6]

:13B
(Address (LIST))

Effective address of LIST[R6] = A (LIST) + 4 · C(R6)
= $13B_{16}$ + 4 · 6 = $13B_{16}$ + 18_{16} = 153_{16}

Figure 7.1   An example of indexed addressing mode

the PC, which would be the address of the next operand mode byte, AF, plus four times the contents of R6. The second operand specifier, 83 AF, is a PC-relative BYTE offset, with 83, or -125 (decimal) as its value.

Only one more explanation of syntax is required. Many programmers routinely use one as the minimum value of the subscripts for their arrays; in fact, early versions of FORTRAN forced you to use that convention. While Pascal allows other values as the smallest array subscript, many programmers still use one; it seems to be the most natural value. In indexing, however, the concept of arrays is more understandable if the lower-bound subscripts are always zero.

Because the address of the first location in an array is only the base address, the first value of the index register must be zero. Using this convention, the address of the second element of an array is one times the size of its elements plus the base address, the address of the third element is two times the element size plus the base address, and so on. Therefore, always think of arrays in Macro as having subscripts that begin at zero, although we could generalize our method to work properly for any other lower bound.

7.3.2   Indexing Operation

We are now ready to write the Macro code to sum the elements of a LONGWORD integer array named LIST.

. . . .

Example 7.2: Summing a LONGWORD Array in Macro

```
LIST: .BLKL    100
SUM:  .LONG    0
         .
         .
         .
      CLRL     SUM
;
; FOR REG := 0 TO 99 DO
;
      CLRL     R6
LOOP:
;
;     ADD LIST[REG] TO SUM
;
      ADDL2    LIST[R6], SUM
      AOBLEQ   #99, R6, LOOP
;
; END-FOR
;
```

To add a list of bytes together, we could use the code in the following example.

. . . .

Example 7.3: Summing a BYTE Array in Macro

```
LIST: .BLKB    100
SUM:  .BYTE    0
         .
         .
         .
      CLRB     SUM
;
; FOR REG := 0 TO 99 DO
;
      CLRL     R6
LOOP:
;
;     ADD LIST[REG] TO SUM
;
      ADDB2    LIST[R6], SUM
      AOBLEQ   #99, R6, LOOP
```

```
;
; END-FOR
;
```

. . . .

Note that the syntax of indexing is unaffected by the size of the operand being addressed. The VAX notes by the context of [R6] that the operand is a byte and uses a multiplier of one (it can simply avoid the multiplication in this case) to form the correct offset.

Indexing allows us to vastly increase the scope of the problems that we can handle using our relatively small collection of instructions and addressing modes.

A complete example should be helpful at this point.

. . . .

Example 7.4

: *Problem Statement*

In: An integer, LENGTH, followed by LENGTH-integers. LENGTH will be <= 100.

Out: The integer percentage of input data that are greater than the integer average of those data.

We will use some of the Pascal syntax in our pseudocode that deals with arrays. The pseudocode for Example 7.4 is relatively simple, so we will present it with little discussion.

:• *Pseudocode Solution*

Initialize SUM and COUNT (for values > average)
Get LENGTH
Set LIMIT to LENGTH − 1
FOR REG : = 0 TO LIMIT DO
    Get next value into LIST[REG]
    Add LIST[REG] to SUM
END-FOR
Compute AVERAGE
FOR REG : = 0 TO LIMIT DO
    IF LIST[REG] > AVERAGE
        THEN increment COUNT
    ENDIF
END-FOR
Compute % of data > AVERAGE
Print %
End-of-program

Note that we had to use a separate variable, LIMIT, as the FOR loop limit, instead of LENGTH. While the loops must be executed LENGTH times, the index must start at zero, so the limit has to be LENGTH $- 1$, which is computed before the loop begins.

Note that we use REG as the FOR variable in our pseudocode; that variable will also be used as an array subscript, or index.

:: *Macro Solution*

```
; PERCENTAGE OF INPUT DATA GREATER
; THAN ITS AVERAGE
; IN:   AN INTEGER LENGTH, FOLLOWED BY
;       LENGTH-INTEGERS
;       LENGTH WILL BE LESS THAN OR EQUAL TO 100.
; OUT:  THE PERCENTAGE OF DATA THAT ARE > AVERAGE
        .PSECT   EXAMPLE, LONG
SUM:       .BLKL   1     ; SUM OF ALL DATA
LIST:      .BLKL   100   ; ARRAY FOR ALL DATA
LENGTH:    .BLKL   1     ; NUMBER OF INPUT VALUES
AVERAGE:   .BLKL   1     ; AVERAGE OF ALL INPUT DATA
PERCENT:   .BLKL   1     ; % OF DATA > AVERAGE
LIMIT:     .BLKL   1     ; FOR AOBLEQ (LENGTH-1)
COUNT:     .BLKL   1     ; NUMBER OF VALUES > AVERAGE
;
        .ENTRY   EX_7_4, 0
        INIT_IO
        CLRL     SUM
        CLRL     COUNT
        READ_L   LENGTH
;
; SET LIMIT TO LENGTH - 1
;
        SUBL3    #1, LENGTH, LIMIT
;
; FOR REG := 0 TO LIMIT DO
;
        CLRL     R6
        CMPL     R6, LIMIT
        BLEQ     LOOP1
        BRW      LOOP1_END
```

```
LOOP1:
;
;      GET NEXT VALUE INTO LIST[REG]
;
       READ_L   LIST[R6]
;
;      ADD LIST[REG] TO SUM
;
       ADDL2    LIST[R6], SUM
       AOBLEQ   LIMIT, R6, LOOP1
;
; END-FOR
; COMPUTE AVERAGE
;
LOOP1_END:
       DIVL3    LENGTH, SUM, AVERAGE
;
; FOR REG := 0 TO LIMIT DO
;
       CLRL     R6
       CMPL     R6, LIMIT
       BLEQ     LOOP2
       BRW      LOOP2_END
LOOP2:
;
;      IF LIST[REG] > AVERAGE
;
       CMPL     LIST[R6], AVERAGE
       BLEQ     ENDIF
;
;              THEN INCREMENT COUNT
;
       INCL     COUNT
;
;      ENDIF
;
ENDIF:
       AOBLEQ   LIMIT, R6, LOOP2
;
; END-FOR
; COMPUTE % OF DATA THAT ARE > AVERAGE
;
```

Continued

```
LOOP2_END:
      MULL3    #100, COUNT, R7
      DIVL3    LENGTH, R7, PERCENT
      PRINT_L  ^'PERCENTAGE OF DATA > AVERAGE=', -
               PERCENT
      $EXIT_S
      .END     EX_7_4
```

· ·

Since the instructions that deal with the array LIST in this example all deal with longwords, the effective address is computed by adding four times the index register to the base array address. For example, in the instruction,

```
CMPL LIST[R6], AVERAGE
```

since the op code CMPL compares longwords, the effective address of the first operand is computed as

A(LIST) + (4 · R6)

where A(LIST) means the address value of the symbol LIST. If the op code had been CMPW, instead of CMPL, the address used would have been computed as

A(LIST) + (2 · R6)

Note that indexed address operands can be read and printed directly using READ__L and PRINT__L.

We will now present another example that uses indexing.

· ·

Example 7.5

: *Problem Statement*

   In: A list of positive integers, followed by a negative integer. The length of the list will be < 101, and the values in the list will be < 10000.

   Out: The input, sorted into ascending order, using the exchange sort algorithm.

In a simple exchange sort algorithm, the first value in the list is compared with the second. If the two are in order, nothing is done. If they are out of order, they are interchanged. Then the first value, which may now be the original value from the second position, is compared with the third value. Once again, if they are out of order, they are interchanged.

This process continues until the value in the first position has been compared with all of the other values in the list. (In reality a succession of values usually occupies the first position.) The process now has found the smallest value in the list and placed it in the first position.

The whole process is then repeated for the second element of the list. When completed, the second smallest value will have been placed in the second position in the list. After the process is repeated for all but the last element of the list, you have a list whose values are in ascending order.

Since the data values for Example 7.5 are in the WORD range we will use words to store them. We can now write out the pseudocode solution to our problem.

:• *Pseudocode Solution*

```
Initialize REG to zero
Get the first VALUE
WHILE VALUE > = 0 DO
    Move VALUE to LIST[REG]
    Increment REG
    Get VALUE
END-DO
Set LENGTH to REG
Set TOP_LIMIT to LENGTH − 2
Set BOT_LIMIT to LENGTH − 1
FOR TOP_REG : = 0 TO TOP_LIMIT DO
    Set BOT_START to TOP_REG + 1
    FOR BOT_REG : = BOT_START TO BOT_LIMIT DO
        IF LIST[TOP_REG] > LIST[BOT_REG]
            THEN interchange them
        ENDIF
    END-FOR
END-FOR
FOR REG : = 0 TO BOT_LIMIT DO
    Print LIST[REG]
END-FOR
End-of-program
```

Before continuing, you should convince yourself that the algorithm shown in this pseudocode actually represents the algorithm we explained.

Note that the exchange sort we have developed here is not a fast method of ordering data. Although much faster techniques exist, we have chosen the exchange sort because of its simplicity.

We can now give the Macro version of the solution.

:: Macro Solution

```
; EXCHANGE SORT OF INPUT DATA INTO ASCENDING ORDER
; IN:   A LIST OF POSITIVE INTEGERS,
;       FOLLOWED BY A NEGATIVE INTEGER.
;       THERE WILL BE FEWER THAN 101
;       INTEGERS IN THE LIST AND THEY WILL ALL BE
;       LESS THAN 10000.
; OUT:  THE VALUES OF THE INPUT, SORTED INTO
;       ASCENDING ORDER, USING AN EXCHANGE SORT.
;
        .PSECT   EXAMPLE, LONG
VALUE:          .BLKW       1        ; BUFFER FOR INPUT &
                                     ; OUTPUT
LIST:           .BLKW     100        ; THE ARRAY OF INPUT
LENGTH:         .BLKL       1        ; THE NUMBER OF
                                     ; INPUT VALUES
BOT_START:      .BLKL       1        ; INIT FOR INNER
                                     ; LOOP VAR
TOP_LIMIT:      .BLKL       1        ; LIMIT FOR THE
                                     ; OUTER LOOP
BOT_LIMIT:      .BLKL       1        ; LIMIT FOR THE
                                     ; INNER LOOP
;
        .ENTRY  EX_7_5, 0
        INIT_IO
;
; INITIALIZE REG TO ZERO  AND GET FIRST VALUE
;
        CLRL    R6
        READ_W  VALUE
;
; WHILE VALUE >= 0 DO
;
LOOP:
        TSTW    VALUE
        BLSS    END_DO
;
; MOVE VALUE TO LIST AND INCREMENT REG
;
        MOVW    VALUE, LIST[R6]
        INCL    R6
```

```
        READ_W  VALUE
        BRW     LOOP
;
; END-DO
; MOVE REG TO LENGTH
;
END_DO:
        MOVL    R6, LENGTH
;
; SET TOP_LIMIT TO LENGTH-2 & BOT_LIMIT TO LENGTH - 1
;
        SUBL3   #2, LENGTH, TOP_LIMIT
        SUBL3   #1, LENGTH, BOT_LIMIT
;
; FOR TOP_REG := 0 TO TOP_LIMIT DO
;
        CLRL    R6
        CMPL    R6, TOP__LIMIT
        BLEQ    OUTER_LOOP
        BRW     O_LOOP_END
OUTER_LOOP:
;
;       SET BOT_START TO TOP_REG + 1
;
        ADDL3   #1, R6, BOT__START
;
;       FOR BOT_REG := BOT_START TO BOT_LIMIT DO
;
        MOVL    BOT_START, R7
INNER_LOOP:
;
;            IF LIST[TOP_REG] > LIST[BOT_REG]
;
        CMPW    LIST[R6], LIST[R7]
        BLEQ    ENDIF
;
;                THEN INTERCHANGE THEM
;
        MOVW    LIST[R6], R8
        MOVW    LIST[R7], LIST[R6]
        MOVW    R8, LIST[R7]
;
```

Continued

```
;              ENDIF
;
ENDIF:
       AOBLEQ  BOT_LIMIT, R7, INNER_LOOP
;
;       END-FOR (FOR BOT_REG)
;
I_LOOP_END:
       AOBLEQ  TOP_LIMIT, R6, OUTER_LOOP
;
; END-FOR (FOR TOP_REG)
;
O_LOOP_END:
       PRINT_L ^'SORTED LIST'
;
; FOR REG := 0 TO BOT_LIMIT DO
;
       CLRL    R6
       CMPL    R6, BOT_LIMIT
       BLEQ    P_LOOP
       BRW     P_LOOP_END
P_LOOP:
       PRINT_W ^' ', LIST[R6]
       AOBLEQ  BOT_LIMIT, R6, P_LOOP
;
; END-FOR (FOR REG)
;
P_LOOP_END:
       $EXIT_S
       .END    EX_7_5
```

7.4   *The INDEX Instruction* : : : : : : : : : : : : : : : : :

The INDEX instruction provides *subscript range-checking* for both single-
and multi-dimensioned array accesses. The general form of this instruction is:

INDEX subscript, lower-bound, upper-bound, element-size, index-in,
     index-out

The subscript operand is the index of the desired element, assuming a
lower bound of zero. The lower-bound and upper-bound operands are spec-

ified, and if the given subscript is outside the given range, a subscript range trap (error) is caused. All of the operands of INDEX are longwords. The index-in operand is used for arrays whose lower bound is not zero and for multi-dimensioned array access; in single-dimensioned arrays, the lower bound is zero, and we use a zero literal for this operand. The index-out operand is usually a register where the INDEX instruction puts the address index that can then be used to address the array element. The action of INDEX is perhaps best described by the following pseudocode:

Set index-out to (index-in + subscript) · element-size
IF subscript < lower-bound OR subscript > upper-bound
    THEN subscript range error trap
ENDIF
End-of-instruction

When index-in is zero, the first line becomes:

Set index-out to subscript · element-size

The primary reason to use INDEX is to implement range checking. Because we would normally use indexing to address the elements of single-dimensioned arrays of standard VAX data types, we would not need the multiplication of the element size by the subscript, because it is implicit in indexing.

INDEX sets the N indicator bit if the index-out is negative and the Z bit if index-out is zero.

In the following example, we want to print an element of an array of longwords, LIST, whose index range is 0–99. The index of the element we want to print is in COUNT, and we want to check the value in COUNT before we use it.

```
INDEX    COUNT, #0, #99, #1, #0, R5
PRINT_L  ^'COUNT ELEMENT OF LIST=', LIST[R5]
```

When the lower bound of the index of an array is not zero, the index-in operand is used to allow INDEX to operate correctly. Because index-out is computed as index-in + subscript, we can use the negative of the lower bound as index-in to get the correct result. For example, suppose we had an array of longwords whose index range was −5 to +5. To use INDEX for subscript range-checking, we would compute the index register value with the following:

```
INDEX    SUBSCRIPT, #-5, #5, #1, #5, R5
```

In this case R5 would be set to the value of index-in + subscript, or 5 + SUBSCRIPT. For a SUBSCRIPT of −2, R5 would be 5 − 2 = 3, which is correct: The −2 element of that array would be the fourth element, which is the one addressed by an index register value of 3.

7.5 *Matrices* :

Matrices are two-dimensioned arrays, a very common form. In many applications they are used to store tabular information or to store the coefficients of linear systems of equations. While matrices are always visualized in two dimensions, they are stored in a computer in single-dimensioned arrays. To do this, a mapping function is used to convert references to matrices into address offsets in the single-dimensioned array.

Although some programming languages use other matrix storage methods, we will discuss the most common method, *row major order*. Row major order means that the elements of the matrix are stored by rows. For example, the matrix

2	1	6
3	4	2
0	5	3

is stored in row major order as

2
1
6
3
4
2
0
5
3

References to elements of matrices in most programming languages consist of the name of the matrix and two subscript values, the row index and the column index. To map matrix references to indices in a single-dimensioned array, the following function can be used:

f(row, column) = (row · number-of-columns + column) · element-size

This is easy to compute in Macro, because the VAX indexing mechanism takes care of multiplying by the element size. The following example should clarify matrix accessing. The matrix is a 50-row by 10-column matrix of WORD integers.

. . . .

Example 7.6: Matrix Access

```
         MAXROWS = 50
         MAXCOLS = 10
MAT:     .BLKW   MAXROWS * MAXCOLS
```

```
ROW:      .BLKL   1
COL:      .BLKL   1
            .
            .
            .
          MULL3   ROW, #MAXCOLS, R5
          ADDL2   COL, R5
          PRINT_W ^'ROW, COL ELEMENT OF MAT =', -
                  MAT[R5]
```

. . . .

If subscript range-checking is desired, INDEX can be used to compute addresses for the matrix elements. Since INDEX checks the range of only one subscript, we must use it twice for matrices. The first INDEX instruction checks the row index value for range and multiplies it by the number of columns, using the number of columns as the element size operand. The second INDEX checks the range of the column index and adds it to the output of the first INDEX. This operation is shown in the following example, which duplicates the last example with the addition of subscript range-checking.

. . . .

Example 7.7: Using INDEX for Matrix Access

```
      MAXROWS = 50
      MAXCOLS = 10
MAT:      .BLKW   MAXROWS * MAXCOLS
ROW:      .BLKL   1
COL:      .BLKL   1
            .
            .
            .
          INDEX   ROW, #0, #<MAXROWS-1>, -
                  #MAXCOLS, #0, R5
          INDEX   COL, #0, #<MAXCOLS-1>, #1, -
                  R5, R5
          PRINT_W ^'ROW, COL ELEMENT OF MAT=', -
                  MAT[R5]
```

. . . .

As you can see, using INDEX does not decrease the complexity of computing an address into a matrix; in fact, it is less efficient. The advantage of INDEX lies in its use for subscript range-checking.

Chapter Summary :

1. The single-dimensioned array is a fundamental structure in the majority of computer programs.

2. Addressing array elements involves adding an offset value to the base address of the array. This process is implemented in most computers by placing the offset value in a register. The offset value is then added to the base array address by hardware at execution time. This is called indexing or index register address modification.

3. The VAX assembler and the VAX hardware combine to provide a facility for implementing indexing easily.

4. In Macro, the index register is specified on an operand by placing it in square brackets just after the base address operand. The data type of the op code indicates the size of the operand in bytes. This size is multiplied by the index register value, and the result is added to the operand base address to get the memory address of the operand.

5. When implementing arrays using index registers in Macro, we usually think of the subscripts as beginning at zero. In loops that process arrays, one register is used for both the FOR loop variable and the index register address modifier.

6. INDEX provides a convenient tool to compute addresses for array elements when subscript range-checking is desired.

New Terms

Base array address	Matrices
Indexing	Row major order
Instruction set orthogonality	Subscript range-checking

Chapter 7 Problem Set :

1. What expression describes the address of the INDEX element of a single-dimensioned array whose smallest subscript is five and whose element size is eight?

2. Explain the basic process of indexing at the instruction level.

3. Suppose that the address of the symbol LIST is 23B in hex and the value of R8 is five. What are the addresses of the values moved by the following instructions?

   a. MOVB LIST[R8], RESULT
   b. MOVL LIST[R8], RESULT
   c. MOVW LIST[R8], RESULT

Write and debug structured Macro programs for the following problems:

4. *In:* An integer, LENGTH, followed by LENGTH-integers, where LENGTH will be < 101.
  Out: The list of input values with all of the negative values preceding all of the positive values in the order in which they were input.

5. *In:* A list of fewer than 100 negative integers, followed by a positive integer.
  Out: The percentage of input data that are within five of the average of the data. For example, if the average is 243, we want the percentage of data that are > 237 and < 249.

6. *In:* A list of positive integers, in ascending order, followed by a negative integer, followed by five more positive integers. There will be fewer than 100 total positive integers.
  Out: The input list with the five additional integers inserted into their correct positions in the original ordered list.

7. *In:* A list of positive integers, all < 1000, followed by a negative integer.
  Out: A list of the unique numbers from the input. There will be fewer than 100 unique numbers in the input.

Note: You must use a WORD array for the data of this problem.

8. *In:* An integer, LENGTH, followed by LENGTH-integers, all in the range of − 100 to + 100. LENGTH will be < 100.
  Out: **a.** A list of the positive values of the input.
        b. A list of the negative values of the input.

Notes: **a.** *The zeros in the input are to be ignored.*
     b. *You must build two new arrays, one for the positive values and one for the negative values, before you produce the output. The value of this problem is in building the new arrays, not in printing lists.*
     c. *You must use all BYTE integers in this problem.*

9. *In:* An integer, LENGTH, followed by two lists of integers, each of length LENGTH. Both lists are in ascending order. LENGTH will be < 101.

  Out: A list of all of the input data in ascending order.

Note: You are not to simply place all of the input values in one array and then sort it. You must read the input directly into two separate arrays. Each data value must then be moved into its correct position in the final array with just one move.

10. *In:* A list of integers in the range of 0–99, followed by −1.

  Out: The distribution of the input, by computing and printing the number of input values in the ranges 0–9, 10–19, . . . 90–99.

Note: Use the input value, after some manipulation, as a subscript into an array of ten counters.

11. *In:* A number, LENGTH, followed by LENGTH-integers, where LENGTH is < 101.

  Out: The reverse of the input.

Note: You must first place all input in an array, rearrange the array into reverse order, and then print it starting at the beginning.

12. *In:* A list of < 51 positive integers, followed by −1.

  Out: The input data, after sorting into descending order using a bubble sort algorithm.

Note: A bubble sort algorithm is similar to an exchange sort. The difference is that all comparisons are done between adjacent elements. The order of comparisons is as follows: first to second, second to third, . . . , second-to-last to last, first to second, second to third, . . . , third-to-last to second-to-last, first to second, . . .

13. *In:* A number, LENGTH, followed by LENGTH-integers, where LENGTH will be < 101.

  Out: **a.** The number of input values that are greater than the average of the even subscripted input values (first, third, and so on).

  b. The number of input values that are smaller than the average of the odd subscripted input values (second, fourth, and so on).

14.   *In:* Two integers, ROW and COL, followed by (ROW·COL) – LONGWORD integers, one value per line. ROW and COL will both be < = six.

    Out: *a.* The sum of each row of the input matrix.

        b. The sums of both diagonals of the input matrix.

Note: You must use INDEX for all accesses to the matrix, except for its input.

15.   *In:* Same as Problem 14, except with two matrices instead of one, both of the same size.

    Out: The matrix sum of the two input matrices, one value per line.

Note: Do not use INDEX for this problem.

8
INDIRECT ADDRESSING

Assembly languages have nearly always allowed and often required the use of *indirect addressing*. Contemporary high-level programming languages such as PL/I, C, Pascal, and Ada all provide some facility for using this technique. This chapter introduces the concept, VAX methods, and some of the uses of indirect addressing.

Although we introduce a powerful new concept here and detail a variety of ways of specifying it in Macro, the primary applications of this concept appear only in Chapters 9 and 10. Therefore, as this chapter shows you new ways of forming operand expressions, we will tell you repeatedly that you must wait to discover the best uses for them.

8.1 The Concept of Indirect Addressing : : : : : : : : :

Consider the employment situation of the professional arsonist (a person who sets property on fire for monetary gain). Because such a person does only this one thing, he or she learns to set fires with a high degree of professionalism. The employment problem for an arsonist, however, is considerable. Because the profession is obviously immoral, unethical, and illegal, potential employers are not anxious to associate publicly with arsonists.

One employer solved this communication problem in the following manner. Suspecting his phone was tapped, he wished to avoid calling the arsonist to relay the address of the structure he wanted burned and was even less anxious to tell him or her in person. Therefore, he would call the arsonist and give the address of a phone booth where he had written the target address on page 100 of the phone book. Once the arsonist was informed of the technique, the process worked very effectively: It was impossible to connect the employer's conversations with the fires.

The employer in this tale had invented the process of indirect address-ing: Instead of relaying the address that he wanted burned, he gave the address of a place where the target address could be found. This process of indirect addressing has been part of computer architectures for several decades.

The primary purpose of indirect addressing is to add a higher degree of flexibility to addressing operands, especially when dealing with struc-tured data. The process is also fundamental to the parameter passing mechanics of many programming languages. In programming languages, indirect addressing means that an operand specifies the address of the operand value, not the value itself.

8.2   *Register-Deferred Addressing Mode* : : : : : : : :

Indirect addressing can be used in several ways in Macro, the simplest of which is called register-deferred addressing. (*Deferred addressing* is used in the DEC literature for indirect addressing.) An operand that is to be addressed using this mode has its address in a register. That the register is to be used as the address of the operand, rather than as the operand itself, is indicated by placing the register reference in parentheses. For example,

```
MOVL     VALUE, (R3)
```

moves the longword in location VALUE to the memory location whose address is in R3. Consider the following example.

. . . .

Example 8.1: Register-Deferred Addressing Mode

```
0000 1735 :R3
0000 19FB :1735

MOVL     R3, R4
MOVL     (R3), R5
```

. . . .

In this example, the effective address of the first operand of the first MOVL instruction is R3, while the effective address of the first operand of the second MOVL instruction is the contents of R3. When these instructions are executed, R4 gets the hex value 1735, and R5 gets the LONGWORD value at address 1735, or 19FB. These operations are illustrated in Figure 8.1.

The machine language format for the register-deferred addressing mode is a single byte with the code 6 in the left nibble, and the register number in the right nibble. For example, the Macro instruction below is followed by its machine language version:

```
MOVL    (R5), R6
```

```
  2   1   0
┌────┬────┬────┐
│ 56 │ 65 │ D0 │
└────┴────┴────┘
```

Clearly, if we are to use this version of indirect addressing, we must have a technique for getting meaningful addresses into registers. To do this in Macro, we use the move address instructions.

MOVAx moves the address of its first operand to the location specified by the second operand. In this instruction, *x* can be B for byte, W for word, L for longword, or Q for quadword. For example,

```
MOVAB   VALUE, R5
```

moves the address of the BYTE integer VALUE to R5.

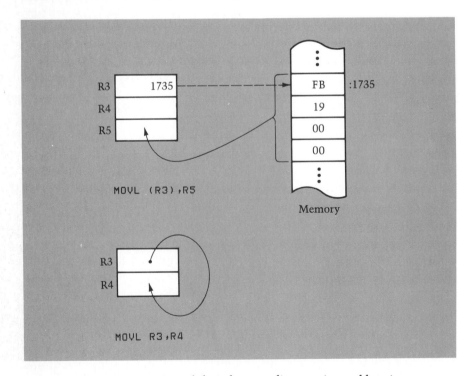

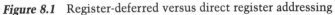

Figure 8.1   Register-deferred versus direct register addressing

In a sense, MOVx is an indirect version of MOVAx. MOVAx moves the value of a symbol, which is an address, while MOVx moves the contents of a memory location, which is specified by the symbolic version of its address.

Because the value that MOVAx moves is always an address, it is always a longword. This is true regardless of the data type of the first operand or the type specified by the x character in the op code.

Because it does not make sense to move the address of a register, using a register name for the first operand of a MOVAx instruction is illegal. The same is true for short literals.

These instructions commonly use a symbol as the first operand. Because the size of the operand shouldn't matter, you may wonder why there are four different MOVAx instructions. Although the size doesn't matter in most cases, using a particular version of the MOVAx instruction increases the readability of your program. Furthermore, Section 8.3 will introduce two new addressing modes that in rare circumstances must use the correct version.

In machine language, the operands of MOVAx appear exactly as they do for other instructions, such as MOVx. At runtime, however, instead of using the computed operand address to access memory, the computer uses the computed address as the operand.

Indirect addressing is often used as an alternative to indexing. The following example shows how the technique is used to input a list of LONGWORD values and to place them into an array.

. . . .

Example 8.2: *Register-Deferred Addressing Mode*

```
LENGTH:  .BLKL    1
LIST:    .BLKL    100
COUNT:   .BLKL    1
             .
             .
             .
         PRINT_L  ^'LIST LENGTH:'
         READ_L   LENGTH
         MOVAL    LIST, R5
;
; FOR COUNT := 1 TO LENGTH DO
;
         MOVL     #1, COUNT
         CMPL     COUNT, LENGTH
         BLEQ     LOOP
         BRW      OUT_LOOP
```

Continued

```
LOOP:
;
;       GET NEXT VALUE INTO LIST
;
        PRINT_L  ^'NEXT VALUE:'
        READ_L   (R5)
        ADDL2    #4, R5
        AOBLEQ   LENGTH, COUNT, LOOP
;
; END-FOR
;
OUT_LOOP:
              •

              •

              •
```

When indexing is possible, to use indirect addressing is not usually a good idea. The indexed version is much easier to read and does not require the explicit increment, which you could easily get wrong or forget altogether. However, indirect addressing is not useless. In its more complex forms, indirect addressing is far more flexible than indexing when you must address complicated data structures.

8.3   Autoincrement and Autodecrement Addressing Modes :

The one inconvenience to using register-deferred addressing is that we must increment the register that contains the address each time the loop is executed. The autoincrement mode eliminates this inconvenience. This mode is specified by placing a plus sign (+) following an operand already specified by register-deferred mode as shown below:

```
MOVL     VALUE, (R5)+
```

The difference between register-deferred and autoincrement addressing is that in autoincrement mode the specified register is incremented after the effective address of the operand has been computed and used. Therefore, the quantity that is added to the register depends on the size of the operand being addressed, or the context of the instruction as determined by the op code. In the instruction above, the contents of R5 are first used as the address of the operand, and then four is added to R5 because the instruction context indicates that the operand is a longword. If the op code had been MOVB instead of MOVL, R5 would have been incremented by one instead of four.

Using autoincrement in Example 8.2, we could replace the two instructions

```
READ_L   VALUE, (R5)
ADDL2    #4, R5
```

with

```
READ_L   VALUE, (R5)+
```

Autoincrement increases the usefulness of indirect addressing by making it easier to employ and less prone to error. Indirect addressing for simple array processing, however, still lacks readability: To find out what is being addressed by an autoincrement operand, you must search through the previous code to see where the register was set to its initial value. Autoincrement addressing is, however, significantly more efficient than indexing because the effective address computation is so simple.

You occasionally will find it convenient to step through an array of elements backwards, rather than forward. For this capability, the VAX architecture provides the autodecrement mode, which decrements a register used in indirect addressing. In autodecrement mode, the register is altered before it is used. To specify autodecrement mode on an operand, you place a minus sign ($-$) before the parenthesized register. The amount that is subtracted from the register is determined by the size of the addressed operand. If the op code indicates that the operand is a word, then two is subtracted; if the op code indicates that the operand is a longword, then four is subtracted; and so forth.

The following example should clarify the autoincrement and autodecrement addressing modes. For comparison, we have written the code to sum the 100 elements of a WORD array three times, once using autoincrement, once using autodecrement, and once using an index register.

. . . .

Example 8.3: Autoincrement and Autodecrement Addressing Modes

```
SUM:      .BLKW    1
LIST:     .BLKW    100
COUNT:    .BLKL    1
            .
            .
            .
;
; SUM USING AUTOINCREMENT
;
          MOVAW    LIST, R5
          CLRW     SUM
;
```

Continued

```
; FOR COUNT := 1 TO 100 DO
;
        MOVL      #1, COUNT
LOOP1:
;
;     ADD ELEMENT TO SUM
;
        ADDW2     (R5)+, SUM
        AOBLEQ    #100, COUNT, LOOP1
;
; END-FOR
;

            .
            .
            .

;
; SUM USING AUTODECREMENT
;
        MOVAW     LIST+200, R5
        CLRW      SUM
;
; FOR COUNT := 1 TO 100 DO
;
        MOVL      #1, COUNT
LOOP2:
;
;     ADD ELEMENT TO SUM
;
        ADDW2     -(R5), SUM
        AOBLEQ    #100, COUNT, LOOP2
;
; END-FOR
;

            .
            .
            .

;
; SUM USING INDEXING
;
        CLRW      SUM
;
```

```
; FOR REG := 0 TO 99 DO
;
        CLRL    R5
LOOP3:
;
;     ADD ELEMENT TO SUM
;
        ADDW2   LIST[R5], SUM
        AOBLEQ  #99, R5, LOOP3
;
; END-FOR
;
```

. . . .

A quick look at these three code segments shows us that indexing requires one fewer instructions than either autoincrement or autodecrement. Indexing is also the most readable. Autodecrement is probably the most error-prone, because the register must be started with the correct value. In Example 8.3, this is especially easy because the length of the array is a constant. If it were a program variable, say LENGTH, then this variable would have to be first multiplied by two and then added to the register, a process that takes another instruction and is easy to do incorrectly.

Note that when using indexing, we normally use a register both for the FOR loop counter and for the index register, as we would in a high-level language. However, when using register-deferred, autoincrement, or autodecrement modes, the loop counter has nothing to do with array addressing.

The machine language operand for autoincrement is a single byte, with the code 8 in the left nibble, and the register number in the right nibble. The machine language operand for autodecrement is also a single byte, with the code 7 in the left nibble and the register number in the right nibble. The Macro instruction below is followed by its machine language equivalent:

```
MOVL    -(R5), (R6)+
```

    2   1   0

86	75	D0

All three of the indirect addressing modes discussed can also be indexed. The computation of effective addresses in these cases requires explanation.

When indexing and register-deferred modes are combined, the base address is computed exactly as if indexing were not included. Then indexing is applied as it is when the base is PC-relative addressed. For example, consider the following program fragment.

. . . .

Example 8.4: Combining Register-Deferred and Indexing Modes

```
LIST:      .WORD    7, 9, 11, 12
A:         .BLKW    1
B:         .BLKW    1
C:         .BLKW    1
             .
             .
             .
           MOVL     #2, R1
           MOVAL    LIST, R5
           MOVW     (R5)[R1], A
           MOVW     -(R5)[R1], B
           MOVW     (R5)+[R1], C
             .
             .
             .
```

. . . .

Assume that the address of LIST is 542, so we have:

LIST[0]	0007	:542
LIST[1]	0009	:544
LIST[2]	000B	:546
LIST[3]	000C	:548

If the Example 8.4 code segment were executed, the first two instructions would set R1 to two and R5 to 542.

The first operand of the third instruction (MOVW   (R5)[R1], A) has an effective address of 546, or the base address of 542 plus the contents of R1 (two) times the element size (two). So the value 11 (decimal) is moved to location A.

The first operand of the fourth instruction (MOVW   −(R5)[R1], B) has an effective address of 544, or the base address of 540 (542 − 2) plus the contents of R1 (two) times the element size (two). So the decimal value nine is moved to location B.

The first operand of the fifth and last instruction (MOVW   (R5)+[R1], C) has an effective address that is the same as that of the fourth instruction (544) because the address is computed before the autoincrement is done. Therefore, the fifth instruction moves the decimal value nine to location C and then adds two to R5.

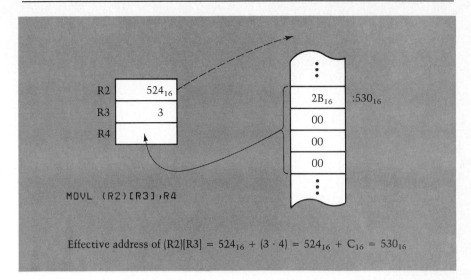

Figure 8.2 Combination of register-deferred and indexed addressing modes

Figure 8.2 should help clarify operand addressing that involves both indirect addressing and indexing.

The machine language for an operand that is specified by a combination of indexing and register-deferred, autoincrement, or autodecrement addressing has two bytes. The first is the index byte with the code 4 in the left nibble and the index register number in the right nibble. The second byte is the indirect addressing byte, which appears in the forms described earlier.

For example, the Macro instruction below is followed by its machine language equivalent:

```
SUBL2    (R5)+[R3], R6
```

3	2	1	0
56	85	43	C2

We could use the combination of indirect and indexed addressing modes to process arrays, as the following example shows.

. . . .

Example 8.5: Array Processing with Indexed and Register-Deferred Addressing

```
LIST:     .BLKL    100
SUM:      .LONG    0
            .
            .
            .
          MOVAL    LIST, R5
;
; SUM THE FIRST 50 ELEMENTS OF "LIST"
; FOR REG := 0 TO 49 DO
;
          CLRL     R6
LOOP:
;
;         ADD ELEMENT TO SUM
;
          ADDL2    (R5)[R6], SUM
          AOBLEQ   #49, R6, LOOP
;
; END-FOR
;
```

. . . .

Recall our earlier statement that the op code choice for MOVAx would be important in some cases. We can now explain those cases. In autoincrement and autodecrement modes that have no explicit operand size, the assembler must be able to determine how much is to be added to or subtracted from the register. Because operand size can be determined from the op code, the MOVAx instruction includes the different op codes. For example, in the instruction

```
MOVAW    -(R5), ADDR
```

two must be subtracted from R5 before it is used.

Finally, note that when you use the combination of autoincrement or autodecrement with indexing, two different registers must be used, one for indexing and one for autoincrement or autodecrement. For register-deferred indexed addressing, the same register can be used for both purposes.

8.4   *Displacement Mode* :

Often data to be processed appear as lists of records called files. These records are often a mix of different kinds of data: some integers, some other numeric forms, and some character information. Because we are discussing only integer forms of data, we will present an example of data processing that involves just integers.

Suppose we have student data records that include social security numbers, class levels, ages, grade point averages or GPAs (as integers in the range of 0–400, for 0.0–4.0 averages), and sex (coded as zero for female and one for male). The form of these records is shown below:

Byte number

3	2	1	0

Social security number			:RECORD
GPA	Age	Class	:RECORD + 4
		Sex	:RECORD + 8

A convenient method of accessing the various parts of this structure uses the *displacement* addressing mode.

Using displacement simply involves preceding a register-deferred operand by an offset value or expression called displacement. The effective address of an operand specified by the displacement mode is computed by adding the value of the displacement to the specified register. This operation is demonstrated in Figure 8.3.

Using the displacement addressing mode, we can conveniently access any of the fields in the student data record. For example, if the address of the record is in R5 and we have the following direct assignment statements in the program,

```
SSN_O = 0
CLASS_O = 4
AGE_O = 5
GPA_O = 6
SEX_O = 8
```

then we can move the fields to other locations with the following instructions:

```
MOVL    SSN_O(R5), SOC_NUM
MOVB    CLASS_O(R5), CLASS
MOVB    AGE_O(R5), AGE
MOVW    GPA_O(R5), GPA
MOVB    SEX_O(R5), SEX
```

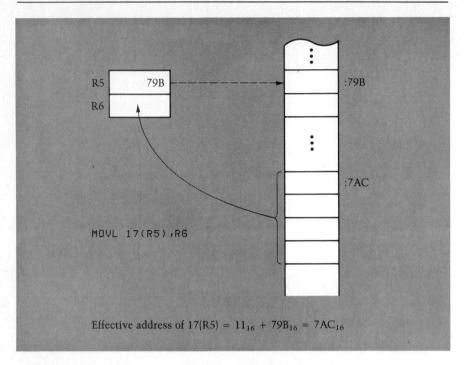

Figure 8.3 Displacement mode addressing

The displacement can be specified in Macro as any operand expression. If the size of the displacement is known, the assembler chooses the smallest size (longword, word, or byte) that will suffice. If the size is unknown because the displacement is relocatable or defined later in the source program, the assembler uses a word to store it. The LINK program subsequently reports an error if the displacement value does not fit its specified size. Section 8.5 explains how to specify the sizes of displacements, as well as offsets used in PC-relative address operands.

Note that PC-relative is a special case of displacement mode addressing that uses the PC. An operand expression specified without a parenthesized register name indicates that the PC is to be used and that the assembler must compute the offset value. An operand expression that includes a parenthesized register name means that we have already computed the offset value and the specified register is to be used instead of the PC.

The machine language for displacement mode operands consists of two to five bytes; the format is exactly like that used for PC-relative operands, except the mode byte specifies the register that is deferred instead of the PC. The first byte has the mode coded in the left nibble: A for BYTE displacement, C for WORD displacement, and E for LONGWORD displacement. The right nibble of the first byte has the number of the specified register. Subsequent bytes store the actual displacement. The Macro instruction below is followed by its machine language equivalent:

```
ADDB2    42(R3), R4
```

```
 3  2   1   0
```
54	2A A3	80

8.5 *Relative Deferred Mode* : : : : : : : : : : : : : : : : :

When a number of addresses must be stored and used indirectly to address operands, relative-deferred addressing mode is used. In the relative-deferred mode, the location containing the address is a PC-relative addressed longword. The operand is specified as relative-deferred when it is preceded with an at sign (@). The addressing method is the same as if a register had been used. In the following example, the last two move instructions move the same word:

```
MOVAW    KOUNT, R1
MOVAW    KOUNT, ADDR_KOUNT
MOVW     (R1), RESULT
MOVW     @ADDR_KOUNT, RESULT
```

The machine language version of a relative-deferred mode operand uses a mode nibble of F for LONGWORD offset, D for WORD offset, and B for BYTE offset. (Note that these codes are one larger, respectively, than the regular displacement addressing mode nibbles of E, C, and A.) Because the PC is used in relative-deferred addressing, it is specified in the register nibble as in PC-relative addressing.

The machine code version of the last instruction in the example fragment (MOVW   @ADDR__KOUNT, RESULT) is:

```
 4   3   2   1   0
```
42	AF	3B	BF	D0

Byte 1 specifies that the PC is to be used (F) and that a BYTE offset is to be used (B) to compute the address of the address of the operand. Byte 2 shows that the offset value is 3B, or 59 in decimal. Bytes 3 and 4 specify PC-relative addressing using the BYTE offset value of 42, or 66 in decimal. The two offset values are, of course, meaningless without the addresses of the instruction and the data.

.ADDRESS is a directive that allocates a LONGWORD location and initializes it to the address of its operand, as shown below:

```
ADDR_KOUNT:     .ADDRESS KOUNT
```

The operand of .ADDRESS can also be a list of address expressions, as shown below:

```
ADDR_TABLE:     .ADDRESS    SUM, KOUNT, RESULT
```

This directive allocates three longwords of storage and initializes them to the addresses of SUM, KOUNT, and RESULT.

In the Example 8.6 program fragment, we use relative-deferred addressing to print the elements of a BYTE array of length 50.

. . . .

Example 8.6: Relative-Deferred Addressing Mode

```
LIST:           .BLKB       50
ADDR_LIST:      .ADDRESS    LIST
COUNT:          .BLKW       1
                .
                .
                .
;
; FOR COUNT := 1 TO 50 DO
;
        MOVW    #1, COUNT
LOOP:
        PRINT_W ^'NEXT VALUE=', @ADDR_LIST
;
;       INCREMENT ADDRESS
;
        INCL    ADDR_LIST
        ACBW    #50, #1, COUNT, LOOP
;
; END-FOR
;
                .
                .
                .
```

. . . .

Note that we must add one to ADDR__LIST each time through the loop. Because this is both an inconvenience and a source of possible error, relative-deferred addressing should be restricted to situations where indexing cannot be used.

As with the other forms of indirect addressing, indexing can be included in a relative-deferred operand. In the following example, the last move instruction moves the third longword from TABLE to RESULT.

. . . .

Example 8.7: Combining Relative-Deferred Addressing and Indexing

```
TABLE:      .BLKL     100
ADDR_TAB:   .ADDRESS TABLE

              .

              .

              .

            MOVL      #2, R5
            MOVL      @ADDR_TAB[R5], RESULT
```

. . . .

This example is used to illustrate how relative-deferred addressing works with indexing. Normally, you would address TABLE with indexing alone.

Combined relative-deferred and indexed addressing is used when the address of an array is passed to a subprogram as a parameter. In this case, as will be discussed in Chapter 10, all addressing of the array must be indirect. Furthermore, if several arrays that require indexing are subprogram parameters, memory locations rather than registers are often used to store their addresses.

Figure 8.4 illustrates the operation of combined relative-deferred addressing and indexing.

8.6   *Two Levels of Indirectness* : : : : : : : : : : : : : : : :

So far we have been discussing single-level indirect addressing. Situations sometimes arise, especially in the handling of addresses passed as parameters to subprograms, in which a second level of indirectness is useful. In *two-level indirect addressing*, operand contains the address of the address of the operand value.

Two addressing modes already introduced can be modified to denote two-level indirect addresses: autoincrement and displacement. The operands are specified to be deferred twice by preceding them with at signs (@), as in @(R5)+ and @42(R6). These modes are referred to as autoincrement-deferred and displacement-deferred, respectively.

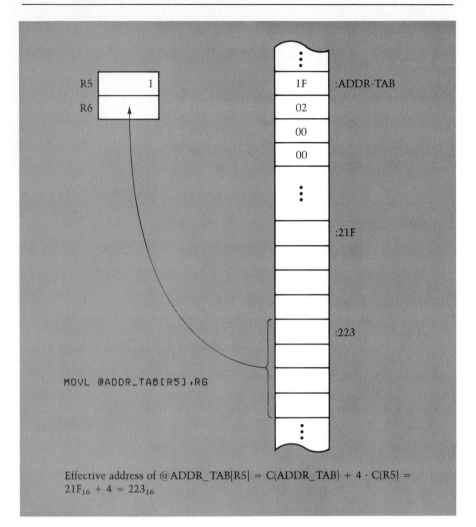

$$\text{Effective address of } @\text{ADDR\_TAB[R5]} = C(\text{ADDR\_TAB}) + 4 \cdot C(R5) =$$
$$21F_{16} + 4 = 223_{16}$$

Figure 8.4   Combination of relative-deferred and indexed addressing modes

Because the actual displacement can be omitted if zero is the offset value, register-deferred addresses can also be preceded by @ and used as two-level indirect addresses. Therefore, we have three operand forms to specify two-level indirect addressing. We will refer to deferred zero-value displacement as register-deferred deferred.

The effective address for an autoincrement-deferred operand is calculated as follows. The value in the specified register is used to address a memory location. The LONGWORD contents of that location are used as a memory address; this becomes the effective address of the operand,

and the specified register is incremented by four. For example, consider the following:

```
0000 18F0 :R5
0000 5163 :358
0000 0358 :18F0
```

```
MOVW     @(R5)+, RESULT
```

The effective address of the first operand of this MOVW instruction is the contents of the location that is specified as the contents of R5; that is, it is 358, as specified in location 18F0, which is specified as the contents of R5. This move instruction moves the contents of this address, the value 5163 (hex), to location RESULT, and then four is added to R5. Recall that two would have been added to R5 if this were ordinary autoincrement addressing, since R5 then would have been pointing at a word. In the autoincrement-deferred case, however, R5 is pointing at an address, which is always a longword. Therefore, the added value must be four.

Figure 8.5 shows the operation of the MOVW instruction in autoincrement-deferred mode.

To further understand two-level indirect addressing, consider the following example. Figure 8.6 shows the situation before this code is executed.

. . . .

Example 8.8: *Register-Deferred Deferred Addressing Mode*

```
; MOVE 48 BYTES FROM THE LOCATION WHOSE ADDRESS
; IS POINTED TO BY R7 TO THE LOCATION
; WHOSE ADDRESS IS POINTED TO BY R8
;
COUNT:          .BLKW     1
        .
        .
        .
;
; FOR COUNT := 1 TO 6 DO
;
        MOVL     #1, COUNT
LOOP:
;
;      MOVE A QUADWORD & MOVE POINTERS
;
        MOVQ     @(R7), @(R8)
        ADDL2    #8, (R7)
```

Continued

```
        ADDL2    #8, (R8)
        ACBW     #6, #1, COUNT, LOOP
;
; END-FOR
;
```

· ·

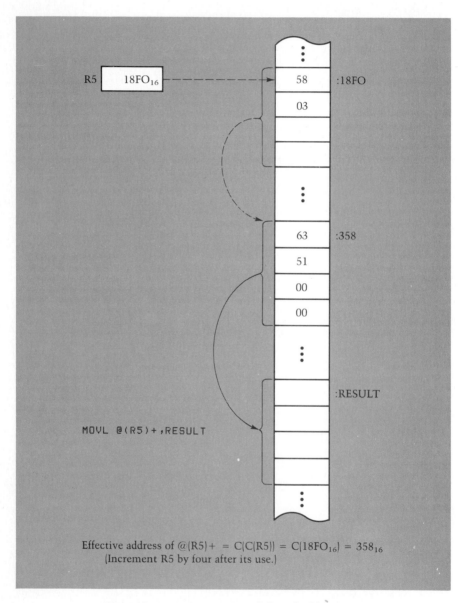

Effective address of @(R5)+ = C(C(R5)) = C(18FO$_{16}$) = 358$_{16}$
(Increment R5 by four after its use.)

Figure 8.5   Autoincrement-deferred addressing

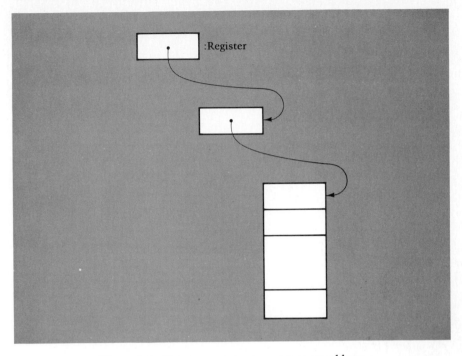

Figure 8.6   Using a register to point at an address

To examine the ordinary displacement-deferred mode, consider the following example.

```
0000 0420 :R5
0000 15FB :244
0000 7F00 :420
0244 1562 :424
0015 0000 :428
0000 0015 :42C
```

```
MOVL    @6(R5), RESULT
```

The result of this move instruction is that RESULT gets the LONGWORD value 0000 15FB. The effective address, 244, is computed by adding six to the contents of R5 to get 426; at 426, the LONGWORD value is 0000 0244. The contents of the longword at 244 is 0000 15FB.

All three of the two-level indirect addressing operand forms can be indexed. We would index these forms if the effective address were an array. The following example shows the combined indexed register-deferred deferred mode.

. . . .

Example 8.9: Combining Register-Deferred Deferred Addressing and Indexing

```
0000 0850 :R5
0000 0007 :758
0000 0005 :75C
0000 0010 :760
0000 0003 :764
0000 0006 :768
0000 0758 :850
              •
              •
              •
          CLRL     SUM
;
; FOR REG := 0 TO 4 DO
;
          CLRL     R6
LOOP:
;
;      ADD ELEMENT TO SUM
;
          ADDL2,   @(R5)[R6], SUM
          AOBLEQ   #4, R6, LOOP
;
; END-FOR
;
```

. . . .

The value in SUM at the end of this loop is 7 + 5 + 16 (decimal) + 3 + 6, which is 37 (decimal). In this loop, R5 starts at 850 and remains at that value, while R6 moves in one-step increments of one from zero to four; the effective addresses for the first operand of the add instruction are 758, 75C, 760, 764, and 768.

The requirement that you use two registers in combined autoincrement addressing and indexing also applies to the deferred mode.

8.7 Controlling the Sizes of Displacements : : : : : :

In both kinds of displacements or offsets used in the VAX addressing modes, PC-relative and displacement, the assembler chooses the size of the displacement.

For PC-relative operands, if the value of the expression is known, the assembler chooses the smallest possible size among longword, word, and byte. If the expression contains symbols defined later in the source program or in a different program section using the .PSECT directive, the assembler considers the value of the expression unknown and uses the default size, or longword. This default can be changed with the .DEFAULT directive.

The general form of the .DEFAULT directive is:

.DEFAULT DISPLACEMENT, keyword

where keyword is LONG, WORD, or BYTE.

Macro also allows the programmer to specify the desired size of the displacement on any or all PC-relative operands. This is done by preceding the operand with a unary operator that is the syntactic reverse of those used to specify the radix. (The unary operators for binary radix constants are ^B, ^W, and ^L.) The operator B^ specifies that a BYTE offset is to be used, W^ specifies a WORD offset, and L^ specifies a LONGWORD offset.

In general, you should let the assembler choose the size of a PC-relative offset, assuming that most of your operands have known values. It is also a good idea to reset the default offset size to WORD for all but the very largest of programs; otherwise, the PC-relative operands that have unknown values will use LONGWORD offsets. Recall that WORD offset allows you to address any location within 32,767 bytes of the instruction, quite a large range of addresses.

For displacement and displacement-deferred mode operands where the value of the operand is known, the assembler again chooses the smallest possible size among byte, word, and longword. If the value is unknown, the assembler uses a WORD displacement. This default to WORD cannot be changed. If it turns out to be too small, the LINK process detects this and an error message appears on the terminal.

However, the programmer can specify the size of the displacement to be used for these operands in exactly the same way as for PC-relative operands. For example,

```
MOVW      B^CLASS_O(R5), R6
```

specifies that the displacement value CLASS__O is to be placed in a byte of the instruction as the offset. This assumes that CLASS__O will be assigned a BYTE value that is unknown at the time this instruction is being assembled. When instructions specify displacement sizes that are too small, the LINK process catches the error and produces an error message.

Because displacements are often in the BYTE range, it is worthwhile to specify the B^ operator. Also, when you know a displacement will be larger than a word, specifying the L^ operator saves a run of the assembler and linker and therefore is worth the effort.

Chapter Summary :

1. Indirect addressing is the process of specifying addresses of operands instead of the operands themselves.

2. In register-deferred mode, the simplest form of indirect addressing, the address of the operand is placed in a register, and that register's name is then placed inside parentheses.

3. Autoincrement mode is register-deferred mode with a built-in increment, the size of which is determined by the instruction context. Although this mode is intended for array addressing, indexing is preferable when the application allows its use.

4. Autodecrement mode is register-deferred mode with a built-in decrement, the size of which is also determined by the instruction context. This mode is useful for addressing the elements of an array in reverse order.

5. Register-deferred, autoincrement, and autodecrement mode operands all can include indexing. Combined with these modes, indexing works exactly as it does in PC-relative mode; that is, the rest of the operand determines a base array address, and the index is added at runtime to produce the effective address.

6. Displacement mode allows an offset to be specified with register-deferred mode. It is useful for addressing fields within data records.

7. Relative-deferred mode uses the PC-relative mechanism to specify indirect addresses. The mode is specified by preceding the operand with an @ and can also be indexed.

8. Two-level indirect addressing means that the operand specifies an address where the address of an operand value can be found. This can be specified in register-deferred, displacement, and autoincrement mode operands by preceding these operands with the indirect operator, @. The resulting modes are called register-deferred deferred, displacement-deferred, and autoincrement-deferred.

9. The sizes of displacements in PC-relative mode operands and displacement mode operands can be controlled by the instruction, using unary operators and the .DEFAULT directive.

New Instructions

MOVAB   MOVAL   MOVAQ   MOVA W

New Directives

.ADDRESS   .DEFAULT

New Addressing Modes

Autodecrement   Displacement-deferred
Autoincrement   PC-relative deferred
Autoincrement-deferred   Register-deferred
Displacement   Register-deferred deferred

New Operand Specifier Operators

B^   L^   W^

New Terms

Deferred addressing   Indirect addressing
Displacement   Two-level indirect addressing

Chapter 8 Problem Set :

1. Explain why the VAX has four different MOVAx instructions.

2. Explain why it is better, when possible, to use indexing to access the elements of an array than to use register-deferred mode.

3. What are all of the differences between the autoincrement and autodecrement addressing modes?

4. When indexing and register-deferred addressing are combined, is the address modification caused by indexing done first or last?

5. In register-deferred mode, is it legal to use the same register for both the index and the base address computation?

6. What is one of the most common uses of displacement mode?

7. Explain the relationship between displacement mode and PC-relative mode.

8. Why does the VAX have relative-deferred mode when it already has register-deferred mode?

9. Explain how an effective address is computed when register-deferred deferred and index modes are combined.

10. Define the circumstances when the assembler considers the value of a PC-relative operand address expression unknown.

11. How do you change the default displacement size that the assembler uses when it encounters a displacement expression whose value is unknown?

12. Translate the following Macro instructions to machine code and follow each with the hex values of each source operand (not the address). Assume the following values for registers and memory locations:

```
0000 0109 : R1
0000 0108 : R2
0000 0100 : R3
0000 010C : R4
0000 0104 : R5
0000 0001 : R6

0000 010C :104
0000 010A :108
0000 0108 :10C
```

   a. SUBL2   (R2), R5
   b. CLRW   B^3(R1)
   c. INCW   @W^4(R3)
   d. ADDL2   (R5)+, −(R4)
   e. MULL2   L^8(R3)[R6], R4
   f. DIVW2   W^8(R3), R2

Write and debug structured Macro programs for the following problems.

13.   *In:*   An integer, LENGTH, followed by LENGTH-integers, where LENGTH will be < 101.
     Out: The list of input values with all of the negative values preceding all of the positive values in the order in which they were input.

Note: You cannot use indexing in this program.

14.   *In:*   A list of fewer than 100 negative integers, followed by a positive integer.
     Out: The percentage of input data that are within five of the average of the data. For example, if the average is 243, we want the percentage of data that are > 237 and < 249.

Note: You cannot use indexing in this program.

15.   *In:*   A list of positive integers, in ascending order, followed by five more positive integers. There will be fewer than 100 total positive integers.
     Out: The input list with the five additional integers inserted into their correct positions in the original ordered list.

Note: You must use indirect addressing to address the base of the array, but you must also use indexing to address the array elements.

16. *In:* A list of positive integers, all < 1000, followed by a negative integer.
  Out: A list of the unique numbers from the input. There will be fewer than 100 unique numbers in the input.

Note: You must use a WORD array for the data of this problem. You must use indirect addressing to address the base of the array, but also indexing to address the array elements.

17. *In:* An integer, LENGTH, followed by LENGTH-integers, all in the range of − 100 to + 100. LENGTH will be < 100.
  Out: **a.** A list of the positive values of the input.
    b. A list of the negative values of the input.

Note: The zeros in the input are to be ignored. You must use indirect addressing to address the elements of the input array and the array of positive values, but cannot use it for the array of negative values.

18. *In:* An integer, LENGTH, followed by two lists of integers, each of length LENGTH. Both lists are in ascending order.
  Out: A list of all of the input data, in ascending order.

Note: You are not to simply place all of the input values in one array and then sort it. Each data value must be moved into its correct position in the final array with one move. Also, you cannot use indexing at all in this program.

19. Rewrite Problem 17 by placing the addresses of the two arrays in a table, moving the address of the table into a register, and then using displacement-deferred mode for all accesses to the two arrays.

20. Rewrite Problem 18, using register-deferred deferred addressing for all accesses to the three arrays (two input and one output).

9

CHARACTER MANIPULATION

At one time, people regarded computers as remarkably fast and accurate machines that dealt, however, only with numbers. Until now, we too have been dealing exclusively with integer values and integer operations. But digital computers, of course, are capable of dealing with many different kinds of data.

One of the most common forms of data processed by contemporary computers is text, or strings of coded characters. Computers have been dealing with text routinely since the early 1950s when the first language translators were created. This is because translating high-level programming languages, or assembly languages for that matter, to machine code involves a good deal of text processing.

9.1   Character Codes and Character Data : : : : : : : :

Computer registers and memory locations cannot store graphical representations of characters. Even if they could, it would be extremely wasteful. Because we must deal with a relatively small character set, we can simply associate an integer with each character and use these numerical encodings for character data. A byte can store 256 different values, allowing a set of 256 characters to be encoded. This is adequate for most current applications.

VAX computers use the American Standard Code for Information Interchange (ASCII) character code. ASCII was developed by the American

National Standards Institute as the standard coding for all data transmission connections, including terminal-computer connections over common carriers such as telephone lines, as well as short distance connections between computers and their peripheral equipment. The ASCII character set includes upper- and lowercase alphabetic characters, the decimal digits, the punctuation characters used in English and the more common programming languages, and a collection of special characters to indicate various control signals between devices. Some representative ASCII codes are shown below:

Character	Hex Code
A	41
B	42
.	.
.	.
.	.
Z	5A
a	61
b	62
.	.
.	.
.	.
z	7A
0	30
1	31
.	.
.	.
.	.
9	39
+	2B
,	2C
/	2F
FF (form feed)	0C
LF (line feed)	0A

The complete set of ASCII character codes can be found in Appendix C.

As an example of an ASCII character string, the sentence "Macro is fun!" is shown below as it would appear in memory, starting at address 300 (hex):

Character	Byte	Address
M	4D	:300
a	61	:301
c	63	:302
r	72	:303
o	6F	:304
space	20	:305
i	69	:306
s	73	:307
space	20	:308
f	66	:309
u	75	:30A
n	6E	:30B
!	21	:30C

Character strings used as Macro instruction operands are specified by *descriptors* that include two quantities: the address of the first byte and the length of the string in bytes, as an unsigned word. Note that character strings are stored with the leftmost character in the lowest address, which is the opposite of the order in which the bytes of a LONGWORD integer are stored.

Macro has several directives for creating character strings at assembly time. The simplest of these, .ASCII, allocates a byte for each character in its operand. The operand must be delimited by some character that does not appear in the string. The delimiter can be any printable character except a space, a tab, an equal sign, a semicolon, or a less-than symbol (<). The characters in the string can be any character except null (0), carriage return (13 in decimal), or line feed (10 in decimal). To create a string that uses these characters at either end of the operand, you must assign their ASCII values to symbols by using direct assignment directives and then place them within pointed brackets on the desired end of the operand. Example 9.1 illustrates these rules.

. . . .

Example 9.1: The .ASCII Directive

```
        CR  =  13
        LF  =  10
STRING_1:       .ASCII      'MERRY CHRISTMAS'<CR><LF>
STRING_2:       .ASCII      *IT'S TOO EARLY?*
STRING_3:       .ASCII      %***NO IT ISN'T***%
```

. . . .

To use character strings, we usually will need to know the lengths of the strings in bytes. We can determine the length of a constant character string in a number of ways. We can count them ourselves, or we can place a label on the line following the .ASCII directive and then set a new symbol to the difference between the address values of the two. A method more accurate than the former and less cumbersome than the latter uses a variation of the .ASCII directive, .ASCIC.

The .ASCIC directive uses the same operand as .ASCII to build an ASCII coded string of bytes, but it also counts the number of bytes in the string and places that number in the byte preceding the first character code. In Example 9.2, STRING_1 and STRING_2 are equal.

. . . .

Example 9.2: .ASCII versus .ASCIC

```
STRING_1:       .ASCIC      'VAX FOR PRESIDENT'
STRING_2:       .BYTE       17
                .ASCII      'VAX FOR PRESIDENT'
```

. . . .

We could also build ASCII strings with a .BYTE directive by looking up all of the codes for the characters in the string we wanted and listing them one at a time in the operand of the directive. However, that would be a boring and error-prone task.

Character strings can be used as literal operands in certain Macro instructions. The form of a string literal is:

#^ a delimited-string

The string cannot be longer than the size of the operand for which it is being used; for example, if a string is used as the source operand in a MOVW, it cannot contain more than two characters. When a string literal is too short, zeros are added to pad it out to the required length. Note that these are numeric zeros, not ASCII codes for zero (30 in hex).

In the following move instruction, R7 receives the value shown:

```
MOVL      #^A/VAX/, R7
```

in the ASCII codes:

```
 3   2   1   0
┌──────────────────┐
│ 00  58  41  56   │  :R7
└──────────────────┘
```

or the characters:

```
  3    2    1   0
┌──────────────────┐
│ null  X   A   V  │  :R7
└──────────────────┘
```

9.2   *Character Input/Output* : : : : : : : : : : : : : : : : : :

Now that we can build character constants, we need to get the character data into memory for processing. The READ__A instruction allows you to read a character string into memory. It has only one operand: the address where it is to put the string. For example,

```
READ_A    MESSAGE
```

gets all characters from the terminal, up to but not including the carriage return and line feed, and places their ASCII codes into memory starting at address MESSAGE. The longest string that can be read with READ__A is 80 characters. If READ__A receives more characters than the area at the given address can store, the input string simply overwrites the following memory area.

The PRINT__A instruction prints a string of ASCII characters. It has three parameters: a literal label for the output, the length of the string as an unsigned word, and the address of the string to be printed. The following example prints POEM TITLE: MARY HAD A LITTLE LAMB.

. . . .

Example 9.3: The PRINT__A Instruction

```
MESSAGE:  .ASCIC    'MARY HAD A LITTLE LAMB'
LENGTH:   .BLKW    1
             .
             .
             .
    MOVZBW  MESSAGE, LENGTH
    PRINT_A ^'POEM TITLE:', LENGTH, MESSAGE+1
```

Note the convenience of using the .ASCIC directive to get the length of a string. However, we often will have to compute string length in some other way, especially when we are building strings for output.

9.3   *Character Manipulation* : : : : : : : : : : : : : : : : :

This section explains how to sort alphanumeric data, scan for and skip characters in text, and search strings for specific substrings.

9.3.1   *Sorting Character Data*

Sorting data is among the most common uses of computers. Although many sorting tasks involve lists of numeric data, others involve alphanumeric or textual data. Therefore, most computers have the capability of sorting lists of coded alphabetic data.

The *collating sequence* of a character code is the order of its elements. The collating sequence of ASCII has the codes for the alphabet in numeric order: The code for A is less than the code for B, and so forth. Instructions for comparing strings of alphabetic data are designed to affect indicator bits, just as the CMPx instructions the VAX uses for comparing integers. Because most sorting algorithms involve interchanging elements in the list being sorted, we also need move instructions that move character strings, such as the MOVx instructions for integer data.

The VAX has two instructions that compare character strings, one with three operands (CMPC3) and one with five operands (CMPC5). The general form of CMPC3 is:

CMPC3   length, string-1, string-2

Length is treated as an unsigned word that contains the length in bytes of each of the two character string operands, both of which are given as addresses.

CMPC3 is used to compare the characters of the two string operands one pair at a time, left to right. If an unequal pair is found, the Z and N indicators are affected and the operation is terminated. The N indicator is set if the character in the first string is less than the character in the second string; otherwise it is cleared. If all of the character pairs are equal (that is, the strings are equal), the Z indicator is set; otherwise, it is cleared. These indicator values give the conditional branch instructions natural meaning, consistent with their use in the integer compare instructions.

The CMPC3 instruction, like the other character manipulation instructions, also uses some of the lower numbered registers. This register alteration is called the *side effects* of an instruction. Some of the altered registers are left with useful information concerning the outcome of the instruction execution.

The CMPC3 instruction uses R0 and R2 as counters for the number of characters that have not been compared and found equal in the first and second string operands, respectively. The registers will be set to zero only if the strings are equal. Because the two operand strings are the same length, R2 always will be left with the same value as R0. After CMPC3 is executed in Example 9.4, both R0 and R2 will contain the value of four.

. . . .

Example 9.4: The CMPC3 Instruction

```
STR_1:    .ASCII    'MARYANNE'
STR_2:    .ASCII    'MARYLYNN'
             .
             .
             .

          CMPC3     #8, STR_1, STR_2
```

. . . .

CMPC3 uses R1 and R3 as pointers into the two strings being compared, R1 into the first string and R3 into the second string. After execution, the address of the character in the first string operand that terminated the operation (that is, the first character that was not equal to its counterpart in the second string operand) is in R1. The address of the corresponding character in the second string operand is in R3. If the two string operands are equal, R1 has the address of the first byte past the end of the first string operand, and R3 has the address of the first byte past the end of the second string operand. In the Example 9.4 code fragment, R1 would get the address of STR_1 plus four, and R3 would get the address of STR_2 plus four.

Now you can understand why all of our previous example programs have used middle registers for indexing and indirect addressing. You should use the lower numbered registers only when you need them for a short time, such as for intermediate results of arithmetic expression evaluation.

We often need to compare two strings of unequal length. For example, suppose we are examining words in some sort of text, a poem or a program, and wish to keep a table of the unique words we find. To do this, we must compare all newly found words with the words that are already in the table. Obviously, we cannot expect all of these words to have the same length.

The CMPC5 instruction was designed for this purpose. The general form of CMPC5 is:

CMPC5   length-1, string-1, fill-char, length-2, string-2

The first two operands provide the length in bytes, as an unsigned word, and the address of the first string operand. The third operand specifies a fill character to be used when the shorter of the two strings runs out of characters. The last two operands specify the length and address of the second string operand in the same way as the first two operands.

CMPC5 operates exactly like CMPC3 when the two strings have equal lengths. When the strings are of unequal length, the comparison progresses as it would with CMPC3 until the shorter string is exhausted or a pair of characters that are different is found. If the shorter string is exhausted before an unequal pair is found, CMPC5 continues by comparing the remaining characters of the longer string with the specified fill character. The indicators are affected the way they are with CMPC3.

Consider the following example.

. . . .

Example 9.5: The CMPC5 Instruction

```
STR_1:   .ASCIC   'MARY'
STR_2:   .ASCIC   'MARYLOU'
LEN_1:   .BLKW    1
LEN_2:   .BLKW    1
            .
            .
            .
         MOVZBW   STR_1, LEN_1
         MOVZBW   STR_2, LEN_2
         CMPC5    LEN_1, STR_1+1, #^A/ /, LEN_2, STR_2+1
```

. . . .

The compare operation stops when the L in MARYLOU is compared with the fill character, a blank. Because L has an ASCII code of 4C in hex and a blank has an ASCII code of 20 in hex, the N indicator would be set and the Z indicator would be cleared. The set N indicator indicates that the first string is ahead of the second string in alphabetic order. This typical use of CMPC5 in effect extends the shorter string with blanks out to the length of the longer string.

CMPC5 affects the first four registers in a way similar to CMPC3. R0, a counter for the first string operand, is set to the number of characters left in the first string operand including the character that terminated the operation. R0 is set to zero only if the two string operands were of equal length and composition or if the first string operand was completely used before the comparison operation was completed.

R1, a pointer into the first string operand, is set to the address of the character in the first string operand that terminated the operation. If the comparison operation used all of the characters of the first string operand, R1 will have the address of the first character past the end of the first string.

R2 is the counter associated with the second string operand, and R3 is the pointer associated with the second string operand.

In Example 9.5, R0 would be set to zero; R1 would be set to the address of STR_1 plus five; R2 would be set to three (the number of remaining characters including the one that stopped the comparison operation); and R3 would be set to the address of STR_2 plus five.

The MOVC3 and MOVC5 instructions are closely related to the CMPC3 and CMPC5 instructions. The MOVC3 has three operands, a string length and two string addresses, and MOVC5 has five operands that include a fill character.

The general form of MOVC3 is:

MOVC3   length, string-1, string-2

The length operand is treated, as in the CMPCx instructions, as an unsigned word. The two strings are specified by addresses. In Example 9.6, the MOVC3 instruction moves the entire contents of the text of STR__1 to STR__2.

. . . .

Example 9.6: The MOVC3 Instruction

```
STR_1:    .ASCIC   'APPLES ARE GOOD FOR YOU'
STR_2:    .BLKB    23
LENGTH:   .BLKW    1

            .

            .

            .

          MOVZBW   STR_1, LENGTH
          MOVC3    LENGTH, STR_1+1, STR_2
```

. . . .

MOVC3 uses the first six registers. R1 is set to the address of the first byte past the end of the first string operand; R3 is set to the address of the first byte past the end of the second string operand. Therefore, these registers are set to the beginning address of their respective string operands plus the length of the moved string. Although R0, R2, R4, and R5 are all used by MOVC3, they do not retain any useful information.

The MOVC5 instruction is used to move shorter strings to longer locations and vice versa. The general form is:

MOVC5   length-1, string-1, fill-char, length-2, string-2

Length-1 is the unsigned word length of the string at string-1, length-2 is the unsigned word length of the string at string-2, and fill-char is an ASCII constant that is to be used when the source string (string-1) is shorter than the destination string (string-2). If the source string is longer than the destination string, the excess characters in the source string are not moved.

As an example, consider the following code fragment.

. . . .

Example 9.7: The MOVC5 Instruction

```
STR_1:   .ASCIC   'CHOPIN'
STR_2:   .ASCIC   'BEETHOVEN'
STR_3:   .BLKB    8
STR_4:   .BLKB    8
LEN_1:   .BLKW    1
LEN_2:   .BLKW    1
           .
           .
           .
     MOVZBW   STR_1, LEN_1
     MOVZBW   STR_2, LEN_2
     MOVC5    LEN_1, STR_1 + 1, #^A/*/, #8, STR_3
     MOVC5    LEN_2, STR_2 + 1, #^A/*/, #8, STR_4
```

. . . .

After execution of these two MOVC5 instructions, STR__3 would contain CHOPIN**, STR__4 would contain BEETHOVE, and the N would not have been moved anywhere.

In addition to moving strings to locations of different lengths than the source strings, MOVC5 can be used to fill blocks of memory with certain characters. The following instruction

```
MOVC5   #0, STR_2, #^A/ /, #100, STR_2
```

places 100 blanks in memory, starting at the address STR__2.

Note that all of the character manipulation instructions implicitly specify a single BYTE context. Therefore, if indexing, autoincrement, or autodecrement modes are used to address any of the operands, the single BYTE context causes no modification of the index register in indexing, and increments and decrements of one for autoincrement and autodecrement, respectively.

We are ready to write a complete program example using what we have learned about character manipulation in Macro.

. . . .

Example 9.8

: Problem Statement

> *In:* An integer, LENGTH, followed by LENGTH-names, where each
> name has up to 20 characters, and LENGTH will be < 101.
>
> *Out:* The input sorted into ascending alphabetic order using an
> exchange sort algorithm.

Our pseudocode solution to this problem implements the same
exchange sort that we used in the solution to Example 7.2.

:• Pseudocode Solution

```
Get LENGTH
Get input NAMES
Set TOP__LIMIT TO LENGTH − 2
Set BOT__LIMIT TO LENGTH − 1
FOR TOP__REG : = 0 TO TOP__LIMIT DO
    Set BOT__START TO TOP__REG + 1
    FOR BOT__REG : = BOT__START TO BOT__LIMIT DO
        IF NAMES[TOP__REG] > NAMES[BOT__REG]
            THEN interchange them
        ENDIF
    END-FOR
END-FOR
Print sorted list
End-of-program
```

The Macro program for Example 9.8 uses the MOVC3, MOVC5, and
CMPC3 instructions. The major complication in sorting lists of strings
not encountered in sorting numbers is that strings are more difficult to
address than numbers. Because the numbers we have dealt with were
standard data types on the VAX, the indexing scheme of the VAX allowed
a simple way of addressing them. Strings, however, cannot be a standard
data type: No single string length would be appropriate for a wide range
of applications. Therefore, indexing cannot be used to address the elements of a list of character strings directly, nor can autodecrement and
autoincrement. For the exchange sort algorithm, we need two nested FOR
loops to control the process. Although these FOR loop variables cannot
be used to address the strings being sorted directly, they can be used
indirectly.

If range-checking is desired, the INDEX instruction introduced in
Chapter 7 could be used. Because the array of strings is logically single-
dimensioned and we can use a lower bound of zero, we do not need the

index-in operand. To get the correct index register value, we simply give the index and the element size of 20. The lower-bound and upper-bound operands will be zero and 99.

For example, to print the 15th 20-character string in an array named LIST, we could use the following code:

```
INDEX #14, #0, #99, #20, #0, R6
PRINT_A ^'FIFTEENTH WORD =', #20, LIST[R6]
```

Note that this works correctly only because LIST is a BYTE variable and PRINT__A specifies a BYTE context. If the LIST[R6] operand were used on an instruction with a nonBYTE context, the effective address computation would be incorrect.

If range-checking is not desired, we can compute the correct index register values with a multiply instruction. For example, to again print the 15th 20-character string in an array named LIST, we could use the following code:

```
MULL3   #14, #20, R6
PRINT_A  ^'FIFTEENTH WORD =', #20, LIST[R6]
```

In the exchange sort program we will use INDEX to address the strings in the sort operation.

We also must address the strings to get them into memory and to print the results of the sort. For this, we will use relative-deferred addressing, which is more efficient than indexing and also demonstrates the use of indirect addressing once more. For this addressing, we will simply load the addresses of the strings into pointer locations and then increment them by 20 to get to the next locations in the arrays.

The Macro program for the exchange sort of the list of names should help clear up any confusion about how these addressing schemes work.

:: *Macro Solution*

```
; EXCHANGE SORT OF A LIST OF NAMES
; IN:  AN INTEGER LENGTH, FOLLOWED BY LENGTH-
;      NAMES, WHERE EACH NAME HAS UP TO 20
;      CHARACTERS, AND LENGTH WILL BE LESS THAN 101.
; OUT:  THE INPUT, AFTER SORTING IT INTO ASCENDING
;      ALPHABETIC ORDER, USING AN EXCHANGE
;      SORT ALGORITHM.
;
      .PSECT  EXAMPLE, LONG
      MAX_NUM_NAMES = 100
LENGTH:    .BLKL   1  ; NUMBER OF INPUT NAMES
TOP_LIMIT:.BLKL    1  ; MAXIMUM FOR OUTER SORT PTR
BOT_LIMIT:.BLKL    1  ; MAXIMUM FOR INNER SORT PTR
```

Continued

```
BOT_START:.BLKL    1   ; LOWER BOUND FOR INNER LOOP
NAMES:      .BLKB   20*MAX_NUM_NAMES  ;
                        ; STORAGE FOR NAMES
TEMP_NAME:.BLKB    20  ; TEMPORARY FOR A NAME
NAME_PTR: .BLKL    1   ; ADDRESS PTR FOR A NAME
COUNTER:  .BLKL    1   ; COUNTER FOR I/O OF DATA
;
      .ENTRY  EX_9_8, 0
      INIT_IO
;
; GET LENGTH
;
      PRINT_L  ^'LIST LENGTH PLEASE'
      READ_L   LENGTH
;
; GET NAMES
;
      MOVAB    NAMES, NAME_PTR
;
; FOR COUNTER := 1 TO LENGTH DO
;
      MOVL     #1, COUNTER
      CMPL     COUNTER, LENGTH
      BLEQ     READ_LOOP
      BRW      OUT_READ_LOOP
READ_LOOP:
;
;     GET A NAME
;
      MOVC5    #0, NAMES, #^A/ /, #20, @NAME_PTR
      PRINT_L  ^'NEXT NAME PLEASE'
      READ_A   @NAME_PTR
      ADDL2    #20, NAME_PTR
      AOBLEQ   LENGTH, COUNTER, READ_LOOP
;
; END-FOR
; SET TOP_LIMIT TO LENGTH-2 AND
; BOT_LIMIT TO LENGTH-1
;
OUT_READ_LOOP:
      SUBL3    #2, LENGTH, TOP_LIMIT
      SUBL3    #1, LENGTH, BOT_LIMIT
;
; FOR TOP_REG := 0 TO TOP_LIMIT DO
;
```

```
        CLRL      R6
        CMPL      R6, TOP_LIMIT
        BLEQ      OUTER_LOOP
        BRW       OUT_OUT_LOOP
OUTER_LOOP:
;
;     SET BOT_START TO TOP_REG+1
;     & COMPUTE THE TOP NAME ADDRESS (R8)
;
        ADDL3     #1, R6, BOT_START
        INDEX     R6, #0, #99, #20, #0, R8
;
;         FOR BOT_REG := BOT_START TO BOT_LIMIT DO
;
        MOVL      BOT_START, R7
IN_LOOP:
;
;             IF NAMES[TOP_REG] > NAMES[BOT_REG]
;             (FIRST COMPUTE ADDRESS OF BOTTOM NAME (R9))
;
        INDEX     R7, #0, #99, #20, #0, R9
        CMPC3     #20, NAMES[R8], NAMES[R9]
        BLEQ      ENDIF
;
;                 THEN INTERCHANGE THEM
;
        MOVC3     #20, NAMES[R8], TEMP_NAME
        MOVC3     #20, NAMES[R9], NAMES[R8]
        MOVC3     #20, TEMP_NAME, NAMES[R9]
;
;             ENDIF
;
ENDIF:
        AOBLEQ    BOT_LIMIT, R7, IN_LOOP
;
;         END-FOR
;
        AOBLEQ    TOP_LIMIT, R6, OUTER_LOOP
;
; END-FOR
;
OUT_OUT_LOOP:
;
; PRINT SORTED LIST
;
```

Continued

```
        PRINT_L   ^'SORTED LIST'
        PRINT_L   ^' '
        MOVAB     NAMES, NAME_PTR
;
; FOR COUNTER := 1 TO LENGTH DO
;
        MOVL      #1, COUNTER
        CMPL      COUNTER, LENGTH
        BLEQ      PRINT_LOOP
        BRW       OUT_PRINT_LOOP
PRINT_LOOP:
        PRINT_A   ^' ', #20, @NAME_PTR
        ADDL2     #20, NAME_PTR
        AOBLEQ    LENGTH, COUNTER, PRINT_LOOP
;
; END-FOR
;
OUT_PRINT_LOOP:
        $EXIT_S
        .END      EX_9_8
```

9.3.2 Finding Words

You will often need to find words in text. This occurs in programs that do all sorts of translations, whether translations of Macro programs into VAX machine code or translations of Canadian legislative activities from English to French. Also, programs that do language analysis of any kind must be able to find the words in given text. For example, a text's word frequencies and correlations between pairs of words can help determine its author, since writers use word patterns that act like fingerprints.

We first will deal with a simple case of word-finding. When finding words in text in which the only legal word separators are blanks, a word is defined as a string of nonblank characters. To find a word means to find its first character, its last character, and then compute its length.

We begin by looking at characters, one at a time, left to right, through the given text. The first nonblank character we find will be the first character of the word. We continue from there, looking until we find a blank. That blank will be the terminating character for the word, and the address of the character to its immediate left will be the address of the last character in the word.

The VAX has two instructions that were designed for finding words: LOCC (*locate* character) and SKPC (*skip* character). The general form of LOCC and SKPC is:

op-code character, string-length, string-address

The character is usually specified as an ASCII literal, the string-length is an unsigned word, and the string-address is any expression that has an address value.

LOCC is used to compare a given character with each of the characters of a given string, one at a time, left to right, until either the string is exhausted or one of the character pairs matches. We find out how the execution of LOCC ended by checking the Z indicator bit: If a matching character was found, Z is cleared; otherwise, it is set. LOCC sets R0 to the number of characters in the given string that were not passed over or to zero if no characters matched. R1 is set to the address of the matching byte or to the address of the first byte past the operand string if no byte matched.

SKPC is strongly related to LOCC; it causes the same sort of action that LOCC causes, except that it compares characters until it finds a mismatch. If a mismatch is found, Z is cleared; otherwise, Z is set. Once again, R0 is set to the number of characters in the given string that were not skipped, and R1 is set to the address of the first unskipped character or the address of the first byte past the string if no mismatch is found.

Example 9.9 should help you understand these two instructions.

. . . .

Example 9.9: The LOCC Instruction

```
STRING:  .ASCII   "XXX!!!YY"
          .
          .
          .
          LOCC     #^A/!/, #8, STRING
```

. . . .

Now, the Z indicator is cleared, R0 contains the value five, and R1 points to the first !.

Next, consider the following instruction, executed just after the LOCC in Example 9.9:

```
SKPC     #^A/!/, R0, (R1)
```

The three exclamation points are skipped. The Z indicator is cleared, R0 contains the value two or the number of characters not skipped in the string, and R1 points to the first Y in the string.

In Example 9.9, we used LOCC and SKPC to find a kind of word, although a string of exclamation points embedded in uppercase letters is a somewhat peculiar word. The simple case of word-finding posed at the beginning of this section is quite similar to this example. We can use SKPC to find the first character of a word and LOCC to find the last character by using a blank as the given character for the instructions.

If a given string of text contains only one word, the problem is quite simple, as Example 9.10 shows.

. . . .

Example 9.10

: *Problem Statement*

In: A character string that contains a single nonblank substring.
Out: The nonblank substring, after it is moved to a new string location.

The pseudocode solution to Example 9.10 describes the process we outlined earlier.

:• *Pseudocode Solution*

Get string
Find the beginning of the nonblank substring
Find the end of the nonblank substring
Move the substring to WORD
Print WORD
End-of-program

The Macro program for this algorithm naturally contains more details than the pseudocode version.

:: *Macro Solution*

```
; FIND, MOVE, AND PRINT THE NONBLANK SUBSTRING
;         OF A GIVEN STRING
; IN:  A CHARACTER STRING THAT CONTAINS A SINGLE
;      NONBLANK SUBSTRING
; OUT:  THE NONBLANK SUBSTRING, AFTER IT'S MOVED
;       TO A NEW STRING LOCATION.
;
          .PSECT   EXAMPLE, LONG
LINE:        .BLKB 80      ; INPUT STRING
WORD:        .BLKB 25      ; THE NONBLANK SUBSTRING
LINE_PTR:  .ADDRESS  LINE  ; POINTER INTO LINE
LENGTH:      .LONG 80      ; LENGTH OF LINE
SKIPPED:     .BLKL 1       ; NUMBER OF SKIPPED CHAR
;
          .ENTRY   EX_9_10, 0
          INIT_IO
          MOVC5    #0, LINE, #^A/ /, #80, LINE
          READ_A   LINE
;
```

```
; FIND THE BEGINNING OF THE WORD
;
        SKPC    #^A/ /, LENGTH, LINE
;
; RESET THE ADDRESS POINTER AND THE
;   LENGTH OF THE REMAINING STRING
;
        MOVL    R0, LENGTH
        MOVL    R1, LINE_PTR
;
; FIND THE END OF THE WORD
;
        LOCC    #^A/ /, LENGTH, @LINE_PTR
;
; MOVE THE WORD TO THE LOCATION "WORD"
;
        SUBL3   R0, LENGTH, SKIPPED
        MOVC3   SKIPPED, @LINE_PTR, WORD
        PRINT_A  ^'THE WORD IS:', SKIPPED, WORD
        $EXIT_S
        .END    EX_9_10
```

. . . .

This operation is complicated by the need to keep track of the length of the remaining string and the address of the first unskipped character.

Figure 9.1 shows how the SKPC and LOCC instructions in the Example 9.10 program would operate on a simple input line.

To find all of the words in a given line of text, you simply embed the Example 9.10 code in a WHILE loop that depends on the pointer staying within the given line.

We will complicate the word-finding problem by including other characters as word delimiters, a common application to account for the various punctuation characters used to terminate words in English. If we had to use LOCC and SKPC to find words in English text, separate code would be necessary for each possible word terminator. To simplify this, the VAX has two instructions that are related to LOCC and SKPC: SCANC and SPANC.

The problem facing the designer of these kinds of instructions is how much of the instruction should be transparent to the user. For example, an instruction could specify a list of characters to search for or the programmer could build code sequences for the desired operation. The design-

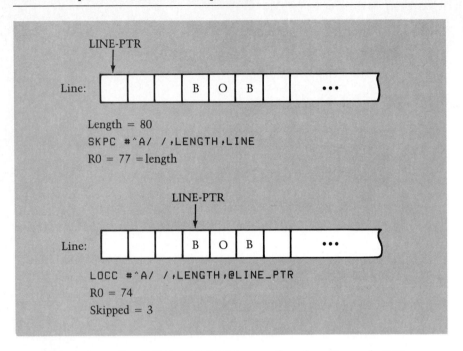

LINE-PTR

Line:

Length = 80
SKPC #^A/ /,LENGTH,LINE
R0 = 77 = length

LINE-PTR

Line:

LOCC #^A/ /,LENGTH,@LINE_PTR
R0 = 74
Skipped = 3

Figure 9.1   The SKPC and LOCC instructions from Example 9.10.

ers of the VAX took the middle ground, providing two instructions that require the programmer to supply a block of storage and to deal with some aspects of the operation.

For the SCANC and SPANC instructions, we must supply a 256-byte translate table. Each position in the table corresponds to one of the possible values in a byte, 96 of them corresponding to the ASCII character codes. In each table position, we must place a value that indicates whether an action should be taken when a character corresponding to that position is found in the string being scanned.

Each bit in these bytes can be used to indicate an action by either a SCANC or a SPANC instruction. Therefore, the 256 codes can be divided into eight different categories. Note that those categories are not mutually exclusive.

For example, if we want the SCANC instruction to stop scanning the given string when it finds a comma or a period, we would place a value that has one of the bits set in the 45th and the 47th table positions and a value in all other table locations that has that bit cleared (the ASCII codes for comma and period are 44 and 46 in decimal). The code 1 could be used in the 45th and 47th table positions, and 2 in all others. We would then use 1 in the SCANC instruction to indicate that we want it to stop when it finds a comma or a period.

SCANC uses the characters of the given string, one at a time, left to right, as indices into the table. The corresponding value found in the table is compared with the value specified in the instruction using a logical AND operation. The AND operation compares all eight bit pairs. The result is nonzero if at least one of the bit pairs has both bits set. When the AND operation produces a nonzero value, the operation halts and the Z indicator is cleared. If no character in the string causes the AND operation to produce a nonzero value, Z is set.

R0 is set to the number of unskipped characters in the string, including the one that produces the match, or to zero if no match is found. Because R0 is tested to affect the Z indicator, it is cleared when a match is found and set otherwise. R1 is set to the address of the character in the string that produces the match or to the address of the first byte past the end of the string if no match is found. R2 and R3 are also used, but do not retain any useful information.

Table bytes can have one of their bits set by using the values 1, 2, 4, 8, 16, 32, 64, or 128. They can have multiple bits set by using other values, which is useful when certain characters are used in more than one way. For example, if a program uses SCANC in one situation to scan for punctuation characters, we would want all punctuation characters in the table to have a particular bit set. But if later we wished to scan for just periods, the period entry in the table would have a different code that also has the bit that was the code for all punctuation characters set. For example, by using 3 for the period code and 1 for the other punctuation characters, the SCANC for punctuation characters would use 1, while the SCANC for periods would use 2.

SPANC operates exactly like SCANC, except that it continues until the AND operation between a table entry and the value specified on the instruction produces a zero result. This happens when the two bytes being compared (with AND) have no pairs of corresponding bits in which both bits are set. A zero result clears the Z indicator; otherwise, Z is set. The first four registers are set exactly as they are with SCANC.

For example, to skip over a substring of commas and periods, we would use a SPANC with a code of 1, along with the table we described for the SCANC operation, to find the first comma or period.

The general form of the SCANC and SPANC instructions is:

op-code   length, string, table, value

The length is that of the string and is treated as an unsigned word. The string and table operands are treated as addresses. The value is always a BYTE integer.

The table can be built by using the .BYTE directive and making use of the repetition factor option.

Example 9.11 should help clarify the use and actions of the SCANC and SPANC instructions.

. . . .

Example 9.11

:   Problem Statement

> *In:* A string of characters that contains a substring of lowercase letters.
>
> *Out:* The substring of lowercase letters.

This example is similar to Example 9.10, except that we will allow the word to contain only lowercase alphabetic characters. Also, instead of using blanks as the stop characters for the scanning instructions, we will use the set of lowercase alphabetic characters to span and scan to find the ends of the word.

First, we must build the table. We will use 1 for the positions associated with the ASCII lowercase alphabetic characters and 2 elsewhere. We can then specify 1 for the word delimiters in each of the SCANC and SPANC instructions, SCANC to the first lowercase letter and SPANC to the first character that is not a lowercase letter.

:• Pseudocode Solution

The pseudocode for Problem 9.11 is so similar to the pseudocode for Problem 9.10, we will not repeat it here.

:: Macro Solution

```
; FIND AND PRINT THE LOWERCASE SUBSTRING
; IN:  A STRING WHICH CONTAINS A LOWERCASE
;      SUBSTRING
; OUT:  THE LOWERCASE SUBSTRING
;
          .PSECT  EXAMPLE, LONG
TABLE:    .BYTE    2[97], 1[26], 2[133]
;                  TRANSLATE TABLE
LINE:     .BLKB    80    ; INPUT STRING
LINE_PTR: .ADDRESS LINE  ; ADDR OF FIRST
;                          UNSCANNED CHAR
LENGTH:   .LONG    80    ; LENGTH OF THE
;                          REMAINING STRING
SKIPPED:  .BLKL    1     ; NUMBER OF SKIPPED
;                          CHARACTERS
WORD:     .BLKB    25    ; THE FOUND SUBSTRING
;
```

```
        .ENTRY   EX_9_11, 0
        INIT_IO
        MOVC5    #0, LINE, #^A/ /, #80, LINE
        READ_A   LINE
;
; FIND THE BEGINNING OF THE SUBSTRING
;
        SCANC    LENGTH, @LINE_PTR, TABLE, #1
;
; RESET ADDRESS POINTER AND REMAINING LENGTH
;
        MOVL     R0, LENGTH
        MOVL     R1, LINE_PTR
;
; FIND THE END OF THE SUBSTRING
;
        SPANC    LENGTH, @LINE_PTR, TABLE, #1
;
; MOVE THE SUBSTRING TO "WORD"
;
        SUBL3    R0, LENGTH, SKIPPED
        MOVC3    SKIPPED, @LINE_PTR, WORD
        PRINT_A  ^/'THE WORD IS:', SKIPPED, WORD
        $EXIT_S
        .END     EX_9_11
```

. . . .

As with the Macro solution to Example 9.10, this program could become the heart of a program that finds all of the words in given text. Although that would involve a little more bookkeeping, such as making sure the search ends when a string has no more words, you have the basic tools for this and similar tasks.

9.3.3   Finding Substrings

Finding a particular substring in a given string is a common task for a text editor. It is also useful in other situations, such as looking up entries in tables of strings. Example 9.12 is a simple problem that requires finding substrings.

. . . . = ...

Example 9.12

: **Problem Statement**

> *In:* An integer, LENGTH, followed by LENGTH-words, where each
> has < 26 characters. LENGTH will be < 101.
> *Out:* A table of unique words from the input, with their frequencies
> of occurrence in the input.

For this problem we need not find words in text because the input is
already in word form. The central task is to look words up in the table. If
the word is already in the table, its frequency counter must be incremented. If the word is not in the table, it must be placed in the table and
its frequency counter set to 1. We could easily write a Macro program for
Example 9.12, using the string compare and move instructions already
discussed. We could also write a Macro program that searches a text string
for a certain substring using only what we have already covered. However,
a better way exists for doing both of these tasks using the VAX character
instruction MATCHC. The general form of MATCHC is:

MATCHC   target-length, target, source-length, source

The lengths, as usual, are treated as unsigned words, and the target and
source operands are treated as addresses.

Using MATCHC, the given source string is searched for the given
target string. If the target string is found, the Z indicator is set; otherwise,
it is cleared. The first four registers are affected by MATCHC. R2 is set to
the number of bytes left in the searched source string if the target string
is found, and to zero otherwise. R3 is left with the address of the first byte
past the last matching character in the source string if the target string is
found and to the address of the first byte past the source string otherwise.
R0 and R1 are used but are not left with useful information.

Now we will return to Example 9.12.

:• **Pseudocode Solution**

```
Get LENGTH
FOR COUNT : = 1 TO LENGTH DO
    Get WORD
    IF WORD is not in the TABLE
        THEN put WORD in TABLE
    ENDIF
    Increment WORD's frequency count
END-FOR
Print TABLE and the frequencies
End-of-program
```

Although this problem must address the elements of an array of strings, there is no reason to use INDEX because the array will not be searched by index.

:: *Macro Solution*

```
; A WORD FREQUENCY TABLE FROM WORD INPUT
; IN:  AN INTEGER LENGTH, FOLLOWED BY LENGTH-
;      WORDS, WHERE EACH HAS FEWER THAN
;      26 CHARACTERS.  LENGTH WILL BE LESS
;      THAN 101.
; OUT: A TABLE OF UNIQUE WORDS FROM THE INPUT,
;      ALONG WITH THEIR FREQUENCIES OF
;      OCCURRENCE IN THE INPUT
.PSECT   EX, LONG
TABLE:        .BYTE     ^A/ / [2500]   ; THE TABLE OF WORDS
TAB_LEN:      .BLKL     1              ; LENGTH OF WORD TABLE
                                       ; IN BYTES
TAB_ADDR: .ADDRESS      TABLE          ; ADDRESS OF THE WORD
                                       ; TABLE
NUM_ENTRIES: .BLKL      1              ; THE NUMBER OF
                                       ; TABLE ENTRIES
WORD:         .BLKB     25             ; AN INPUT WORD
LENGTH:       .BLKL     1              ; LENGTH OF THE INPUT LIST
COUNT:        .BLKL     1              ; COUNTER FOR INPUT/OUTPUT
FREQ:         .BYTE     0[100]         ; WORD FREQUENCIES
;
         .ENTRY  EX_9_12, 0
         INIT_IO
         CLRL     TAB_LEN
         CLRL     NUM_ENTRIES
         PRINT_L  ^'NUMBER OF WORDS, PLEASE'
         READ_L  LENGTH
;
; FOR COUNT := 1 TO LENGTH DO
;
         MOVL     #1, COUNT
         CMPL     COUNT, LENGTH
         BLEQ     LOOP
         BRW      OUT_LOOP
```

Continued

```
LOOP:
        MOVC5    #0, WORD, #^A/ /, #25, WORD
        PRINT_L  ^'NEXT WORD PLEASE'
        READ_A   WORD
;
;       IF TABLE IS EMPTY
;
        TSTL     TAB_LEN
        BNEQ     ELSE
;
;                THEN
;                  PUT WORD IN TABLE, COUNT IT, & SET
;                  FREQ TO 1
;
        MOVC3    #25, WORD, TABLE
        ADDL2    #25, TAB_LEN
        MOVL     #1, NUM_ENTRIES
        MOVB     #1, FREQ
        BRW      ENDIF
;
;                ELSE IF WORD IS NOT IN THE TABLE
ELSE:
        MATCHC   #25, WORD, TAB_LEN, TABLE
        BEQL     ITS_THERE
;
;                        THEN PUT THE WORD IN TABLE
;                        (AT (R3))
;
        MOVC3    #25, WORD, (R3)
        ADDL2    #25, TAB_LEN
        INCL     NUM_ENTRIES
;
;                    ENDIF
;                INCREMENT FREQUENCY COUNT
; (ITS ADDRESS IS ((R3 - TABLE-ADDRESS - 1) / 25))
;
ITS_THERE:
        SUBL2    TAB_ADDR, R3
        DECL     R3
        DIVL2    #25, R3
        INCB     FREQ[R3]
;
;       ENDIF (IF TABLE IS EMPTY)
```

```
;
ENDIF:
        AOBLEQ  LENGTH, COUNT, LOOP
;
; END-FOR
;
OUT_LOOP:
        PRINT_L  ^'FREQUENCY TABLE'
        CLRL    R7
;
; FOR COUNT := 1 TO NUM_ENTRIES DO
;
        MOVL    #1, COUNT
        CMPL    COUNT, NUM_ENTRIES
        BLEQ    P_LOOP
        BRW     OUT_P_LOOP
P_LOOP:
        PRINT_A ^' ', #25, @TAB_ADDR
        PRINT_B ^' ', FREQ[R7]
        ADDL2   #25, TAB_ADDR
        INCL    R7
        AOBLEQ  NUM_ENTRIES, COUNT, P_LOOP
;
; END-FOR
;
OUT_P_LOOP:
        $EXIT_S
        .END    EX_9_12
```

. . . .

Note that this program was meant to demonstrate the use of MATCHC. Using a FOR loop and indexing to address the elements in this problem would be a more machine-efficient method.

Several VAX instructions for dealing with characters were not included in this chapter. These instructions for converting between numeric values and character strings will be covered in Chapter 12.

Chapter Summary :

1. ASCII is a code for characters that is used by the VAX for all character handling operations.

2. ASCII constants can be built with the .ASCII directive or the .ASCIC directive, which also counts the constant's length.

3. Character constants can be used as literal operands by delimiting them and placing the unary operator ^A in front of them.

4. CMPC3 provides a method of comparing equal length character strings. CMPC5 is used to compare unequal length strings.

5. MOVC3 moves a character string to a string location of the same size. MOVC5 moves a character string to a string location of a different size. A fill character is used to lengthen the string, if necessary, and excess characters are ignored.

6. LOCC and SKPC allow the scanning of a string to the first occurrence or nonoccurrence, respectively, of a given character.

7. SPANC and SCANC allow the scanning of a string to the first occurrence or nonoccurrence, respectively, of a set of characters.

8. MATCHC provides a mechanism for finding a given target string in a given source string.

New Instructions

CMPC3	MATCHC	MOVC5	SKPC
CMPC5	MOVC3	SCANC	SPANC
LOCC			

New Directives

.ASCIC   .ASCII

New Operand Operators

^A

New Input/Output Instructions

PRINT_A   READ_A

New Terms

Collating sequence   Side effects
Descriptor

Chapter 9 Problem Set :

1. What is the difference between .ASCII and .ASCIC?

2. Describe character constant literals.

3. How is R0 used in the execution of CMPC3?

4. How are R0 and R2 used in the execution of CMPC5?

5. How is R1 used in the execution of MOVC3?

6. How is the Z indicator affected by the execution of MOVC5?

7. How is R1 used in the execution of LOCC?

8. How is the Z indicator affected by the execution of SKPC?

9. Describe completely the actions of SCANC.

10. How is the Z indicator affected by the execution of SPANC?

11. How is R1 affected by the execution of SCANC?

12. How is R2 affected by the execution of MATCHC?

13. How is the Z indicator affected by the execution of MATCHC?

14. In what way is the setting of the Z indicator consistent across all of the string instructions?

Write and debug structured Macro programs for the following problems.

15.   *In:* Five lines of text.
     Out: The number of occurrences of the lowercase letters a and b.

16.   *In:* A line of characters that may contain a substring that is delimited (on both ends) by a period, where there are exactly two periods, or maybe none.
     Out: The delimited substring, if it occurs.

17.   *In:* Some number of lines of text, terminated by a line that begins with five Zs. The input text contains words, as strings of letters, that are always delimited by blanks.
     Out: A list of all of the words of the input, in a column.

18.   *In:* Some number of lines of text, terminated by a line that
      begins with three periods. The input contains words, con-
      sisting of letters, that are delimited by either blanks or
      quotes (") at their beginnings and either blanks, periods,
      commas, or quotes at their ends. Also, words can begin in
      the first character position and/or end in the last column.
     Out: The words of the input, in a column.

19.   *In:* Same as Problem 16.
     Out: A list of the unique words of the input, along with their
      frequencies of occurrence.

20.   *In:* Same as Problem 17.
     Out: Same as Problem 18.

21.   *In:* Some number of lines of text, consisting of lowercase words
      separated by blanks, followed by a line that begins with
      three periods.
     Out: The input text, with all occurrences of the word "apple"
      replaced by the word "orange."

22.   *In:* Same as Problem 20.
     Out: The input text, with all occurrences of the word "prune"
      deleted. Instances of the word "prune" are not to be replaced
      by blanks—they are only removed.

23.   *In:* Same as Problem 20, except that two additional lines pre-
      cede the other input. Each of these two lines contains a
      single word.
     Out: The input, except that all occurrences of the word on the
      first input line are replaced by the word on the second
      input line.

24.   *In:* A single line of text, followed by two integers on a second
      line.
     Out: The input text, with the substring starting at the position
      indicated by the first input number whose length is indi-
      cated by the second input number removed.

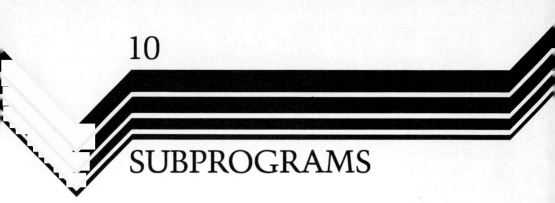

10

SUBPROGRAMS

Subprograms are clearly one of the most important mechanisms of programming, whether in a high-level programming language or in an assembly language, for at least two fundamental reasons. First, subprograms allow us to avoid repeating both the creation and the recording of program parts. Once the code for a process is written and debugged, it can be used in all future programs that require that process. We don't have to retype the code because it can be stored on a magnetic medium.

Second, and most significant, subprograms allow us to decompose programs into pieces that are both logically separate and manageably small. Large programs are made feasible only because they can be broken into relatively small parts.

Now that we have established the importance of subprograms, this chapter will explain how they can be implemented in Macro. We start by discussing the *stack* and the instructions for manipulating it because the stack is used to establish the linkage between calling programs and the programs they call.

10.1   Stack Operations :

A stack is a fundamental data structure that is used in a broad spectrum of computer applications, ranging from operating systems to computerized accounting systems. One of the stack uses that is most relevant to us is its use in linking programs to called subprograms. Therefore, before we discuss the construction of Macro subprograms, we must discuss the VAX stack operations.

A stack is a list of storage locations of some type, similar to a single-dimensioned array. The basic difference between a stack and a single-dimensioned array is the way in which their elements are accessed. Access to the elements of an array is random; that is, any element can be accessed at any time and, therefore, in any order. In contrast, access to the elements of a stack is highly restricted. Stacks always begin with no relevant data and in that condition are said to be empty. Data can be added to and removed from the stack only at one end. Therefore, data in a stack grow and shrink in number of elements at the same end. The active end is called the stack top, or top.

Logically, we push data down into a stack the way we push clean trays into a spring-loaded tray stack in a cafeteria. The more trays you place on the stack, the more they weigh and the farther down they squeeze their supporting spring; the one on top is always at about the same height. We think of data stacks in a computer in the same way, as if the stack top were stationary and the other end moved up and down as data are removed and added.

In fact, having a physical stack in a computer memory that behaved exactly like that logical picture would be highly inefficient. Every addition and every deletion from such a stack would require movement of all of the other stack elements. It is far more efficient to anchor the bottom of the stack instead of the top. In the VAX, the bottom of the stack is the first element of a block of storage. The stack top is a pointer that floats up and down as data are added and removed from the stack. This is easy to implement: We use a LONGWORD integer variable for the stack top and initialize it with the beginning address of the stack.

By convention on the VAX, stacks grow toward smaller addresses. This means that stack top pointers are always initialized to point at the highest address in the block of storage that is to be used for the stack.

The *push* operation decrements the stack top pointer by the element size and then places the value to be pushed in the location pointed to by the new top pointer value. The *pop* operation moves the value pointed to by the stack top pointer to a specified location and then increments the top pointer by the element size. The stack pop and push operations on a stack of LONGWORD values are shown in Figure 10.1.

The push and pop operations can be implemented easily in Macro by using the autoincrement and autodecrement addressing modes. We use a register for the stack top and initialize it to the address of the last element of the block being used for the stack. Then a MOVx instruction using autodecrement with the stack top register as the second operand would effectively push the first operand onto the stack. Likewise, a MOVx instruction using autoincrement with the stack top register as the first operand would effectively pop the top stack element from the stack and

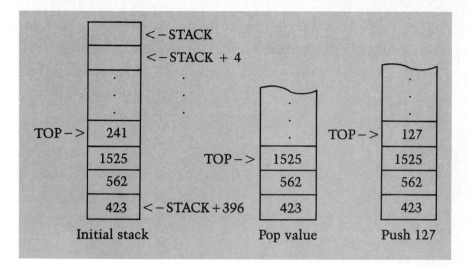

Figure 10.1 Register Top Stack Operations

into the second operand. Consider the following example.

. . . .

Example 10.1: Register Top Stack Operations

```
STACK:    .BLKL   100
            .
            .
            .
          MOVAL   STACK+400, R6
          MOVL    #42, -(R6)
          MOVL    #426, -(R6)
            .
            .
            .
          MOVL    (R6)+, VALUE
```

. . . .

This code initializes a stack of 100 longwords to the empty condition
with the MOVAL instruction. Note that the stack top, R6, is initialized
to the address of the first byte past the end of the block allocated for the
stack. This is always the initial condition of a stack, its empty condition.

The first two MOVL instructions push two values onto the stack, 42
and 426. The stack top is decremented by four in each of these two operations. Each operation leaves the stack top pointer pointing at the element
currently at the top of the stack.

The last MOVL instruction removes this top element from the stack (426) and places it in location VALUE. It then increments the stack top pointer so that it points at the new top element (42).

While this method works admirably, most of the stack operations in Macro deal with a particular stack and use convenient stack manipulation instructions. Henceforth, when we use the term stack, we will be referring to this stack.

The system allocates storage for the stack at the time the linker creates the executable program image. The stack top pointer is R14, which is usually referred to as SP for *stack pointer*. The system initializes SP before program execution. Therefore, to use the stack, we need only use SP as the stack pointer and not worry about allocating stack storage or initializing the stack top pointer.

One restriction on use of the stack is that all of the specialized stack instructions deal with longwords. Since much of the data we will want to store on the stack are addresses, this is not a severe restriction.

The PUSHL instruction is used to push longwords onto the stack. It has one operand and operates like a MOVL instruction whose second operand is − (SP). PUSHL's operand specifies the longword that is to be pushed onto the stack. For example,

```
PUSHL #42
```

decrements SP by four and then places the LONGWORD value 42 (decimal) onto the stack.

The POPL instruction does the opposite of PUSHL. It removes, or pops, a LONGWORD value from the stack and places that value in the location specified by its operand. It then increments SP by four. For example,

```
POPL    VALUE
```

removes the LONGWORD element currently being pointed to by SP, places it in location VALUE, and then adds four to SP.

Actually, the VAX does not have a machine language instruction for POPL. When "POPL operand" is encountered in a Macro program, a "MOVL (SP)+, operand" instruction is built. PUSHL, on the other hand, is a real VAX instruction.

Because we often need to store addresses on the stack, the VAX has the PUSHAx collection of instructions to push the addresses of their respective operands onto the stack. The x can be B, W, L, or Q to indicate that the address of a byte, word, longword, or quadword is to be pushed. In all of these cases, SP is decremented by four, and then the address of the operand as a 32-bit quantity is placed at the address specified by SP.

We highly recommend that you save the registers that a subprogram uses before the subprogram code executes. If the register values are not saved, any values that the calling program had in those registers will be destroyed. Saving a register means storing it in memory just before a subprogram is entered and restoring it just before control is returned to the calling program. To simplify these operations for the programmer, the VAX has provided a neat pair of instructions.

Both POPR and PUSHR instructions use the same form of operand, which is different from any we have seen. The general form of this operand is:

^M<register-list>

This operand is called a *register mask*. It creates a 16-bit string, or word, in which each bit represents one of the 16 registers. Any register whose name appears in the register list inside the pointed brackets has its corresponding bit set. All other bits in the mask are cleared. When the register mask operand is used on a PUSHR or POPR instruction, the following register names can appear in the register-list: R0–R12, AP, FP, and SP. Note that PC cannot be named and that one of the registers can be named by either of its names, R12 or AP. When used as the operand of a POPR or PUSHR instruction, the register mask must be used as a literal, that is, preceded by a #.

In the following example, the values of the specified registers are first pushed onto the stack and then later removed from the stack and placed back in the registers.

. . . .

Example 10.2: *Saving and Restoring Registers*

```
PUSHR     #^M<R2, R7, R8>
          .
          .
          .
POPR      #^M<R2, R7, R8>
```

For this pair of instructions to operate correctly, a special process must take place. To enable the POPR instruction to restore the correct values to the proper registers, the PUSHR and POPR instructions must push and pop the register values in opposite orders. PUSHR pushes the registers specified in its register mask beginning with the high-numbered registers. POPR pops the values off the stack into the low-numbered registers first. Note that the order that register names are listed in the register mask is irrelevant. For example, the following two instructions save and then restore the specified registers.

. . . .

Example 10.3: *Unordered Register Masks*

```
PUSHR     #^M<R7, R3, R10>
          .
          .
          .
POPR      #^M<R3, R7, R10>
```

10.2   Simple Subprograms : : : : : : : : : : : : : : : : : : :

We now will investigate the methods the VAX uses to implement subprograms. The simplest kinds of VAX subprograms are called *subroutines*. They are characterized as using limited and informal parameter passing methods, and providing no error-handling capability.

VAX subroutines communicate data from and to their callers by using two globally accessible locations, R0 and R1. Because they are often used by the system (such as for the character string instructions), R0 and R1 are the least safe places to put anything. Therefore, they are natural places for handling temporary data communication between calling and called programs.

To implement any kind of subprogram we need some mechanism for transferring control to the subprogram and then back to the calling program when the subprogram has completed its task. Getting to a subprogram is simple: We could use a BRW instruction. However, getting back is a little more complex. For subroutines that are not allowed to be used recursively, we could pass the return address along to the subroutine, have it save the address somewhere, and then have it branch indirectly to that location when it wanted to return; this assumes we have an indirect branch instruction. (We will discuss recursive subprograms in Section 5 of this chapter.) To provide more flexibility, however, it is better to use the stack to store the return address. The VAX includes several methods of building the linkage to and from subprograms.

For subroutines, three different instructions are available to save the return address on the stack and then branch to the specified subroutine address. The choice of three allows us to select the smallest that can handle the task at hand.

BSB*x* pushes the PC onto the stack and then does a PC-relative branch to its specified operand. The *x* in BSB*x*, which can be either B for BYTE or W for WORD, is used to specify the size of the offset to be added to the PC to get the effective address.

For example,

```
BSBB      SUB1
```

pushes the PC onto the stack and then uses a BYTE offset to address the subroutine SUB1. Note that the value of the PC is exactly the return address (the address of the instruction following the BSBB). BSBB is useful only for subroutines that are within 127 bytes of the instruction. Because this is a severe limitation, we place BSBB in the same category as ACBB, an instruction to be avoided in most cases. Even if the subroutine is within byte range at the time you write the code, later changes and additions will frequently move it out of that range.

BSBW can call subroutines that are within 32,767 bytes of the instruction. This will certainly suffice for the vast majority of situations. In those cases where a subroutine is more than 32,767 bytes away, the JSB instruction can be used. Since the need for JSB is rare, we will postpone its discussion until Chapter 15.

The RSB instruction provides the mechanism for transferring control back to the calling program when a subroutine has completed its task. RSB is rather unusual in that it does not have operands: It simply pops the top longword from the stack into the PC. Because the instruction that transferred control to the subroutine (BSBx) pushed the value of PC onto the stack, this results in a transfer of control to the instruction following the BSBx. This transfer occurs only if the subroutine has not used the stack and failed to restore it to its condition upon subroutine entry (the return address on top).

The following example illustrates the construction of a subroutine.

. . . .

Example 10.4

⠒ *Problem Statement*

> *In:* An integer.
> *Out:* A message indicating whether the input value is prime.
> *Method:* A subroutine must be used to decide whether the input value is prime.

We will use a very unsophisticated method to solve this problem. We will divide the input value first by two and then by all odd integers in the range of three to half of the input. If the number is not prime, it will have at least one divisor among that group.

Note that this process also works if you divide by values up to the square root of the input, instead of half of the input. However, our main interest here is Macro subroutines and not numeric methods, so we will not worry about computing and using the square root.

⠒ *Pseudocode Solution*

Set DIVISOR to 3
Compute LIMIT as INPUT / 2 (setting REMAINDER)
WHILE (DIVISOR < LIMIT) AND (REMAINDER <> 0) DO
    Divide INPUT by DIVISOR (setting REMAINDER)
    Add 2 to DIVISOR
END-DO
IF REMAINDER <> 0
    THEN set RESULT to 1
    ELSE set RESULT to 0
ENDIF
End-of-program

The most noteworthy aspect of this algorithm is that it contains our first use of a *compound condition* (the condition on the WHILE statement uses an AND operator). This is not as simple to code as it may appear, because we must code the logical inverse of conditionals.

The logical inverse of a condition with two relational expressions and an AND operator is the inverses of the two relational expressions connected by an OR operator. For example, the logical inverse of

(A > B) AND (C <= D)

is

(A <= B) OR (C > D)

If the first of these conditions appeared in a WHILE construct, we would code it in Macro, assuming that the variables were all longwords, as follows:

```
CMPL      A , B
BLEQ      OUT_LOOP
CMPL      C , D
BGTR      OUT_LOOP
```

In the case of a condition that contains two relational expressions and an OR operator, the inverse condition is the inverses of the two relational expressions connected by an AND operator. To code the inverse of such a condition in Macro, we must test both relational expressions every time. For example, the logical inverse of

(A > B) OR (C <= D)

is

(A <= B) AND (C > D)

The Macro code for the first condition, if it were the condition on a WHILE statement, would be as follows:

```
          CMPL      A , B
          BLEQ      SECOND
          BRW       SKIP
SECOND:
          CMPL      C , D
          BGTR      OUT_LOOP
SKIP:
```

This is clearly messier than the code for a compound condition with an AND operator, so be sure you study it until you are comfortable with the process.

These methods of inverting the logic of the AND and OR expressions are direct applications of two of the fundamental laws of Boolean algebra, called DeMorgan's theorems.

One final note: When a compound expression is used to control a WHILE loop, it is sometimes necessary to know which condition caused loop termination. You learn this by adding an IF construct after the loop. Our pseudocode for Example 10.4 sets the result according to whether the loop was terminated by the first relational expression or the second.

The Macro subroutine version of our pseudocode for Example 10.4 uses the EDIV instruction for the division operations because the shorter versions of the divide instructions do not save the remainder. We have embedded the subroutine in a small calling program that tests it.

:: *Macro Solution*

```
; A PROGRAM TO DECIDE PRIME NUMBERS
; IN:   A POSITIVE NUMBER
; OUT:  A MESSAGE INDICATING WHETHER THE NUMBER IS
;         PRIME
; METHOD:  A SUBROUTINE THAT DIVIDES BY ODD VALUES
;
; MAIN PROGRAM DATA AREA
;
        .PSECT   EXAMPLE, LONG
VALUE:           .BLKL   1 ; INPUT VALUE
;
; SUBPROGRAM PRIME
;
; IN:   A POSITIVE INTEGER IN R1
; OUT:  IF THE INPUT IS PRIME R0 = 1, ELSE R0 = 0
; METHOD:  DIVISION BY 2 AND ALL ODD NUMBERS <
;             VALUE/2
;
PRIME:
;
; SET DIVISOR TO 3
;
      MOVL     #3, DIVISOR
;
; COMPUTE LIMIT AS INPUT / 2
;
      CLRL     DIVIDEND + 4
      MOVL     R1, DIVIDEND
      EDIV     #2, DIVIDEND, LIMIT, REMAINDER
;
; WHILE (DIVISOR < LIMIT) AND (REMAINDER <> 0) DO
;
```

Continued

```
LOOP:
        CMPL     DIVISOR, LIMIT
        BGEQ     OUT_LOOP
        TSTL     REMAINDER
        BEQL     OUT_LOOP
;
;     DIVIDE INPUT BY DIVISOR
;
        EDIV     DIVISOR, DIVIDEND, QUOTIENT, -
                 REMAINDER
;
;     ADD 2 TO DIVISOR
;
        ADDL2    #2, DIVISOR
        BRW      LOOP
;
; END-DO
;
OUT_LOOP:
;
; IF REMAINDER <> 0
;
        TSTL     REMAINDER
        BEQL     ELSE
;
;     THEN SET RESULT TO 1
;
        MOVL     #1, R0
        BRW      ENDIF
;
;     ELSE SET RESULT TO 0
;
ELSE:
        CLRL     R0
;
; ENDIF
;
ENDIF:
;
; RETURN
;
        RSB
;
```

```
; SUBROUTINE DATA AREA
;
DIVISOR:      .BLKL      1
DIVIDEND:     .BLKQ      1
LIMIT:        .BLKL      1
REMAINDER:    .BLKL      1
QUOTIENT:     .BLKL      1
;
; BEGIN MAIN PROGRAM CODE
;
      .ENTRY  EX_10_4, 0
      INIT_IO
      PRINT_L  ^'PLEASE ENTER VALUE TO BE TESTED'
      READ_L   VALUE
;
; ENACT SUBPROGRAM PRIME
;
      MOVL     VALUE, R1
      BSBW     PRIME
;
; IF RESULT (R0) = 1
;
      CMPL     R0, #1
      BNEQ     ELSE2
;
;     THEN VALUE IS PRIME
;
      PRINT_L ^'INPUT VALUE IS PRIME'
      BRW      ENDIF2
;
;     ELSE VALUE IS NOT PRIME
;
ELSE2:
      PRINT_L ^'INPUT VALUE IS NOT PRIME'
;
; ENDIF
;
ENDIF2:
      $EXIT_S
      .END     EX_10_4

            . . . . . . . . . . . . . . . . . . . . . . . . . .
```

The subprogram form we have discussed in this section and used in the solution to Example 10.4 is highly restricted. The parameter passing mechanism puts a severe limit on the number of parameters that can be passed and on how the subprogram can be called, that is, not recursively. Furthermore, subprograms in this form cannot be called from programs written in other programming languages.

10.3 Passing Parameters with a General Argument List :

Two methods of parameter passing and subprogram linkage use the standard interface that is used between all VAX subprograms. Subprograms linked in this way are called *procedures*. Of the two procedure linkage methods, the one that uses what is called a general argument list is actually the least general.

The general argument list method places the parameters in a block of storage and then passes the address of that block to the procedure. Before we explain the general argument list in detail, we must explain the following common methods of passing parameters.

Call by value is a parameter passing method that transmits the actual value of the parameter to the called program. This technique implements a one-way communication of data to the called program: The called program cannot return data through a parameter passed by this method. Call by value is the default method of passing parameters in Pascal.

Call by reference is a parameter passing method that transmits the address of an argument to the called program. This implements a two-way communication of data between the calling and the called programs: Because the called program is given an address, it can both take data from that location and place new values in it. Call by reference, the optional parameter passing method used in Pascal, is specified in that language by preceding formal parameters by the keyword VAR. It is also the standard means of passing parameters in FORTRAN.

A third parameter passing method, *call by descriptor*, is sometimes used in VAX languages to pass a description of a data location, including its size, type, and structure. This is the method normally used for passing character strings.

Now we can return to the general argument list call mechanism. The general form of the CALLG instruction that calls a procedure using this technique is:

CALLG   argument-list-address, procedure-address

Before we explain how CALLG operates, we should look at the structure of the general argument list, which is shown below:

arg-count	<- argument-list
argument 1	<- argument-list + 4
argument 2	<- argument-list + 8
· · ·	· · ·
argument n	<- argument-list + 4·n

The number of parameters, or arguments, in the general argument list is specified by an unsigned byte in the first position in the list. The remaining three bytes of the first longword must be zeros. That each parameter occupies one longword in the list allows for storage of call by reference parameters, or addresses, and call by value parameters, each of which occupies part or all of a longword.

For example, if we needed to pass the address of an array named LIST and the value of its length, the argument list could be constructed as follows:

```
ARG_LIST:
          .LONG      2        ; NUMBER OF PARAMETERS
          .ADDRESS   LIST     ; ARRAY ADDRESS
LEN:      .BLKL      1        ; VALUE OF LIST'S LENGTH
```

A procedure named SORT can now be called with the following code:

```
MOVL     LENGTH, LEN
CALLG    ARG_LIST, SORT
```

Note that we moved the value of LENGTH, which we assumed contained the number of elements in LIST, into the argument list just before the CALLG instruction. The alternative would be to use the longword in the argument list as the regular home for the LENGTH value.

Keep in mind that all of the arguments in an argument list, including the number of parameters, must be longwords, even though only the first byte of those longwords is used. Also, if other calls to SORT should use different parameters (for example, a different array is to be sorted), either a different argument list must be created and used, or the values in the first list must be modified before each call.

A number of different data values are pushed onto the stack when a CALLG instruction is executed. The area of the stack into which these values are pushed is the *call frame*. Because it is assumed that most procedures will need to use registers in addition to R0 and R1, a mechanism has been built in for saving registers. Rather than have the procedure push these register values onto the stack at the beginning and then pop the values back into the registers before returning, these actions are implicit in the linkage instructions.

The first line of a procedure is an .ENTRY directive that includes both the name of the procedure and an entry mask indicating the registers that are to be saved on the stack, as well as the trap enable bits DV and IV, for decimal and integer overflow, respectively, that are to be set while in the procedure. The ^M operator is used as the second operand of the .ENTRY directive to build the 16-bit entry mask. For example, the first line of a procedure SORT that uses R5, R6, R7, and R8 and sets the integer overflow trap enable would be:

```
.ENTRY   SORT,  ^M<IV, R5, R6, R7, R8>
```

The CALLG instruction then fetches the word built by the mask operator and pushes the indicated registers onto the stack, highest number first. Note that certain registers cannot be specified in this mask, namely, R0, R1, AP, FP, SP, and PC.

The other information that CALLG saves in the call frame precedes the saved registers. The general form of the call frame is shown below:

Exception handler
SPA S 0   Mask   PSW   00000
Saved AP
Saved FP
Saved PC
Saved registers

The first longword of the call frame is the address of an *exception handling* routine. This longword is set to zero by the CALLG instruction. The system transfers control to the given address when an exception occurs during execution of the procedure code. Unless it is important that a specified action be taken when an exception occurs in a procedure, this field will be left at zero. When it is important, the procedure places in that longword the address of the code it wants executed if an exception occurs.

The second longword contains a variety of information tidbits. Because SPA is a two-bit field used by the system and not by the programmer, we need not explain it here. The S field is a single bit that indicates whether this is a CALLG call or the CALLS call that we will discuss in the next section; an S bit value of 1 indicates that the procedure was called with a CALLS. The bit following S and the five lowest-order bits are not used and are always zeros. The mask field stores bits 0–11 of the entry mask specified in the first word of the called program. The right or lower-order word stores bits 5–15 of the PSW, as it appeared when CALLG started execution.

The third, fourth, and fifth longwords of the call frame store the AP, FP, and PC registers, respectively. Following the PC are the registers specified by the entry mask. Because the stack grows toward smaller addresses, the push instructions that build the call frame are in the reverse of the order of the frame's contents.

We now can describe all of the pertinent actions of CALLG in pseudocode terms as follows:

Fetch the entry mask from the second operand of CALLG
Push all registers specified in the entry mask
    (highest numbered registers first)
Push   PC
Push   FP
Push   AP
Push a longword consisting of:
    SPA
    S = 0 (means this is a CALLG)
    #0 (a single bit)
    Bits 0–11 of the entry mask
    Bits 5–15 of the PSW
    #0 (five bits)
Push a longword zero (exception handler address)
Set FP to SP
Clear condition code bits
Set AP to the first operand of CALLG
Set trap enable bits according to the entry mask
Clear the FU bit of the PSW
Set PC to the second operand of CALLG plus two

Finally, we can discuss how a procedure is written. Addressing the parameters is the primary process we must explain.

Because the AP register is left with the address of the general argument list, we can address any of the parameters as a constant offset plus AP, which is used as an indirect address. While in the procedure, the number of parameters that were passed is at (AP); the first parameter is at 4(AP), the second parameter is at 8(AP), and so forth. We can address call by value parameters using those operand expressions. For call by reference parameters, we simply precede the operand expression by the indirect operator, @, to get a second level of indirectness.

To restore the system to its condition before the procedure was called and to return to the instruction following CALLG, we use the RET instruction, which has no operands. RET removes the entire call frame, restores the saved values to all saved registers, and transfers control to the instruction immediately after the CALLG that started its execution.

Now, we are ready to write a procedure and exercise it with the CALLG instruction.

. . . .

Example 10.5

: Problem Statement

> *In:* An integer, LENGTH, followed by LENGTH-integers, where LENGTH will be < 101.
> *Out:* The input list of integers, after they have been sorted into descending order.
> *Method:* A procedure must be used to implement a simple exchange sort.

:• Pseudocode Solution

The pseudocode for the sort operation is exactly the same as that used for the character string sort we did in Chapter 9, so we will not repeat it here.

:: Macro Solution

```
; PROGRAM TO SORT AN ARRAY OF INTEGERS
; IN:   AN INTEGER, LENGTH, FOLLOWED BY LENGTH-
;       INTEGERS
; OUT:  THE INPUT INTEGERS, IN DESCENDING ORDER
; METHOD:  A PROCEDURE THAT IMPLEMENTS AN EXCHANGE
;            SORT
;
; MAIN PROGRAM DATA AREA
;
        .PSECT  EXAMPLE, LONG
LIST:   .BLKL 100   ; INPUT DATA
LENGTH: .BLKL 1     ; LENGTH OF INPUT LIST
LIMIT:  .BLKL 1     ; LIMIT FOR I/O LOOPS
;
```

```
; ARGUMENT LIST FOR SUBPROGRAM SORT
;
ARG_LIST:
          .LONG     2        ; NUMBER OF PARAMETERS
          .ADDRESS LIST      ; ARRAY ADDRESS
LEN:      .BLKL     1         ; LOCATION FOR ARRAY LENGTH
;
; SUBPROGRAM SORT
;
      .ENTRY   SORT, ^M<R7, R8>
      ARRAY = 4
      ARRAY_LEN = 8
;
; SET TOP_LIMIT TO LENGTH-2 & BOT_LIMIT TO LENGTH-1
;
;
      SUBL3    #2, ARRAY_LEN(AP), TOP_LIMIT
      SUBL3    #1, ARRAY_LEN(AP), BOT_LIMIT
;
; FOR TOP_REG := 0 TO TOP_LIMIT DO
;
      CLRL     R7
      CMPL     R7, TOP_LIMIT
      BLEQ     OUTER_LOOP
      BRW      OUT_OUTER_LOOP
OUTER_LOOP:
;
;       SET BOT_START TO TOP_REG + 1
;
      ADDL3    #1, R7, BOT_START
;
;       FOR BOT_REG := BOT_START TO BOT_LIMIT DO
;
      MOVL     BOT_START, R8
IN_LOOP:
;
;           IF ARRAY[TOP_REG] > ARRAY[BOT_REG]
;
      CMPL     @ARRAY(AP)[R7], @ARRAY(AP)[R8]
      BGEQ     ENDIF
;
```

Continued

```
;                  THEN INTERCHANGE THEM
;
      MOVL     @ARRAY(AP)[R7], -(SP)
      MOVL     @ARRAY(AP)[R8], @ARRAY(AP)[R7]
      MOVL     (SP)+, @ARRAY(AP)[R8]
;
;         ENDIF
;
ENDIF:
      AOBLEQ   BOT_LIMIT, R8, IN_LOOP
;
;       END-FOR (FOR BOT_REG = BOT_START)
;
      AOBLEQ   TOP_LIMIT, R7, OUTER_LOOP
;
; END-FOR (FOR TOP_REG := 0)
; RETURN
;
OUT_OUTER_LOOP:
      RET
;
; SUBPROGRAM SORT DATA AREA
;
TOP_LIMIT: .BLKL   1   ; LIMIT FOR TOP_REG
BOT_START: .BLKL   1   ; BEGINNING VALUE FOR
                       ; BOT_REG
BOT_LIMIT: .BLKL   1   ; LIMIT FOR BOT_REG
;
; BEGIN MAIN PROGRAM
;
      .ENTRY   EX_10_5, 0
      INIT_IO
      READ_L   LENGTH
;
; COMPUTE LIMIT FOR I/O LOOPS
;
      SUBL3    #1, LENGTH, LIMIT
;
```

```
; FOR REG := 0 TO LIMIT DO
;
        CLRL      R7
        CMPL      R7, LIMIT
        BLEQ      READ_LOOP
        BRW       OUT_READ_LOOP
READ_LOOP:
        READ_L    LIST[R7]
        AOBLEQ    LIMIT, R7, READ_LOOP
;
; END-FOR
; SORT DATA
;
OUT_READ_LOOP:
        MOVL      LENGTH, LEN
        CALLG     ARG_LIST, SORT
        PRINT_L ^' SORTED LIST'
        PRINT_L ^' '
;
; FOR REG := 0 TO LIMIT DO
;
        CLRL      R7
        CMPL      R7, LIMIT
        BLEQ      PRINT_LOOP
        BRW       OUT_PRINT_LOOP
PRINT_LOOP:
        PRINT_L     ^' ', LIST[R7]
        AOBLEQ    LIMIT, R7, PRINT_LOOP
;
; END-FOR
;
OUT_PRINT_LOOP:
        $EXIT_S
        .END      EX_10_5
```

. . . .

A few features of this program are noteworthy. First, we moved the length of the array into the argument list just before calling the procedure, rather than having it always there. Although in this program it would have been shorter to have it a permanent part of the argument list, that is a less flexible method; if we needed to sort two different arrays, putting in the second length would destroy the length of the first.

Second, because the array elements include addresses in several places in the procedure, we could have shortened the operands and the execution time by moving the array address to a register that would then be used as a single-level indirect address. The instruction

```
MOVL    ARRAY(AP), R9
```

would move the array address to R9, which then could be used as shown in the following:

```
CMPL    (R9)[R7], (R9)[R8]
```

The CALLG form has several disadvantages. One of these is that the parameters must be located in an area away from the CALLG instruction; this decreases readability because, when you find a CALLG, you must search through the rest of the program to find the parameters. Another drawback is that CALLG cannot be used in recursive calls to subprograms. On the other hand, CALLG is a very efficient method of subprogram linkage.

10.4   *Passing Parameters in the Stack* : : : : : : : : : :

The VAX alternative to CALLG for calling procedures is CALLS. Instead of placing the parameters in a block of storage and passing the block's address, we use CALLS to place the parameters in the stack and pass the number of parameters as an operand.

The general form of CALLS is:

CALLS   number-of-parameters, procedure-address

The action of CALLS is similar to that of CALLG. In fact, the only difference in the call frame portion of the stack is that the S bit is set instead of cleared (to indicate that this is a CALLS instruction, not CALLG).

When CALLS is executed, the parameters have already been pushed onto the stack. CALLS pushes the value of its first operand, the number of parameters, onto the stack, builds the call frame in the stack as CALLG does, but then sets AP to point at the LONGWORD value of the number of parameters in the stack. This arrangement makes the stack area where the parameters are stored appear exactly as the general argument list that CALLG uses.

In the procedure, the only significant difference between the way the system handles CALLS and CALLG calls is in the action of RET. For CALLS calls, RET must remove the parameters from the stack before control is returned to the calling code. RET knows when to take this action by checking the S bit in the call frame.

For example, we could use CALLS to call the SORT procedure of Section 10.3, as shown in the following:

```
PUSHL    LENGTH
PUSHAL   LIST
CALLS    #2, SORT
```

Note that once again things are backwards. Because the stack grows toward smaller addresses, in a sense growing backwards, and the procedure addresses the parameters as if they were stored in memory in the forward direction, the calling program must push the parameters onto the stack in reverse order. In SORT, AP points at the number of parameters, AP + 4 points at the array address, and AP + 8 points at the array length. This is true whether SORT is called with CALLG or CALLS. As this example shows, we use PUSHL to pass call by value parameters, and PUSHAx to pass call by reference parameters.

Pascal and other high-level languages that allow recursive subprograms use a stack to pass parameters. On the VAX, all Pascal procedure calls are made with CALLS.

Another feature required of recursive procedures is that local storage must be dynamically allocated with each call to the procedure. Our SORT procedure simply uses a block of memory for data storage at its end. Because there is no reason for this procedure to be called recursively, this is fine. However, procedures that are called recursively, along with others that dynamically allocate local storage, must allocate storage from the stack.

Recall that FP has the address of the address of the exception handling subprogram. This stack position is also the last used longword of the stack. Therefore, we could use FP and negative offsets to address locations in the stack. The actual storage is allocated by subtracting the required number of bytes from the SP.

For example, suppose a procedure named FINDER needed four local variables: two longwords named MAX and MIN, and two WORD integers named COUNT and LIMIT. The following code would set up the required storage.

. . . .

Example 10.6: Dynamic Storage Allocation

```
.ENTRY   FINDER, ^M<,,,>
MAX  = -4
MIN  = -8
COUNT  = -10
LIMIT = -12
ADDL2    #LIMIT, SP
```

Now, the four locals can be addressed as:

MAX(FP), MIN(FP), COUNT(FP), and LIMIT(FP)

Every time FINDER is called, the four locals will be allocated in the stack. Because we did not change FP in allocating the storage for the four locals, and RET uses FP to find the beginning of the call frame, RET will automatically deallocate whatever is used for local storage as long as it is allocated and referenced in the way we just described. Any Macro procedure that allocates its local storage from the stack can call itself with CALLS.

Note that we could have used a subtract instruction to move SP around our dynamic storage area, but using the last constant as an operand is somewhat safer.

10.5   *Recursive Procedures* : : : : : : : : : : : : : : : : : : :

In simple terms, a recursive function or subprogram is one that calls itself. If you have had no previous exposure to *recursion*, it may sound like a peculiar concept with only esoteric applications. On the contrary, recursion is both natural and commonly applicable.

For problems that can be solved by either conventional iteration or recursion, most computers will execute the iterative algorithm faster. The exceptions would be stack machines such as the Burroughs B5000, B6000, and B7000 series computers. However, machine efficiency is not always the primary concern. In fact, readability and ease of programming are far more important criteria when choosing implementation techniques. Note that most applications programs are written in high-level languages, even though assembly language implementations are much more machine efficient.

Recursion is chosen as a technique over iteration where the algorithm is more naturally expressed with recursion. The most elementary textbook example of recursion is the factorial function, which is described using recursion as follows:

$$f(0) = f(1) = 1$$
$$f(n) = n \cdot f(n - 1)$$

Although the factorial function is naturally expressed using recursion, it is a poor example for a recursive procedure, because it can be implemented so simply using iteration. Consider the following pseudocode.

. . . .

Example 10.7: Pseudocode for the Factorial Function, Computed Iteratively

```
Get N
Set FACT to 1
FOR COUNT : = 2 TO N DO
    Set FACT to FACT * COUNT
END-FOR
Print FACT
End-of-program
```

Most examples of recursion that are realistic, both in terms of being a natural means of expressing a process and in terms of being reasonably efficient, are too complicated for our purposes here. Although the example we are about to present is usually implemented using iteration, its recursive implementation is both natural and efficient.

. . . .

Example 10.8

: ***Problem Statement (for a function)***

In: Parameters:
1. The address of an ascending LONGWORD array.
2. The value of the upper-bound index of the array to be searched.
3. The value of the lower-bound index of the array to be searched.
4. The value to be found in the array.

Out: The position of the given value in the array, in R0, assuming the positions begin at zero.

Method: A recursive version of a binary search.

A binary search takes advantage of the fact that the list is in numeric order. By comparing the target, or the value to be found, with the middle array element, the algorithm can decide which half of the list the target occupies; the other half of the list can be eliminated from the subsequent search. This process is then repeated on the remaining half of the list. In this way, the algorithm takes an average of the base two logarithm of the list's length comparisons to find any one of its elements. Contrast this with the number of comparisons that a linear search takes, on average half the list length. (A linear search searches the list by comparing the target with each list element, one at a time, until the target is found.) For long lists, the binary search is far faster than a linear search. For example, to find one value in a list of 1000 elements, the binary search uses 50 times fewer comparisons, on average, than a linear search.

After each comparison in a binary search, the algorithm is reapplied to the half of the remaining list in which the target has been found to reside. These reapplications of the search process are naturally implemented as recursive calls to the process.

The pseudocode algorithm for the recursive binary search (BINSER) is shown below in the form of a function. Macro functions, by convention, return their functional values in R0.

:• **Pseudocode Solution**

Function BINSER(LIST, LOWER__BOUND,
    UPPER__BOUND, TARGET)
IF LOWER__BOUND > UPPER__BOUND
    THEN set R0 to −1 (TARGET is not in LIST)
    ELSE
        Compute MID as (UPPER__BOUND + LOWER__BOUND)/ 2
        IF TARGET = LIST[MID]
            THEN set R0 to MID
            ELSE IF TARGET < LIST[MID]
                THEN set R0 to BINSER(LIST, LOWER__BOUND,
                            MID − 1, TARGET)
                ELSE set R0 to BINSER(LIST, MID + 1,
                            UPPER__BOUND, TARGET)
            ENDIF
        ENDIF
ENDIF
Return
End-of-function

The first IF construct in this algorithm determines when the target is not in the list. Obviously, all such algorithms must take this case into account. Our algorithm sets the functional value, R0, to minus one to indicate the error to the calling program.

We will now write the Macro code for the binary search, but this time we will not include a main program to test the subprogram. After the code, however, we will show a calling sequence for the procedure.

:: *Macro Solution*

```
        ,PSECT  EXAMPLE, LONG
; FUNCTION BINSER
; A RECURSIVE BINARY SEARCH
;
; PARAMETERS:
;     (1) THE ADDRESS OF AN ORDERED LONGWORD ARRAY
;     (2) THE VALUE OF THE LOWER-BOUND INDEX OF
;         THE ARRAY INDICES TO BE SEARCHED
;     (3) THE VALUE OF THE UPPER-BOUND INDEX OF
;         THE ARRAY INDICES TO BE SEARCHED
;     (4) THE VALUE OF THE TARGET LONGWORD
;
        LIST = 4
        LOWER_BOUND = 8
        UPPER_BOUND = 12
        TARGET = 16
        MID = -4
;
        ,ENTRY  BINSER, ^M<R2>
;
; ALLOCATE A LONGWORD FOR THE 'MID' POINTER
;
        ADDL2   #MID, SP
;
; IF LOWER_BOUND > UPPER_BOUND
;
        CMPL    LOWER_BOUND(AP), UPPER_BOUND(AP)
        BLEQ    ELSE1
;
;    THEN SET R0 TO -1 (TARGET IS NOT IN LIST)
;
        MOVL    #-1, R0
        BRW     ENDIF1
;
;    ELSE
;            COMPUTE MID AS
;            (UPPER_BOUND+LOWER_BOUND)/2
;
```

Continued

```
ELSE1:
      ADDL3    UPPER_BOUND(AP), LOWER_BOUND(AP), R2
      DIVL3    #2, R2, MID(FP)
;
;                IF TARGET = LIST[MID]
;
      MOVL     MID(FP), R2
      CMPL     TARGET(AP), @LIST(AP)[R2]
      BNEQ     ELSE2
;
;                   THEN SET R0 TO MID
;
      MOVL     MID(FP), R0
      BRW      ENDIF2
;
;                      ELSE IF TARGET < LIST[MID]
;         NOTE THAT THE INDICATORS ARE STILL SET)
;
ELSE2:
      BGEQ     ELSE3
;
;                         THEN SET R0 TO BINSER(LIST,
;                         LOWER_BOUND, MID - 1, TARGET)
;
      PUSHL    TARGET(AP)
      SUBL3    #1, MID(FP), -(SP)
      PUSHL    LOWER_BOUND(AP)
      PUSHL    LIST(AP)
      CALLS    #4, BINSER
      BRW      ENDIF3
;
;                         ELSE SET R0 TO BINSER(LIST,
;                         MID+1,UPPER_BOUND,TARGET)
;
ELSE3:
      PUSHL    TARGET(AP)
      PUSHL    UPPER_BOUND(AP)
      ADDL3    #1, MID(FP), -(SP)
      PUSHL    LIST(AP)
      CALLS    #4, BINSER
;
```

```
;                    ENDIF (IF TARGET < LIST[MID])
;
ENDIF3:
;
;        ENDIF (IF TARGET = LIST[MID])
;
ENDIF2:
;
; ENDIF (IF LOWER_BOUND > UPPER_BOUND)
;
ENDIF1:
        RET
```

. . . .

Note that to access the parameters we used named constants built with direct assignments for the offsets from AP. The MID constant is the negative offset from FP that is used to access the longword that is dynamically allocated with each call to BINSER. These constants provide highly readable operands in the instructions that deal with the parameters.

Although we compute the subscript of the list value that is to be compared with the target in the dynamic location MID(FP), we move a copy of it to R2 where we actually address the value. This is only a convenience; indexing is such a natural mode that it should be used whenever possible.

Because LIST(AP) is the address, we must use PUSHL to get the address of the list onto the stack. If we had used PUSHAL, the address of the address of the list would have been placed onto the stack.

When we needed to push MID + 1 or MID − 1 onto the stack, we used add and subtract instructions, respectively, with autodecrement SP destinations rather than computing the value in a register and then pushing the register. Our method uses one instruction rather than two. Pushes and pops can often be done in this convenient way.

Although this program has IF constructs nested three deep, it is still readable. Readability is enhanced by both indenting the nested pseudocode statements and labeling the ENDIFs.

An example of a nonrecursive, or external, call to BINSER follows.

. . . .

Example 10.9: An External Call to BINSER

```
;
; FIND POSITION OF 'VALUE' IN 'STUDENT_NUMS'
;
        PUSHL    VALUE
        PUSHL    #<LENGTH - 1>
        PUSHL    #0
        PUSHAL   STUDENT_NUMS
        CALLS    #4, BINSER
;
; IF R0 >= 0
;
        TSTL     R0
        BLSS     ELSE
;
;       THEN PRINT R0
;
        PRINT_L  ^'POSITION OF "VALUE" IS:', R0
        BRW      ENDIF
;
;       ELSE PRINT ERROR MESSAGE
;
ELSE:
        PRINT_L  ^'*** ERROR, "VALUE" IS NOT IN'
        PRINT_L  ^'"STUDENT_NUMS"'
;
; ENDIF
;
ENDIF:
```

                             ·
                             ·
                             ·

. . . .

Note that recursive calls to BINSER (those in BINSER) use PUSHL to pass the array address, but the nonrecursive call in Example 10.9 used PUSHAL. This is because the nonrecursive call must pass the actual address of the array, whereas recursive calls have only the array's address, not its name, and so simply pass it along as is.

Reentrant code is code that is not self-modifying in any way. It is not allowed to change its instructions, nor can it contain data locations that get changed. This enables reentrant code to be shared by two or more users in a multiprogramming environment. For example, the text editor that you use in creating your Macro programs is reentrant code: Regardless of how many users are simultaneously using the same editor, they all use the same copy. Not only does this provide a huge savings of memory, but if the editor contained data locations that changed, the system could not keep track of to which user the current version belongs.

The BINSER subprogram is an example of a reentrant program. All of its local storage, except R2, is dynamically allocated from the stack. R2, which is saved on the stack by the CALLS/RET mechanisms, is also dynamic.

10.6   Subprogram Libraries : : : : : : : : : : : : : : : : : : :

Now we can examine the best method of storing and using subprograms. Once a subprogram is written and debugged, it can be used as part of the system for which it was written, as well as for other systems. The best way to implement this flexibility is to assemble the subprograms separately, once they are debugged, and to keep their object or machine language forms in a subprogram library. Then the library can be included in the LINK operation to bring them into the executable image.

The only change that must be made to a subprogram used in this way is to convert any of its symbols that will be accessed by other programs into *global symbols*. All of the labels we have been using are local to the assembly process in which they are written. To make a local label accessible to the LINK program, we simply add a second colon after its name. A single colon specifies a local label, and a double colon specifies a global symbol.

Direct assignment statements that define globally accessible symbols must use two equal signs. For example,

```
FLAG == 5
```

makes the symbol FLAG available to all object code during the linking process.

Note that it is not a good programming practice to allow symbols that are defined in a subprogram to be available to other programs. Parameter passing should be used for such needs.

To place a subprogram in a library, we first must assemble it. Then we can place it in a library with the following DCL or VAX/VMS command:

```
$ LIBRARY/CREATE library-name object-program-list
```

The library name can be any legal filename. The object-program-list is a list of names of assembled programs that you want placed in the library. Groups of programs that are used on the same project are usually gathered together in a library.

Once the library is created, it can be used by specifying its name on the LINK command. For example, if we wanted the binary search subprogram to be placed in a library and then used in an execution of a program named SORTER, we could use the following commands:

```
$ MACRO BINSER
$ LIBRARY/CREATE SERLIB BINSER
$ MACRO SORTER
$ LINK SORTER, SERLIB/LIB
$ RUN SORTER
```

10.7   Subprograms and the Debugger : : : : : : : : : :

Two of the VAX/VMS debugging facilities that pertain to subprograms are the CALL command and the subprogram trace operation.

The general form of the CALL command is:

CALL subprogram-name [(argument-list)]

Any subprogram that was included on the LINK command can be executed under the debugger with CALL.

To trace subprogram use in the debugger, tracepoints can be set at all subprogram call and return instructions with the following command:

```
DBG>SET TRACE/CALL
```

Chapter Summary :

1.   The VAX stack is allocated by the system. Its top is the user-accessible register, SP, which is initialized by the system.

2.   PUSHR and POPR are used to store registers on the stack and pop them back off the stack, respectively. The operand of both of these is a register mask, built with the unary operator ^M.

3.   PUSHL and POPL are used to store longwords on the stack and pop them back off the stack, respectively.

4.   A quick-and-dirty method of building and calling subprograms is provided on the VAX with the BSBB, BSBW, JSB, and RSB instructions. This method requires the user to ensure that the stack's integrity is maintained during execution of the subprogram's code. Parameters are passed only through registers R0 and R1.

5.   The two methods of constructing procedures on the VAX are used for all of the available languages on the VAX.

6.   CALLG is used to pass parameters as a block of storage in the calling program. It also builds an area of the stack, the call frame, where registers and status information are saved.

7. Using CALLS is the most general method of calling procedures on the VAX. Parameters are passed in the stack, a technique that allows both recursive and reentrant procedures.

8. Parameters in procedures are accessed by using the AP register, with an offset, as an indirect address.

9. Subprograms can be assembled separately, placed in libraries, and then brought in by the LINK operation for inclusion in the executable image.

10. Symbols can be defined for global access by using two colons instead of one in instructions and directives that define symbols with labels and by using two equal signs instead of one in direct assignment statements.

11. Subprogram calls and returns can be traced, and subprograms can be executed individually in the debugger.

New Instructions

BSBB	CALLS	PUSHAB	PUSHAW	RET
BSBW	POPL	PUSHAL	PUSHL	RSB
CALLG	POPR	PUSHAQ	PUSHR	

New Operand Operators

^M

New Terms

Call by descriptor	Pop
Call by reference	Procedures
Call by value	Push
Call frame	Recursion
Compound conditions	Register mask
Exception handling	Stack
Global symbols	Subroutines

Chapter 10 Problem Set :

1. In what direction does the VAX system stack grow, toward address zero or toward higher addresses?

2. Does the PUSHL instruction generate its own op code?

3. Does the POPL instruction generate its own op code?

4. How can WORD integers be pushed on the stack?

5. What are all of the versions of the PUSHAx instruction?

6. Describe the register mask operator.

7. In what order are the registers pushed by PUSHR?

8. In what order are the registers popped by POPR?

9. Describe all of the actions of BSBW.

10. Write the Macro code for the following pseudocode statements.

    a. WHILE (A > B) AND (C <= D) DO

    b. IF (A <= B) OR (C = D) THEN
           Increment COUNT
      ENDIF

    c. IF (A <> B) AND (C <= D)
          THEN print RESULT
          ELSE print error message
      ENDIF

11. What is the order of the register storage in the call frame?

12. What bits of the PSW are saved in the call frame?

13. What are the criteria for choosing between CALLG and CALLS?

14. What is the difference between a subprogram that is to be called with CALLS and the same subprogram that is to be called with CALLG?

15. Describe how storage can be dynamically allocated in a subprogram.

16. Why are subprograms written to be reentrant?

17. How can a symbol that is assigned to a LONGWORD integer with .LONG be made globally accessible?

Write and debug structured Macro subprograms for the following problems. For testing purposes, write a calling program for each subprogram.

18. *Parameters:*
    a. The address of an array of longwords.
    b. The length, as a LONGWORD value, of the array.

    Result: Use an exchange sort to put the array into descending order.

Note: You must use CALLG to test this subprogram.

19. *Parameters:*

    a. The address of an ordered array of WORD integers.
    b. The address of the array's length.
    c. The value of a WORD integer.

    Result: The value from parameter (c) must be inserted into the array of parameter (a). The array's length from parameter (b) must be changed.

Note: You must use CALLG to test this subprogram.

20. *Parameters:*

    a. The address of a line of English text containing < 100 characters. All words are separated by blanks, and there are no punctuation characters, just lowercase alphabetics and blanks.
    b. The address of a character string of length 25.
    c. The address of a BYTE integer.

    Result: The third word in the string of parameter (a) is to be found and placed in the string of parameter (c). The string of parameter (a) may or may not actually contain three words. If it does not, parameter (c) is to be set to 1, otherwise to 0.

21. *Parameters:*

    a. The address of an array of BYTE integers.
    b. The address of the length of the array.

    Result: All duplicate values are to be removed from the array, without reordering its elements. The length is to be set to the new correct value.

22. *Parameters:*

    a. The address of an array of WORD integers.
    b. The value of the length of the array, as a longword.
    c. The address of a WORD integer.

    Result: The median of the array parameter (a) is to be computed and placed in parameter (c).

Note: You are to use a second subprogram, similar to that of Problem 18, to sort the input array.

23. *Parameters:*

 a. A non-negative LONGWORD integer (ARG__1).
 b. A non-negative LONGWORD integer (ARG__2).

Result: The evaluation of Ackerman's function, which is defined as:

A(0, ARG__2)   = ARG__2 + 1 for all ARG__2 > 0
A(ARG__1, 0)   = A(ARG__1 − 1, 1) for ARG__1 > 0
A(ARG__1, ARG__2)= A(ARG__1 − 1, A(ARG__1, ARG__2 − 1))
                                      for ARG__1 and ARG__2 > 0

Note: This subprogram must be recursive. Also, note that this program will require large amounts of stack space for large parameter values. Therefore, you should test it on relatively small values (that is, < 10).

24. *Parameters:*

 a. The address of a character string of ASCII decimal digits.
 b. The value of the length of the string.

Result: The value of the ASCII string, in R0.

Note: This subprogram must implement a recursive procedure for this conversion. (Note that the numeric value of a single ASCII decimal digit is the ASCII value minus 30 (hex), and the numeric value of a two-character ASCII string is the numeric value of the first character times ten plus the numeric value of the second character.)

25. *Parameters:*

 a. A positive LONGWORD integer, N.
 b. A positive LONGWORD integer, M.

Result: The number of ways the sum of M positive integers is equal to N. This is called the partition problem, whose solution can be computed using the following recursive equations:

$$P(N, M) = 0 \text{ for } N < M$$

$$P(M,M) = P(N,1) = 1$$

$$P(N, M) = \sum_{I=M-1}^{n-1} P(I, M\text{-}1) \text{ for } N > M$$

11

MACROS

This chapter introduces the general concept of a macro and discusses the details of building macros in Macro. Macros are mechanisms that significantly extend the power of a computer's assembly language by allowing additions to the instruction set. No serious study of assembly language programming is complete without an understanding of the process of creating and using macros.

11.1   The Macro Concept :

You should try to avoid confusing the three uses of the word macro. A macro is a language construct that is common to nearly all assembly languages. The word Macro refers to the assembly language of the VAX. And the word MACRO refers to the VMS system command that invokes the VAX assembler program.

A macro is, in a sense, an assembly time subprogram. A macro definition, like a subprogram definition, is a prescription for a process. However, macros describe how text, whether code or data, is to be written into a program, as well as use parameters to specify textual variations of a particular call, or instantiation.

The fundamental difference between macros and subprograms is that the computer executes the code of a subprogram at execution time when it encounters a call instruction; upon completion, control returns to the instruction immediately following the call. Macros, on the other hand, are invoked at assembly time as if they were assembler directives; they then generate text in the position of the call, such as code to be executed in line with the surrounding code. The macro also may generate directives to allocate data storage areas at assembly time.

In some situations, we must choose between macros and subprograms. Macro code is in-line; that is, it appears where the macro definition was invoked and so has no linkage overhead, making it more time efficient. Subprogram code requires only one copy and so is more space efficient. In most cases, the decision to use a macro will be a matter of convenience and not one of efficiency.

The primary use of macros is to extend the instruction set of the machine we are programming and to provide additional directives for the assembler we are using. Macros can not only create new instructions from the existing set, but also can redefine real instructions for the particular needs of certain programs. The input/output instructions you have been using are all macros, used to extend the VAX instruction set by building calls to procedures. Although procedure calls often require several lines of code to deal with parameter passing, our macros are single lines, making them far more convenient to use.

11.2   Parameterless Macros : : : : : : : : : : : : : : : : : : :

We will begin our discussion of the construction of VAX macros with the simplest case: macros without parameters. Although these macros are not useful in most situations, we want to introduce the concept of a macro without the additional mechanics of parameter passing.

The general form of a parameterless macro definition is.

.MACRO macro-name
— macro-body —
.ENDM   [macro-name]

.MACRO is a directive to the assembler that what follows is a macro definition. It also provides the name of the macro, which can take the form of any other symbol in Macro. (Note that we now have four uses for the word macro.)

The macro-body is a collection of text, usually Macro instructions that specify what text the macro is to create when invoked. These instructions can be executable, nonexecutable, or both.

The .ENDM directive is used to mark the end of the macro definition. Although the optional macro-name on .ENDM is rarely useful to the assembler, it does aid readability. We recommend its inclusion on all .ENDM directives.

To call a macro, we place its name on a program line as if it were an op code. The assembler will then replace the call with the macro body text. The text that is generated by a macro call is a *macro expansion.*

As an example of a macro, consider the following definition.

. . . .

Example 11.1: A Parameterless Macro

```
.MACRO QUAD_R3
MULL2 R3, R3
MULL2 R3, R3
.ENDM QUAD_R3
```

. . . .

This macro definition includes the code to produce the fourth power of the value in R3, leaving the result in R3. When called, QUAD__R3 produces the following code:

```
MULL2 R3, R3
MULL2 R3, R3
```

Remember that macro definitions do not exist at runtime. They are assembly time entities that build assembly language text that either affects the assembly process or is assembled into machine code and executed at runtime. They are abstractions in the sense that subprograms are abstractions. Macros, however, are physically replaced by their actual definitions at assembly time, whereas subprograms are logically replaced by their definitions at runtime. Once the code produced by a macro is placed in a listing generated by the assembler, the abstraction ceases to exist, whereas subprograms remain abstractions in the listings.

When the assembler encounters a macro definition, it simply copies it to a macro definition storage area. No further assembler processes are applied until a call to the macro is found.

Macros can redefine VAX op codes. For every string of characters that the assembler finds and determines to be an op code (from its context), the assembler searches the macro definitions found in the program, any specified macro libraries, and the system macro library, all before it looks in the instruction op code table. Therefore, an op code is assumed to be a VAX instruction only after the assembler has determined that it is not the name of a macro. This can be a useful feature for special applications. In most cases, however, we will define macros to provide additional facilities, not to redefine existing instructions.

Now that you have been introduced to the macro concept, we can add the parameter mechanism.

11.3 *Passing Parameters to Macros* : : : : : : : : : : : :

Because macro expansion is an assembly time event, we obviously cannot send the values of variables as parameters to macros. The only data available for parameters at assembly time are the symbols and their address values in the symbol table. Because the assembler can handle strings as well, they can also be parameters.

The correspondence between actual parameters and formal parameters in subprograms is usually by value or by address. Neither of these two mechanisms is suited to macros. Because macros create text, the only correspondence technique that is viable is textual substitution: The actual parameters, provided on the macro call instruction, are textually substituted wherever their corresponding formal parameters occur in the macro definition.

11.3.1 *Simple Macro Parameters*

The basic form of a macro formal parameter list is shown in the following:

.MACRO   macro-name   parameter-list

The parameters within the parameter-list can be separated by commas, spaces, or tabs, although commas are usually used. The parameter-list can be separated from the macro-name also by a comma, a space, or a tab. The following example shows the basic form of both formal and actual parameters.

. . . .

Example 11.2: A Simple Swap Macro

```
.MACRO   SWAP_L  V1, V2, V3
MOVL     V1, V3
MOVL     V2, V1
MOVL     V3, V2
.ENDM    SWAP_L
```

The macro call

```
SWAP_L  LIST[R7], LIST[R8], TEMP
```

produces the following code:

```
MOVL     LIST[R7], TEMP
MOVL     LIST[R8], LIST[R7]
MOVL     TEMP, LIST[R8]
```

. . . .

This macro is used to extend the Macro language by defining an inter-change instruction for longwords, which does not exist in Macro. This normally would be done only if the swap operation were required more than once in a program.

If too many parameters are passed in a macro call, the assembler will produce an error message. On the other hand, if a call does not provide an adequate number of actual parameters, those that are missing or absent will default to the empty string. For example, the following call to SWAP__L

```
SWAP_L   LIST[R7], LIST[R8]
```

will produce the following code:

```
MOVL       LIST[R7],
MOVL       LIST[R8], LIST[R7]
MOVL        , LIST[R8]
```

Although in this example the absent parameter will quickly cause other syntax errors, you sometimes will want parameters to be erased from the macro definition.

11.3.2   *Default Parameters*

Absent parameters occasionally indicate that some default value is to be used. This can be specified in the formal parameter list of the macro definition. For example, we can let the V3 parameter of SWAP__L default to the name TEMP by defining it as follows:

```
.MACRO   V1, V2, V3 = TEMP
```

Now, if we expand SWAP__L with the same incomplete call used in Sec-tion 11.3.1, we get:

```
MOVL       LIST[R7], TEMP
MOVL       LIST[R8], LIST[R7]
MOVL       TEMP, LIST[R8]
```

This is the same code that was produced by our expansion of SWAP__L in Section 11.3.1. If TEMP is used on most calls to SWAP__L, it makes the calls slightly simpler to use TEMP as the default value rather than always including it in the call.

Default parameters are most valuable where a macro uses a large num-ber of parameters in nearly always the same way. Note that if an absent parameter is not at the end of the parameter list, as it was earlier, you simply leave out the actual parameter. All of the comma separators must be present in the parameter list, however, or the assembler will associate the actual parameters with the formal parameters incorrectly.

11.3.3   *Keyword Parameters*

Errors can be avoided in the correspondence between actual and formal
parameters by using keyword parameters rather than forming the correspondence strictly by position. Keyword actual parameters are specified
by replacing an actual parameter with an assignment of an actual parameter to the formal parameter name. Consider the following example:

```
SWAP_L  V2 = LIST[R8],  V1 = LIST[R7],  V3 = TEMP
```

The code that is created by this call is exactly the same as the code created
in the previous sections.

The use of formal parameter names obviates the need for ordering the
actual parameters. Keyword parameters help prevent errors when calling
macros with large numbers of parameters, because it is difficult to keep
more than six parameters in the correct order. Keyword parameters are
used extensively for the input/output macros that are part of the VMS
system software, which we will discuss in Chapter 14.

11.3.4   *String Parameters*

When a macro parameter is a string, rather than a symbol or constant, we
often must delimit the actual parameter. The normal delimiters for string
parameters are pointed brackets, < and >. However, if the string contains
either of these characters, a different method is clearly required. In these
cases, you can specify any other character as the delimiter (to be used at
both ends of the string) by preceding it with a circumflex (^). This is the
method you have been using for specifying the literal label on all of your
PRINT__*x* macro calls. String parameters that do not contain the usual
parameter separators (commas, spaces, or tabs) need not be delimited.

The use of string parameters in the PRINT__*x* instructions is typical.
These instructions build ASCII constant strings for their first parameters,
as the following example shows.

. . . .

Example 11.3: String Parameters

```
         .MACRO  PRINT_L  LABEL,  ...
             .
             .
             .
  LAB:   .ASCII   @LABEL@
             .
             .
             .
         .ENDM
```

The calls to such a macro should be familiar to you by now.

11.3.5   Catenation of Parameters

Macro parameters can also be catenated, either with constant strings or with other parameters. The apostrophe (') is used as the catenation operator for macro parameters. When a parameter is to be catenated with a constant string, a single apostrophe is used. When two parameters are to be catenated together, two apostrophes are used. Note that two apostrophes are not the same as a quote ("). Although a quote looks like two apostrophes, it is a single character.

We can use the catenation feature of macro parameters to make SWAP__L more flexible. Rather than restrict it to LONGWORD values, we can use it with bytes, words, longwords, and quadwords by passing the operand size as an additional parameter. The size parameter, which can be a single character, is catenated onto the basic MOV op code to form the correct instruction.

The new definition of this macro, now called SWAP, is shown below:

. . . .

Example 11.4: Default Parameters

```
.MACRO   SWAP V1, V2, V3 = TEMP, SIZE = L
MOV'SIZE V1, V3
MOV'SIZE V2, V1
MOV'SIZE V3, V2
.ENDM
```

An example call to SWAP, and the code it generates, follows:

```
SWAP     LIST[R7], LIST[R8],,Q

MOVQ     LIST[R7], TEMP
MOVQ     LIST[R8], LIST[R7]
MOVQ     TEMP, LIST[R8]
```

11.3.6   Unique Symbol Generation

If a macro builds a label in an expansion, it will build the same label for every call. Because any program that contains two or more calls to such a macro would have multiple definitions for the same label, a problem occurs.

Although one solution to this problem is to pass the label to the macro as an actual parameter, a much better solution exists that is common to many assembly languages. Because the assembler can easily maintain a counter for all macro expansions on a given translation, we let it create unique labels for us using the expansion counter value plus the number 29999 as part of the label. The labels generated by this method are called local labels. The form of local labels is an integer constant followed by a dollar sign ($). Because the local labels generated by the assembler use the constants 30000, 30001, and so on (29999 + 1, 29999 + 2, and so on), the generated labels are 30000$, 30001$, and so on. We will discuss local labels in Chapter 15.

To get the assembler to build a unique local label for each macro call, we place our required labels at the end of the list of formal parameters and precede each label with a question mark (?). We then use those labels as we normally would, without worrying about duplications in multiple calls, because the assembler will replace the labels we use by local labels. Actual parameters in the macro call cannot correspond to these label formal parameters. The labels are excess parameters and must be independent of any relationship to the actual parameters.

The following macro builds ASCII strings, as well as a branch to get around them.

. . . .

Example 11.5: Unique Symbol Generation

```
        .MACRO   STRING_BUILDER   STRING, -
                 STRING_LABEL, ?ARND
        BRB      ARND
STRING_LABEL:    .ASCII   /STRING/
ARND:
        .ENDM
```

Two example calls to STRING__BUILDER, and the code that they produce, follow:

```
        STRING_BUILDER  ^'WILL THIS EVER END?', -
                 QUESTION

        BRB       30000$
QUESTION:    .ASCII   /WILL THIS EVER END?/
30000$:
        STRING_BUILDER   ^'SOON, SOON.', ANSWER

        BRB       30001$
ANSWER:    .ASCII   /SOON, SOON./
30001$:
```

. . . .

Macros commonly are used to call procedures. Although procedures are the most space-efficient methods of abstracting code, their calling code is cumbersome, especially when using the stack to pass parameters.

Suppose we have a procedure that prints a fixed-length ASCII string of ten characters and a longword. (This would be a highly restricted version of PRINT__L.) The parameters for this procedure, which we will call PRINT, are the address of the ASCII string and the longword value. A macro to call PRINT could be written as follows.

. . . .

Example 11.6: Print a Ten-Character Label and a Longword

```
        .MACRO   PRINT_L   STRING, VALUE, ?ARND, -
                           ?LABEL
        BRB      ARND
LABEL:  .ASCII  @STRING@
ARND:
        PUSHL    VALUE
        PUSHAB   LABEL
        CALLS    #2, PRINT
        .ENDM
```

11.4 *String Operations in Macros* : : : : : : : : : : : : : :

The Macro language provides three built-in functions that process ASCII strings. These functions are legal only within macro definitions and within repeat blocks, which we will discuss in Section 11.5.

The function %LENGTH returns the length of a given parameter. The call to %LENGTH appears as follows:

%LENGTH(string)

where the string is either a macro parameter or a constant string, delimited by pointed brackets or by a new delimiter character. For example, consider the following:

```
%LENGTH(STRING)
LEN__FRUIT = %LENGTH(<APPLES AND GRAPES>)
%LENGTH(^*ERROR - TABLE OVERFLOW*)
```

The first line finds the length of the macro parameter STRING. The other two do the same counting that you could do while you typed the function parameter (the second assigns the length to a symbol by direct assignment). The primary use of %LENGTH is to find the length of macro parameters.

The function %LOCATE is an assembly time version of MATCHC. The form of the call to %LOCATE is as follows:

%LOCATE(string__1, string__2 [, symbol])

The first parameter, string__1, is the target of the search. It can be either a macro parameter or a delimited constant string. The second parameter, string__2, is the source string and is also either a macro parameter or a delimited constant string. The third parameter, which is optional, indicates where in the source string the search is to begin. Positions in the source string are indicated by integers, the position of the first character being zero. This third parameter must be either an absolute symbol or a decimal constant.

For example, the value of

```
%LOCATE(<JOE>, ^'JOE JOEFFRIES', 2)
```

is four because the second occurrence of JOE begins in that position; the first occurrence is skipped because we specified that the search begin in position two (the first E). If %LOCATE does not find the target in the source string, it returns the length of the source string. For example, the value of the following function call is seven:

```
%LOCATE(^'MARY', <MARTINI>)
```

Note that when the third parameter is absent, the search begins in position zero of the source string.

The %EXTRACT function extracts a substring from a given string. The general form of a call to %EXTRACT is as follows:

%EXTRACT(symbol-1, symbol-2, string)

The first parameter, symbol-1, is an absolute symbol or a decimal constant that specifies the starting position in the string that is to be extracted. The second parameter, symbol-2, is an absolute symbol or a decimal constant that specifies the length of the substring to be extracted. The third parameter, string, is the source string from which the substring is to be removed; the string is either a macro parameter or a delimited ASCII constant string.

The following example of the use of %EXTRACT

```
%EXTRACT(0, 4, <ALKA-SELTZER>)
```

has a value of

ALKA

11.5   *Assembly Time Loops and Conditional Assembly* :

Although the facilities described in this section may at first seem a bit peculiar, they are powerful tools that can be used to great advantage in assembly language programs.

11.5.1   Repeat Loops

An assembly time repeat loop contains Macro instructions that are to be written into the program more than once. While these loops often appear inside macro definitions, they can appear anywhere in a Macro program.

To build a loop that we want repeated a number of times, we use the .REPEAT directive, the general form of which is:

.REPEAT expression

The expression must be an absolute expression. The instructions that are to be repeated are terminated by another directive, .ENDR. The number of times the instructions that appear between .REPEAT and .ENDR are to be written into the program is indicated by the value of the expression parameter on the .REPEAT directive. If the value of the expression is less than or equal to zero, the instructions in the .REPEAT range are not written at all. .REPEAT is, therefore, a pretest loop construct.

For example, we could skip ten lines in the output of a program by coding the following.

. . . .

Example 11.7: A Simple Repeat Loop

```
.REPEAT 10
PRINT_L ^' '
.ENDR
```

This loop builds ten PRINT_L instructions.

11.5.2   Values of Symbols as Parameters

We said earlier that values of memory locations and registers cannot be sent to macros as parameters because such values cannot be determined at assembly time. The only numeric values associated with symbols that can be used as actual parameters to macros are the address values of symbols. The only symbols with address values that are meaningful to us are those that are assigned to addresses with direct assignment statements. We have used such symbols as names for constants; these constants were the address values associated with them in the symbol table.

You sometimes will want to send the address value of a symbol to a macro rather than the symbol's actual ASCII string name. Consider the problem of building instructions that deal with register operands for which the register number is not known until the macro is called. We could handle this situation by assigning a symbol the register number as an address value. This address value can be specified in an actual macro parameter by preceding it with a backward slash (\). The macro expansion then converts the address value of the actual parameter to a decimal ASCII string, which is textually substituted for all occurrences of the formal parameter in the macro definition.

For example, suppose that we want to build code to clear a number of sequentially numbered registers, starting at R0. If we have a macro that can build a CLRL instruction for a variable register name, we could place a call to that macro in a repeat loop that has a counter. The following is such a macro.

. . . .

Example 11.8: *Catenation of Parameters to Constant Strings*

```
.MACRO    CLREG    REG_NUM
CLRL      R'REG_NUM
.ENDM
```

The code to use this macro in the way we described follows:

```
REG_NUM = 0
.REPEAT 5
CLREG     \REG_NUM
REG_NUM = REG_NUM + 1
.ENDR
```

The following code is generated by this call:

```
CLRL      R0
CLRL      R1
CLRL      R2
CLRL      R3
CLRL      R4
```

11.5.3   *List-Directed Repeat Loops*

You often will need to build assembly time loops that use a different element of the list in each repetition. The general form of the .IRP (*indefinite repeat*) directive is:

.IRP   symbol, <argument-list>

The .IRP directive is similar to a macro with a single parameter. This single parameter (symbol) takes on the value of the first element of the argument-list and generates the code between itself and the next .ENDR directive. It repeats this process after taking on the value of the second element of the argument list (assuming there are at least two). This continues until the argument list is exhausted (or the machine is exhausted, whichever comes first). The symbol is used like a macro parameter symbol: It has no value of its own, but takes on the values from the argument list, one at a time, until there are no more.

The following macro produces a call to a procedure that prints a literal string and four LONGWORD values. This is again a restricted version of

PRINT__L. The parameters of the procedure, again named PRINT, are the length of the literal string (as a longword), the address of the literal, and the values of the four longwords.

. . . .

Example 11.9: Print a Label and Four Longwords

```
        .MACRO   PRINT_L STRING, VAL1, VAL2, VAL3, -
                              VAL4, ?STR, ?ARND
        .IRP     ARG, <VAL4, VAL3, VAL2, VAL1>
        PUSHL    ARG
        .ENDR
        PUSHAB   STR
        PUSHL    #<%LENGTH(STRING)>
        CALLS    #6, PRINT
        BRB      ARND
STR:    .ASCII   @STRING@
ARND:
        .ENDM
```

. . . .

In this macro we used the .IRP loop to build the four PUSHL instructions for placing the four LONGWORD values on the stack. To enable the literal string to have a variable length, we use the %LENGTH function in the macro to compute its length, which is then passed to the procedure.

Another indefinite repeat loop construct is less frequently used. Instead of repeatedly taking symbols from a given list, one for each loop transit, the .IRPC (indefinite *repeat* *character*) repeatedly takes characters from a given string. The general form of .IRPC is:

.IRPC   symbol, <string>

The string is delimited either by pointed brackets or by circumflex-defined delimiters.

The .IRP and .IRPC directives allow for a certain kind of *conditional assembly*. Conditional assembly allows blocks of Macro code to be assembled only when a specified condition is true.

11.5.4 Assembly Time Selection Structures

Sometimes a program has two or more separate sections that are mutually exclusive: If one is used on a particular run of the program, the other is not. Such a program wastes the storage for the code of the unused part. Although in a virtual memory machine like the VAX this is not a serious problem, it does make sense to include in an assembly program listing and its object code only those sections that are being used. Macro has an

assembly time selection structure that allows such selective generation
of code.

The general form of the assembly time selection directive follows:

.IF   condition   operand(s)

The block of code that is to be conditionally assembled is ended by another
directive, .ENDC. The .IF directive has one or two parameters, depending
on the particular condition being tested.

If the directive has a single operand that is an absolute expression, the
possible conditions are EQUAL (EQ), NOT__EQUAL (NE), GREATER (GT),
LESS__THAN (LT), GREATER__EQUAL (GE), and LESS__EQUAL (LE). If
the operand is a simple symbol, the possible conditions are DEFINED
(DF) and NOT__DEFINED (NDF). If the directive has two operands, they
are considered macro parameters; the possible conditions are IDENTICAL
(IDN) and DIFFERENT (DIF). For single macro parameter operands, the
possible conditions are BLANK (B) and NOT__BLANK (NB).

As an example of assembly time selection, consider the following variation of the SWAP macro we wrote in Example 11.2.

· ·

Example 11.10: Assembly Time Selection

```
.MACRO   SWAP      V1, V2, V3
.IF      BLANK V3
MOVL     V1, -(SP)
MOVL     V2, V1
MOVL     (SP)+, V2
.ENDC
.IF      NOT_BLANK V3
MOVL     V1, V3
MOVL     V2, V1
MOVL     V3, V2
.ENDC
.ENDM
```

· ·

When the third parameter is absent, the first block of code is assembled
and the second block is ignored. When the third parameter is present, the
first block is ignored and the second block is assembled.

Assembly time selection can also be used when we need to selectively
assemble or not assemble blocks of code at several places in the program.
No matter how many such blocks are in a program, they can all be controlled by a single direct assignment statement to a flag symbol upon
which the selections depend.

The Macro language also has directives that allow the equivalent of an ELSE clause to be placed on the assembly time selection structure. The directive .IF__FALSE is used to mark the beginning of the code for the ELSE clause, assuming that the THEN clause is selected by a positive logic condition. Otherwise, the directive .IF__TRUE is used. If you want to be able to turn on the code generation process no matter what the conditional is, the .IF__TRUE__FALSE directive is used.

We will now rewrite Example 11.10 with an ELSE clause instead of two conditionals.

. . . .

Example 11.11: ELSE Clauses in Assembly Time Selections

```
.MACRO   SWAP      V1, V2, V3
.IF      BLANK V3
MOVL     V1, -(SP)
MOVL     V2, V1
MOVL     (SP)+, V2
.IF_FALSE
MOVL     V1, V3
MOVL     V2, V1
MOVL     V3, V2
.ENDC
.ENDM
```

. . . .

We could conditionally assemble a single instruction with the .IF directive, but this would require three lines of code. A simpler method is provided by the .IIF (*immediate if*) directive, the general form of which is:

.IIF   condition   operand(s), instruction

The condition and operand(s) parameters are the same as those for the .IF directive. The instruction can be any Macro instruction. The .IIF is a one-line version of .IF. Because only one line of Macro code can be conditionally assembled, no .ENDC is required. The following builds an instruction to clear the LONGWORD location COUNT, but only if FLAG has a symbol table value of zero:

```
.IIF     EQUAL    FLAG, CLRL COUNT
```

11.6 *More Directives* :

If we want to conditionally exit from a macro expansion, we use the
directive. .MEXIT as shown below:

```
.IIF    EQUAL   FLAG,  .MEXIT
```

.MEXIT can also be used to exit from assembly time repeat loops. Note
that if .MEXIT is used in a nested macro or nested repeat loop, it transfers
control to the next higher level of expansion.

The .NARG directive is useful for building very flexible macros. The
general form of the .NARG directive is:

.NARG symbol

The action of .NARG is simple: It counts the number of actual parameters
on the call to the macro in which it is placed and puts that count in the
given symbol (as an address value). .NARG is legal only in macros, having
no use outside them.

The general form of the .NCHR directive is as follows:

.NCHR   symbol, <string>

.NCHR is used to place the number of characters in the given string in
the given symbol as its address value in the symbol table. The string must
be delimited by pointed brackets unless it contains a comma, space, tab,
or semicolon, in which case circumflex-defined delimiters must be used.

Note that while .NARG is legal only inside macro definitions, .NCHR
is legal anywhere in a Macro program.

The macro that builds the call to the procedure you have been using
to print LONGWORD values uses conditional assembly and the .NARG
directive to count parameters. The procedure requires the following
parameters:

The number of LONGWORD values to be printed
The length of the literal string
The address of the literal string
The values of the longwords to be printed

The following is the macro definition for PRINT__L.

. . . .

Example 11.12: The Complete PRINT__L Macro

```
.MACRO   PRINT_L STRING,  V1,  V2,  V3,  V4,  -
                          V5,  V6,  ?LAB,  ?ARND
.NARG    COUNT
.IRP     ARG,  <V6,  V5,  V4,  V3,  V2,  V1 >
.IIF     NOT__BLANK,  ARG,  PUSHL ARG
.ENDR
```

```
        PUSHAB  LAB
        PUSHL   #<%LENGTH(STRING)>
        PUSHL   #<COUNT - 1>
        CALLS   #<COUNT + 2>, PRINT
        BRB     ARND
LAB:    .ASCII  @STRING@
ARND:
        .ENDM
```

Note that both the procedure parameter for the number of values to be printed and the first operand of the CALLS instruction must use the result of the .NARG directive. The immediate conditional directive .IIF is used to push the values of all passed LONGWORD values onto the stack.

11.7   *Macro Listing Control* : : : : : : : : : : : : : : : : : : :

The default case is that the code generated by a macro expansion is not placed in the program listing produced by the assembler. Two different levels of macro code can be forced into the assembler's listing file: the executable instructions alone or all of the instructions. The .SHOW directive is used for both levels; the difference is specified by different parameters. The general form of the .SHOW directive is:

.SHOW   parameter

The two parameters are EXPANSIONS (or ME, for *macro expansions*) and BINARY (or MEB, for *macro expansions binary*). EXPANSIONS specifies that all generated code be placed in the listing. BINARY specifies that only the generated instructions that are executable be placed in the listing.

   The .SHOW directive can be disabled by a subsequent .NOSHOW directive. For example, if the directive

```
.SHOW     EXPANSIONS
```

has appeared, and you now want its action disabled, you can use the following directive:

```
.NOSHOW   EXPANSIONS
```

   Note that several additional parameters can be used on .SHOW and .NOSHOW. They are described in the VAX-11 Macro Language Reference Manual. Note also that the .LIST and .NLIST directives have the same effects as the .SHOW and .NOSHOW directives, respectively.

Chapter Summary :

1. Macros are assembly time abstractions. They provide the software means of extending the instruction set of a computer.

2. The .MACRO and .ENDM directives begin and end macro definitions, respectively. The macro's name and its formal parameters appear as operands on the .MACRO directive.

3. An absent actual parameter defaults to the empty string in a macro expansion. Default values of formal parameters can be assigned using the .MACRO directive. Keyword parameters have their values assigned to formal parameter names on the macro call.

4. Strings can be passed as actual macro parameters, although they often require delimiters. Formal parameters can be catenated to other parameters using two apostrophes as an operator and to constant strings using a single apostrophe as an operator.

5. The address value of a symbol can be sent as an actual macro parameter by preceding it with a backward slash character.

6. Unique labels can be generated in a macro by placing each label's name in the formal argument list and preceding it with a question mark. Each call to the macro will then produce different values for these labels.

7. The %LENGTH, %LOCATE, and %EXTRACT functions are assembly time functions on strings that are available only within macro definitions and repeat blocks. %LENGTH returns the length, in characters, of its string parameter. %LOCATE is an assembly time version of MATCHC. %EXTRACT removes a substring from a given string.

8. The .REPEAT directive creates an assembly time loop that is repeated a specified number of times. The .IRP directive creates an assembly time loop in which the number of repetitions depends on the length of its argument list. .IRPC is the same as .IRP, except that it uses a string whose length determines the number of repetitions instead of an argument list.

9. The .IF and .IIF directives provide assembly time selection constructs for either blocks or single instruction bodies.

10. The .NARG directive is used to determine the number of arguments passed to a macro. .NCHR is used to assign the length of a given string to a symbol as its symbol table value.

11. The EXPANSIONS parameter on the .SHOW and .NOSHOW directives controls the listing of all Macro code generated by macro expansions. The BINARY parameter controls the listing of executable Macro code.

New Directives

.ENDC	.IF__TRUE	.MACRO
.ENDM	.IF__TRUE__FALSE	.MEXIT
.ENDR	.IIF	.NARG
.IF	.IRP	.NOSHOW
.IF__FALSE	.IRPC	.REPEAT

New Functions and Operators

\ (value-of operator)	%LENGTH
%EXTRACT	%LOCATE

New Terms

Conditional assembly   Macro expansion

Chapter 11 Problem Set :

1. What are the criteria that must be considered when choosing between subprograms and macros?

2. What is the difference between the BINARY and EXPANSIONS parameters for the .SHOW and .NOSHOW directives?

3. What happens when a macro call includes more actual parameters than the macro definition has formal parameters?

4. What happens when a macro call includes fewer actual parameters than the macro definition has formal parameters?

5. What is the form of all actual parameters that are substituted for the formal parameters in the macro definition?

6. What is the difference between keyword parameters and default values for formal parameters?

7. What characters cannot be used as delimiters on strings used as actual parameters to macros?

8. How can a parameter be catenated to another parameter in a macro?

9. When would you want to pass the value of a symbol as an actual parameter to a macro?

10. Is it legal to use the %LENGTH function outside a macro definition?

11. Explain the arguments and actions of the %EXTRACT function.

12. What is the difference between the actions of the .IRP and the .REPEAT directives?

13. List and explain all of the possible operands of the .IIF directive.

14. When would you want to use the .NARG directive?

Write and debug structured macros for the following problems.

15. *Parameters:* Two values, BEGIN and END, and a symbol.
   Result: To generate a LONGWORD constant for each value between BEGIN and END, with the first having the parameter symbol as a label.

16. *Parameters:* Two values, BEGIN and END, and a symbol.
   Result: To save the registers numbered from BEGIN to END at the given symbolic address.

17. *Parameters:* Two symbols, FROM and TO, and a value LENGTH.
   Result: To move LENGTH longwords, using MOVL instructions, from FROM to TO.

18. *Parameters:* Two symbols, TEST__VALUE and TARGET.
   Result: To branch to TARGET, using a BRW instruction, if the word at TEST__VALUE has the value zero.

19. *Parameters:* A symbol and a value.
   Result: To raise the longword whose label is the input symbol to the power indicated by the second parameter.

20. *Parameters:* Two symbols and two values.
   Result: The code for the top of a FOR-TO loop, using the first symbol as the FOR variable, the second symbol as the label, and the two values as the initial and terminal values of the FOR variable. Your code should not assume that the loop has at least one repetition.

21. *Parameters:* Four symbols and a relational operator (for example, =, <>, and so on).
   Result: The code for the top of a WHILE loop, where the first symbol is a label for the top of the loop, the second is a label for the bottom of the loop, and the next two symbols are the LONGWORD locations to be compared.

12

FLOATING POINT AND DECIMAL INSTRUCTIONS

In addition to instructions for dealing with integer data, most larger mini-computers and all mainframe computers have instructions for manipulating floating point and decimal data.

Floating point data have two parts, fraction and exponent, that allow computers to store numeric values over a very large range by using only the most significant digits of those values. VAX computers have instructions for many of the operations that are often needed for floating point data.

Decimal data are stored in strings as codings of decimal digits. Because decimal data are required for business application programs, any computer meant for such environments must have data types and instructions for decimal data. The VAX computers, designed to be applicable to both scientific and business problems, include instructions for manipulating such data.

12.1 Single-Precision Floating Point Numbers : : : :

The VAX has two standard floating point data types: single-precision and double-precision. This section will discuss representation and instructions for the single-precision data type.

12.1.1   Single-Precision Floating Point Notation

Floating point notation represents a numeric value as a fraction and an exponent. This notation is a slight modification of *scientific notation*. One difference is that scientific notation uses one digit on the left side of the decimal point, whereas floating point notation uses an implied zero there. Another difference is that the exponents in VAX floating point notation are powers of two, whereas scientific notation exponents are powers of ten. The following are examples of numbers in scientific notation, with their conventional decimal values in parentheses:

1.378 E 5 (137,800)
−2.57361 E −6 (−0.00000257361)

The exponents (E 5 and E −6) are usually shown as tens with superscripts (10^5 and 10^{-6}). In many programming languages, however, the E notation is used, primarily because card punch machines and terminal keyboards do not have superscripts.

The VAX storage layout of single-precision floating point data is shown in Figure 12.1. This layout looks strange because the fraction representation has been divided and spread over two words. This format was chosen for its compatibility with that used by the PDP-11 computers. The least significant bit of the fraction is in bit 16; the most significant bit is in bit 6. To see how these fit together, imagine the left word of the representation removed from its present position and attached, in the same order, to the right end of bit 0.

Bit 15 is the sign of the fraction, with 0 used as positive and 1 used as negative. The eight bits from bit 7 to bit 14 are used for the exponent, which is a power of two. Instead of using twos complement notation for the exponent, an unsigned notation called *excess 128* is used to allow both positive and negative values. To convert an exponent from signed to excess 128 notation, 128 is added to the exponent value. To convert from excess 128 to signed notation, 128 is subtracted from the value. For example, if the eight-bit exponent of a floating point number has a decimal value of 141, its actual value is 13. Likewise, if the exponent in floating point notation is 120, its actual value is minus eight.

Although the eight-bit exponent field can store values of 0–255, zero is reserved for special use. In excess 128 notation, the values 1–255 represent exponents in the range of −127 to +127. Because the exponent represents a power in base two, the range of numbers that can be represented in single-precision floating point notation on the VAX is from about the −127th power of two to the 127th power of two.

The VAX uses 24 bits for the fraction in single-precision floating point notation; that is about seven decimal digits. However, there is room for only 23 bits in the four-byte representation. This apparent discrepancy can be explained. All floating point values are normalized after every operation, which means that any leading zeros on the fraction are discarded

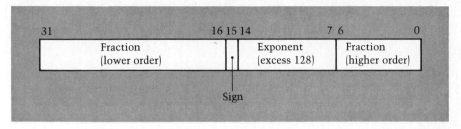

Figure 12.1 Single-precision floating point data format

while the exponent is decreased by the number of discarded zeros to compensate. Because this operation always results in a bit with a value of one in the highest position, assuming the fraction is not zero, why store that bit? The VAX simply assumes that the 23-bit fraction that is stored in bits 6–0 and 31–15 actually has a bit that always has a value of one appended to its most significant end. Therefore, bit 6 is actually the second most significant bit in the fraction.

For example, suppose that a floating point arithmetic operation results in the following:

Fraction: 00001001001100001101 1011
Exponent: 135 (decimal)

Normalization of this value decreases the exponent by four and shifts the fraction to the left by four bits. With the leftmost bit now implied, the value is:

Fraction: 00100110000110110110000
Exponent: 131 (decimal)

When the result of an operation has a fraction of zero, the result is zero, regardless of the value of the sign or the exponent. For this result, the VAX standard floating point version of zero is used.

Two special values can reside in a single-precision floating point location, one with the exponent, the sign, and the fraction having a zero value, in which case it represents zero. The other has a zero exponent and a fraction value of one, in which case it represents a reserved value that will cause a reserved operand failure when used. These two are shown below:

Single-precision floating point zero:
00000000 00000000 00000000 00000000
Reserved single-precision floating point value:
00000000 00000001 00000000 00000000

Figure 12.2 shows how to determine the decimal value of a given number in floating point notation.

Floating point value in hex: 000041F8
Floating point value in binary:

$$\underbrace{0000\ 0000\ 0000\ 0000}_{\substack{\text{Fraction}\\\text{(lower order)}}},\ \underset{\substack{\uparrow\\\text{Sign}}}{0}\ \underbrace{100\ 0001\ 1}_{\text{Exponent}},\ \underbrace{111\ 1000}_{\substack{\text{Fraction}\\\text{(higher order)}}}$$

Sign = 0 (fraction is positive)
Exponent in excess 128 = 83_{16} = 131_{10}
Exponent = 131_{10} − 128_{10} = 3
Fraction = 0.11111000 0000 0000 0000 0000$_2$
Value   = fraction$^{(-3)}2$
             = 111.11_2
Decimal value = $7 + \frac{1}{2} + \frac{1}{4}$
             = 7.75

Figure 12.2   Determining the decimal value of a floating point notation number

Given decimal number = −5.5
Binary equivalent = −101.1
Normalized version = $-0.1011^{(3)}2$
Fraction = 0.0110 . . . 0
Sign = 1
Exponent = 3_{10} = 11_2
Excess 128 exponent = 131_{10} = 1000 0011$_2$
Binary value (complete): $\underbrace{0000\ 0000\ 0000\ 0000}_{\substack{\text{Fraction}\\\text{(lower order)}}},\ \underset{\substack{\uparrow\\\text{Sign}}}{1}\ \underbrace{100\ 0001\ 1}_{\text{Exponent}},\ \underbrace{011\ 0000}_{\substack{\text{Fraction}\\\text{(higher order)}}}$

Hex value (complete): 0000 C1B0

Figure 12.3   Determining the hex floating point value of a given decimal number

Figure 12.3 shows how to find the hex floating point notation value for a given decimal number.

The precision of all operations on single-precision floating point data values is 24 bits, or about seven decimal digits. The actual range of decimal values that can be stored in this notation is from 0.29 E −38 to 1.7 E 38. While this range is certainly sufficient for most needs, the precision is not, which is why VAX has a double-precision floating point data type, to be discussed in Section 12.2.

12.1.2 Floating Point Constant Notation

Floating point constants can be written in several different forms in a Macro program. In the following examples, "sod" represents a string of decimal digits:

[sign]sod.
[sign]sod.sod
[sign]sod E [sign]sod
[sign]sod. E [sign]sod
[sign]sod.sod E [sign]sod

Some examples of numbers in these respective forms follow:

$-32.$
4.654
$45 E -5$
$+2. E 27$
$-2754.3 E +8$

Allocating space for floating point variables is similar to allocating space for LONGWORD integers. The .BLKF directive allocates the number of single-precision floating point data locations that its operand specifies and sets them all to zero.

The .FLOAT directive, which is also called .F__FLOATING, is used in the same way as .LONG. The operands cause locations to be allocated and the operand floating point values placed in them.

As examples, consider the following:

```
SUM:      .FLOAT   0.
PI:       .FLOAT   3.141593
CHARGE:   .FLOAT  -2.71 E -27
LIST:     .BLKF   10
```

The .FLOAT directive rounds given values when they have too much significance (for example, 3.14159265). For single-precision floating point directives, this default rounding can be overridden by placing a directive in the program. This directive as shown below causes these constants to be truncated rather than rounded:

```
.ENABLE TRUNCATION
```

The parameter TRUNCATION can be abbreviated as FPT.

12.1.3 Floating Point Non-Arithmetic Operations

The more common operations that we have discussed for dealing with integer data on the VAX have counterparts for floating point data. The instructions simply use F in place of the integer codes B, W, L, and Q.

The MOVF instruction does to floating point operands what MOVL does to longwords. The only difference is in how the validity of the operands is checked. Although the MNEGF instruction also negates its first operand and then moves that value to its second operand, the negation of a floating point operation is drastically different than negating an integer. The former simply requires that one bit, bit 15, be complemented, whereas the latter involves forming the twos complement of the value.

The MOVAF instruction has the same effect as the MOVAL instruction: The address of the first operand is placed in the second operand. In fact, both of these instructions are assembled into the same machine op code.

The TSTF instruction affects the Z and N indicators according to the value in the location specified by its operand. This instruction, of course, is different than TSTL because the data representation is quite different. For floating point operands, CMPF has the same effect as CMPL.

The PUSHAF instruction, as with the MOVAF instruction, actually encodes its LONGWORD cousin (PUSHAL) in machine code. When you need to push a floating point value onto the stack, the PUSHL instruction can be used.

We will demonstrate the use of some of these instructions in Section 12.1.4.

12.1.4   Floating Point Arithmetic Instructions

Again, the floating point arithmetic instructions are varieties, using F, of the symbolic op codes you learned for integer data.

The CLRF instruction sets its operand to the floating point zero value, which has the same form as the LONGWORD integer zero. In fact, the CLRF instruction is translated into the same machine op code as CLRL.

The ADDF2 and ADDF3 instructions add single-precision floating point values; the first places the result in the location specified as the second operand, and the second places the result in the third operand.

The SUBF2 and SUBF3 instructions are the two- and three-operand forms of the single-precision floating point subtract operation. The MULF2 and MULF3 instructions are the two- and three-operand forms of the single-precision floating point multiplication operation. The DIVF2 and DIVF3 instructions are the two- and three-operand forms of the single-precision floating point division operation. Note that should you have a divisor of zero, these instructions produce unpredictable results.

The results of all single-precision floating point operations are rounded when they have more than 24 significant bits of fraction.

Floating point operations set the condition indicators in ways analogous to their integer counterparts. Therefore, all of the conditional branches covered so far will work after floating point instructions in the same way as they did after integer operations.

Floating point constants can be used as operands on floating point instructions. Like their integer counterparts, floating point constants can be in either short literal or immediate form. The assembler chooses the form if the operand has not specified it. We will explain in Chapter 15 how to specify a particular form.

The syntax of a floating point constant operand is simply the floating point constant preceded by a pound sign (#) as shown below:

```
MOVF      #4.32, RESULT
ADDF2     #-10.632, SUM
```

Sometimes counter-controlled loops will have a loop variable that is a floating point value. This happens either when the loop variable is used in a computation that involves floating point data or when the loop variable must move in non-integer increments. Although the Pascal FOR statement provides increment and decrement operations only on an integer loop variable, we can generalize our pseudocode FOR construct to allow floating point parameters. Coding this construct is simple with the VAX, using the ACBx instruction for single-precision floating point data, ACBF. As an example of ACBF, consider the following loop skeleton.

. . . .

Example 12.1: Use of ACBF

```
;
; FOR VAR := 0.0 TO 1.5 STEP 0.1 DO
;
          MOVF      #0.0, VAR
LOOP:
            .
            .
            .
          ACBF      #1.5, #0.1, VAR, LOOP
;
; END-FOR
;
```

. . . .

The value of the variable VAR is 0.0 the first time through the loop, 0.1 the second time, 0.2 the third time, and so on, until VAR has been through the loop with the value of 1.5.

Keep in mind that the usual problems of floating point operations apply in Macro, as they do in FORTRAN or Pascal. For example, floating point notation is approximate. Adding 0.1 ten times to the cleared location SUM does not necessarily produce the value 1.0 because of rounding errors.

Often integer values will become involved in arithmetic expressions with floating point values. In a high-level language such as FORTRAN or Pascal, the integer value is automatically converted to floating point form. Because this conversion is automatic, many beginning programmers believe that computers can do mixed mode operations. They cannot, however: Arithmetic instructions either deal with integer operands and produce integer results or deal with floating point operands and produce floating point results. The VAX has a full complement of conversion instructions with which to convert the VAX integer data types to single-precision floating point.

The CVTBF, CVTWF, and CVTLF instructions respectively convert BYTE, WORD, and LONGWORD integer values, as specified in their first operands, to single-precision floating point values and then place those values in their second operands. For BYTE and WORD values, the converted result is an exact representation because single-precision floating point values store about seven decimal digits of precision and BYTE and WORD values have at the most about three and five decimal digits, respectively. LONGWORD values, which can have up to about ten decimal digits, must be rounded to seven decimal digits when necessary.

The VAX also has conversion instructions to convert single-precision floating point values to integers. The CVTFB, CVTFW, and CVTFL instructions convert single-precision floating point values, as specified in their first operands, to integer bytes, words, and longwords, respectively. When the floating point value has more digits of precision than the target integer location can store, the floating point value is truncated; that is, the extra lower-order digits are discarded. When the target is a longword, an alternative instruction rounds the floating point value to fit into the ten digits of the longword. The Macro op code for this instruction is CVTRFL, for *convert rounded floating* point to *longword*.

Having discussed most of the VAX instructions for dealing with single-precision floating point data, we can now develop an example program. We have not built any macro instructions for getting floating point values into and out of the VAX through a terminal or disk file. Therefore, we will use a subprogram to demonstrate the use of floating point operations. Chapter 14 will discuss how to build input/output routines for floating point data.

. . . .

Example 12.2

∶ *Problem Statement*

> *In:* A floating point value.
> *Out:* The sine of the input parameter, in R0.

We will write a function subprogram for this problem. The method we will use to compute the sine function of the given argument is the Taylor series expansion. Because single-precision floating point data in the VAX keeps only the seven most significant decimal digits, we can stop the iterative process when we have reached that precision.

The following is the formula of the Taylor series for the sine function:

$$\text{SINE}(X) = X - X^3/3! + X^5/5! - X^7/7! + \ldots$$

If enough terms are included, the series represents the exact value of the sine function. Because the number of terms required for a given precision varies with the value of the argument, a fixed number of terms cannot yield the desired precision for any argument. The maximum error that results from not including enough terms to get the exact functional value is bounded by the absolute value of the first excluded term. If we include terms in a loop until the absolute value of the next term is less than 0.000001, we should have the value of the sine function, or at least within 0.000001 of it.

Note that, although the Taylor series expansion is not the best way to compute the sine function, it does provide a good environment in which to demonstrate the use of floating point arithmetic on the VAX.

The exclamation points in the formula denote the factorial function, a common mathematical function that is defined on the non-negative integers in the following recursive formulae:

$$\text{FACTORIAL}(N) = N \cdot \text{FACTORIAL}(N - 1)$$
$$\text{FACTORIAL}(0) = \text{FACTORIAL}(1) = 1$$

Although the factorial function is defined as a recursive function, we will implement it iteratively in a function subprogram. Note that not only is the factorial defined on integers, but the value of the function is also an integer. However, because its value quickly becomes too large to be stored in a longword, we will implement it as a floating point function.

The heart of the sine subprogram is a loop that adds another term to the series each time it is repeated. The pseudocode for the sine function follows.

:• *Pseudocode Solution*

Set SIGN to -1
Set OLD__TERM to X (the argument)
Set SINE to X
Set NEW__TERM to $-X^3/3!$
Set POWER to 3
WHILE the absolute value of NEW__TERM > 0.0000001 DO
    Add NEW__TERM to SINE
    Set OLD__TERM to NEW__TERM
    Set SIGN to $-1 \cdot$ SIGN
    Add 2 to POWER
    Set NEW__TERM to SIGN $\cdot$ X^{POWER} / POWER!
END-DO
Add NEW__TERM to SINE
End-of-algorithm

Because the terms of the sine series have alternating signs, we must build this into the computation. We do this by keeping a variable named SIGN that alternates its sign each time through the loop. The new terms are multiplied by SIGN, causing their signs to alternate.

:: *Macro Solution*

```
; FUNCTION SUBPROGRAM SINE
;
; PARAMETER:   A SINGLE-PRECISION FLOATING POINT
;              VALUE
; FUNCTIONAL VALUE:  THE SINE OF THE PARAMETER, IN
;     R0, ASSUMING THE PARAMETER IS AN ANGLE IN
;     RADIANS.
;
      .ENTRY  SINE, ^M<R2>
      ARG = 4
;
; SET SIGN TO -1, OLD TERM TO ARG, SIGN TO ARG,
;     AND POWER TO 3
;
      MOVF    #-1.0, SIGN
      MOVF    ARG(AP), OLD_TERM
      MOVF    ARG(AP), SINE__VALUE
      MOVF    #3.0, POWER
;
```

```
; COMPUTE SECOND TERM & PLACE IT IN NEW TERM
;     (-ARG**3 / 3!)
;
      PUSHL   POWER
      CALLS   #1, FACTORIAL
      MULF3   ARG(AP), ARG(AP), R2
      MULF2   ARG(AP), R2
      MNEGF   R2, R2
      DIVF3   RO, R2, NEW_TERM
;
; COMPUTE ABS_NEW_TERM AS THE ABSOLUTE VALUE OF
; NEW_TERM
;
      MOVF    NEW_TERM, ABS_NEW_TERM
;
; IF NEW TERM < 0
;
      TSTF    NEW_TERM
      BGEQ    LOOP
;
;     THEN MAKE IT POSITIVE
;
      MNEGF   ABS_NEW_TERM, ABS_NEW_TERM
;
; ENDIF
; WHILE ABS_NEW_TERM > 0.000001 DO
;
LOOP:
      CMPF    ABS_NEW_TERM, #0.000001
      BGTR    IN_LOOP
      BRW     END_DO
IN_LOOP:
;
;     SET NEW_TERM TO SINE VALUE &
;     NEW_TERM TO OLD_TERM
;
      ADDF2   NEW_TERM, SINE_VALUE
      MOVF    NEW_TERM, OLD_TERM
;
```

Continued

```
;       SET SIGN TO -1 * SIGN & ADD 2 TO POWER
;

        MULF2    #-1.0, SIGN
        ADDF2    #2.0, POWER
;
;       SET NEW_TERM TO SIGN * ARG ** POWER / POWER!
;

        PUSHL    ARG(AP)
        PUSHL    POWER
        CALLS    #2, EXP
        MOVF     R0, R2
        PUSHL    POWER
        CALLS    #1, FACTORIAL
        MULF2    SIGN, R2
        DIVF3    R0, R2, NEW_TERM
;
;       COMPUTE ABS_NEW_TERM AS THE ABSOLUTE VALUE
;       OF NEW_TERM
;

        MOVF     NEW_TERM, ABS_NEW_TERM
;
;       IF NEW_TERM < 0
;

        TSTF     NEW_TERM
        BGEQ     OK
;
;          THEN MAKE ABS_NEW_TERM POSITIVE
;

        MNEGF    ABS_NEW_TERM, ABS_NEW_TERM
;
;       ENDIF
;
OK:
        BRW      LOOP
;
; END-DO
; ADD LAST TERM TO SINE & RETURN
;
END_DO:
        ADDF2    NEW_TERM, SINE_VALUE, R0
        RET
;
```

```
; DATA AREA FOR SUBPROGRAM SINE
;
SIGN:        .BLKF   1 ; AN ALTERNATOR FOR SERIES TERMS
OLD_TERM:  .BLKF   1 ; THE SECOND LAST TERM OF THE SERIES
NEW_TERM:  .BLKF   1 ; THE LAST TERM OF THE SERIES
SINE_VALUE.BLKF   1 ; THE CURRENT VALUE OF THE SERIES
POWER:       .BLKF   1 ; THE CURRENT POWER OF THE NEW TERM
ABS_NEW_TERM: .BLKF  1 ; ABSOLUTE VALUE OF NEW TERM
;
; END OF SUBPROGRAM SINE
;
; SUBPROGRAM FACTORIAL
;
; PARAMETER:  A SINGLE-PRECISION FLOATING POINT
;             VALUE
; FUNCTIONAL VALUE:  FACTORIAL OF THE PARAMETER,
;                    IN R0
;
      .ENTRY  FACTORIAL, 0
      ARG = 4
      MOVF    #1.0, RESULT
;
; FOR COUNT := 2 TO ARG DO
;
      MOVF    #2.0, COUNT
      CMPF    COUNT, ARG(AP)
      BLEQ    F_LOOP
      BRW     OUT_F_LOOP
F_LOOP:
;
;   MULTIPLY RESULT BY THE NEXT FACTOR
;
      MULF2   COUNT, RESULT
      ACBF    ARG(AP), #1.0, COUNT, F_LOOP
;
; END-FOR
```

Continued

```
; MOVE RESULT TO R0 & RETURN
;
OUT_F_LOOP:
      MOVF     RESULT, R0
      RET
;
; SUBPROGRAM FACTORIAL DATA AREA
;
RESULT: .BLKF  1 ; THE CURRENT VALUE OF FACTORIAL
COUNT:  .BLKF  1 ; THE LOOP COUNTER FOR FACTORIAL
;
; END OF SUBPROGRAM FACTORIAL
;
; SUBPROGRAM EXP
;
; PARAMETERS:
;      (1) A SINGLE-PRECISION FLOATING POINT
;          EXPONENT
;      (2) A SINGLE-PRECISION FLOATING POINT
;          VALUE
; FUNCTIONAL VALUE:   THE VALUE, RAISED TO THE
;                     EXPONENT POWER
;
      .ENTRY  EXP, 0
      EXPONENT = 4
      VALUE = 8
      MOVF     VALUE(AP), R0
;
; FOR COUNTER := 2 TO EXPONENT DO
;
      MOVF     #2.0, COUNTER
      CMPF     COUNTER, EXPONENT(AP)
      BLEQ     E_LOOP
      BRW      OUT_E_LOOP
E_LOOP:
;
;     MULTIPLY RESULT BY VALUE
;
      MULF2    VALUE(AP), R0
      ACBF     EXPONENT(AP), #1.0, COUNTER, E_LOOP
;
```

```
; END-FOR
; RETURN
;
OUT_E_LOOP:
      RET
;
; SUBPROGRAM EXP DATA AREA
;
COUNTER:   .BLKF  1 ; THE LOOP COUNTER
;
; END OF SUBPROGRAM EXP
```

. . . .

The one remaining floating point arithmetic instruction in the VAX set is a complex and powerful instruction called POLYF. POLYF implements a process of evaluating polynomials called Horner's Rule that uses the minimum number of arithmetic operations. The general form of the POLYF instruction is as follows:

POLYF   argument, degree, coefficient-table-address

The general form of a polynomial in one variable, which is the form that POLYF evaluates, is:

$$f(x) = a0 + a1 \cdot x + a2 \cdot x^2 + a3 \cdot x^3 + \ldots$$

where the *a* terms are the coefficients and *x* is the variable. For POLYF, the coefficients and the variable must be the same data type.

The first operand of POLYF is the variable. The second operand is the degree of the polynomial, which is the highest power of the variable that occurs in the polynomial; this operand is given as a WORD integer. The third operand of POLYF is the address of the table of coefficients, which is a list of the coefficients of the polynomial with the coefficient of the highest degree term first. The result is placed in R0.

Suppose we need to evaluate the following polynomial:

$$f(x) = 5.63 + 2.79 \cdot x + 12.13 \cdot x^2 - 0.32 \cdot x^3$$

The coefficient table for this polynomial is:

```
COEF_TAB:
         .FLOAT  -0.32
         .FLOAT  12.13
         .FLOAT  2.79
         .FLOAT  5.63
```

We can evaluate the polynomial with the following single instruction:

```
POLYF   X, #3, COEF_TAB
```

12.2   Double-Precision Floating Point Data : : : : : :

Double-precision floating point is used for computing those mathematical functions that require more than the seven decimal digits of precision in single-precision arithmetic. The presence of two floating point forms is common to high-level programming languages used for numerical computations, such as FORTRAN.

The format of VAX double-precision floating point values is shown in Figure 12.4. This format is a simple extension of the single-precision form: It has two additional words of fraction capacity. The last two words of the fraction belong, logically, to the right of the single-precision form. The least significant bit of the fraction is bit 0 of the last word, and the most significant bit of the fraction is bit 6 of the first word.

While the range of values that can be stored in double-precision is the same as that for single-precision, the precision is increased to about 16 decimal digits.

To allocate double-precision data locations, the .BLKD version of .BLKx is used. It allocates a number of quadword locations equal to the value of its operand and initializes them all to zero values. Zero values are indicated for the double-precision form in the same way they are for single-precision, that is, all zeros. Therefore, .BLKD does the same operation as .BLKQ.

To both allocate and initialize one or more double-precision floating point data locations to nonzero values, the .DOUBLE directive is used. Note that .D__FLOATING is equivalent to .DOUBLE.

Double-precision constants are specified in the same way as single-precision constants with one exception: When the exponential form is used, the exponent is prefaced with D instead of E.

The following examples illustrate the directives we just described:

```
SUM:     .DOUBLE 1.24625 D -4, -0.00005683, -
                 4.257 D 5 [6]
LIST:    .BLKD 100
```

SUM is the address of the first of eight double-precision locations, which is initialized to 0.000124625; the second is initialized to −0.00005683 and the last six to 425700. LIST is the address of the first of a block of 100 eight-byte locations, all of which are initialized to zero.

Because the instructions that deal with double-precision floating point data are so similar to those for manipulating single-precision data, we will only describe them briefly.

The ADDx2, ADDx3, SUBx2, SUBx3, DIVx2, DIVx3, MULx2, MULx3, MOVx, CLRx, MNEGx, CMPx, PUSHAx, TSTx, and MOVAx instructions all have versions for double-precision operands, with the x taking on the form D. D versions also exist for the ACBx and POLYx instructions, and the family of CVTxx instructions has versions for converting B, W, L, and F (single-precision floating point) types to and from D types. Finally, the

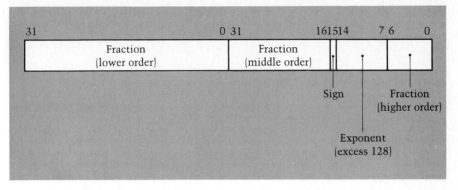

Figure 12.4 Double-precision floating point data format

CVTRDL instruction rounds a double-precision value to a LONGWORD location.

An option available on VAX systems provides two more floating point forms.

The G floating point form, which is eight bytes long, provides slightly less precision than double-precision but a much larger range of possible exponents. G operations keep about 15 decimal digits and can store a range of values from 0.56 E −308 to 0.9 E 308.

The H floating point form, which is 16 bytes long, provides a large degree of precision and a huge range of possible exponents. H operations keep about 33 decimal digits of precision, and the range of possible values is from 0.84 E −4932 to 0.59 E 4932. The H form should satisfy the most demanding number cruncher.

Because the instructions for G and H floating point data are similar to those for F and D values, we will not describe them here. Note, however, that the G and H instructions are substantially slower than their F and D relatives. Not only do they deal with larger operands, but they are implemented in microcode rather than in hardware and do not use the VAX floating point accelerator. Future VAX machines may implement these operations in hardware.

12.3 *Dealing With Decimal Data* : : : : : : : : : : : : :

Many computer applications require exact arithmetic on a wide range of numeric data without demanding extremely high speed. Most business applications fall into this category where calculations on values that represent amounts of money must be exact but are not themselves extensive. The majority of required operations in many business applications involve input/output.

Most business applications programs are written in COBOL (*common business-oriented language*). Computers that are destined to have COBOL compilers usually include decimal data formats and decimal arithmetic instructions. Because some of these operations are also useful outside of business applications, we will discuss one such application after we have covered the data formats and instructions for dealing with decimal data.

12.3.1 Decimal Data Formats

The VAX uses several data formats for storing decimal values. Some are useful only for input/output, and others can be used as operands for the decimal instruction set.

Strings of ASCII unpacked decimal digits, or those in which each digit occupies one byte, are called numerics. Numeric strings are not stored in byte-backwards order as are integers; the first byte of a numeric string that contains a digit has the most significant digit. Numeric strings come in two categories in the VAX.

In a *leading separate numeric*, the sign byte precedes the most significant digit. Legal sign bytes are the ASCII codes for +, −, and blank, or 2B, 2D, and 20 in hex, respectively. (The blank implies positive.) The ASCII codes for the decimal digits are 30−39 in hex. For example, the leading separate numeric representations of the numbers −27 and 341 are:

2D3237
2B333431

All of your program inputs have been read with the READx macros in leading separate numeric form. Section 12.3.3 will explain how to convert this form of data to other forms more suitable for manipulation.

Leading separate numeric operands are specified by the address of the sign byte and a length as the number of digits, not counting the sign. For example, the lengths of 2D3237 and 2B333431 are two and three, respectively. Legal lengths for leading separate numerics are 0−31.

In a *trailing numeric*, the sign is superimposed over the last digit of the representation (if positive, the sign can be left out). Note that the unsigned form is not the same as the leading separate numeric form, which always has a sign byte.

The two techniques for specifying the sign of a trailing numeric value are called *zoned* and *overpunch*. In both of these cases, all but the least significant digits are stored in the ASCII decimal digit codes. The hex values for the least significant digits in the zoned sign and overpunch sign forms are shown on page 299.

Digit	Zoned Hex Format	Overpunch Hex Format
+0	30	7B
+1	31	41
+2	32	42
+3	33	43
+4	34	44
+5	35	45
+6	36	46
+7	37	47
+8	38	48
+9	39	49
-0	70	7D
-1	71	4A
-2	72	4B
-3	73	4C
-4	74	4D
-5	75	4E
-6	76	4F
-7	77	50
-8	78	51
-9	79	52

Because trailing numeric values do not require a separate byte for the sign, their lengths are both the number of digits and the number of bytes they occupy. The two VAX instructions that deal with trailing numeric operands will operate on either of the two sign forms.

The VAX also uses a string format for storing decimal data called *packed decimal*. In packed decimal, two digits are packed into each byte. The last nibble contains the sign. Although the hex digit C is normally used to represent the plus sign, and D to represent the minus sign, the hex digits A, E, and F are also interpreted as plus, while B is also interpreted as minus.

The length of a packed decimal string is the number of digits it contains; note that this length does not include the sign. A packed decimal string with an even number of digits leaves no room for the sign nibble. Therefore, a zero is added as the most significant digit. The values of the following examples

    531C
    027D
    06315C

are 531, -27, and 6315, respectively.

A packed decimal string with zero length is represented by the sign nibble with a zero attached on its left. For example, 0C is a zero length packed decimal string with the value of zero.

The Macro directive .PACKED is used to build a single packed decimal constant. Because you sometimes will want to have the length of a packed decimal constant in symbolic form, the operand of the .PACKED directive provides that as an option. The general form of this directive is:

[label] .PACKED decimal-string [, symbol]

Decimal-string can contain from 0–31 decimal digits and can be preceded by a sign. Symbol, when present, represents the length in digits of the constant. Note that no facility exists for using literal packed decimal strings as operands.

Following are examples of the .PACKED directive, in the second of which LEN__CASH is assigned the value three:

```
DEBT:      .PACKED -5631
CASH:      .PACKED 956, LEN_CASH
```

While LONGWORD integers are always stored byte-backwards, packed decimal strings are stored with the bytes in their customary order and the nibbles within each byte in reverse order. For example, the value of the variable DEBT is stored as:

```
1D6305  :  DEBT
```

The nibbles are not actually backwards. They just appear to be reversed because they are stored in pairs.

12.3.2   Instructions for Decimal Data

The set of VAX instructions that use decimal operands is limited; nearly all instructions deal with packed decimal data.

Packed decimal strings can be moved with the MOVP instruction, whose general form is:

MOVP   length, source, destination

The length operand is the number of digits, not counting the sign, in the string to be moved; this length is given as a word. The source and destination operands are addresses of memory locations.

Note that the MOVP instruction uses R0–R3 as address pointers and counters. Therefore, values in these registers are destroyed by this operation.

In Example 12.3, the value of the packed decimal string at SALARY is moved to PAYROLL.

. . . .

Example 12.3: The MOVP Instruction

```
SALARY:     .PACKED    18520
PAYROLL:    .BLKB      3
              •

              •

              •
            MOVP    #5, SALARY, PAYROLL
```

. . . .

The VAX has instructions for the four basic arithmetic operations on packed decimal data. Addition and subtraction operations come in both two- and three-operand forms, while the multiplication and division instructions use three operands.

As we saw with the MOVP instruction, to specify a single packed decimal operand requires two actual Macro operands: the length and the address of the packed decimal value. Therefore, the names of the addition and subtraction instructions for packed decimal operands contain either 4 or 6 to indicate two or three operands, respectively.

The general forms of the two packed decimal add instructions are:

ADDP4   addend-length, addend-address, sum-length, sum-address
ADDP6   addend-length, addend-address, add-op2-length,
        add-op2-address, sum-length, sum-address

In ADDP4, the addend string is added to the sum string. In ADDP6, the addend string is added to the add-op2 string, and the resulting string is placed in the destination string as specified by sum-length and sum-address.

If the destination string is too short to hold the sum, the overflow V indicator is set. The Z and N indicators are affected according to the value of the sum string. ADDP4 destroys R0–R3, and ADDP6 destroys R0–R5.

The two subtract instructions for packed decimal strings are similar to their counterparts for addition. Their general forms are:

SUBP4   subtrahend-length, subtrahend-address, difference-length,
        difference-address
SUBP6   subtrahend-length, subtrahend-address, minuend-length,
        minuend-address, difference-length, difference-address

In SUBP4, the first operand string, the subtrahend, is subtracted from the second operand string, and the result replaces the second operand string. In SUBP6, the subtrahend string is subtracted from the second operand string, the minuend, and the resulting string is placed in the destination string, the difference.

As with the ADDPx instructions, SUBP4 destroys R0–R3, and SUBP6 destroys R0–R5. Also, the N, Z, and V indicators are set as they are with the integer subtract instructions.

The general forms of the divide and multiply instructions for packed decimal data are:

DIVP   divisor-length, divisor-address, dividend-length,
            dividend-address, quotient-length, quotient-address
MULP   multiplier-length, multiplier-address, multiplicand-length,
            multiplicand-address, product-length, product-address

The DIVP instruction divides the dividend string by the divisor string and places the result in the quotient string. The Z, N, and V indicators are set by DIVP the same as they are by DIVL. Also, an error occurs if the divisor is zero, which, as in the case of integer division, cannot be masked. R0–R5 are destroyed by DIVP. Note that DIVP does not provide a means of retrieving the remainder of the divide operation.

The MULP instruction multiplies the multiplicand string by the multiplier string and places the result in the product string. Like DIVP, it sets the N, Z, and V indicators and destroys R0–R5.

For multiplications and divisions by powers of ten, you can use the ASHP (*arithmetic shift and round packed*) instruction, which shifts packed decimal numbers to the left or right. Its general form is:

ASHP   count, source-length, source-address, round,
            destination-length, destination-address

The count operand specifies both the direction and the number of digits of the shift. It represents the power of ten by which the source value is multiplied (if positive) or divided (if negative). A shift left by two is equivalent to multiplication by 100, and a shift right by three is equivalent to division by 1000. A zero value count has no effect on the destination operand.

The round operand specifies the exact nature of the rounding to be done for right shifts or division. Bits 0–3 having the value of the round operand are added to the most significant lower-order digit that is shifted out. If the result of this addition is greater than nine, one is added to the shifted value, which is then placed in the destination operand. For example, if the leftmost digit that is shifted out is a seven, and the value of the round operand is five, their sum is 12. This is greater than nine and produces a decimal carry of one that is added to the result of the shift.

Because the usual threshold value for rounding is five, five is normally used as the round operand. Note that if the result of the shift is negative, the round operand value is also considered negative. A round operand that is zero results in truncation. The round operand is a byte, and the lengths of the two packed decimal operands are words.

The only advantage in using ASHP instead of MULP or DIVP is that it is much faster.

Packed decimal strings can be compared with the CMPP3 and CMPP4 instructions. CMPP3 is used to compare two packed decimal strings of equal length, and CMPP4 is used to compare two packed decimal strings of unequal length. The general forms of these instructions are:

CMPP3   length, value-1-address, value-2-address

CMPP4   value-1-length, value-1-address, value-2-length,
               value-2-address

The only effect of both CMPP3 and CMPP4 is to set the condition indicators: The two packed decimal strings are compared and the condition indicators are affected.

12.3.3   Conversion Instructions for Decimal Data

The last instructions involved with decimal data are those for converting data values between the decimal formats, and between packed decimal strings and LONGWORD integers.

The CVTLP and CVTPL instructions convert values between longwords and packed decimal strings. The general forms are:

CVTLP   longword, packed-length, packed-address

CVTPL   packed-length, packed-address, longword

CVTLP converts the given longword to packed decimal form and places the result in the packed decimal string specified by its second and third operands. After execution, R0–R2 contain zeros, and R3 has the address of the byte that contains the most significant digit of the packed decimal string. The N, Z, and V indicators are affected, with the V indicator set when the packed decimal string is too short to hold the value from the longword. Because a longword can contain up to ten decimal digits, using ten for the string operand will ensure that overflow does not occur.

CVTPL converts the packed decimal string specified by its first two operands to a longword and places that value in its third operand. After execution, R0, R2, and R3 contain zeros, and R1 has the address of the byte containing the most significant digit in the packed decimal string. However, any register from R0–R3 can be used as the destination of CVTPL. As with CVTLP, the N, Z, and V indicators are affected, with the V indicator set when the packed decimal string has a value outside the range that LONGWORD locations can store, which is −2,147,483,648 to 2,147,483,647.

The CVTPS and CVTSP instructions convert between packed decimal strings and leading separate numeric strings. Note that the letter S is used to indicate the leading separate numeric data type. The general forms of these two conversion instructions are:

CVTPS   packed-length, packed-length, leading-length,
               leading-address

CVTSP   leading-length, leading-address, packed-length,
               packed-address

CVTPS converts the packed decimal string specified by its first two operands to a leading separate numeric string and places it in the location specified by its last two operands. Remember that the lengths of both packed decimal and leading separate numeric strings are the number of digits, not including the sign. The N, Z, and V indicators are affected as usual. After execution, R0 and R2 contain zeros, R1 contains the address of the byte of the packed decimal string that has the most significant digit, and R3 contains the address of the sign byte of the leading separate numeric string. The sign byte of the leading separate numeric string is either an ASCII + or −. As with the other decimal conversion and arithmetic instructions, negative zero values are not built by CVTPS. In such cases, the sign is changed to +.

CVTSP converts the leading separate numeric string specified by its first two operands to a packed decimal string and places it in the location specified by its last two operands. This instruction checks for several kinds of errors in its operands. A reserved operand fault occurs if either operand string has a specified length outside the range of 0−31; if any of the digit bytes of the leading separate numeric string is not among the ASCII codes for zero through nine; or if the sign byte is not the ASCII code for a blank, +, or −.

CVTSP also affects the N, Z, and V indicators. After execution of a CVTSP instruction, R0 and R2 contain zeros, R1 has the address of the sign byte of the leading separate numeric string, and R3 has the address of the byte containing the most significant digit of the packed decimal string.

The last two decimal instructions convert values between trailing numeric and packed decimal strings. The general forms of these instructions are:

CVTPT packed-length, packed-address, table, trailing-length, trailing-address

CVTTP trailing-length, trailing-address, table, packed-length, packed-address

The table operand in these instructions is used to provide the translation for the last byte of the trailing numeric string, which contains the different forms of the superimposed sign. The table, which is 256 bytes long, is used as a translation table in much the same way as the translation table is used for the SPANC and SCANC instruction: The byte to be translated is used as an unsigned index into the table, and the value found at the indexed location is the translation for the given byte.

For CVTPT, the table must have an entry for each possible value of the highest address byte in a packed decimal string. This byte is always a sign nibble and a decimal digit. Because all hex symbols with values greater than nine are legal sign nibbles, 60 meaningful entries are required in the table. These are placed in the hex locations A0, . . . , A9, B0, . . . ,

B9, ... , F0, ... , F9. Each of these locations must contain a translation in the form of the byte that has the least significant digit and the sign in a trailing numeric string. For example, if zoned sign is desired in the trailing numeric string, the A5 (hex) position in the table must contain the hex value 35, as must the C5, E5, and F5 positions (the other legal forms of +5 in a packed decimal string). Note that the table is used exclusively for translating the one byte of the packed decimal string that contains the sign. The other digits of the packed decimal string are translated to ASCII decimal digits.

The N and Z indicators are affected according to the sign and value of the packed decimal string. The V indicator is set if the trailing numeric string does not have enough space for the value of the packed decimal string. After CVTPT execution, R0 and R2 have zero values, R1 has the address of the byte containing the most significant digit of the packed decimal string, and R3 has the address of the most significant digit of the trailing numeric string.

CVTTP uses the translation table to convert the byte of the trailing numeric string that contains the least significant digit and the sign. That byte is used as an unsigned index into the table. The byte found at that location is used as the highest address byte of the packed decimal string. For example, table locations 4B and 72 (hex) both must contain D2, which is the code for minus two in the packed decimal string. 4B is the hex code of the overpunch format for minus two, and 72 is the hex code of the zoned format for minus two.

CVTTP checks for several kinds of illegal operands and produces a reserved operand error when one is detected. Illegal operands have lengths that are outside the range of 0–31; a byte in any but the lowest-order position of a trailing numeric string that is not a valid ASCII decimal digit; or translations of the least significant digit using an invalid packed decimal digit or sign nibble.

After execution of a CVTTP instruction, R0 and R2 have zero values, R1 has the address of the most significant digit of the trailing numeric string, and R3 has the address of the byte containing the most significant digit of the packed decimal string.

Table 12.1 contains all of the VAX data conversion instructions.

	BYTE	WORD	LONG	Single Fl. Pt.	Double Fl. Pt.	Leading Separate	Trailing Numeric	Packed Decimal
BYTE		CVTBW	CVTBL	CVTBF	CVTBD			
WORD	CVTWB		CVTWL	CVTWF	CVTWD			
LONG	CVTLB	CVTLW		CVTLF	CVTLD			CVTLP
Single-Precision Floating Point	CVTFB	CVTFW	CVTFL CVTRFL		CVTFD			
Double-Precision Floating Point	CVTDB	CVTDW	CVTDL CVTRDL	CVTDF				
Leading Separate Numeric								CVTSP
Trailing Numeric								CVTTP
Packed Decimal			CVTPL			CVTPS	CVTPT	

Table 12.1 VAX Data Conversion Instructions

The following example demonstrates the use of some of the decimal instructions.

. . . .

Example 12.4

: Problem Statement

> In: A string of no more than 20 characters, all of which are blank except for a signed decimal number that has fewer than four digits.
>
> Out: The cube of the input decimal number, as a longword.

Note that the number in the input is in leading separate numeric form. Although the solution to this problem is fairly straightforward, we will spell it out in pseudocode before we present the Macro version.

:· Pseudocode Solution

> Get input string
> Find beginning of the number
> Find end of the number
> Convert the number to packed decimal
> Compute the cube of the number
> Convert the result to longword
> Print result
> End-of-program

:: *Macro Solution*

```
; DECIMAL CONVERSIONS & ARITHMETIC
; IN:  A STRING OF FEWER THAN 20 CHARACTERS, ALL
;      OF WHICH ARE BLANKS EXCEPT FOR A SIGNED
;      DECIMAL NUMBER THAT HAS FEWER THAN FOUR DIGITS.
; OUT:  THE CUBE OF THE INPUT NUMBER, AS A
;       LONGWORD.
;
      .PSECT  EXAMPLE, LONG
IN_STRING: .BYTE   ^A/ /[20]   ; INPUT STRING
IN_S:      .BLKB   5   ; INPUT AS LEADING SEPARATE
IN_P:      .BLKB   2   ; INPUT AS A PACKED DECIMAL
SQUARE:    .BLKB   4   ; SQUARE OF INPUT
CUBE:      .BLKB   5   ; CUBE OF INPUT
OUT:       .BLKL   1   ; OUTPUT LOCATION
LENGTH:    .BLKL   1   ; LENGTH OF INPUT STRING
      .ENTRY  EX_12_4, 0
      INIT_IO
      READ_A  IN_STRING
;
; FIND BEGINNING & END OF NUMBER
;
      SKPC    #^A/ /, #20, IN_STRING
      MOVL    RO, R2
      MOVL    R1, R3
      LOCC    #^A/ /, RO, (R1)
      SUBL3   RO, R2, LENGTH
      DECL    LENGTH
;
; CONVERT THE NUMBER STRING TO PACKED DECIMAL
;
      CVTSP   LENGTH, (R3), #3, IN_P
;
; COMPUTE THE CUBE OF THE NUMBER
;
      MULP    #3, IN_P, #3, IN_P, #6, SQUARE
      MULP    #3, IN_P, #6, SQUARE, #9, CUBE
;
```

Continued

```
; CONVERT THE RESULT TO A LONGWORD
;
        CVTPL    #9, CUBE, OUT
        PRINT_L  ^'INPUT CUBED =', OUT
        $EXIT_S
        .END     EX_12_4
```

Chapter Summary :

1. Single-precision floating point is a VAX data type for scientific applications programs. It is a version of scientific notation in which values are represented by fractions and exponents. The precision of single-precision floating point is about seven decimal digits, and the range is 0.29 E -38 to 1.7 E 38.

2. .FLOAT is the directive for creating single-precision floating point locations with specified initial values, and .BLKF is the directive for allocating one or more such locations with zero initial values.

3. Single-precision floating point values can be moved with MOVF and MNEGF, tested with TSTF, compared with CMPF, have their addresses moved with MOVAF and PUSHAF, and placed on the stack with PUSHL. Such locations can be cleared with CLRF, added with ADDF2 and ADDF3, subtracted with SUBF2 and SUBF3, divided with DIVF2 and DIVF3, and multiplied with MULF2 and MULF3. Results of these arithmetic operations are rounded.

4. ACBF allows counter-controlled loops with single-precision floating point parameters.

5. Single-precision floating point values can be converted to bytes, words, and longwords with CVTFB, CVTFW, and CVTFL, respectively. CVTRFL rounds a floating point value before converting it to a longword. Bytes, words, and longwords can be converted to single-precision floating point values with CVTBF, CVTWF, CVTLF, respectively.

6. Double-precision is the second standard VAX floating point data type. It provides about 16 decimal digits of precision in the same range as single-precision.

7. The three different VAX data types for decimal values are leading separate numeric, trailing numeric, and packed decimal. The first two are unpacked, using one byte per digit, and the last is packed, storing two digits per byte.

8. The only instructions for the unpacked decimal data types are those for converting them to and from packed decimal: CVTPS, CVTSP, CVTPT, and CVTTP.

9. Packed decimal values can be created with the .PACKED directive, moved with MOVP, added with ADDP4 and ADDP6, subtracted with SUBP4 and SUBP6, divided with DIVP, multiplied with MULP, and compared with CMPP3 and CMPP4. They can also be shifted left or right with the ASHP instruction. Packed decimal values can be converted to and from longwords with CVTLP and CVTPL.

New Instructions

ACBD	CMPP4	CVTLP	DIVF3	MULP
ACBF	CVTBD	CVTPL	DIVP	POLYD
ADDD2	CVTBF	CVTPS	MNEGD	POLYF
ADDD3	CVTDB	CVTPT	MNEGF	PUSHAD
ADDF2	CVTDF	CVTRDL	MOVAD	PUSHAF
ADDF3	CVTDL	CVTRFL	MOVAF	SUBD2
ADDP4	CVTDW	CVTSP	MOVD	SUBD3
ADDP6	CVTFB	CVTTP	MOVF	SUBF2
ASHP	CVTFD	CVTWD	MOVP	SUBF3
CLRD	CVTFL	CVTWF	MULD2	SUBP4
CLRF	CVTFW	DIVD2	MULD3	SUBP6
CMPD	CVTLD	DIVD3	MULF2	TSTD
CMPF	CVTLF	DIVF2	MULF3	TSTF
CMPP3				

New Directives

.BLKD	.ENABLE TRUNCATION
.BLKF	.F__FLOATING
.D__FLOATING	.FLOAT
.DOUBLE	.PACKED

New Terms

Excess 128 notation	Scientific notation
Leading separate numeric	Trailing numeric
Overpunch sign	Zoned sign
Packed decimal	

Chapter 12 Problem Set :

1. How many significant decimal digits are saved in each single-precision floating point arithmetic operation?

2. How many significant decimal digits are saved in each double-precision floating point arithmetic operation?

3. Assuming the default situation, are the constants built by .FLOAT that have too many digits of significance rounded or truncated?

4. Explain how the single-precision data format stores 24 bits of fraction in only 23 bit positions.

5. What is the exact format for a single-precision floating point value of zero?

6. What is the binary form of the single-precision floating point representation of the following numbers?

    a. 67   *b.* −42   *c.* 161   *d.* 17

7. What are the decimal values of the following single-precision floating point values (hex)?

    a. 00004240
    b. 0000C2A8
    c. 00004148
    d. 0000C190

8. What action is taken when the first operand of a CVTFB has the value 285?

9. Why did we use a floating point computation to get the factorial function value in Example 12.2, although factorial is defined as an integer function?

10. Does your VAX system have the G and H floating point data types?

11. In what programming language are found the most common uses of the decimal instructions?

12. Show the form of the number −4276 in leading separate numeric format.

13. Show the form of the number −4276 in trailing numeric format.

14. Show the form of the number −4276 in packed decimal format.

15. How can the ASHP instruction be used to produce division operations that truncate fractional results?

16. Build a 256-byte translation table to be used with CVTTP.

Write and debug structured Macro programs for the following problems.

17.   *In:*   A positive LONGWORD integer.
   Out: The integer value of the square root of the input value,
         using the following iterative formula, with an initial guess
         of (input + 1) / 2:

NEXT__GUESS := OLD__GUESS + (((INPUT / OLD__GUESS) –
               OLD__GUESS) / 2)

Note: You must use floating point instructions for all calculations done in this program. Stop the iteration when a NEXT__GUESS is greater than or equal to the OLD__GUESS. This iterative scheme is named the Newton-Raphson method.

18.   *In:*   A floating point value.
   Out: The natural antilog function of the input, using the Taylor
         series:

$$e^x := 1 + x + x^2 / 2! + x^3 / 3! + \ldots$$

Note: Write this program as a function subprogram with only one parameter: the argument to the antilog function. Stop summing series terms when the last added term has a value smaller than 0.00001.

19.   *In:*   A list of integers in the range of five to nine digits.
   Out: The sum of the squares of the input values.

Note: You must convert all input values to packed decimal before squaring them. The output can be printed in leading separate numeric form using PRINT__A.

20.   *In:*   A list of integers from the terminal in the range of 20 to
         30 decimal digits, starting in the first position of the input
         lines.
   Out: The median input value.

Note: All input and output must be done with PRINT__A and READ__A. All comparisons and moves must be done in packed decimal format. The median is the middle element of a sorted list. If the list has an even number of elements, the median is the average of the two middle elements.

21.   *In:*   A list of positive floating point numbers followed by a negative value.
   Out: The number of the input values that are greater than the
         average of all of the input data.

13

BIT AND LOGIC OPERATIONS

In a variety of situations, you will find it convenient, and often necessary, to be able to deal with individual bits of a string and to extract or analyze bit substrings. For example, consider the disassembly process that the debugger must implement for the STEP and EXAMINE/INSTRUCTION commands. Both of these commands require software to construct a Macro instruction from a VAX machine instruction, which is after all only a string of bits.

Logic operations can be used for a variety of applications, including applications in pure logic and set operations where sets are represented as bit strings.

Although we have postponed discussing the bit and logic operations until now, no course of study of any machine and its machine language is complete without a familiarity with such operations.

13.1   Bit String Data :

The last VAX data type we will introduce is the *bit string*. Bit strings are simply strings of bits. In fact, the bit string is not a legitimate data type in the same sense that WORD and LONGWORD are data types. The VAX cannot index to bit strings, nor can we allocate bit strings of various sizes with Macro directives. Bit strings in the VAX environment are more accurately defined as substrings of other data types.

The full specification of a bit string requires three instruction operands: a base address, a bit offset, and a size. The base address is an address

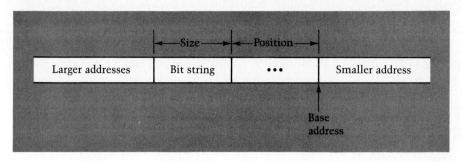

Figure 13.1 The general form of a bit string data location

of a byte, which can be specified with any of the VAX addressing modes. The size is a BYTE value, and the offset is a signed longword; both of these can be specified by any VAX addressing mode. The position is determined by a bit offset from bit 0 of the byte at the base address to bit 0 at the beginning of the string. Because it is signed, the string can be on either side of the base address. The offset is a 32-bit quantity, which is considered a signed 29-bit BYTE offset plus a bit offset of three bits within that byte. The size of a bit string is restricted to the range of 0–32 bits. In most cases, an operand that specifies a size outside that range will cause a reserved operand fault.

This somewhat strange base-and-offset addressing mode is used for bit strings because bit addresses in the VAX do not fit into a 32-bit longword. The whole 32 bits are needed to address a byte in the virtual address space. Because the bit within a byte requires another three bits, it would take 35 bits to form a complete bit address. Therefore, the two part addresses are used.

Because we will often need to deal with bit fields within registers, the base address may be a register as well as a memory location, as long as the position or offset operand is in the range of 0–31. Note that this is the only case in the VAX architecture where an address operand can specify a register.

The general form of a bit string is shown in Figure 13.1.

13.2 Bit String Operations :

When data occupy single bit locations, the required operations are often very simple: The data values are indicators, and testing is the most common function. The VAX has several instructions for conditional branching that are based on single bit locations. For example, you can determine, within a procedure, how that procedure had been called (by CALLS or CALLG) by conditionally branching on the S bit in the information longword of the call frame.

Two categories of conditional branch instructions use general bit addressing: those that only perform a conditional branch, called BBx (*branch bit*), and those that perform a conditional branch as well as affect the tested bit, called BBxx. Because the bit string that is tested with these instructions is actually a single bit, the size portion of the bit string specification is unnecessary.

The general form of the BBx instructions is:

BBx   position, base, address

The two op code possibilities are BBC and BBS for branching on bit clear and branching on bit set, respectively. The position operand is a LONG-WORD bit offset from the second operand, the base address. The last operand is the target address of the branch. As with other conditional branch instructions, the target is addressed with a BYTE offset, which restricts the distance between the instruction and the target to fewer than 128 bytes.

As an example of the machine code for a BBx instruction, consider the following:

```
BBC       R7, (R6), OUT
```

    3   2   1   0

42	66	57	E1

This instruction tests the addressed bit by using the contents of R7 as a bit offset from the byte addressed by the contents of R6. If the bit is clear, 42 (hex) is added to the PC to produce the address value of the symbol OUT.

The following use of BBC branches to the label CALLG if the S bit in the call frame indicates that the currently executing procedure was called by CALLG. Recall that the S bit is in position 29 of the second longword of the call frame, which is pointed to by FP.

```
BBC       #29, 4(FP), CALLG
```

Four VAX instructions in the BBxx, or the test and modify form, first test a bit for either set or clear, and then cause the same bit to be either set or cleared. The general form of these instructions is the same as that of the BBx instructions. The four op codes are BBCC (*branch on bit clear and clear*), BBSC (*branch on bit set and clear*), BBSS (*branch on bit set and set*), and BBCS (*branch on bit clear and set*). You may wonder why you would test for a bit value and then place that same value into the bit. Although the branch is conditional, the modification of the bit is not. For example, BBSS sets the addressed bit regardless of whether the bit was previously clear or set.

The general form of the BB*xx* instructions is:

BB*xx*   position, base, address

The first two operands specify the bit address to be tested, and the third operand specifies the target address of the branch.

Occasionally, the bit to be tested is the lowest-order bit of a memory byte or register. The VAX has two instructions for this situation: BLBC (*b*ranch on *l*ow-order *b*it *c*lear) and BLBS (*b*ranch on *l*ow-order *b*it *s*et). The general form of these instructions is:

BLB*x* source, address

The source is addressed with any addressing mode and treated as a longword for addressing purposes. As with other conditional branch instructions, the target address is coded as a BYTE displacement, so it must be within 127 bytes of the instruction.

When each bit of a bit string stores an independent data value, you may need to locate the first set or cleared bit. For example, suppose each bit of the string when set indicates that a location in an array is currently being used. When an available location is needed, we would need to find a cleared bit in the string.

The VAX has two instructions for implementing this sort of bit search: FFS (*f*ind *f*irst bit *s*et) and FFC (*f*ind *f*irst bit *c*lear). The general form of these instructions is:

FF*x*   position, size, base, result

The position, size, and base operands specify a bit string. Again, position is a signed longword, base is an address, and size is a byte with a value in the range of 0–32. The bit string is first removed from the indicated address and then scanned, right to left, for the first occurrence of the indicated bit value (set if FFS and cleared if FFC). If the indicated bit value is found, the Z indicator is cleared and the position of the found bit relative to the base address operand is placed in the result operand, which is a longword. If the indicated bit value is not found, the Z indicator is set and the result operand gets the position of the first bit past the searched bit string. Note that if the size operand is zero, the Z indicator is set and the result operand is set to the value of the first operand (the position of the first bit in the bit string).

The FF*x* instructions can be used to scan long bit strings. Suppose, for example, that we have an array of 512 elements that uses a bit string to indicate each element's current use status. Because the starting position (the first operand) of FF*x* can be greater than 31 when the bit string is in memory, we would simply place an FF*x* with a size of 32 bits in a loop. If we use the same location for both the start position and the result, each FF*x* that failed would cause an increment of the start position by 32, which would move it to the beginning of the next longword of data.

If we assume that a cleared bit means an available location, the code fragment in Example 13.1 will find the position of the first available location in FLAGS by searching the bit string. The found position is placed in POSITION, which is also used for the starting position. This code is a good example of a posttest logical loop. We will use such a loop, modeled in pseudocode on the Pascal REPEAT construct, for this example.

. . . .

Example 13.1: The FFC Instruction

```
FLAGS:     .BLKL 16   ; THE BIT STRING
FENCE:     .BYTE 0    ; TO MAKE SURE SEARCH LOOP ENDS
POSITION: .BLKL 1     ; THE START & RESULT POSITION
                 •
                 •
                 •
        CLRL      POSITION
;
; REPEAT
;
LOOP:
;
;      SEARCH 32 BITS OF FLAGS
;
        FFC       POSITION, #32, FLAGS, POSITION
        BEQL      LOOP
;
; UNTIL Z IS CLEAR
;
```

. . . .

We can test to see if the 16 longwords of FLAGS contained a cleared bit by comparing POSITION with 512. If POSITION is less than 512, then it shows the bit position of the first cleared bit. Otherwise, FLAGS did not contain a cleared bit.

Another group of instructions is used for comparing and moving bit strings. Each of these instructions deals with groups or fields of bits, and each has a V in its op code to indicate this. V was chosen because bit fields are variable lengths.

The INSV instruction is used to move a substring from the bottom of a longword to a bit field. Its general form is:

INSV   source, position, size, base

The first operand is the longword whose lower-numbered bits are to be moved. The other three operands specify the bit field and the size of the string to be moved. For example,

```
INSV    #^XFOFF, #4, #8, R3
```

moves the first eight bits (all ones, in this case) from the first operand to bit position four in R3. The machine code version of this instruction is shown below:

8	7	6	5 4 3 2	1	0
53	08	04	0000F0FF	8F	F0

The operation of the INSV instruction is shown in Figure 13.2.

The reverse operation to INSV is to move a bit field to a longword. The VAX has two such instructions, called extract instructions: One sign-extends the field to 32 bits (EXTV), and one zero-extends the field to 32 bits (EXTZV). The general form of these instructions is:

op code   position, size, base, destination

The first three operands specify the bit field, and the last specifies the longword destination. The operation of the EXTV and EXTZV instructions is demonstrated in Figure 13.3.

In each of the INSV, EXTV, EXTZV, and FFx instructions, a reserved operand fault results from a size specification that is greater than 32.

As an example of how an extract instruction is used, consider the problem of converting a given LONGWORD integer to ASCII hex form.

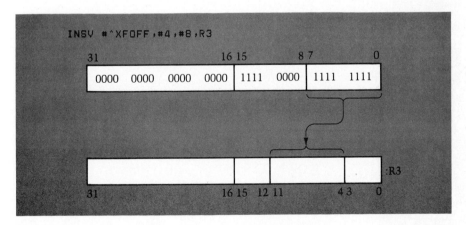

Figure 13.2 The INSV instruction

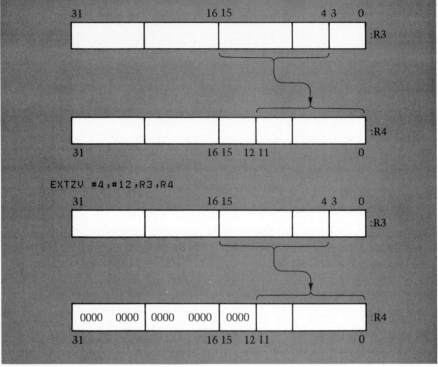

Figure 13.3 The EXTV and EXTZV instructions

You can make this conversion by extracting the nibbles of the longword, one at a time, and using them as indices into a table of ASCII codes for the hex symbols, as shown in Example 13.2.

. . . .

Example 13.2

፧ *Problem Statement*

    In: A LONGWORD integer.
    Out: The input integer in hex.

፧• *Pseudocode Solution*

Get a longword
FOR DIGIT : = 7 DOWNTO 0 DO
    Extract a NIBBLE
    Convert NIBBLE to hex ASCII and place it in OUTPUT
END-FOR
Print OUTPUT
End-of-program

:: *Macro Solution*

```
; CONVERT A LONGWORD TO HEXADECIMAL ASCII
; IN: A LONGWORD INTEGER
; OUT:  THE INPUT INTEGER IN HEXADECIMAL
;
      .PSECT  EXAMPLE, LONG
HEX_ASCII:  .ASCII /0123456789ABCDEF/ ; TRANSLATE
;                     TABLE (NIBBLES TO ASCII)
INPUT:     .BLKL  1 ; THE INPUT INTEGER
OUTPUT:    .BLKB  8 ; THE OUTPUT STRING
OUT_PTR:   .BLKL  1 ; A POINTER INTO THE OUTPUT
DIGIT:     .BLKL  1 ; LOOP COUNTER
;
      .ENTRY  EX_13_2, 0
      INIT_IO
      PRINT_L ^'INPUT VALUE PLEASE:'
      READ_L  INPUT
      MOVAB   OUTPUT, OUT_PTR
;
; FOR DIGIT := 7 DOWNTO 0 DO
;
      MOVL    #7, DIGIT
LOOP:
;
;     EXTRACT A NIBBLE
;
      MULL3   #4, DIGIT, R0
      EXTZV   R0, #4, INPUT, R1
;
;     CONVERT NIBBLE TO HEX ASCII
;
      MOVB    HEX_ASCII[R1], @OUT_PTR
      INCL    OUT_PTR
      SOBGEQ  DIGIT, LOOP
;
; END-FOR
;
      PRINT_A ^'HEX VALUE:', #8, OUTPUT
      $EXIT_S
      .END    EX_13_2

        . . . . . . . . . . . . . . . . . . . . . . . . .
```

Note that this program could be made slightly more efficient, both in terms of space and speed, by using a register to point into OUTPUT. We could then use autoincrement mode for the second operand of the MOVB.

There are two VAX instructions for comparing a bit string or field with a longword. Obviously, these instructions were meant for fields of fewer than 32 bits because CMPL works nicely when comparing two full longwords. Furthermore, most bit string comparisons involve one field value and one literal rather than two field values. Because literal strings are most efficiently represented in longwords, they have been chosen as the type of the second operand.

For CMPV, the field is sign-extended to 32 bits before the comparison; the highest-order bit of the field is considered the sign bit. For CMPZV, the field is zero-extended to 32 bits before the comparison. The general form of these instructions is:

op code   position, size, base, comparand

The position, size, and base operands specify the bit field, and the comparand operand specifies the longword with which the field is to be compared.

For example, consider the following:

```
CMPV    #4, #4, FIRST, SECOND
CMPZV   #8, #4, FIRST, SECOND
```

The first of these removes the four-bit field beginning in bit position four of FIRST (the second nibble), sign-extends it to 32 bits, and then compares it with the longword at SECOND. The second instruction removes the third nibble from FIRST, zero-extends it to 32 bits, and compares it to the longword at SECOND.

Note that these two compare instructions are equivalent to extract instructions that are followed by CMPL.

13.3 Shift Instructions :

Shift instructions move the contents of registers or memory locations left or right: They do to bits what ASHP does to packed decimal strings. These operations are of less value in the VAX than they were in most earlier machines that lacked the bit string instructions just discussed. On such machines, shifts were used to do many packing, unpacking, and conversion operations.

The ASHx instructions perform arithmetic shifts, which means that the sign of the value being shifted is preserved. The general form of these two instructions, ASHL and ASHQ, is:

ASHx   count, source, destination

The first operand specifies both the number of times the value is to be shifted by one bit and the direction of the shift. For example, a count value of five specifies a shift left of five bits, bringing five zero bits into the right end of the location. A count value of minus three specifies a right shift of three bits, bringing three copies of the sign bit into the left end of the location; this preserves the sign of the value. A zero value for count causes no shift to take place. The count operand is a byte location.

The source and destination operands specify the location of the value to be shifted and the location where the shifted value is to be placed, respectively. Note that the source value is unaffected by the shift instruction; that is, after the execution of a shift instruction, the source operand value is the same as it was before the instruction was executed.

ASHL uses longwords for the source and destination operands, and ASHQ uses quadwords. In both cases, the overflow indicator is set if a left shift moves a bit into or through the sign bit position that differs from the original sign bit value of the source.

The following should help explain the actions of the ASHx instructions:

| 11111111 | 11111111 | 11110000 | 11110000 | : VALUE |

```
ASHL    #5, VALUE, VALUE
```

| 11111111 | 11111110 | 00011110 | 00000000 | : VALUE |

```
ASHL    #-8, VALUE, VALUE
```

| 11111111 | 11111111 | 11111110 | 00011110 | : VALUE |

The ASHx instructions can be used to replace some of the multiplication and division operations in code that must run at maximum speed.

Consider the ASHP shift operation on decimal numbers. A shift of n-digits to the right is equivalent to division by ten raised to the power of n. A shift of n-digits to the left is equivalent to multiplication by ten to the power n. This same phenomenon occurs in shifts of binary values by binary digits or bits, in which the effective multiplication and division operations are by powers of two.

For example, a left shift of four bits has the same effect as multiplication by the fourth power of two or 16. Likewise, a right shift of three bits has the same effect as division by the third power of two or eight. However, shift instructions can replace multiplication or division instructions only when the multiplication or division is by a power of two.

The only reason for replacing a multiplication or division instruction by a shift instruction is speed. A shift is many times faster than either multiplication or division. Note also that an ASHL with a count value greater than or equal to 32 effectively clears the destination operand. However, CLRL is both a faster and a more readable means of clearing a location.

In Example 13.2, we could replace the following multiplication instruction by the shift instruction shown below it:

```
MULL3     #4, DIGIT, R0
ASHL      #2, DIGIT, R0
```

The ASHx instructions simply discard the bits that are shifted out of the location being shifted. For example,

```
ASHL      #10, VALUE, VALUE
```

loses the leftmost ten bits of VALUE.

Occasionally, you will want to have the shift operation be circular; that is, the bits being shifted out are brought into the other end of the value. On the VAX, this operation can be done with the ROTL (*rotate longword*) instruction, whose general form is the same as the ASHx instructions. The operands of ROTL are identical to those for ASHx. Note that no rotate instructions exist for quadwords or any other data type.

The following shows two examples of the ROTL instruction.

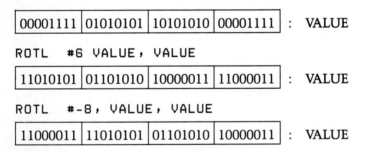

```
| 00001111 | 01010101 | 10101010 | 00001111 |  :  VALUE

ROTL    #6 VALUE, VALUE

| 11010101 | 01101010 | 10000011 | 11000011 |  :  VALUE

ROTL    #-8, VALUE, VALUE

| 11000011 | 11010101 | 01101010 | 10000011 |  :  VALUE
```

ROTL is used to reverse the order of the two words of a longword as shown below:

```
ROTL      #16, address, address
```

13.4   *Logic Operations* :

This section begins with a description of the basic logic operations on single bit operands shown on page 323.

		Second operand	
		0	1
First	0	0	1
operand	0	1	1

Inclusive OR

		Second operand	
		0	1
First	0	0	1
operand	1	1	0

Exclusive OR

		Second operand	
		0	1
First	0	0	0
operand	1	0	1

AND

In addition to *inclusive OR, exclusive OR,* and *AND,* there is one more basic logic operation, *complement.* The complement of a bit is its other value; that is, the complement of zero is one, and the complement of one is zero. Because these operations are useful, both for actual applications involving logic (for example, circuit design) and for masking operations, most computers have instructions for them.

The logic instructions of a computer typically deal with standard data types rather than individual bits. In these cases, the logic operations are performed, bit by bit, on all of the bits of the operand or operands. For example, an AND operation between two bytes ANDs each of eight pairs of corresponding bits, as is shown below:

$$
\begin{array}{r}
10010110 \\
\text{AND}\ \underline{10101101} \\
\text{RESULT}\ 10000100
\end{array}
$$

The complement operation has three VAX instructions, one for bytes, one for words, and one for longwords. The general form of these instructions is:

MCOMx   source, destination

For the op codes MCOMB, MCOMW, and MCOML, the operands are bytes, words, and longwords, respectively. Note that MNEGL is not equivalent to MCOML. MNEGL computes the twos complement of the source operand, whereas MCOML computes the ones complement, which is just the complement.

The exclusive OR operation has six VAX instructions with both two- and three-operand forms for BYTE, WORD, or LONGWORD operands. Their general forms are:

XORx2   mask, destination
XORx3   mask, source, destination

The x can be B for byte, W for word, or L for longword. The first operand is called mask because it is frequently used as a mask when searching for differences in values. For example, in the instruction

```
XORB3    #^XF0, VALUE, RESULT
```

RESULT will be zero only if VALUE is equal to F0 (hex). Any set bits in RESULT indicate differences. This can be useful for analyzing bit data.

The VAX instructions for inclusive OR and AND were designed, respectively, for setting and clearing particular bits of locations. Therefore, inclusive OR is named BIS (*bit set*). In the case of AND, the actual AND operation is not implemented, rather the complemented AND, in which the first operand is complemented and then ANDed with the second operand. The result of these two operations is, in effect, a bit clearing operation. Therefore, the complemented AND instructions are named BIC (*bit clear*).

The general forms of the inclusive OR operation are:

BISx2   mask, destination
BISx3   mask, source, destination

For BISx2, the mask operand is inclusively ORed with the destination operand. For BISx3, the mask operand is inclusively ORed with the source operand and the result is placed in the destination operand. The x in these instructions can be B for BYTE operands, W for WORD operands, and L for LONGWORD operands.

To set any bit or pattern of bits in a location, you can use a BIS instruction whose mask operand has those desired bits set. For example, to set bits 4 and 6 of the byte at VALUE, we would use the following instruction:

```
BISB2    #^B01010000, VALUE
```

The other bits of the byte at VALUE are unaffected by this instruction.

The general forms of the instructions for complemented AND are:

BIC*x*2   mask, destination
BIC*x*3   mask, source, destination

For BIC*x*2, the mask is complemented and then ANDed with the destination. For BIC*x*3, the mask is complemented and then ANDed with the source operand and the result is placed in the destination. The *x* in these instructions can be B for BYTE operands, W for WORD operands, or L for LONGWORD operands.

The bits in the destination operand that correspond to the set bits in the mask operand are cleared. When you have three operands, the other bits of the destination will have the same values as their corresponding bits in the second operand; they retain their original values in the two-operand case. For example, consider the following.

. . . .

Example 13.3: A BIC Instruction

```
VALUE:    .BYTE    ^B11001101
          .
          .
          .
          BICB3    #^B00001111, VALUE, RESULT
```

RESULT gets the value 11000000 because the BICB3 clears the bits in the right nibble of VALUE. The BIC instructions can be used to clear any bit or pattern of bits in any byte, word, or longword.

To AND a value with another, we must complement the first value before we use the BIC instruction. The second complement then restores the mask to its original value for the AND operation. For example, consider the following, in which we extract the right nibble from a byte.

. . . .

Example 13.4: An AND Operation

```
VALUE:    .BYTE    ^B11011100
MASK:     .BYTE    ^B11110000
          .
          .
          .
          MCOMB    MASK, MASK
          BICB3    MASK, VALUE, RESULT
```

RESULT gets the value 11010000. Note that in many machines the AND operation is used extensively for extracting bits or bit strings. On the VAX, however, this function is performed more easily with the EXT instructions, which is why the AND operation is buried in the bit clearing instructions.

The following example illustrates the uses of many of the instructions introduced in this chapter. It demonstrates how a floating point number can be dismantled so that it can be printed.

. . . .

Example 13.5

: *Problem Statement*

Parameters:

    a. A single-precision floating point value.

    b. The address of a longword (FRACTION).

    c. The address of a word (EXPONENT).

    d. The address of a byte (SIGN).

Result: The value of the fraction portion of parameter (a) in parameter (b), including the implied bit; the value of the exponent in parameter (c), not in excess 128 notation; and the value of the sign bit in parameter (d).

:· *Pseudocode Solution*

Place a copy of the floating point value in FRACTION
Clear bits 7–15 and set bit 7 of FRACTION
Interchange the two words of FRACTION and shift it left eight bits
Extract EXPONENT and unbias it
Extract SIGN
End-of-procedure

:: *Macro Solution*

```
; PROCEDURE TO PRODUCE THE COMPONENTS OF A
; SINGLE-PRECISION FLOATING POINT VALUE
; PARAMETERS:
;     A. A SINGLE-PRECISION FLOATING POINT VALUE
;     B. THE ADDRESS OF A LONGWORD (FRACTION)
;     C. THE ADDRESS OF A WORD (EXPONENT)
;     D. THE ADDRESS OF A BYTE (SIGN)
; RESULT: PARAMETERS B, C, AND D, GIVEN PARAMETER A
;
```

```
        .ENTRY   DISMANTLE, ^M<R2>
        INPUT = 4
        FRACTION = 8
        EXPONENT = 12
        SIGN = 16
;
; PLACE A COPY OF THE FLOATING POINT VALUE IN
; 'FRACTION'
;
        MOVF     INPUT(AP), @FRACTION(AP)
;
; CLEAR BITS 7-15 & SET BIT 7 OF 'FRACTION'
;
        BICL2    #^XFF80, @FRACTION(AP)
        BISL2    #^X80, @FRACTION(AP)
;
; INTERCHANGE THE TWO WORDS OF THE FRACTION &
; SHIFT LEFT 8 BITS
;
        ROTL     #16, @FRACTION(AP), @FRACTION(AP)
        ASHL     #8, @FRACTION(AP), @FRACTION(AP)
;
; EXTRACT EXPONENT & UNBIAS IT
;
        EXTZV    #7, #8, INPUT(AP), R2
        SUBW3    #128, R2, @EXPONENT(AP)
;
; EXTRACT SIGN
;
        EXTZV    #15, #1, INPUT(AP), @SIGN(AP)
        RET
```

. . . .

Our last group of logic instructions actually do an AND operation, but they do not save the result. They only set the N and Z condition indicators. The three forms of the BIT (*bit test*) instruction are BITB for BYTE operands, BITW for WORD operands, and BITL for LONGWORD operands. The general form of BIT is:

BITx   mask, source

The two operands are ANDed, the result is tested to affect the Z and N indicators, and the result is discarded. Neither operand is affected.

The BIT instructions are similar to the conditional branch instructions for bit strings (BBx), except that here we are testing bit patterns in standard data types and only setting the indicators rather than conditionally branching. However, our reason for setting the Z and N indicator bits is to affect subsequent conditional branches.

As an example of a BIT instruction, consider the following:

```
BITB     #^B00100101, VALUE
```

We set the Z indicator only if bits 0, 2, and 5 of the byte at VALUE are all zeros. This example instruction can never set the N indicator because the sign position bit of the mask is zero.

Chapter Summary :

1. Bit strings are pseudo data types: They are treated as if they were bona fide data types, but they are in fact only parts of other standard data types.

2. A bit string is specified by a base address, a bit offset from that base address, and a length that is less than 33.

3. The BBx instructions are used to conditionally branch on the state of a particular bit.

4. The BBxx instructions are similar to the BBx instructions, except that they also modify the tested bit.

5. The FFx instructions are used to search a bit string for the first bit in the specified state.

6. Five VAX instructions deal with bit strings rather than individual bits. CMPV and CMPZV are used to compare bit strings with specified longwords. INSV is used to build a bit string from part of a longword. EXTV and EXTZV are used to move a bit string to a longword.

7. The ASHx instructions perform arithmetic shifts, either left or right, on longwords and quadwords. ROTL rotates a longword either left or right.

8. MCOMx computes the ones complement of its first operand. XORx2 and XORx3 compute the exclusive OR function. The BISx2 and BISx3 instructions perform the inclusive OR operation, which is often used to set one or more bits. The BICx2 and BICx3 instructions first complement and then AND their first operand with their second operands; they are frequently used to clear one or more bits.

9. The BITx instructions are used to test particular bits or bit patterns. They only set the condition indicators; they do not branch.

New Instructions

ASHL	BICB3	BISW2	CMPZW	MCOMW
ASHQ	BICL2	BISW3	EXTV	ROTL
BBC	BICL3	BITB	EXTZV	XORB2
BBCC	BICW2	BITL	FFC	XORB3
BBCS	BICW3	BITW	FFS	XORL2
BBS	BISB2	BLBC	INSV	XORL3
BBSC	BISB3	BLBS	MCOMB	XORW2
BBSS	BISL2	CMPV	MCOML	XORW3
BICB2	BISL3			

New Terms

AND	Exclusive OR
Bit strings	Inclusive OR
Complement	

Chapter 13 Problem Set :

1. Describe exactly how a bit string operand is specified in Macro.

2. What is the difference between the BBS and BBSS instructions?

3. What is the size of the offset used to address the target of a BBC instruction?

4. Explain the exact operation of the FFS instruction, including the effect on the Z indicator.

5. What is the difference between CMPV and CMPZV?

6. Why would a shift be used instead of a multiplication by a power of two?

7. What is the difference between ASHL #8, COUNT, COUNT and ROTL #8, COUNT, COUNT?

8. Perform the following operations:

a.	11010101	*b.*	10001000	*c.*	10101011
AND	10101000	AND	01011011	OR	10001100

d.	01101111	*e.*	10101110	*f.*	10101110
OR	10110001	XOR	01100001	XOR	11101010

9.   What is the difference between the actions of MNEGB and MCOMB?

10. Write the Macro instructions to perform the AND operation between the words at ALPHA and BETA, placing the result at GAMMA.

Write and debug structured Macro programs for the following problems.

11. *In:* A longword.
     Out: The bit reverse of the input.

12. *In:* Two longwords.
     Out: The two longwords, as a quadword, shifted left by five bits.

13. *In:* A longword integer.
     Out: The binary value of the input, using only PRINT__A for output.

14. Suppose, for a certain project, that sets are represented as bit strings of length 256, where each bit reflects the presence or absence of a particular element. For example, if the set elements are ASCII characters and the bit corresponding to A in a particular bit string is set, it indicates that A is present in that set. Write a procedure as follows:
     Parameters: **a.** The address of the first byte of a 32-byte string representing a set.
     b. The address of a byte.
     Result: The byte in parameter (b) is set to 1 if the set was empty and to 0 otherwise.

15. Write a procedure as follows:
     Parameters: **a.** The address of the first byte of a 32-byte string representing a set, where elements of the set are the integers from 1–256.
     b. Same as (a), except for a different set.
     c. The address of a 32-byte string.
     Result: A 32-byte string representing the set union of the two input parameters, stored at the address in parameter (c).

16. Write a procedure as follows:
     Parameters: Same as Problem 15.
     Result: A 32-byte string representing the set intersection of the two input parameters, stored at the address in parameter (c).

17. *In:* **a.** The address of the first byte of a 10-byte string representing a set, where the set elements are the integers from 1–80.
     b. An integer.
     Out: If the integer is in the range of 1–80, a message indicating whether it is an element of the input set. If the integer is outside the range of 1–80, an error message.

18. *In:* An eight-digit hex number, in ASCII.
Out: The decimal value of the input, using PRINT__L.

19. *In:* An eight-digit hex number, in ASCII.
Out: The binary value of the input, using PRINT__A.

20. *In:* A LONGWORD integer.
Out: The number of set bits in the input.

21. *In:* A list of ten integers in the range 0–7.
Out: A longword consisting of all input, packed together, with bits 30 and 31 cleared.

22. Write a procedure as follows:
Parameters: **a.** A single-precision floating point value.
b. The address of a longword.
Results: The integer value of the first parameter, converted to a longword, in parameter (b). If the floating point value does not fit in the longword, the overflow indicator must be set in the calling program's PSW. You cannot use CVTFL.

23. Write a procedure as follows:
Parameters: **a.** A LONGWORD integer value.
b. An address.
Results: The input longword, converted to single-precision floating point notation and placed at the address in the second parameter, without using CVTLF.

14

VAX INPUT/OUTPUT

A detailed description of input/output on the VAX could easily fill a volume the size of this book. This chapter will very briefly discuss the structure and some of the uses of one of the input/output methods available in the VAX/VMS system software package.

14.1 Overview of VAX-11 RMS : : : : : : : : : : : : : : :

VAX-11 RMS (record management services), a subsystem of the VAX/VMS operating system, is a method of communicating data between a VAX computer and its peripheral devices. All of its data transfers take place in units of data called records. Henceforth we will refer to VAX-11 RMS simply as RMS.

RMS is used indirectly in the input/output operations for all of the high-level languages available on the VAX. In this chapter, however, we will learn to use RMS directly from Macro programs.

Although RMS has the facilities for dealing with both magnetic tape and disk storage devices, we will restrict our discussion to the disk device. Data that are stored on peripheral devices can be arranged in a variety of ways, all of them involving units called *records*. A record is a collection of data items, or *fields*, that logically belong together (for example, all of the information that an employer keeps on one employee). On a terminal device, a record is a line.

All of the records of a particular kind are collected into groups called *files* (for example, all of a company's employee records). Files are stored on disk devices on a VAX in 512-byte blocks. A block is the actual unit that moves between main memory and a disk.

Records can be written on a disk device in three different formats: fixed length, variable length, or variable length with fixed length control. This chapter will deal exclusively with the simplest of these, fixed length. Records can be arranged within files in any of three file organizations: sequential, relative, or indexed.

In *sequential file organization,* the simplest method of organizing a file, records are written next to each other, first to last. This organization restricts the processing of a file's records to either sequential order or random order by a record's file address; in some high-level languages, sequential files can be accessed only in sequential order. Sequential access means that, to read the tenth record of the file, you must first read the nine records that precede it. New records are added at the end of the file; adding a record between two existing records requires that a new file be created. One of the advantages of sequential file organization is that it does not waste any disk space.

Relative and indexed file organizations provide for nonsequential processing of a file's records, but require more complex accessing software and are less efficient in their use of disk space. Although these methods are important to VAX users, a discussion of them is beyond the scope of this book. We will restrict this chapter to dealing with sequential files.

All input/output processes on the VAX are controlled by the system software rather than by the user programs. This is essential when the system is multiprogrammed (allows multiple simultaneous users). Control is centralized because all users must share the same peripheral devices: A typical VAX system has only one user disk device. Utter chaos would result if all users had direct access to the software that controls traffic to and from such a device. The user software requests input/output operations from the system software by calling the macros in the RMS software system.

RMS input/output processes can be either *asynchronous* or *synchronous:* In the former, the process is started and control returned to the user program, and in the latter, control is returned to the requesting program only when the process is complete. Asynchronous operation allows the user program to continue a computation while the input/output process takes place. In this chapter we will deal only with synchronous input/output processes.

RMS facilities fall into two categories: file level and record level. *File level operations* involve files as units. Many of these operations are provided by VMS. We will discuss RMS file level operations for creating new files, opening existing files for processing, and closing opened files. The RMS *record level operations* that we will discuss are those to read and write records.

14.2   Control Blocks :

Control blocks provide the means of communication between user programs and the RMS routines. Both information about requested RMS operations and information concerning the return status of the requested operation are passed from and to user programs in fields in control blocks.

Although RMS uses four kinds of control blocks, we will discuss only the file access block (FAB) and the record access block (RAB). Every file is required to have a FAB to describe its structure and a RAB to describe the structure of its records.

The user program must allocate space for the required control blocks by using the RMS macros that are described in Section 14.2.1. Another RMS macro provides the actual information that must be placed in a control block before an operation proceeds on the file associated with that block, as we will describe in Section 14.2.3.

14.2.1   Allocation of Space for Control Blocks

The $FAB macro is used to allocate space for a FAB. Although 23 different parameters can be passed to the $FAB macro, most of them have default values. We normally pass only a small number of actual macro parameters. For existing files, the required $FAB parameters are FAC (*file access*) and FNM (*filename*). All parameters are passed to RMS macros by keyword.

The FAC parameter initializes the file access field of the FAB. Its value or values are the RMS functions you intend to perform on the associated file. Any operation that is not included in the file access field of the FAB and is then attempted will be rejected by RMS. The only operations that need to be mentioned are $GET and $PUT, which can be assigned to FAC by the keyword values GET and PUT, respectively. For example, we specify that $GET is to be used on an existing file by including the parameter FAC = GET in the $FAB macro call for that file.

The FNM parameter is used to specify the name of the file. The filename must be enclosed in pointed brackets.

As an example of a FAB macro call, consider the following:

```
INFAB:    $FAB      FAC = GET, FNM = <LIST.DAT>
```

Note that we normally label the $FAB call because later RMS calls must refer to it. In this example, the file LIST.DAT can be read with the $GET macro, assuming that the other required operations are included. The $FAB call simply allocates the space for the FAB and fills in three of its fields. (The FNM parameter fills two fields: the file specification string and the file specification string length.)

For a file that is to be created in the program, a $FAB macro requires three more keyword parameters: ORG, RFM, and MRS.

We must assign a value to the ORG (*organization*) keyword parameter to indicate the desired organization of the file to be created. For sequential organization, that value is SEQ.

We must assign a value to the RFM (*record format*) keyword parameter to indicate the format of the records in the file. For fixed length records, that value is FIX.

We must assign an unsigned word to the MRS (*maximum record size*) keyword parameter whose value indicates the maximum size of the records that will be written to the file. One peculiar aspect of this parameter is that the assigned value is not a literal and is therefore not preceded by a pound sign (#). However, some of the other RMS macros have parameter values that are literals.

Note that we do not need to set the FAC parameter in a $FAB macro that describes a file to be created, because the macro that creates the file ($CREATE, discussed in Section 14.2.2) enables the PUT operation.

For example, consider the following call to $FAB:

```
OUTFAB: $FAB     FNM = <DATA.DAT>, ORG = SEQ, -
                 RFM = FIX, MRS = 50
```

This describes a file named DATA.DAT, sequentially organized, with fixed length records having a maximum length of 50 bytes.

Each RAB is associated with a FAB. Space is allocated for a RAB using the $RAB macro. Although this macro has 18 possible parameters, nearly all of them default to usable values. In fact, only one must be specified on the call.

The one parameter required on a $RAB call is the keyword FAB. We must assign to FAB the address of the FAB with whose file the RAB is to be associated. For example, the following will allocate a RAB that is associated with the file whose FAB is at address INFAB:

```
INRAB:   $RAB     FAB = INFAB
```

14.2.2   File Level Operations

The $CREATE macro is used to construct a new file according to the attributes in the associated FAB. The only parameter required on a $CREATE call is the keyword FAB. We must assign to FAB the address of the FAB whose file is to be created. For example, consider the following:

```
$CREATE FAB = OUTFAB
```

If the FOP (*file process options*) field of the FAB has the value CIF (*create-if*), and a file with the same attributes already exists, the create operation is ignored. As mentioned earlier, the $CREATE macro leaves the file open and enables the PUT operation, even if the $FAB does not specify that action.

The $OPEN macro is used to open an existing file for processing; an unopened file cannot be processed. The only mandatory parameter on the $OPEN call is the FAB keyword. We must assign to FAB the address of the FAB whose file is being opened. For example, we can open the file whose FAB is at INFAB with the following:

```
$OPEN    FAB = INFAB
```

The $CLOSE macro performs the reverse of the $OPEN action: It terminates file processing and closes the file to further processing. The only parameter required on a $CLOSE call is the FAB keyword. We must assign to FAB the address of the FAB associated with the file we want to close.

Executing the code generated by $CLOSE while an operation is under-way will cause an abnormal termination of $CLOSE and will leave the file open. Of course, this cannot happen in synchronous mode. Note also that the close operation is often optional. All files used by a program are automatically closed when the program terminates. Among the actions involved in closing a file is the disconnection of all RABs.

14.2.3   Record Level Operations

The $CONNECT macro establishes the connection between a RAB and a FAB; for sequential files, only a single RAB can be connected to a particular FAB. The $CONNECT macro constructs an internal version of the RAB with which it is associated. This version includes a record pointer, initialized to the first record by the macro code. The macro code also allocates any required buffers, which are temporary storage areas for records involved with the input/output processing of the associated file.

Buffering is used to quicken file access. During file input, for example, if the system buffer can store two of a file's records, then a new record can be gotten while the other record in the buffer is being used. Note that in this case the file's records are actually gotten from disk before the user program requests them.

The only parameter required on a $CONNECT call is the keyword parameter RAB. We must assign to RAB the address of the associated RAB. For example, the following call connects the RAB we allocated earlier in this chapter:

```
$CONNECT   RAB = INRAB
```

Before a disk file can be read, the pertinent information must be placed in its associated RAB. This is done with another macro, $RAB__STORE. The first parameter on a $RAB__STORE call identifies the RAB into which you want to insert information. Although a large number of RAB fields can be set with $RAB__STORE, only two are essential: the address of the record to be used and its length. The keywords for these second and third parameters are different, depending on whether the data are moving in or out. For output operations, the keyword for the record name is RBF and the keyword for that record's length is RSZ. For input operations, the keyword for the record name is named UBF and the keyword for that record's length is USZ.

The following example assumes a user-defined record named INBUF of length 80:

```
$RAB_STORE   RAB = INRAB, UBF = INBUF, USZ = #80
```

This macro places the address of INBUF in the UBF field of the RAB whose address is INRAB. It also places the value 80 in the USZ field of that same RAB. Note that the values given for record length in the $RAB__STORE call are literals, unlike the maximum record size given in the MRS parameter of the $FAB call.

After the $RAB__STORE macro has filled the required fields of the RAB and the RAB has been connected to the FAB, we are ready to perform an input or output operation. We will discuss two RMS macros for actual input/output processes: $GET and $PUT.

The $GET macro calls the system Get service to move a record from a file to the buffer area in a user program. (The actual move is from the system buffer instead of from the file.) The operation recognizes a carriage return as a record terminator when the operation is an input from a terminal. The terminating character of the moved record is placed in STVO, the lower word of the status value field of the RAB, and the length of the input record is placed in a word field whose address is offset from the RAB address by the directly assigned symbol RAB$W__RSZ.

The only parameter required on a $GET call is the keyword RAB, to which we must assign the address of the associated RAB.

For example, consider the following code, which assumes that INBUF is a user-allocated block of length 80:

```
$RAB_STORE   RAB = INRAB, UBF = INBUF, USZ = #80
$GET     RAB = INRAB
MOVW     INRAB + RAB$W_RSZ, LENGTH
```

These instructions get a record from the file connected to the RAB at INRAB and place the length of the fetched record into the word LENGTH.

The $PUT macro calls the system Put service to move the contents of a user-allocated and -filled area to a file. In a sense, it performs the opposite function to that of $GET. The record is always placed at the end of the file if the file's organization is sequential. (Although you can place the new record at a position other than the end, this process moves the end-of-file marker to the position right after the new record, truncating the rest of the file.) The record being moved to the file cannot be longer than the length specified by the file creation command ($CREATE).

Two parameters are required on a $RAB__STORE call to set up a $PUT call: RBF, the address of the record to be written, and RSZ, the length of that record. Consider the following example, in which a record of length 32 at location BUF is written to the file whose RAB is named OUTRAB:

```
$RAB_STORE    RAB = OUTRAB, RBF = BUF, RSZ = #32
$PUT          RAB = OUTRAB
```

14.3   Example Programs :

A number of different errors can occur during a file or record operation. Although a detailed understanding of these problems is beyond the scope of this book, we can check to see if an error has occurred after each operation to avoid continuing when the results cannot be correct.

A status code is placed in R0 after every record and file operation. If the code is an odd number, the operation was error-free. If the code is even, some error has occurred. Therefore, we can test bit 0 of R0 with BLBx to determine whether an error has occurred.

We have now described a sufficient number of RMS macros to allow us to write some example programs involving the creation, writing, and reading of sequential files.

. . . .

Example 14.1

: Problem Statement

In: A list of records from a terminal, where each record consists of:

a. A 20-character name.

b. A 30-character address.

c. A nine-character social security number.

The list is terminated by a name that begins with ZZZZ, with blanks in the other character positions.

Out: A sequential file named PEOPLE.DAT that contains the input data.

Although the solution to this example is not complex, we will show the pseudocode before we write the Macro code.

:* Pseudocode Solution

Build FAB and RAB for the output file
Initialize record counter to zero
Create output file

Get a name
WHILE NAME <> trailer DO
   Get address and social security number
   Write the record to output file
   Increment record counter
   Get next NAME
END-DO
Print number of records written
Close output file
End-of-program

We will use our input/output package to get the input from the terminal. Section 14.4 will describe how terminal input and output is done and demonstrate the process with an example program.

:: *Macro Solution*

```
; CREATE AND WRITE TO A DATA FILE
;
; IN:    A LIST OF RECORDS FROM A TERMINAL, WHERE
;        EACH RECORD CONSISTS OF:
;        (A) A 20-CHARACTER NAME
;        (B) A 30-CHARACTER ADDRESS
;        (C) A NINE-CHARACTER SOCIAL SECURITY
;            NUMBER
; OUT:   A SEQUENTIAL DISK FILE NAMED PEOPLE.DAT
;        THAT CONTAINS THE INPUT DATA
;
        .PSECT   EXAMPLE, LONG
OUT_FAB:    $FAB   FNM = <PEOPLE.DAT>, ORG = SEQ, -
                   RFM = FIX, MRS = 59
OUT_RAB:    $RAB   FAB = OUT_FAB
IOBUF:      .BLKB 59  ; RECORD BUFFER FOR OUTPUT
REC_NUM:    .LONG  0              ; RECORD COUNTER
TRAILER:    .BLKB  #^A/Z/ [4]     ; TRAILER NAME FOR
                                  ; INPUT DATA

        NAME = IOBUF
        ADDRESS = IOBUF + 20
        SSN = IOBUF + 50
        .ENTRY  EX_14_1, 0
        INIT_IO
;
; CREATE AND CONNECT OUTPUT FILE
;                                      Continued
```

```
        $CREATE FAB = OUT_FAB
;
; IF ERROR ON CREATE THEN PRINT ERROR MESSAGE &
; STOP
;
        BLBS     RO, OK_1
        PRINT_L    ^'***ERROR ON CREATE'
        $EXIT_S
;
; ENDIF
;
OK_1:
        $CONNECT  RAB = OUT_RAB
;
; IF ERROR ON CONNECT THEN PRINT ERROR MESSAGE &
; STOP
;
        BLBS     RO, OK_2
        PRINT_L    ^'***ERROR ON CONNECT'
        $EXIT_S
;
; ENDIF
; GET A NAME
;
OK_2:
        MOVC5    #0, IOBUF, #^A/ /, #59, IOBUF
        READ_A   NAME
;
; WHILE NAME <> TRAILER DO
;
LOOP:
        CMPC5    #20, NAME, #^A/ /, #4, TRAILER
        BEQL     END_LOOP
;
;     GET ADDRESS & SOCIAL SECURITY NUMBER
;
        READ_A   ADDRESS
        READ_A   SSN
;
;     WRITE THE RECORD TO THE OUTPUT FILE
;
```

```
        $RAB_STORE          RAB = OUT_RAB, RBF = IOBUF, -
                            RSZ = #59
        $PUT      RAB = OUT_RAB
;
;
;       IF ERROR ON PUT THEN PRINT ERROR MESSAGE &
;       STOP
;
        BLBS      RO, OK_3
        PRINT_L     ^'***ERROR IN FILE WRITE'
        $EXIT_S
;
;       ENDIF
;
OK_3:
        INCL      REC_NUM
        MOVC5     #0, IOBUF, #^A/ /, #59, IOBUF
        READ_A    NAME
        BRW       LOOP
;
; END-DO
;
END_LOOP:
        PRINT_L   ^'NUMBER OF RECORDS WRITTEN =', -
                  REC_NUM
        $CLOSE    FAB = OUT_FAB
        $EXIT_S
        .END      EX_14_1
```

. . . .

Now that we have created a data file of names, addresses, and social security numbers, we will write another program to check to see if the file was written correctly. We include this next example program to demonstrate the RMS code to open and read an existing sequential file.

. . . .

Example 14.2

: *Problem Statement*

   In: The sequential file PEOPLE.DAT that was created in
        Example 14.1
   Out: A listing of the input file on the terminal.

The simplicity of this process dictates that we skip the pseudocode solution and go directly to the Macro solution.

When reading a sequential file we watch for the end-of-file condition, which indicates that no more records are to be read. One of the status codes that the $GET macro leaves in the RAB is used to indicate the end-of-file condition. This status information is located in the RAB at the symbolic offset RAB$L__STS, and the code for the end-of-file condition has been assigned to the symbol RMS$__EOF. Therefore, we compare the longword at the RAB address plus RAB$L__STS with RMS$__EOF after each $GET call, and when they are equal, we know that we have reached the end of the file being read.

∷ *Macro Solution*

```
; READ AND LIST A FILE AT A TERMINAL
;
; IN:   THE SEQUENTIAL DATA FILE PEOPLE.DAT THAT
;       WAS CREATED IN EXAMPLE 14.1
; OUT:  A LISTING OF THE INPUT FILE AT THE
;       TERMINAL
;
        .PSECT  EXAMPLE, LONG
IN_FAB:    $FAB    FNM = <PEOPLE.DAT>, FAC = GET
IN_RAB:    $RAB    FAB = IN_FAB
IN_BUF:    .BLKB   59  ; BUFFER FOR INPUT RECORDS
REC_NUM:   .LONG   0   ; RECORD COUNTER
        NAME = IN_BUF
        ADDRESS = IN_BUF + 20
        SSN = IN_BUF + 50
        .ENTRY  EX_14_2, 0
        INIT_IO
;
; OPEN & CONNECT INPUT FILE
;
        $OPEN   FAB = IN_FAB
;
; IF ERROR IN OPEN THEN PRINT ERROR MESSAGE & STOP
;
        BLBS    RO, OK_1
        PRINT_L   ^'***ERROR IN OPEN'
        $EXIT_S
;
; ENDIF
;
```

```
OK_1:
      $CONNECT            RAB = IN_RAB
;
; IF ERROR IN CONNECT THEN PRINT ERROR MESSAGE &
; STOP
;
      BLBS    R0, OK_2
      PRINT_L   ^'***ERROR IN CONNECT'
      $EXIT_S
;
; ENDIF
; GET A RECORD
;
OK_2:
      $RAB_STORE RAB = IN_RAB, UBF = IN_BUF, -
                 USZ = #59
      $GET    RAB = IN_RAB
;
; IF ERROR IN GET THEN PRINT ERROR MESSAGE & STOP
;
      BLBS    R0, LOOP
      PRINT_L   ^'***ERROR IN GET'
      $EXIT_S
;
; ENDIF
; WHILE NOT EOF ON INPUT FILE DO
;
LOOP:
      CMPL    IN_RAB + RAB$L_STS, #RMS$_EOF
      BNEQ    IN_LOOP
      BRW     END_LOOP
IN_LOOP:
;
;     WRITE RECORD TO TERMINAL
;
      PRINT_A ^'NAME:', #20, NAME
      PRINT_A ^'ADDRESS:', #30, ADDRESS
      PRINT_A ^'SOCIAL SECURITY NUMBER:', #9, SSN
      PRINT_L ^' '
      INCL    REC_NUM
      $GET    RAB = IN_RAB
;
```

Continued

```
;      IF ERROR IN GET THEN PRINT ERROR MESSAGE &
;      STOP
;
       BLBS    R0, OK_3
       PRINT_L   ^'***ERROR IN GET'
       $EXIT_S
;
;      ENDIF
;
OK_3:
       BRW     LOOP
;
; END-DO
;
END_LOOP:
       PRINT_L ^' '
       PRINT_L ^'NUMBER OF RECORDS READ =', REC_NUM
       $EXIT_S
       .END    EX_14_2
```

14.4   *Terminal Input/Output* : : : : : : : : : : : : : : : : : :

This section will show how to get input from the terminal and to move output to the terminal. We have been doing this throughout this book, but the details were hidden in our input/output package.

The differences between terminal input/output and the sequential file disk input/output we have been discussing in this chapter are quite small. Terminal input/output uses standard files that already exist and therefore need not be created. We simply use the standard filenames in our $FAB calls.

The names of the standard input and output files under VMS are SYS$INPUT and SYS$OUTPUT, respectively. Using SYS$INPUT for the filename value on the $FAB macro FNM parameter allows us to $GET input from the terminal. Similarly, we can use SYS$OUTPUT for the filename value on the $FAB macro FNM parameter to allow us to $PUT output to the terminal. Because of the nature of terminals, we must include carriage return and line feed characters to force our output to separate lines. We can do this by using a second $PUT macro call with the ASCII codes for carriage return and line feed characters. In decimal, those codes are 13 and 10, respectively.

An example program should clarify the input/output process for terminals. To ensure it is almost purely an input/output program, we will do no more than input a line of characters from the terminal and then output it right back to the terminal.

. . . .

Example 14.3

⋮ Problem Statement

 In: A line of no more than 80 characters from the terminal.
 Out: The input line to the terminal.

As in the last example, we will skip the pseudocode solution.

∴ Macro Solution

```
; TERMINAL INPUT/OUTPUT
;
; IN:  A LINE OF NO MORE THAN 80 CHARACTERS FROM
;      THE TERMINAL
; OUT:  THE INPUT LINE TO THE TERMINAL
;
      .PSECT   EXAMPLE, LONG
INFAB:   $FAB FAC = GET, FNM = <SYS$INPUT>
INRAB:   $RAB FAB = INFAB
OUTFAB:  $FAB FAC = PUT, FNM = <SYS$OUTPUT>
OUTRAB:  $RAB FAB = OUTRAB
INBUF:   .BYTE   ^A/ / [80]     ; INPUT BUFFER
CLRF:    .BYTE   13, 10         ; CARRIAGE RETURN &
                                ; LINE FEED

      .ENTRY  EX_14_3, 0
      INIT_IO
;
; OPEN & CONNECT THE INPUT AND OUTPUT FILES
;
      $OPEN    FAB = INFAB
      $OPEN    FAB = OUTFAB
;
; IF ERROR ON OPEN THEN PRINT ERROR MESSAGE & STOP
;
      BLBS     R0, OK_1
      PRINT_L   ^/'***ERROR IN OPEN'
      $EXIT_S
;
; ENDIF
;
OK_1:
      $CONNECT  RAB = INRAB
      $CONNECT  RAB = OUTRAB
```

Continued

```
;
; IF ERROR IN CONNECT THEN PRINT ERROR MESSAGE &
; STOP
;
        BLBS    RO, OK_2
        PRINT_L   ^'***ERROR IN CONNECT'
        $EXIT_S
;
; GET THE INPUT STRING
;
OK_2:
        $RAB_STORE   RAB = INRAB, UBF = INBUF, -
                     USZ = #80
        $GET    RAB = INRAB
;
; IF ERROR IN GET THEN PRINT ERROR MESSAGE & STOP
;
        BLBS    RO, OK_3
        PRINT_L   ^'***ERROR IN GET'
        $EXIT_S
;
; ENDIF
;
; PRINT A CARRIAGE RETURN, LINE FEED, AND THE
; INPUT STRING
;
OK_3:
        $RAB_STORE   RAB = OUTRAB, RBF = CRLF, -
                     RSZ = #2
        $PUT    RAB = OUTRAB
        $RAB_STORE   RAB = OUTRAB, RBF = INBUF, -
                     RSZ = #80
        $PUT    RAB = OUTRAB
;
; IF ERROR IN PUT THEN PRINT ERROR MESSAGE & STOP
;
        BLBS    RO, OK_4
        PRINT_L   ^'***ERROR IN PUT'
;
; ENDIF
;
```

```
OK_4:
    $EXIT_S
    .END     EX_14_3
```

. . . .

Note that we included INIT__IO in this program and used the PRINT__L macro to print the error messages. We did this to simplify the program.

A complete description of RMS can be found in the following three Digital Equipment Corporation manuals:

Introduction to VAX-11 Record Management Services
(DEC #AA-D024C-TE)

VAX-11 Record Management Services User's Guide
(DEC #AA-D781C-TE)

VAX-11 Record Management Services Reference Manual
(DEC #AA-D031C-TE)

A complete listing of our input/output package is given in Appendix D. It contains examples of RMS use that are similar to those in this chapter.

Chapter Summary :

1. RMS is one of the methods of input/output that is part of the VAX/VMS system software.

2. Data are stored on disk devices in files, which are collections of records, which in turn are collections of data items. All input/output on the VAX is done by requesting services of the operating system. RMS provides a package of macro instructions for this purpose.

3. Control blocks are the means to communicate input/output parameters between user programs and system service programs. Each file has a FAB to describe the file and a RAB to describe its records. The $FAB macro allocates the FAB and fills some of its fields. The $RAB macro allocates a RAB and fills some of its fields.

4. The $CREATE macro creates a new file, according to the fields of a FAB. The $OPEN macro prepares a file for use. The $CONNECT macro connects a RAB to a file.

5. The $RAB__STORE macro is used to fill fields of a RAB at execution time. $GET moves a record from a file to a user buffer area. $PUT moves a record from a user buffer area to a file.

6. Terminal input/output can be done with RMS in much the same way as disk input/output. We just use the standard filenames SYS$INPUT and SYS$OUTPUT.

New Instructions

$CLOSE	$FAB	$PUT
$CONNECT	$GET	$RAB
$CREATE	$OPEN	$RAB_STORE

New Terms

Asynchronous operations   Record access blocks

Control blocks   Record level operations

Fields   Records

File access blocks   Sequential file organization

File level operations   Synchronous operations

Files

Chapter 14 Problem Set :

1. Explain why users are not allowed direct access to peripheral devices.

2. What purpose do control blocks serve in RMS?

3. What is a FAB and what is its purpose?

4. What is a RAB and what is its purpose?

5. Does a program need both a $CREATE and an $OPEN macro for the same file?

6. What is the difference between filling RAB fields using $RAB and filling them using $RAB_STORE?

7. Although we have not stated it explicitly in this chapter, what file organization, would you guess, is used for SYS$INPUT?

8. Why are files with nonsequential organization available in RMS?

9. Is the constant given as a maximum record length on a call to $FAB a literal?

10. Is the constant given as a record size for the RAB field in a call to $RAB_STORE a literal?

Write and debug structured Macro programs for the following problems.

11.   *In:*   A list of < 30 20-character names from the terminal, terminated by a name that begins with four Zs.

     Out: A sequential disk file of the input, after sorting it into alphabetical order.

12. *In:* The file from Problem 11.

   Out: The input, to the terminal, after sorting into inverse alphabetical order.

13. *In:* A list of < 20 sets of data from the terminal, where each set is of the form:

   a. A 20-character name.
   b. A 30-character address.
   c. A phone number, as a longword.

   Out: Two sequential files, both with the input data. The first file's data are to be in alphabetical order by name. The second file's data are to be in the order of the phone numbers.

14. *In:* *a.* The data file from Problem 11.

   b. A list of fewer than ten 20-character names from the terminal.

   Out: A new sequential data file, with the new names from the terminal inserted into their proper positions.

15. *In:* A list of longwords.

   Out: The sum of the input.

Notes: You cannot use our input/output package for this problem. You can detect the end of the input by the end-of-file status value we used in Example 14.2.

15

REMAINING INSTRUCTIONS

This chapter will discuss those instructions that remain in the VAX repertoire. They are grouped in this loose category either because only a few applications use them or because they do not fit into any other chapter. The primary topics are queue data structures, multiple precision arithmetic, multiple selection structures, and character code translations.

15.1 Queues :

Queues are one of the more common data structures. You are certainly familiar with many natural queues, such as the line you get into at a fast food restaurant. Because computers solve problems by modeling real situations, it is important that they be able to model queues.

Queues also have a number of important uses within an operating system. Operating systems are essentially resource managers; they can use queues to store requests for resources, for example. Unlike most assembly languages, the VAX has instructions for dealing with queue structures.

Queues, like stacks, can be implemented either by adjacency or by noncontiguous methods. Adjacency implementation assumes that logically adjacent elements are also physically adjacent. The primary difficulty with adjacency implementation of queues and other lists is that insertions and deletions require moving other data in the structure. The solution to this problem is to use noncontiguous storage for structure elements and to represent their logical adjacency with pointers between elements. Because such structures have their elements linked together, they are usually called linked lists.

VAX queues are structured in circular, doubly linked lists. In such structures, each element has two pointers or links. Each queue has a header node that consists of two longwords, each of which is a pointer to a node. Each node of a queue consists of three distinct parts: a forward link, a backward link, and a value field. Both links are addresses. The forward link, which we will call FLINK, has the address of the next node logically adjacent in the queue. The FLINK field of the last node in the queue contains the address of the header node. The backward link, which we will call BLINK, contains the address of the previous node logically adjacent in the queue. The BLINK field of the first node of the queue contains the address of the header node. The FLINK is always the first longword of a node, and the BLINK is always the second; the address of a node is the address of its FLINK field. The value field of a node follows the BLINK longword.

Figure 15.1 shows the logical structure of a queue having three nodes whose value fields contain four-character names. Note that the header node does not contain a value field. It is only two longwords: a FLINK and a BLINK.

The primary purpose of the header node is to make it easier to deal with empty queues. An empty queue has both links in its header filled with the header's address, as shown in Figure 15.2.

New nodes are added only at one end of a queue, called the *tail*, and removed only at the other end, called the *head*.

Queues are often used on the VAX for operating system lists that are shared. For this purpose they are implemented in a slightly more general form. Although the instructions for adding and removing nodes from such lists are named as if they operated only on queues, in fact they are designed

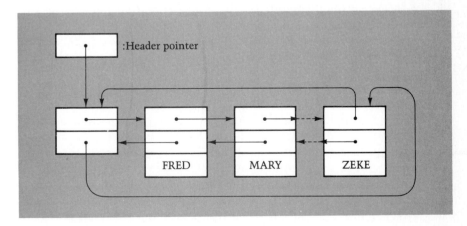

Figure 15.1   The structure of a queue of four-character names

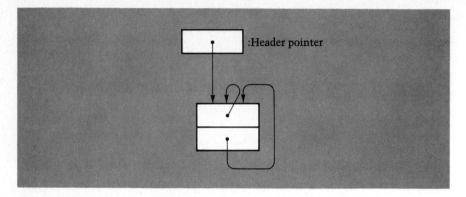

Figure 15.2   An empty queue

for deletions and additions to doubly linked lists in general. Nodes can be added or deleted anywhere in such lists.

The general forms of the queue manipulation instructions are as follows:

INSQUE   entry, predecessor
REMQUE   entry, address

The INSQUE (*insert in queue*) instruction inserts the node indicated by the first operand into the doubly linked list at the position immediately after the node whose address is given in the second operand. A node is inserted at the tail of a queue, an operation called *enqueue*, by specifying the last node of the queue as the second operand of INSQUE. However, nodes can be inserted anywhere in the list. If the list is empty (that is, the node being added is the first), the condition indicator Z is set; otherwise it is cleared.

The REMQUE (*remove from queue*) instruction removes the node specified in the first operand from the doubly linked list and places its address in the second operand. A node is removed from the head of the queue, an operation called *dequeue*, by specifying the first node in the list as the first operand of REMQUE. However, REMQUE can be used to remove any node from the queue. If the removed node was the only node in the list, the condition indicator Z is set; otherwise it is cleared. If the list is empty, an error is indicated by setting the V indicator. If the list is not empty, V is cleared.

Because the INSQUE and REMQUE instructions are often used by separate processes on a shared list, they have some special properties. However, discussion of these properties is beyond the scope of this book. We refer you to the VAX Architecture Handbook for this information.

We will now illustrate the actions of INSQUE and REMQUE. Assume that the node elements consist of three longwords and the data value of each node is a single LONGWORD integer (the other two are the FLINK and BLINK pointers).

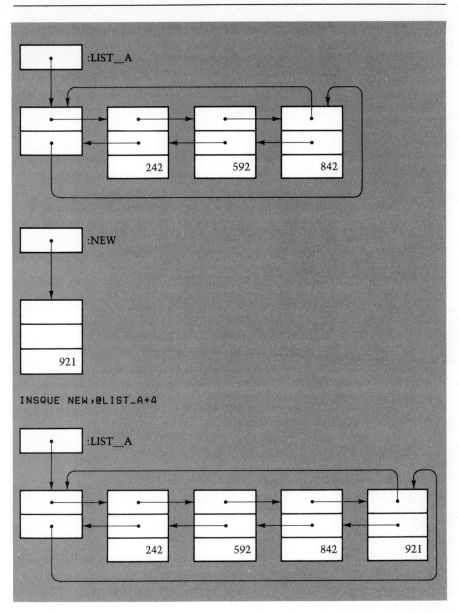

Figure 15.3   Insertion of a node at the end of a list

Figure 15.3 illustrates the enqueue operation. This operation has the following four distinct parts:

1. Set BLINK of NEW to BLINK of LIST_A.
2. Set FLINK of the old last node (pointed to by BLINK of LIST__A) to the address of NEW.
3. Set FLINK of NEW to LIST__A (header).
4. Set BLINK of LIST__A (header) to the address of NEW.

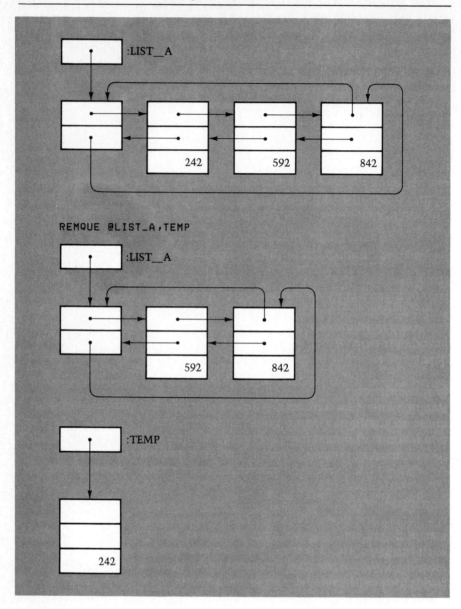

Figure 15.4 Deletion of a node from the head of a list

Figure 15.4 illustrates the dequeue operation. The dequeue operation has the following three separate steps:

1. Set TEMP to FLINK of LIST__A.
2. Set FLINK of LIST__A (header) to FLINK of TEMP.
3. Set BLINK of the node pointed to by FLINK of TEMP to LIST__A (header).

15.2 Local Labels :

Local labels are defined over limited ranges of Macro code. Because of their limited definition range, they can be reused without producing multiple definitions for the same label. Labels that are generated by the macro expander are local labels.

The form of all local labels is a decimal constant in the range of 1–65535, followed by a dollar sign ($). Labels with the decimal values of 30000–65535 are reserved for the macro expander. Those with decimal values of 1–29999 are for user generation.

The range of Macro code over which a local label is defined is called its *local label block*. Local label blocks are delimited in several ways. The beginning of a local label block can be defined by either a normal label, a .PSECT directive, or an .ENABLE directive with the LOCAL__LABEL parameter included. The end of a local label block can be defined by a normal label, a .PSECT directive, or a .DISABLE directive with the LOCAL__BLOCK parameter included, followed by a normal label.

The .ENABLE LOCAL__LABEL directive overrides a normal label being used as a delimiter. Local label blocks that begin with such a directive are terminated only by the first normal label following a .DISABLE LOCAL __LABEL directive. However, the usual way of defining local label blocks is by normal labels.

The following code segment demonstrates the use of local labels:

```
LOOP:
          ▲

10$:
          ▲

OUT_LOOP:
          ▲

10$:
          ▲

LOOP2:
```

Because the local label 10$ is used in two separate local label blocks, the label does not have multiple definitions. To provide this characteristic, local labels are not placed in the normal symbol table.

15.3 Multiple Selection Structures : : : : : : : : : : : : :

Often the logic of a program will require that a selection of a control path be made among more than two targets. Our pseudocode IF construct only allows us to choose one target, or between two targets. Most high-level programming languages include multiple selection structures; for example, Pascal has its CASE construct, and C has its SWITCH construct.

The VAX instruction for implementing the multiple selection structure is not as complicated as it appears. The general form of the CASEx
instruction is as follows:

CASEx selector, base, limit
displacement[0]
displacement[1]

.

.

.

displacement[n]

The selector operand, which is the means of choosing the target, is a
positive integer with a value ranging from that of the base to the value of
the base plus the limit. This selector value chooses a displacement value,
which is a WORD displacement that is added to the PC. The base operand
is the first legal value of the selector; it is subtracted from the selector to
provide a zero-based selection. The limit operand is used to detect errors
when the selector has a value outside the range of legal values. When an
illegal value for the selector is encountered, control is transferred to an
address just beyond the last displacement value. A branch to an area of
error processing code is often placed in this position, although sometimes
only an error message is printed.

The three possible op codes for CASEx are CASEB for BYTE operands,
CASEW for WORD operands, and CASEL for LONGWORD operands. Note
that the displacement values are always WORD values, regardless of the
particular variety of CASEx being used.

Perhaps the best way to explain the use and action of CASEx is by
showing a Pascal CASE instruction and the Macro equivalent.

. . . .

Example 15.1: A Pascal CASE Statement

```
CASE CHOOSE OF
    BEGIN
        1: CAT1 := CAT1 + 1;
        2: CAT2 := CAT2 + 1;
        3: CAT3 := CAT3 + 1
    OTHERWISE
        WRITELN('ERROR IN CASE, CHOOSE =', CHOOSE)
END
```

⦂ *The Macro Equivalent*

```
        CASEL    CHOOSE, #1, #2
1$:     .WORD    10$ - 1$
        .WORD    20$ - 1$
        .WORD    30$ - 1$
        PRINT_L  ^'ERROR IN CASE, CHOOSE =',CHOOSE
        BRW      40$
10$:    INCL     CAT1
        BRW      40$
20$:    INCL     CAT2
        BRW      40$
30$:    INCL     CAT3
40$:
```

∙ ∙

Note the mild confusion that can be caused because the last two operands specify a range for the case variable and the limit value is actually one less than the number of displacement values. If Example 15.1 had specified base and limit values of #1 and #3, and an illegal value had been used for the selector, CASEL would have caused a branch to the address two bytes past the beginning of the error handling code; this will often cause some sort of runtime error.

Note that when the targets are large groups of instructions, they should be replaced by abstractions (in the form of subprograms) for the sake of readability.

15.4   *Multiple Precision Integer Arithmetic* : : : : :

In the early days of minicomputers when typical word lengths were eight, 12, or 16 bits, the machines were often required to do multi-word arithmetic. Because the VAX can do 32-bit integer arithmetic, we have less of a need for such processes. However, situations do arise when addition and subtraction of integers of lengths greater than 32 bits are necessary. To accommodate these needs, the VAX has instructions for adding and subtracting two longwords, including the value of the carry indicator. The general forms of these two instructions are:

ADWC   addend, sum
SBWC   subtrahend, difference

The ADWC (*add* with *carry*) instruction is the same as the ADDL2 instruction, except that the value of the carry indicator is added into the sum.

The SBWC (subtract with carry) instruction is the same as the SUBL2 instruction, except that the value of the carry indicator is subtracted from the second operand. Because the carry indicator is set by a borrow from a previous subtraction, this provides multiple precision subtraction.

Suppose that we have two long integers stored at addresses ALPHA and BETA, and we wish to compute the quantity 2 · ALPHA − BETA and leave the result at location GAMMA. If we assume that the lengths of the two operands, ALPHA and BETA, are equal; that this length (in longwords) is stored as a longword at LEN; and that GAMMA is the address of a sufficiently long block to store the result, the following code computes GAMMA as 2 · ALPHA − BETA.

. . . .

Example 15.2: Multiple Precision Arithmetic

```
;
; FIRST COMPUTE 2 TIMES ALPHA & MOVE ALPHA TO
; GAMMA
;
      DIVL3    #4, LEN, R6
      MOVC3    R6, ALPHA, GAMMA
;
; ADD THE FIRST LONGWORD OF ALPHA TO GAMMA
;
      ADDL2    ALPHA, GAMMA
;
; FOR REG := 1 TO LEN-1 DO
;
      MOVL     #1, R6
      SUBL3    #1, LEN, LIMIT
LOOP1:
;
;     ADD NEXT LONGWORD TO GAMMA
;
      ADWC     ALPHA[R6], GAMMA[R6]
      AOBLEQ   LIMIT, R6, LOOP1
;
; END-FOR
; SUBTRACT FIRST LONGWORD FROM GAMMA
;
      SUBL2    BETA, GAMMA
;
; FOR REG := 1 TO LIMIT DO
;
```

```
        MOVL    #1, R6
LOOP2:
;
;       SUBTRACT NEXT LONGWORD FROM GAMMA
;
        SBWC    BETA[R6], GAMMA[R6]
        AOBLEQ  LIMIT, R6, LOOP2
;
; END-FOR
;
```

Note that this code assumes that the least significant part of these operands is stored first, as is usual with VAX operands. If the lengths of the operands were fixed and relatively short, we could avoid the loops in the code and simply use autoincrement addressing, which would result in less code and faster execution.

15.5   *Character Code Translation* : : : : : : : : : : : : : :

This section will describe two instructions that are used to translate character strings from one code to another. Although these instructions are used primarily for translating character strings between the two major codes, they sometimes have other uses involving other codes. The two major codes are ASCII and EBCDIC (*extended binary coded decimal interchange code*).

One of the code conversion instructions translates fixed length strings. The other converts until it finds a special character in the translation table or runs out of characters, whichever comes first.

The MOVTC (*move translated characters*) instruction is similar to the MOVC5 instruction; the only difference is that characters in transit are translated by serving as indices into a translation table. The general form of the MOVTC instruction is:

MOVTC   source-length, source-address, filler, table, destination-
        length, destination-address

All of these operands are the same as those for MOVC5, except for the table operand that specifies the address of the 256-byte translation table. The first two operands specify the string that is to be moved and translated. The last two operands specify the area where the translated string is to be placed. The filler operand is a character that will be used to complete the destination string should the source string be shorter. When the source string is longer than the destination string, the excess characters of the source string are ignored.

The translation table is used by MOVTC in much the same way it is used for the CVTPT and CVTTP instructions. The source character is used as an index into the table, and the byte at the indexed address is used as the translation of that character. Therefore, each entry of the table that corresponds to a legal character in the source character code must have a value. That value will replace the source character in the destination field.

MOVTC uses the first six registers and leaves them with the following values. R0 has the number of translated bytes remaining in the source string; this will obviously be zero except when the source string is longer than the destination string. R1 is left with the address of the first byte beyond the last byte translated from the source string. R2 and R4 are left with zero values, R3 has the address of the translation table, and R5 has the address of the first byte beyond the last byte in the destination string.

To determine how the instruction terminated, you can test the N and Z indicators. N is set if the source string's length is less than the destination string's length, and Z is set if the lengths of the two strings are equal.

The second character code translation instruction is the MOVTUC (*move translated (until) character*). The actions of MOVTUC are similar to those of MOVTC, except that no fill character is used and the operation can terminate in one additional way. While MOVTC stops translating when one of its two string operands is exhausted, MOVTUC can stop when a specified character is found as a translation in the table. The general form of MOVTUC is:

MOVTUC   source-length, source-address, escape, table,
         destination-length, destination-address

To enable you to determine whether an escape character or the end of one of the strings stopped the MOVTUC execution, MOVTUC sets the V indicator when an escape character is encountered and clears it otherwise. MOVTUC also sets the N indicator if the length of the source string is less than the length of the destination string and Z if the lengths of the two strings are equal.

The first six registers are used by the MOVTUC instruction, which leaves them with the following values. R0 is left with the number of bytes remaining in the source string, including the byte that caused early termination if that occurred. R0 will be zero when no escape character is found and the destination is at least as long as the source. R1 is left with the address of the byte in the source string with which the instruction was dealing when termination occurred. If termination occurred because of an escape character, R1 has the causing character's address; if termination was caused by the end of the destination string, R1 has the address of the last translated character in the source string; and if termination occurred because the source string was completely translated, R1 has the address of the first byte past the end of the source string. R2 is left with a zero value, and R3 has the address of the translation table. R4 is left with the number of bytes remaining in the destination string; it will be zero if the destination string is completely filled. R5 has the address in the destination string of the next character to be received. It will have the address of the first byte past the destination string if early termination does not shorten the destination string.

15.6 The EDITPC Instruction : : : : : : : : : : : : : : : :

The COBOL programming language includes a large number of editing operations that are built into the move statements. These operations, which apply to packed decimal strings, involve removing leading zeros, inserting signs, and floating dollar signs to the left of the most significant digit. The general form of the EDITPC (*edit* packed to *character*) instruction is:

> EDITPC   source-length, source-address, pattern, destination-
> address

The first two operands specify the packed decimal string; the pattern operand specifies the address of the particular editing function or functions to be done; and the last operand specifies the address where the ASCII character string result is to be placed.

Patterns are specified by one or more pattern operators, some requiring operands. These operands often specify character string lengths or fill characters. Pattern operators include: insert, move, fix, load, and control. The list of pattern operators is terminated by the special operator, EO$END.

A complete description of EDITPC can be found in the DEC VAX Architecture Handbook.

15.7 Memory Interlock :

The VAX architecture includes a useful feature that allows writable data structures to be shared. To provide this capability, the relevant instructions must first gain absolute control over the structure and then maintain that control until their execution is completed. On the VAX, this is called *interlocked access*. The VAX has seven instructions that provide interlocked access to certain data structures. We will give only a brief description of these instructions here; complete descriptions can be found in the VAX Architecture Handbook.

Two interlocked access instructions are used to conditionally branch and modify bits. The BBSSI (*branch on bit set and set interlocked*) and BBCCI (*branch on bit clear and clear interlocked*) are identical to the BBSS and BBCC instructions, respectively. The only difference is that the BBSSI and BBCCI instructions lock the byte containing the bit that is to be modified against other processors and devices during their execution.

The ADA WI (*add aligned word interlocked*) instruction is a two-address add instruction for words. It is similar to ADDW2. The differences are that for ADAWI the words being added must be aligned on word boundaries (that is, they must have addresses that are even numbers) and the word operands are interlocked against access by other processors during execution.

Four instructions deal with queues under interlocked conditions. The queues they manipulate differ somewhat from the queues we discussed in Section 15.1. Instead of using actual node addresses as the FLINK and BLINK pointers, these queues use longword address offsets. The four instructions are INSQHI (*insert into queue at head, interlocked*), INSQTI (*insert into queue at tail, interlocked*), REMQHI (*remove from queue at head, interlocked*), REMQTI (*remove from queue at tail, interlocked*). Note that the actions of these instructions are similar to those of the queue instructions we have already discussed. The main differences are that additions to and deletions from these queues can only be done at the ends of the queues; offsets are used instead of actual node addresses; and the structures are interlocked during execution. These four queue operations are also uninterruptible, as are the queue instructions we explained earlier in this chapter.

15.8   *Additional VAX Instructions* : : : : : : : : : : : :

This section will briefly describe the remainder of the VAX instruction set. Some of these instructions are privileged, which means they cannot be used in the usual user mode of VAX execution. The first few, however, are open to the general user of the VAX. They are just not frequently needed.

15.8.1   *User-Accessible Instructions*

When you want to specify how constant operands are to be represented in your programs, you precede them with one of the two operators S^ or I^, for literal and immediate mode, respectively. Recall that, because literal operands are actually stored in the mode byte, they must be very small. Integer values must be in the range of 0–63. Floating point values also must be small in range and precision; the exact range of possibilities is given in the VAX-11 Macro Language Reference Manual. The advantage of using literal form over immediate form is that much less storage is used. Of course, the assembler will always choose the mode that minimizes storage when the value is known. Therefore, the only time you should specify the mode is when an unknown is used as the value and you know that it will fit into the literal format.

JMP is an unconditional branch instruction that can access any address in the VAX virtual memory space. Its operand can use any addressing mode, including indirect addressing and indexing. When PC-relative mode is used and the value of the operand is known, the assembler chooses the smallest offset that will suffice. Except for indirect and indexed branches, you will have little need for JMP.

JSB is related to JMP. In fact, in terms of its operand forms, it is identical. JSB, however, is a subroutine calling instruction like BSBW and BSBB. Again, the only reason to use JSB is if indirect or indexed addressing is needed.

The NOP (*no* operation) instruction does nothing, except take up space (one byte) and use processor time (one cycle).

The MOVPSL (*move PSL*) instruction moves the current value of the PSL to the LONGWORD operand that is specified.

The BICPSW and BISPSW instructions allow the setting and clearing of specific bits and bit patterns in the PSL's user-accessible half, the PSW. These instructions operate in a way similar to the BICW2 and BISW2 instructions, respectively. Each has only one operand, a 16-bit mask, which is specified in Macro with the ^M operator. For BISPSW, the mask is ORed with the PSW. For BICPSW, the mask is complemented and then ANDed with the PSW. These instructions are often used to turn on (or off) trap enable bits of the PSW. For example, the following instruction turns on the integer overflow trap enable bit:

```
BISPSW    #^M<IV>
```

The CRC (*cyclic redundancy check*) is an exotic means of checking the accuracy of character strings that have been transmitted over communications systems. It uses a polynomial and a large amount of arithmetic to compute a value both before and after the transmission; the resulting values are compared. If they are not identical, an error has occurred in transmission.

The BPT (*breakpoint* fault) instruction is used to implement the debugging facilities of the VAX. It has no operands and simply causes a breakpoint fault, which saves the PSL on the stack.

The EMODF and EMODD instructions provide multiplication operations that include eight additional bits of fraction, extending the precision of these results to 32 and 64 bits, respectively. The general form of these instructions is:

> op code   multiplier, multiplier-extension, multiplicand, integer-
> result, fraction-result

The multiplier, multiplicand, and fraction-result data types are indicated by the op code. The multiplier extension is a byte. Because these extended bits are often unknown, zero is often used for this operand. The integer-result is a longword. The steps of these instructions are as follows:

1. Extend the fraction of the multiplier with the byte of the multiplier extension.

2. Multiply the multiplicand by the extended multiplier (32 bits of fraction are saved in the case of EMODF, and 64 bits of fraction are saved in the case of EMODD).

3. The integer part of the result is placed in the integer result location.

4. The rounded fraction part of the result is placed in fraction result location.

These instructions are used primarily to extend the accuracy of numerical calculations, such as the built-in trigonometric subprograms for languages such as FORTRAN.

The VAX has a collection of conditional branch instructions that differ slightly from those we have used throughout this book. Called the unsigned conditional branches, they are used after unsigned operations, such as bit string operations, character string operations, and address comparisons. The unsigned conditional branch instructions are: BLSSU, BLEQU, BEQLU, BNEQU, BGEQU, and BGTRU. The conditions under which these instructions branch are shown below:

Op Code	Condition
BLSSU	C = 1
BLEQU	C = 1 or Z = 1
BEQLU	Z = 1
BNEQU	Z = 0
BGEQU	C = 0
BGTRU	C = 0 and Z = 0

Note that BEQLU and BNEQU are exactly like BEQL and BNEQ, respectively. This makes sense because signs do not affect these operations. In the other four cases, however, the carry indicator is tested rather than the N indicator. This is needed if unsigned integers are being operated upon. Note that the unsigned conditional branch instructions use a BYTE offset, like all of the other VAX conditional branches.

To see the differences between the unsigned conditional branches and their signed counterparts, consider the following instruction:

```
CMPB     #^X80,  #^X7F
```

In this case the N indicator is set. The first operand is negative, because its first bit is set, and the second operand is positive. The result of subtracting 7F (hex) from 80 (hex) is negative. But the carry bit is cleared by the operation, because the carry bit is set by compare instructions only when the first operand is less than the second and both are considered unsigned. As unsigned values, 80 (hex) is certainly not less than 7F (hex). Therefore, after this compare instruction, a BLSSU would fail, and a BLSS would succeed.

Note the difference between how the C indicator is affected by compare instructions and by arithmetic instructions. For arithmetic instructions, the C indicator is set when a carry is produced from the most significant bit (not the sign bit). A comparison instruction has the same kind of effect, except that the most significant bit is now the leftmost bit, because no sign bit is considered present.

The CHMx (*change mode*) instructions are used to change the processor mode of the VAX. CHME changes the mode to executive, CHMK changes the mode to kernal, CHMS changes the mode to supervisor, and the CHMU changes the mode to user. We use these instructions to enter the VMX operating system from a user program to request services.

15.8.2 Privileged Instructions

All of the following instructions are privileged. They are reserved for privileged accounts or for system programmers who are dealing with the system software.

The MFPR (*move from privileged register*) and MTPR (*move to privileged register*) instructions provide access to the set of 30 privileged registers in the VAX. These registers contain such things as the system identification and the interrupt stack pointer.

The LDPCTX (*load process context*) and SVPCTX (*save process context*) instructions are used to restore and save the register and memory management context information of the system. All of the information is saved to and restored from an area called the process control block.

The PROBEx instructions are used to determine whether a given operand is readable (PROBER) or writable (PROBEW). These instructions are used by VMS when execution of a given instruction has been suspended until VMS determines that execution can be completed without interruption by an access problem with one of its operands.

The REI (*return from exception or interrupt*) instruction is used to return from a routine that handles certain kinds of error conditions and interrupts on the VAX.

The XFC (*extended function call*) instruction is used to extend the instruction set of the VAX, according to a particular user group's needs. The new instructions are implemented in either nonstandard microcode or software.

The HALT instruction has no operand. When executed, it stops the CPU. The machine language op code of HALT is 0; therefore, if a program in user mode ever mistakenly attempts to execute a data location with a zero value, it will produce a privileged instruction fault.

We have now at least mentioned every instruction in the standard VAX repertoire.

Chapter Summary :

1. Queues in the VAX system are doubly linked lists. The INSQUE and REMQUE instructions do additions and deletions from these queues, respectively.

2. Local labels are used for relatively short distance references.

3. CASEx is an instruction that implements a multiple selection control structure. Address offsets that follow the CASEx instruction provide the means of finding the selected code.

4. Multiple precision integer arithmetic is possible in Macro using the ADWC and SBWC instructions.

5. The MOVTC and MOVTUC instructions provide a facility for translating character string data from one character code to another. MOVTC translates and moves a specified number of characters, and MOVTUC translates and moves characters until a specified byte appears as the translation of a character.

6. The EDITPC instruction provides the editing functions for packed decimal strings that are required in the translations of COBOL programs.

7. The memory interlock instructions are used by systems programs to manipulate shared data structures.

8. Immediate mode is specified with the ^I operator, and literal mode is specified with the ^S operator.

9. JMP and JSB are used when indexing or indirect addressing modes, respectively, are useful as branch subroutine call targets.

10. The conditional branch instructions are used after unsigned operations to test for different conditions than those we have been using: they check the C indicator instead of the N indicator.

11. The VAX also has a group of privileged instructions for systems programs that include instructions for accessing privileged registers and changing the processor mode.

New Instructions

ADWC	BLSSU	CHMU	JMP	PROBER
BBCCI	BNEQU	CRC	JSB	PROBEW
BBSSI	BPT	EDITPC	LDPCTX	REI
BEQLU	CASEB	EMODD	MFPR	REMQHI
BGEQU	CASEL	EMODF	MOVPSL	REMQTI
BGTRU	CASEW	HALT	MOVTC	REMQUI
BICPSW	CHME	INSQHI	MOVTUC	SBWC
BISPSW	CHMK	INSQTI	MTPR	SVPCTX
BLEQU	CHMS	INSQUE	NOP	XFC

New Terms

Dequeue	Interlocked access
Enqueue	Tail
Head	Local label blocks

Chapter 15 Problem Set :

1. Which end of a queue gets new data elements, the head or the tail?

2. Describe the structure of the header in a VAX queue.

3. What purpose does the header serve in the VAX queue structure?

4. Describe all the actions of REMQUE.

5. Describe all of the actions of INSQUE.

6. What is the difference between CASEB and CASEL?

7. If a CASEx statement has the values seven and 12 as its second and third operands, how many legal values are available for the selector and what are they?

8. Build a multiple selection construct for the following Pascal CASE construct. Assume all variables are LONGWORD integers.

```
CASE SELECT OF
   BEGIN
   3: WRITELN('SUM =', VALUE2);
   4: BEGIN
         INDEX := INDEX + 1;
         WRITELN('SUM =', VALUE3)
      END;
   5: WRITELN('SUM =', VALUE5)
OTHERWISE
   WRITELN('ERROR IN CASE, SELECT =', SELECT)
END
```

9. What are all of the differences between ADDL2 and ADWC?

10. Write a translation table for converting all ASCII decimal digits to ASCII asterisks and all ASCII uppercase letters to ASCII lowercase letters. The table is to be used by MOVTC. It should not affect any of the other characters.

11. Describe the effects of MOVTUC on R4 and R5.

12. What is the purpose of the CRC instruction?

13. What are the differences between the six conditional branches for unsigned operations and their counterparts for signed operations?

A Using the TOYCOM Simulator

The TOYCOM simulator is a high-level language program that makes the computer on which it runs work exactly like TOYCOM. This program has two distinct parts: the TOYCODE assembler and an interpreter for TOYCOM machine language. You can obtain a tape of the TOYCOM simulator by contacting the author or your Benjamin/Cummings representative.

To get into the TOYCOM system, you type RUN TOYCOM. TOYCOM then asks whether you want to work with an existing program stored on a disk or a new program by displaying NEW or OLD ? After you answer NEW or OLD, the system asks for the file name. If it is an old program, you must then give the name you gave with the NEW command when it was created. For a NEW program, you simply make up a name of five or fewer characters, beginning with a letter.

After you have given the file name, TOYCOM will give you the prompt NEXT? to tell you it is ready to accept further commands.

The LIST system command instructs TOYCOM to assemble and produce a listing of the current program.

The RUN command instructs TOYCOM to assemble and execute the current program. RUN can be followed by several options. The LIST option causes TOYCOM to list the program before executing it. The TRACE option tells TOYCOM to print the value of the PC, the ACC, and the current instruction for each instruction it executes, producing an execution trace of the program. This can be very helpful for finding difficult program bugs. It can also be used to see how TOYCOM works. The DUMP option causes TOYCOM to print the contents of its memory exactly as they were when the program completed its execution. This is a way of checking the machine language version of your program. Also included in the dump is the symbol table, which stores the names your program used and the addresses the TOYCOM assembler assigned to them. Only the parts of memory that your program and its data occupied will be included in the dump.

The SAVE command causes TOYCOM to save your current program on disk. The program will be stored under the name you gave in response to the TOYCOM's question after you typed NEW.

If you want to replace an obsolete version of a program with a newer version, your current workspace program, you type REPLACE.

Note that the OLD and NEW commands can be typed any time TOYCOM says NEXT ?, not just at the beginning of a session. However, typing OLD (and thus getting an existing program from second-ary memory) always destroys your current program.

The EXIT command returns control to the operating system.

To facilitate relatively easy additions, deletions, and replacements of TOYCODE instructions, they must be preceded by line numbers. The line numbers can be any unsigned integers less than or equal to 32767.

TOYCOM keeps all TOYCODE instructions in numeric order by the line numbers. Therefore, a new instruction can easily be added anywhere in the program with a line number that fits in numeric order in the spot you want the instruction to be stored. For example, if you want a new instruction between lines 20 and 30, just type it in with a line number greater than 20 and less than 30, like 25. The new line will be placed between lines 20 and 30. You should leave lots of space between the line numbers you use for the initial version of a program. This makes many insertions possible during the lifetime of the program.

Unwanted instructions can be removed from the program by typing their line numbers without replacement instructions.

Instructions can be replaced by typing in the replacements with the same line numbers as the instructions being replaced.

Note that TOYCODE programs cannot be edited with a general text editor such as TECO or EDT. All changes must be made through the process just explained.

B   Hex/Decimal Conversion Table

Hex Digit Position

	8	7	6	5	4	3	2	1
0	0	0	0	0	0	0	0	0
1	268,435,456	16,777,216	1,048,576	65,536	4,096	256	16	1
2	536,870,912	33,554,432	2,097,152	131,072	8,192	512	32	2
3	805,306,368	50,331,648	3,145,728	196,608	12,288	768	48	3
4	1,073,741,824	67,108,864	4,194,304	262,144	16,348	1024	64	4
5	1,342,177,280	83,886,080	5,242,880	327,680	20,480	1280	80	5
6	1,610,612,736	100,663,296	6,291,456	393,216	24,576	1593	96	6
7	1,879,048,192	117,440,512	7,340,032	458,752	28,672	1792	112	7
8	2,147,483,648	134,217,728	8,388,608	524,288	32,768	2048	128	8
9	2,415,919,104	150,994,944	9,437,184	589,824	36,864	2304	144	9
A	2,684,354,560	167,772,160	10,485,760	655,360	40,960	2560	160	10
B	2,952,790,016	184,549,376	11,534,336	720,896	45,056	2816	176	11
C	3,221,225,472	201,326,592	12,582,912	786,432	49,152	3072	192	12
D	3,489,660,928	218,103,808	13,631,488	851,968	53,248	3328	208	13
E	3,758,096,384	234,881,024	14,680,064	917,504	57,344	3584	224	14
F	4,026,531,840	251,658,240	15,728,640	983,040	61,440	3840	240	15

C   ASCII Codes

Hex	Dec	ASCII	Hex	Dec	ASCII	Hex	Dec	ASCII	Hex	Dec	ASCII
00	0	NUL	20	32	SP	40	64	@	60	96	'
01	1	SOH	21	33	!	41	65	A	61	97	a
02	2	STX	22	34	"	42	66	B	62	98	b
03	3	ETX	23	35	#	43	67	C	63	99	c
04	4	EOT	24	36	$	44	68	D	64	100	d
05	5	ENQ	25	37	%	45	69	E	65	101	e
06	6	ACK	26	38	&	46	70	F	66	102	f
07	7	BEL	27	39	'	47	71	G	67	103	g
08	8	BS	28	40	(	48	72	H	68	104	h
09	9	HT	29	41	)	49	73	I	69	105	i
0A	10	LF	2A	42	*	4A	74	J	6A	106	j
0B	11	VT	2B	43	+	4B	75	K	6B	107	k
0C	12	FF	2C	44	,	4C	76	L	6C	108	l
0D	13	CR	2D	45	-	4D	77	M	6D	109	m
0E	14	SO	2E	46	.	4E	78	N	6E	110	n
0F	15	SI	2F	47	/	4F	79	O	6F	111	o
10	16	DLE	30	48	0	50	80	P	70	112	p
11	17	DC1	31	49	1	51	81	Q	71	113	q
12	18	DC2	32	50	2	52	82	R	72	114	r
13	19	DC3	33	51	3	53	83	S	73	115	s
14	20	DC4	34	52	4	54	84	T	74	116	t
15	21	NAK	35	53	5	55	85	U	75	117	u
16	22	SYN	36	54	6	56	86	V	76	118	v
17	23	ETB	37	55	7	57	87	W	77	119	w
18	24	CAN	38	56	8	58	88	X	78	120	x
19	25	EM	39	57	9	59	89	Y	79	121	y
1A	26	SUB	3A	58	:	5A	90	Z	7A	122	z
1B	27	ESC	3B	59	;	5B	91	[	7B	123	{
1C	28	FS	3C	60	(	5C	92	\	7C	124	|
1D	29	GS	3D	61	=	5D	93	]	7D	125	}
1E	30	RS	3E	62	)	5E	94	^	7E	126	~
1F	31	US	3F	63	?	5F	95	_	7F	127	DEL

D Input/Output Macro and Subprogram Package

Macros

```
; MACRO PACKAGE FOR VAX TERMINAL INPUT/OUTPUT FROM MACRO
        .TITLE   IOMAC
        .IDENT   /IO_MACROS/
;
; MACRO INIT_IO
; SETS UP TERMINAL I/O
;
        .MACRO   INIT_IO
        BRW      ARND,,
        .ALIGN   LONG
;
; SET UP INPUT AND OUTPUT RABS & FABS
;
IN.FAB:    $FAB    FAC = GET, FNM = <SYS$INPUT>
IN.RAB::   $RAB    FAB = IN.FAB
OUT.FAB:   $FAB    FAC = PUT, FNM = <SYS$OUTPUT>
OUT.RAB::  $RAB    FAB = OUT.FAB
OUT.BUF::  .BLKB   132      ; OUTPUT BUFFER
IN.BUF::   .BLKB   80       ; INPUT BUFFER
CR.LF::    .BYTE   13,10    ; ASCII CARRIAGE RETURN AND LINE FEED
Q,,::      .BYTE   63       ; ASCII QUESTION MARK
;
; OPEN FILES AND CONNECT RABS
;
ARND,,:
        $OPEN    FAB = IN.FAB
        $OPEN    FAB = OUT.FAB
;
; IF ERROR IN OPEN THEN PRINT ERROR MESSAGE & STOP
;
        BLBS     R0, 20$
        PRINT_L  ^/'*** ERROR IN OPEN IN INIT_IO'
        $EXIT_S
;
; ENDIF
;
20$:
        $CONNECT RAB = IN.RAB
        $CONNECT RAB = OUT.RAB
;
; IF ERROR IN CONNECT THEN PRINT ERROR MESSAGE & STOP
;
```

```
        BLBS    R0, 30$
        PRINT_L ^'*** ERROR IN CONNECT IN INIT_IO'
        $EXIT_S
;
; ENDIF
;
30$:
        .ENDM
;
;****************************************************************
; MACRO PRINT_L
; PRINTS LONGWORD INTEGERS TO THE TERMINAL
;
        .MACRO  PRINT_L LABEL, V1, V2, V3, V4, V5, V6, ?LAB, ?ARND
        .NARG   COUNT...
;
; LOOP TO PUSH ALL PRESENT ARGUMENTS
;
        .IRP    ARG, <V6, V5, V4, V3, V2, V1>
        .IIF    NOT_BLANK, ARG, PUSHL ARG
        .ENDR
;
; SET UP CALL TO PRTL
;
        PUSHAB  LAB
        PUSHL   #<%LENGTH(LABEL)>
        PUSHL   #<COUNT... - 1>
        CALLS   #<COUNT...+2>, PRTL
        BRB     ARND
LAB:    .ASCII  @LABEL@
ARND:
        .ENDM
;
;****************************************************************
; MACRO PRINT_B
; PRINTS BYTE INTEGERS TO THE TERMINAL
;
        .MACRO  PRINT_B LABEL, V1,V2,V3,V4,V5,V6,?LAB,?TEMP,?ARND
        .NARG   COUNT...
;
; LOOP TO PUSH ALL PRESENT ARGUMENTS
;
        .IRP    ARG, <V6,V5,V4,V3,V2,V1>
        .IIF    NOT_BLANK, ARG, CVTBL ARG, TEMP
        .IIF    NOT_BLANK, ARG, PUSHL TEMP
        .ENDR
;
; SET UP CALL TO PRTL
;
        PUSHAB  LAB
        PUSHL   #<%LENGTH(LABEL)>
        PUSHL   #<COUNT... - 1>
```

```
      CALLS    #<COUNT... + 2>, PRTL
      BRB      ARND
LAB:  .ASCII   @LABEL@
TEMP: .BLKL    1
ARND:
      .ENDM
;
;***********************************************************
; MACRO PRINT_W
; PRINTS WORD INTEGERS TO THE TERMINAL
;
      .MACRO   PRINT_W LABEL, V1, V2, V3, V4, V5, V6, ?LAB, -
               ?TEMP, ?ARND
      .NARG    COUNT...
;
; LOOP TO PUSH ALL PRESENT ARGUMENTS
;
      .IRP     ARG, <V6, V5, V4, V3, V2, V1>
      .IIF     NOT_BLANK, ARG, CVTWL ARG,TEMP
      .IIF     NOT_BLANK, ARG, PUSHL TEMP
      .ENDR
;
; SET UP CALL TO PRTL
;
      PUSHAB   LAB
      PUSHL    #<%LENGTH(LABEL)>
      PUSHL    #<COUNT... - 1>
      CALLS    #<COUNT... + 2>, PRTL
      BRB      ARND
LAB:  .ASCII   @LABEL@
TEMP: .BLKL    1
ARND:
      .ENDM
;
;***********************************************************
; MACRO READ_L
; READS LONGWORD INTEGERS FROM THE TERMINAL
;
      .MACRO   READ_L  V1, V2, V3, V4, V5, V6
      .NARG    COUNT...
;
; LOOP TO PUSH ALL ARGUMENTS
;
      .IRP     ARG, <V6, V5, V4, V3, V2, V1>
      .IIF     NOT_BLANK, ARG, PUSHAL ARG
      .ENDR
;
; SET UP CALL TO REDL
;
      PUSHL    #3
      PUSHL    #COUNT...
      CALLS    #<COUNT...+2>, REDL
```

```
        .ENDM
;
;***********************************************************
; MACRO READ_W
; READS WORD INTEGERS FROM THE TERMINAL
;
        .MACRO  READ_W  V1, V2, V3, V4, V5, V6
        .NARG   COUNT...
;
; LOOP TO PUSH ALL PRESENT ARGUMENTS
;
        .IRP    ARG, <V6, V5, V4, V3, V2, V1>
        .IIF    NOT_BLANK, ARG, PUSHAW ARG
        .ENDR
;
; SET UP CALL TO PRTL
;
        PUSHL   #2
        PUSHL   #COUNT...
        CALLS   #<COUNT...+2>, REDL
        .ENDM
;
;***********************************************************
; MACRO READ_B
; READS BYTE INTEGERS FROM THE TERMINAL
;
        .MACRO  READ_B  V1, V2, V3, V4, V5, V6
        .NARG   COUNT...
;
; PUSH ALL PRESENT ARGUMENTS
;
        .IRP    ARG, <V6, V5, V4, V3, V2, V1>
        .IIF    NOT_BLANK, ARG, PUSHAB ARG
        .ENDR
;
; SET UP CALL TO REDL
;
        PUSHL   #1
        PUSHL   #COUNT...
        CALLS   #<COUNT...+2>, REDL
        .ENDM
;
;***********************************************************
; MACRO READ_A
; READS ASCII STRINGS FROM THE TERMINAL
;
        .MACRO  READ_A  STR_ADDR
        PUSHAB  STR_ADDR
        CALLS   #1, REDA
        .ENDM
;
```

```
;****************************************************************
; MACRO PRINT_A
; PRINTS ASCII STRINGS TO THE TERMINAL
;
      .MACRO  PRINT_A LABEL, LENGTH, STR_ADDR, ?LAB, ?TEMP, ?ARND
      PUSHL   #<%LENGTH(LABEL)>
      PUSHAB  LAB
      MOVZWL  LENGTH, -(SP)
      PUSHAB  STR_ADDR
      CALLS   #4, PRTA
      BRB     ARND
LAB:  .ASCII  @LABEL@
ARND:
      .ENDM
;
;****************************************************************
; MACRO DUMP
; DUMPS THE REGISTERS AND A BLOCK OF MEMORY
;
      .MACRO DUMP     START, END
      PUSHAL  END
      PUSHAL  START
      CALLS   #2, DUMPER
      .ENDM
      .END
```

Subprograms

```
; SUBPROGRAM PACKAGE FOR VAX TERMINAL INPUT/OUTPUT FROM MACRO
      .TITLE  IOSUB
      .SUBTITLE       PROCEDURE PRTL--PRINT INTEGERS
      .IDENT  /IO_SUBPROGRAMS/
;
; PROCEDURE PRTL
; PRINTS LONGWORD INTEGERS ON THE TERMINAL
; PARAMETERS:
; 1. THE NUMBER OF VALUES TO BE PRINTED
; 2. THE LENGTH OF THE LITERAL LABEL TO BE PRINTED
; 3. THE ADDRESS OF THE LITERAL LABEL
; 4-?. THE VALUES TO BE PRINTED
; ERRORS:  I/O ONLY
;
      .ENTRY  PRTL, ^M<R2, R3, R4, R5, R6, R7, R8>
      NUM_VALS = 4
      LEN_LIT = 8
      ADDR_LIT = 12
      VALS = 16
;
; CLEAR BUFFER
;
```

```
        MOVC5   #0, OUT.BUF, #^A/ /, #132, OUT.BUF
;
; MOVE THE STRING PARAMETER TO THE OUTPUT BUFFER
;
        MOVC3   LEN_LIT(AP),@ADDR_LIT(AP), OUT.BUF
;
; SET R6 TO ADDRESS OF FIRST VALUE & R7 TO ADDRESS OF BUFFER
;
        ADDL3   #16, AP, R6
        MOVAB   OUT.BUF, R7
        ADDL2   LEN_LIT(AP), R7
        INCL    R7
;
; LOOP TO CONVERT NUMBERS AND PRINT THEM
; FOR KOUNT := NUM_VALS(AP) DOWNTO 1 DO
;
        MOVL    NUM_VALS(AP), KOUNT
        CMPL    KOUNT, #1
        BGEQ    CVT_LOOP
        BRW     OUT_CVT
CVT_LOOP:
;
;       CONVERT NEXT VALUE TO PACKED DECIMAL,
;           AND THEN TO LEADING NUMERIC
;
        CVTLP   (R6), #10, TEMP_BUF
        CVTPS   #10, TEMP_BUF, #11, (R7)
;
;       MOVE POINTERS DOWN
;
        ADDL2   #14, R7
        ADDL2   #4, R6
        ACBL    #1, #-1, KOUNT, CVT_LOOP
;
; END-FOR
; COMPUTE THE FILLED LENGTH OF THE BUFFER IN R7
;
OUT_CVT:
        MOVAB   OUT.BUF, R8
        SUBL2   R8, R7
;
; PRINT IT, AND THEN A CARRIAGE RETURN & LINE FEED
;
        $RAB_STORE  RAB = OUT.RAB, RBF = OUT.BUF, RSZ = R7
        $PUT        RAB = OUT.RAB
;
; IF ERROR IN PUT THEN PRINT ERROR MESSAGE & STOP
;
        BLBS    R0, 10$
        PRINT_A  ^/ /, #27, P_PUT_MESS
        $EXIT_S
```

```
;
; ENDIF
;
10$:
      $RAB_STORE    RAB = OUT.RAB, RBF = CR,LF, RSZ = #2
      $PUT          RAB = OUT.RAB
      RET
;
; LOCAL STORAGE FOR PROCEDURE PRTL
;
P_PUT_MESS:  .ASCII   ' ERROR IN PUT IN PRINT '
TEMP_BUF:    .BLKB   6 ; TEMPORARY STORAGE FOR CONVERSION
KOUNT:       .BLKL   1 ; LOOP COUNTER
      .PAGE
      .SUBTITLE       PROCEDURE REDL--READ INTEGERS
;
;******************************************************************
; PROCEDURE REDL
; GET ASCII INTEGERS FROM THE TERMINAL AND CONVERTS THEM TO
; BYTE, WORD, OR LONGWORD VALUES
; PARAMETERS:
; 1. THE NUMBER OF VALUES TO BE READ
; 2. A CODE TO INDICATE THE TYPE OF THE VALUES
;            (1 MEANS BYTE, 2 MEANS WORD, 3 MEANS LONGWORD)
; 3-? THE ADDRESSES WHERE THE VALUES ARE TO BE PLACED
; ERRORS:  ANY INPUT VALUES THAT ARE TOO LARGE CAUSE AN
;          ERROR MESSAGE TO BE PRINTED AND AN IMMEDIATE RETURN
; NOTE:  ANY ADDRESSES PASSED IN FOR WHICH VALUES WERE
;        NOT FOUND ARE SET TO ZERO
;
      .ENTRY  REDL,^M<R2, R3, R4, R5, R6, R7, R8, R9, R10>
;
; SET R7 TO # OF ADDRESS PARAMETERS, R4 AND R5 TO ADDRESS OF THE
; ADDRESSES, AND 'SIZE' TO TYPE OF ADDRESSED LOCATIONS
;
      MOVL    4(AP), R7
      ADDL3   #8, AP, R4
      MOVL    (R4)+, SIZE
      MOVL    R4, R5
;
; SET ALL PARAMETERS TO ZERO
; FOR COUNT := 1 TO R7 DO
;
      MOVL    #1, COUNT
      CMPL    COUNT, R7
      BLEQ    ZERO_LOOP
      BRW     OUT_LOOP
ZERO_LOOP:
;
;     IF SIZE = 1 THEN
;
```

```
            CMPL    SIZE, #1
            BNEQ    ELSE_1
;
;        CLEAR A BYTE
;
            CLRB    @(R5)+
            BRW     ENDIF_1
;
;        ELSE IF SIZE = 2 THEN
;
ELSE_1:
            CMPL    SIZE, #2
            BNEQ    ELSE_2
;
;            CLEAR A WORD
;
            CLRW    @(R5)+
            BRW     ENDIF_2
;
;        ELSE CLEAR A LONGWORD
;
ELSE_2:
            CLRL    @(R5)+
;
;        ENDIF
;      ENDIF
;
ENDIF_2:
ENDIF_1:
            AOBLEQ  R7, COUNT, ZERO_LOOP
;
; END-FOR
; GET INPUT STRING
;
OUT_LOOP:
            $RAB_STORE   RAB = OUT.RAB, RBF = CR.LF, RSZ = #2
            $PUT         RAB = OUT.RAB
            $RAB_STORE   RAB = OUT.RAB, RBF = Q.., RSZ = #1
            $PUT         RAB = OUT.RAB
;
; IF ERROR IN PUT THEN PRINT ERROR MESSAGE & STOP
;
            BLBS    R0, 20$
            PRINT_A  ^' ', #27, R_PUT_MESS
            $EXIT_S
;
; ENDIF
;
20$:
            $RAB_STORE   RAB = IN.RAB, UBF = IN.BUF, USZ = #80
            $GET         RAB = IN.RAB
```

```
;
; IF ERROR IN GET THEN PRINT ERROR MESSAGE & STOP
;
        BLBS    R0, 30$
        PRINT_A  ^' ', #27, R_GET_MESS
        $EXIT_S
;
; ENDIF
; GET INPUT STRING LENGTH INTO R8 & ADD A BLANK AT THE END
;
30$:
        MOVAB   IN.BUF, R9
        MOVZWL  IN.RAB + RAB$W_RSZ, R8
        ADDL3   R9, R8, R10
        MOVB    #32, (R10)
        INCL    R8
;
; REPLACE ALL COMMAS WITH BLANKS
; FIND FIRST BLANK
;
        MOVL    R8, R6
        LOCC    #^A/,/, R6, IN.BUF
;
; WHILE THERE ARE COMMAS AND MORE INPUT DO
;
COMMA_LOOP:
        TSTL    R0
        BEQL    NO_MORE_COMMAS
        TSTL    R6
        BLEQ    NO_MORE_COMMAS
;
;       REPLACE COMMA WITH A BLANK
;
        MOVL    R1, R10
        MOVB    #^A/ /, (R10)
        INCL    R10
        MOVL    R0, R6
        DECL    R6
;
;    LOOK FOR NEXT COMMA
;
        LOCC    #^A/,/, R6, (R10)
        BRW     COMMA_LOOP
;
; END-DO
;
NO_MORE_COMMAS:
;
; FOR COUNT := 1 TO R7 DO
;
        MOVL    #1, COUNT
```

```
        CMPL      COUNT, R7
        BLEQ      MAIN_LOOP
        BRW       OUT
MAIN_LOOP:
;
;       FIND BEGINNING OF FIRST NUMBER - FIRST FIND FIRST NONBLANK
;
        SKPC      #^A/ /, R8, (R9)
        TSTL      R0
        BNEQ      ARND
        BRW       OUT
ARND:
        MOVL      R0, R8
        MOVL      R1, R9
;
;       R9 IS NOW POINTING AT THE NEXT NUMBER
;       NOW FIND THE FIRST DELIMITER AFTER THE NUMBER
;
        LOCC      #^A/ /, R8, (R9)
;
;       IF IT DOES NOT HAVE A SIGN
;
        CMPB      #^A/-/, (R9)
        BEQL      HAS_SIGN
        CMPB      #^A/+/, (R9)
        BEQL      HAS_SIGN
;
;          THEN GIVE IT A BLANK
;
        DECL      R9
        INCL      R8
        MOVB      #^A/ /, (R9)
;
;       ENDIF
;
HAS_SIGN:
;
;       SET R10 TO LENGTH OF NUMBER (W/O SIGN)
;
        SUBL3     R0, R8, R10
        DECL      R10
;
;       CONVERT NUMBER TO BINARY
;
        CVTSP     R10, (R9), #12, BUF
        CVTPL     #12, BUF, TEMP
;
;       IF OVERFLOW THEN
;
        BVC       OK
```

```
;
;        PRINT MESSAGE AND RETURN
;
      PRINT_L ^'*** ERROR - INPUT VALUE IS TOO LARGE '
      RET
;
;      ENDIF
;
OK:
;
;      IF SIZE = 1 THEN
;
      CMPL    SIZE, #1
      BNEQ    ELSE1
;
;         CONVERT IT TO BYTE
;
      CVTLB   TEMP, @(R4)+
      BRW     ENDIF1
;
;         ELSE IF SIZE = 2 THEN
;
ELSE1:
      CMPL    SIZE, #2
      BNEQ    ELSE2
;
;            CONVERT IT TO WORD
;
      CVTLW   TEMP, @(R4)+
      BRW     ENDIF2
;
;            ELSE MOVE IT AS A LONGWORD
;
ELSE2:
      MOVL    TEMP, @(R4)+
;
;         ENDIF2
;      ENDIF1
ENDIF2:
ENDIF1:
;
;      IF OVERFLOW THEN
;
      BVC     NOT_TOO_BIG
;
;         PRINT ERROR MESSAGE AND RETURN
;
      PRINT_L ^'*** ERROR - INPUT VALUE IS TOO LARGE '
      RET
;
```

```
;      ENDIF
;
NOT_TOO_BIG:
;
;      MOVE R9 (INPUT POINTER) AND R8 (LENGTH REMAINING)
;
       ADDL2    R10, R9
       ADDL2    #2, R9
       SUBL2    R10, R8
       SUBL2    #2, R8
       ACBL     R7, #1, COUNT, MAIN_LOOP
;
; END-FOR
;
OUT:
       RET
;
; LOCAL STORAGE FOR PROCEDURE REDL
;
R_PUT_MESS: .ASCII   ' *** ERROR IN PUT IN READ '
R_GET_MESS: .ASCII   ' *** ERROR IN GET IN READ '
BUF:       .BLKB    12   ; TEMPORARY BUFFER FOR NUMBER CONVERSIONS
COUNT:     .BLKL    1    ; COUNTER FOR BOTH LOOPS OVER INPUT
TEMP:      .BLKL    1    ; TEMPORARY STORAGE FOR VALUE OF A NUMBER
SIZE:      .BLKL    1    ; INPUT SIZE PARAMETER
       .PAGE
       .SUBTITLE        PROCEDURE REDA--READS CHARACTER STRINGS
;
;*******************************************************************
; PROCEDURE REDA
; READS ASCII STRINGS INTO MEMORY
; PARAMETERS:
; 1. ADDRESS AT WHICH TO PLACE INPUT STRING
;
       .ENTRY   REDA, <R2, R3, R4, R5>
       STR_ADDR = 4
;
; GET STRING FROM TERMINAL
;
       $RAB_STORE   RAB=OUT.RAB, RBF = CR.LF, RSZ = #2
       $PUT         RAB = OUT.RAB
;
; IF ERROR IN PUT THEN PRINT ERROR MESSAGE & STOP
;
       BLBS    R0, 10$
       PRINT_A  ^' ', #27, R_PUT_MESS
       $EXIT_S
;
; ENDIF
;
```

```
10$:
      $RAB_STORE    RAB = OUT.RAB, RBF = Q,,, RSZ = #1
      $PUT          RAB = OUT.RAB
;
; IF ERROR IN PUT THEN PRINT ERROR MESSAGE & STOP
;
      BLBS    R0, 20$
      PRINT_A  ^' ', #27, R_PUT_MESS
      $EXIT_S
;
; ENDIF
;
20$:
      $RAB_STORE    RAB = IN.RAB, UBF = IN.BUF, USZ = #80
      $GET          RAB = IN.RAB
;
; IF ERROR IN GET THEN PRINT ERROR MESSAGE & STOP
;
      BLBS    R0, 30$
      PRINT_A  ^' ', #27, R_GET_MESS
      $EXIT_S
;
; ENDIF
;
30$:
      MOVC3    IN.RAB + RAB$W_RSZ, IN.BUF, @STR_ADDR(AP)
      RET
      .PAGE
      .SUBTITLE       PROCEDURE PRTA--PRINT CHARACTER STRINGS
;
;****************************************************************
; PROCEDURE PRTA
; PRINT ASCII STRINGS
; PARAMETERS:
; 1. ADDRESS OF STRING
; 2. LENGTH OF STRING
; 3. ADDRESS OF LITERAL LABEL
; 4. LENGTH OF LITERAL LABEL
;
      .ENTRY  PRTA, ^ M<R2, R3, R4, R5, R7>
      STR_ADDR = 4
      LEN_STR = 8
      ADDR_LIT = 12
      LEN_LIT = 16
;
; CLEAR BUFFER
;
      MOVC5    #0, OUT.BUF, #^A/ /, #132, OUT.BUF
;
; MOVE LITERAL LABEL TO OUTPUT BUFFER
```

```
;
        MOVC3   LEN_LIT(AP), @ADDR_LIT(AP), OUT.BUF
;
; MOVE R7 (BUFFER POINTER) TO POSITION FOR STRING
;
        MOVAB   OUT.BUF, R7
        ADDL2   LEN_LIT(AP), R7
        INCL    R7
;
; MOVE STRING TO BUFFER
;
        MOVC3   LEN_STR(AP), @STR_ADDR(AP), (R7)
        ADDL3   LEN_STR(AP), LEN_LIT(AP), R7
        INCL    R7
;
; PRINT THE BUFFER
;
        $RAB_STORE  RAB = OUT.RAB, RBF = OUT.BUF, RSZ = R7
        $PUT        RAB = OUT.RAB
;
; IF ERROR IN PUT THEN PRINT ERROR MESSAGE & STOP
;
        BLBS    R0, 10$
        PRINT_L ^'*** ERROR IN PUT IN PRINT_A'
        $EXIT_S
;
; ENDIF
;
10$:
        $RAB_STORE  RAB = OUT.RAB, RBF = CR.LF, RSZ = #2
        $PUT        RAB = OUT.RAB
        RET
        .PAGE
        .SUBTITLE       PROCEDURE DUMPER--DUMP REGISTERS & MEMORY
;
;********************************************************************
; PROCEDURE DUMPER
; PRINTS REGISTER CONTENTS & A PORTION OF MEMORY IN HEX
; PARAMETERS:
; 1. BEGINNING MEMORY ADDRESS
; 2. ENDING MEMORY ADDRESS
;
        .ENTRY  DUMPER, <R2, R3, R4, R5, R7>
        MOVL    4(AP), START
        MOVL    8(AP), END
;
; PRINT FIRST EIGHT REGISTERS
;
        MOVQ    R0, VALUE_BUF
        MOVQ    R2, VALUE_BUF+8
```

```
        MOVQ    R4, VALUE_BUF+16
        MOVQ    R6, VALUE_BUF+24
        MOVZBW  LABEL1, LEN
        PRINT_A  ^' ', LEN, LABEL1+1
        $RAB_STORE  RAB = OUT.RAB, RBF = CR.LF, RSZ = #2
        $PUT        RAB = OUT.RAB
        MOVZBW  LABEL2, LEN
        PRINT_A  ^' ', LEN, LABEL2+1
        PUSHL   #8
        CALLS   #1, PRINT_BUF
;
; PRINT LAST EIGHT REGISTERS
;
        MOVQ    R8, VALUE_BUF
        MOVQ    R10, VALUE_BUF+8
        MOVQ    8(FP), VALUE_BUF+16
        MOVL    #0, VALUE_BUF+24
        MOVL    16(FP), VALUE_BUF+28
        MOVZBW  LABEL3, LEN
        PRINT_A  ^' ', LEN, LABEL3+1
        PUSHL   #8
        CALLS   #1, PRINT_BUF
;
; LOOP TO DUMP MEMORY
;
        $RAB_STORE  RAB = OUT.RAB, RBF = CR.LF, RSZ = #2
        $PUT        RAB = OUT.RAB
        MOVZBW  LABEL4, LEN
        PRINT_A  ^' ', LEN, LABEL4+1
;
; CONVERT THE STARTING ADDRESS TO HEX ASCII & PRINT IT
;
        MOVC5   #0, LABEL7+37, #^A/ /, #10, LABEL7+37
        MOVL    #38, R7
;
; FOR DIGIT := 7 DOWNTO 0 DO
;
        MOVL    #7, DIGIT
CONV_LOOP:
;
;       CONVERT A NIBBLE TO HEX ASCII
;
        MULL3   #4, DIGIT, R8
        EXTZV   R8, #4, START, R9
;
;       PUT HEX ASCII BYTE IN OUTPUT BUFFER
;
        MOVB    HEX_ASCII[R9], LABEL7[R7]
        INCL    R7
        ACBL    #0, #-1, DIGIT, CONV_LOOP
```

```
;
; END-FOR
;
OUT_CONV_LOOP:
;
; PRINT STARTING ADDRESS
;
      MOVZBW  LABEL7, LEN
      PRINT_A   ^' ', LEN, LABEL7+1
      $RAB_STORE   RAB = OUT.RAB, RBF = CR.LF, RSZ = #2
      $PUT          RAB = OUT.RAB
      MOVZBW  LABEL5, LEN
      PRINT_A   ^' ', LEN, LABEL5+1
;
; SET START AND END TO MOD 4 BOUNDARIES OF THE MEMORY DUMP
;
      BICL2    #^X2, START
      BICL2    #^X2, END
      ADDL2    #4, END
;
; SET LENGTH TO THE NUMBER OF LINES OF THE DUMP
;
      SUBL3    START,END, LENGTH
      ASHL     #-5, LENGTH, LENGTH
;
; IF LENGTH < 0 THEN
;
      TSTL     LENGTH
      BGEQ     IT_IS_OK
;
;     SET LENGTH TO 0
;
      CLRL     LENGTH
;
; ENDIF
;
IT_IS_OK:
;
; FOR LINE COUNTER := 0 TO LENGTH DO
;
      CLRL     LINE_COUNTER
      CMPL     LINE_COUNTER, LENGTH
      BLEQ     LINE_LOOP
      BRW      OUT_LINE_LOOP
LINE_LOOP:
;
; MOVE EIGHT LONGWORDS TO BUFFER & PRINT THEM
;
      MOVC3    #32, @START, VALUE_BUF+4
      MOVL     START, VALUE_BUF
```

```
        PUSHL   #9
        CALLS   #1, PRINT_BUF
        ADDL2   #32, START
        AOBLEQ  LENGTH, LINE_COUNTER, LINE_LOOP
;
; END-FOR
;
OUT_LINE_LOOP:
        $RABSTORE   RAB = OUT.RAB, RBF = CR,LF, RSZ = #2
        $PUT        RAB = OUT.RAB
        MOVZBW  LABEL6, LEN
        PRINT_A  ^' ', LEN, LABEL6+1
        RET
;
; PROCEDURE PRINT_BUF
; CONVERTS EIGHT LONGWORDS TO HEX ASCII & PRINT THEM
; PARAMETERS:
; 1. FLAG TO INDICATE WHETHER THE EIGHT VALUES ARE IN
; MEMORY OR REGISTERS.  (0 MEANS REGISTERS, 1 MEANS
; MEMORY)
;
        .ENTRY  PRINT_BUF, ^M<R2, R3, R4, R5, R7, R8, R9>
        MOVL    4(AP), NUM_VALUES
        MOVC5   #0, OUT.BUF, #^A/ /, #80, OUT.BUF
        MOVAB   OUT.BUF, OUT_PTR
        MOVAL   VALUE_BUF, VALUE_PTR
;
; IF PARAMETER = 9
;
        CMPL    NUM_VALUES, #9
        BNEQ    EIGHT
;
;       THEN SET LINE PTR FOR 9 VALUES
;
        ADDL2   #72, OUT_PTR
        BRB     ENDIF7
;
;       ELSE SET LINE PTR FOR 8 VALUES
;
EIGHT:
        ADDL2   #63, OUT_PTR
;
; ENDIF
;
ENDIF7:
;
; LOOP TO CONVERT VALUES (EITHER 8 OR 9)
; FOR REG := 0 TO NUM_VALUES DO
;
        CLRL    R7
```

```
        CMPL    R7, NUM_VALUES
        BLEQ    VALUE_LOOP
        BRW     OUT_VALUE_LOOP
VALUE_LOOP:
;
;     CONVERT THE NUMBER FROM BINARY TO HEX ASCII
;     FOR DIGIT := 7 DOWNTO 0 DO
;
        MOVL    #7, DIGIT
DIGIT_LOOP:
;
;        CONVERT A NIBBLE TO HEX ASCII
;
        MULL3   #4, DIGIT, R8
        EXTZV   R8, #4, @VALUE_PTR, R9
;
;        PUT HEX DIGIT IN OUT.BUF & MOVE PTR
;
        MOVB    HEX_ASCII[R9],@OUT_PTR
        INCL    OUT_PTR
        SOBGEQ  DIGIT, DIGIT_LOOP
;
;     END-FOR (FOR DIGIT := 7 DOWNTO 0)
;     MOVE OUT PTR TO LEAVE GAP BETWEEN NUMBERS
;
        SUBL2   #17, OUT_PTR
        ADDL2   #4, VALUE_PTR
        ACBL    NUM_VALUES, #1, R7, VALUE_LOOP
;
; END-FOR (FOR REG := 0 TO NUM VALUES )
;
OUT_VALUE_LOOP:
        $RAB_STORE  RAB = OUT.RAB, RBF = OUT.BUF, RSZ = #80
        $PUT        RAB = OUT.RAB
;
; IF ERROR IN PUT THEN PRINT ERROR MESSAGE & STOP
;
        BLBS    R0, 10$
        PRINT_A ^/ /, #24, D_PUT_MESS
        $EXIT_S
;
;
; ENDIF
;
10$:
        $RAB_STORE  RAB = OUT.RAB, RBF = CR.LF, RSZ = #2
        $PUT        RAB = OUT.RAB
        RET
;
; LOCAL STORAGE FOR PROCEDURES DUMPER AND PRINT BUF
```

```
;
LABEL1: .ASCIC              '                    ***** REGISTER DUMP *****'
LABEL2: .ASCIC -
' R7      R6       R5       R4       R3       R2       R1       R0'
LABEL3: .ASCIC -
' PC      SP       FP       AP       R11      R10      R9       R8'
LABEL4: .ASCIC              '                    ***** MEMORY DUMP *****'
LABEL5: .ASCIC -
'                         ---CONTENTS---                  ADDRESS'
LABEL6: .ASCIC '                  ********** END OF DUMP *********'
LABEL7: .ASCIC '                     STARTING ADDRESS:   '
LEN:            .BLKW   1    ; LENGTH FOR ALL LABELS
D_PUT_MESS:     .ASCII  ' ERROR IN PUT IN DUMP'
HEX_ASCII:      .ASCII  '0123456789ABCDEF' ; CONVERSION TABLE
DIGIT:          .BLKL   1    ; DIGIT COUNTER
START:          .BLKL   1    ; STARTING ADDRESS OF MEMORY DUMP
END:            .BLKL   1    ; ENDING ADDRESS OF MEMORY DUMP
LENGTH:         .BLKL   1    ; LENGTH (IN LINES) OF THE MEMORY DUMP
VALUE_BUF:      .BLKL   9    ; BUFFER OF VALUES TO BE DUMPED (ONE LINE)
VALUE_PTR:      .BLKL   1    ; POINTER TO BUFFER OF VALUES TO BE PRINTED
LINE_COUNTER:   .BLKL   1    ; COUNTER FOR LINES OF MEMORY DUMP
NUM_VALUES:     .BLKL   1    ; NUMBER OF VALUES TO BE CONVERTED
OUT_PTR:        .BLKL   1    ; POINTER INTO THE OUTPUT BUFFER (OUT.BUF)
        .END
```

E Answers to Selected Problems

Chapter 1. **2c.** C − NVALUES <= 0. **2e.** SUMPOS − TOTAL + 47 >= 0. **3c.** C − NVALUES > 0. **3e.** SUMPOS − TOTAL + 47 < 0.

Chapter 2. **1b.** 11101. **1e.** 101100. **1h.** 11. **2b.** E4F. **2e.** 1FF6. **2h.** 6F54. **3b.** 31. **4c.** 00111111. **4d.** 10011100. **5b.** 26179. **5e.** 510. **6b.** 0010 0011 1010 1010. **7b.** 9B9. **8b.** 1765. **9b.** −23. **9e.** −86. **9i.** 127.

Chapter 3. **1.** The range of legal addresses of a machine is called its address space. **4.** A connotative symbol is one that makes clear its use. **6.** Longwords are stored backwards in memory so that their lower order half and lowest order byte can also be used as operands when the stored value is sufficiently small. **9.** The size of an immediate mode operand is dictated by the op code of the instruction. For example, an immediate operand in a MOVL instruction is five bytes long, a mode byte and a longword value. Literal mode operands are all two bytes long, a mode byte and a single byte value. Thus, literal mode can be used only for very small values.
11.

```
        FDFF CF 53 D0 : 454
   FDFB CF 55 FDF7 CF C1 : 459
```

Chapter 4 **3.** The body of a posttest loop is executed once before it is determined that any execution is desired.
7.

```
; IF KOUNT <= LENGTH
        CMPL     KOUNT, LENGTH
        BGTR     ELSE
;
;       THEN ADD NEXT TO SUM AND INCREMENT KOUNT
;
        ADDL2    NEXT, SUM
        INCL     KOUNT
        BRW      ENDIF
;
;       ELSE SET RESULT TO SUM AND SET KOUNT TO ZERO
;
ELSE:
        MOVL     SUM, RESULT
        CLRL     KOUNT
```

```
;
;  ENDIF
;
ENDIF:
```
10.
```
;  WHILE IN DATA > O DO
;
LOOP:
        TSTL    IN_DATA
        BLEQ    OUT_LOOP
;
;       SET SUM TO IN_DATA * IN_DATA / 2
;
        MULL3   IN_DATA, INDATA, SUM
        DIVL2   #2, SUM
;
;       GET IN_DATA
;
        READ_L  IN_DATA
        BRW     LOOP
;
;  END-DO
;
OUT_LOOP:
```
11.
```
;  FOR KOUNT := 1 TO 100 DO
;
        MOVL    #1, KOUNT
LOOP:
;
;       GET VALUE AND ADD VALUE TO SUM
;
        READ_L  VALUE
        ADDL2   VALUE, SUM
        AOBLEQ  #100, KOUNT, LOOP
;
;  END-FOR
;
```

Chapter 5. **2.** AFTER:*n* allows the first $n - 1$ encounters with the breakpoint to be ignored. **6.** An EXAMINE without parameters examines the longword immediately following the last examined longword. (This assumes that the default type is LONG.) **9.** Exiting the debugger with control/C allows restarting (with DEBUG or CONTINUE) with the same parameter settings and points set. Exiting with EXIT also transfers control out of the debugger, but you can only begin again with all points canceled and with the default parameter settings.

Chapter 6.   **3.** None of the WORD instructions affect the upper half of registers that are used as destination operands. **5.** Either now, or after a subsequent addition of code, the target will be too far away for BYTE offset addressing. **7.** In the instruction MOVL IN__DATA__4, OUT, the longword whose address is four bytes before the address IN__DATA is moved to OUT. In the instruction SUBL3 #4, IN__DATA, OUT, four is subtracted from the longword at IN__DATA and the result is placed at OUT.

Chapter 7.   **1.** BASE+(INDEX-5)*8. **3a.** 23B+5 = 240. **3c.** 23B+(5*2) = 23B+A = 245.

Chapter 8.   **2.** Indexing has a great advantage in readability over register-deferred mode. **5.** While it is illegal to use the same register for both indexing and either autoincrement or autodecrement in an operand, it is legal to use the same register for both indexing and register-deferred mode. **9.** First the base address is computed by using the longword at the location pointed to by the register-deferred deferred register. Then that address is modified with the index register, either by adding the index register's value, or a multiple of it, as dictated by the op code.

```
12a.  55 62 C2          12c.  0004 D3 B6
      0000 010A                0000 010C
12e.  54 00000008 E3 46 C4
      0000 0108
      0000 0108
```

Chapter 9.   **3.** R0 is used in CMPC3 as a character counter in the first string operand. It is initialized to the length of the string and is decremented each time a pair of equal characters are found (in the two strings). **7.** R1 is used in LOCC as a pointer into the searched strings. It is initialized to the address of the first character of the string and is incremented each time the comparison fails (on unequal). **11.** R1 is used with SCANC as a pointer into the source string. It is initialized to the address of the first character of the string and incremented each time a translation is ANDed with the specified byte and zero results. **14.** Z is always set when search instructions fail. When Z is set by the compare instructions, it means that they failed to find any difference between the two strings.

Chapter 10.   **4.** WORD integers can be pushed on the stack by pushing the longword of which they are a part with PUSHL.
10b.
```
; IF (A <= B) OR (C = D) THEN
;
      CMPL    A , B
      BGTR    SECOND
      BRW     DO_IT
```

```
SECOND:
        CMPL     C, D
        BNEQ     NEXT
;
;       INCREMENT COUNT
;
DO_IT:
        INCL     COUNT
;
; ENDIF
;
NEXT:
```

13. CALLG is clearly more machine efficient than CALLS, but when recursion is being used, or it is inconvenient to use CALLG (because of the details of loading the general argument list), CALLS should be used. **16.** Subprograms are written to be reentrant only when they are to be shared among simultaneous users.

Chapter 11. **3.** Too many actual parameters in a macro call causes an error message. **5.** All actual macro parameters have the form of ASCII strings. **10.** The %LENGTH function can be used outside macro definitions, but only in repeat blocks. **14.** The .NARG directive is used to determine the number of passed parameters in a macro. It was very useful in the macros of the VAX terminal input/output package.

Chapter 12. **2.** Approximately 16 decimal digits of accuracy are saved by the double-precision floating point operations.
6a. 0000 0000 0000 0000 0100 0011 1000 0110
6c. 0000 0000 0000 0000 0100 0100 0010 0001
7a. 12 **7c.** 3.125 **12.** 2D34323736 **14.** 04276D

Chapter 13. **2.** BBS branches if the addressed bit is set. BBSS branches if the addressed bit is set, but also sets the addressed bit. **6.** The shift operation is much faster than multiplication. **8a.** 10000000
8c. 10101111 **8e.** 11001111
10. MCOMW   ALPHA, R7
       BICW3   R7, BETA, GAMMA

Chapter 14. **1.** Since there is often far more demand than supply of peripheral devices, an impartial arbiter is needed to regulate their use. **5.** The $CREATE macro also leaves the file open, so an $OPEN is unnecessary. **8.** Nonsequential file organization is available in RMS for applications in which fast random access to records is required.

Chapter 15. **3.** The header node of a VAX queue structure assures that there is a fixed location where accesses to the queue can begin. Furthermore, the header node provides a convenient way of handling empty queues. **7.** The legal selector values for a CASEx with seven and 12 as its second and third operands are 7, 8, 9, 10, 11, 12, and 13. (This assumes that there are seven displacement values specified.) **12.** The CRC instruction is used to check the accuracy of character strings that have been transmitted between two devices.

F VAX Instruction Summary

OP	MNEMONIC	DESCRIPTION	ARGUMENTS	N	Z	V	C
9D	ACBB	Add compare and branch byte	limit.rb, add.rb, index.mb, displ.bw	•	•	•	–
6F	ACBD	Add compare and branch double	limit.rd, add.rd, index.md, displ.bw	•	•	•	–
4F	ACBF	Add compare and branch floating	limit.rf, add.rf, index.mf, displ.bw	•	•	•	–
F1	ACBL	Add compare and branch long	limit.rl, add.rl, index.ml, displ.bw	•	•	•	–
3D	ACBW	Add compare and branch word	limit.rw, add.rw, index.mw, displ.bw	•	•	•	–
58	ADAWI	Add aligned word interlocked	add.rw, sum.mw	•	•	•	•
80	ADDB2	Add byte 2-operand	add.rb, sum.mb	•	•	•	•
81	ADDB3	Add byte 3-operand	add1.rb, add2.rb, sum.wb	•	•	•	0
60	ADDD2	Add double 2-operand	add.rd, sum.md	•	•	•	0
61	ADDD3	Add double 3-operand	add1.rd, add2.rd, sum.wd	•	•	•	0
40	ADDF2	Add floating 2-operand	add.rf, sum.mf	•	•	•	0
41	ADDF3	Add floating 3-operand	add1.rf, add2.rf, sum.wf	•	•	•	0
C0	ADDL2	Add long 2-operand	add.rl, sum.ml	•	•	•	•
C1	ADDL3	Add long 3-operand	add1.rl, add2.rl, sum.wl	•	•	•	0
20	ADDP4	Add packed 4-operand	addlen.rw, addaddr.ab, sumlen.rw, sumaddr.ab, [R0-3.wl]	•	•	•	0
21	ADDP6	Add packed 6-operand	add1len.rw, add1addr.ab, add2len.rw, add2addr.ab, sumlen.rw, sumaddr.ab, [R0-5.wl]	•	•	•	0
A0	ADDW2	Add word 2-operand	add.rw, sum.mw	•	•	•	•
A1	ADDW3	Add word 3-operand	add1.rw, add2.rw, sum.ww	•	•	•	0
D8	ADWC	Add with carry	add.rl, sum.ml	•	•	•	•
F3	AOBLEQ	Add one and branch on less or equal	limit.rl, index.ml, displ.bb	•	•	•	–
F2	AOBLSS	Add one and branch on less	limit.rl, index.ml, displ.bb	•	•	•	–
78	ASHL	Arithmetic shift long	count.rb, src.rl, dst.wl	•	•	•	0
F8	ASHP	Arithmetic shift and round packed	count.rb, srclen.rw, srcaddr.ab, round.rb, dstlen.rw, dstaddr.ab, [R0-3.wl]	•	•	•	0
79	ASHQ	Arithmetic shift quad	count.rb, src.rq, dst.wq	•	•	•	0
E1	BBC	Branch on bit clear	pos.rl, base.vb, displ.bb, [field.rv]	–	–	–	–
E5	BBCC	Branch on bit clear and clear	pos.rl, base.vb, displ.bb, [field.mv]	–	–	–	–
E7	BBCCI	Branch on bit clear and clear interlocked	pos.rl, base.vb, displ.bb, [field.mv]	–	–	–	–
E3	BBCS	Branch on bit clear and set	pos.rl, base.vb, displ.bb, [field.mv]	–	–	–	–
E0	BBS	Branch on bit set	pos.rl, base.vb, displ.bb, [field.rv]	–	–	–	–
E4	BBSC	Branch on bit set and clear	pos.rl, base.vb, displ.bb, [field.mv]	–	–	–	–
E2	BBSS	Branch on bit set and set	pos.rl, base.vb, displ.bb, [field.mv]	–	–	–	–
E6	BBSSI	Branch on bit set and set interlocked	pos.rl, base.vb, displ.bb, [field.mv]	–	–	–	–
1E	BCC	Branch on carry clear	displ.bb	–	–	–	–
1F	BCS	Branch on carry set	displ.bb	–	–	–	–
13	BEQL	Branch on equal	displ.bb	–	–	–	–
13	BEQLU	Branch on equal unsigned	displ.bb	–	–	–	–
18	BGEQ	Branch on greater or equal	displ.bb	–	–	–	–
1E	BGEQU	Branch on greater or equal unsigned	displ.bb	–	–	–	–
14	BGTR	Branch on greater	displ.bb	–	–	–	–
1A	BGTRU	Branch on greater unsigned	displ.bb	–	–	–	–

Copyright © Digital Equipment Corporation. All rights reserved.

OP	MNEMONIC	DESCRIPTION	ARGUMENTS	COND. CODES N	Z	V	C
8A	BICB2	Bit clear byte 2-operand	mask.rb, dst.mb	•	•	0	–
8B	BICB3	Bit clear byte 3-operand	mask.rb,src.rb, dst.wb	•	•	0	–
CA	BICL2	Bit clear long 2-operand	mask.rl, dst.ml	•	•	0	–
CB	BICL3	Bit clear long 3-operand	mask.rl, src.rl, dst.wl	•	•	0	–
B9	BICPSW	Bit clear processor status word	mask.rw	•	•	•	•
AA	BICW2	Bit clear word 2-operand	mask.rw,dst.mw	•	•	0	–
AB	BICW3	Bit clear word 3-operand	mask.rw, src.rw, dst.ww	•	•	0	–
88	BISB2	Bit set byte 2-operand	mask.rb, dst.mb	•	•	0	–
89	BISB3	Bit set byte 3-operand	mask.rb, src.rb, dst.wb	•	•	0	–
C8	BISL2	Bit set long 2-operand	mask.rl, dst.ml	•	•	0	–
C9	BISL3	Bit set long 3-operand	mask.rl, src.rl, dst.wl	•	•	0	–
B8	BISPSW	Bit set processor status word	mask.rw	•	•	•	•
A8	BISW2	Bit set word 2-operand	mask.rw,dst.mw	•	•	0	–
A9	BISW3	Bit set word 3-operand	mask.rw, src.rw, dst.ww	•	•	0	–
93	BITB	Bit test byte	mask.rb, src.rb	•	•	0	–
D3	BITL	Bit test long	mask.rl, src.rl	•	•	0	–
B3	BITW	Bit test word	mask.rw, src.rw	•	•	0	–
E9	BLBC	Branch on low bit clear	src.rl, displ.bb	–	–	–	–
E8	BLBS	Branch on low bit set	src.rl, displ.bb	–	–	–	–
15	BLEQ	Branch on less or equal	displ.bb	–	–	–	–
1B	BLEQU	Branch on less or equal unsigned	displ.bb	–	–	–	–
19	BLSS	Branch on less	displ.bb	–	–	–	–
1F	BLSSU	Branch on less unsigned	displ.bb	–	–	–	–
12	BNEQ	Branch on not equal	displ.bb	–	–	–	–
12	BNEQU	Branch on not equal unsigned	displ.bb	–	–	–	–
03	BPT	Break point fault	[−(KSP).w*]	0	0	0	0
11	BRB	Branch with byte displacement	displ.bb	–	–	–	–
31	BRW	Branch with word displacement	displ.bw	–	–	–	–
10	BSBB	Branch to subroutine with byte displacement	displ.bb, [−(SP).wl]	–	–	–	–
30	BSBW	Branch to subroutine with word displacement	displ.bw, [−(SP).wl]	–	–	–	–
1C	BVC	Branch on overflow clear	displ.bb	–	–	–	–
1D	BVS	Branch on overflow set	displ.bb	–	–	–	–
FA	CALLG	Call with general argument list	arglist.ab,dst.ab, [−(SP).w*]	0	0	0	0
FB	CALLS	Call with argument list on stack	numarg.rl,dst.ab, [−(SP).w*]	0	0	0	0
8F	CASEB	Case byte	selector.rb, base.rb, limit.rb, displ.bw-list	•	•	0	•
CF	CASEL	Case long	selector.rl, base.rl, limit.rl, displ.bw-list	•	•	0	•
AF	CASEW	Case word	selector.rw, base.rw, limit.rw, displ.bw-list	•	•	0	•
BD	CHME	Change mode to executive	param.rw, [−(ySP).w*] $y = $ MINU(E, PSL$_{current-mode}$)	0	0	0	0
BC	CHMK	Change mode to kernal	param.rw, [−(KSP).w*]	0	0	0	0
BE	CHMS	Change mode to supervisor	param.rw, [−(ySP).w*] $y = $ MINU(S, PSL$_{current-mode}$)	0	0	0	0
BF	CHMU	Change mode to user	param.rw, [−(SP).w*]	0	0	0	0
94	CLRB	Clear byte	dst.wb	0	1	0	–
7C	CLRD	Clear double	dst.wd	0	1	0	–

OP	MNEMONIC	DESCRIPTION	ARGUMENTS	COND. CODES N	Z	V	C
D4	CLRF	Clear floating	dst.wf	0	1	0	-
D4	CLRL	Clear long	dst.wl	0	1	0	-
7C	CLRQ	Clear quad	dst.wq	0	1	0	-
B4	CLRW	Clear word	dst.ww	0	1	0	-
91	CMPB	Compare byte	src1.rb, src2.rb	•	•	0	•
29	CMPC3	Compare character 3-operand	len.rw, src1addr.ab, src2addr.ab, [R0-3.wl]	•	•	0	•
2D	CMPC5	Compare character 5-operand	src1len.rw, src1addr.ab, fill.rb, src2len.rw, src2addr.ab, [R0-3.wl]	•	•	0	•
71	CMPD	Compare double	src1.rd, src2.rd	•	•	0	0
51	CMPF	Compare floating	src1.rf, src2.rf	•	•	0	0
D1	CMPL	Compare long	src1.rl, src2.rl	•	•	0	•
35	CMPP3	Compare packed 3-operand	len.rw, src1addr.ab, src2addr.ab, [R0-3.wl]	•	•	0	0
37	CMPP4	Compare packed 4-operand	src1len.rw, src1addr.ab, src2len.rw, src2addr.ab, [R0-3.wl]	•	•	0	0
EC	CMPV	Compare field	pos.rl, size.rb, base.vb, [field.rv], src.rl	•	•	0	•
B1	CMPW	Compare word	src1.rw, src2.rw	•	•	0	•
ED	CMPZV	Compare zero-extended field	pos.rl, size.rb, base.vb, [field.rv], src.rl	•	•	0	•
0B	CRC	Calculate cyclic redundancy check	tbl.ab, initialcrc.rl, strlen.rw, stream.ab, [R0-5.wl], dst.wl	•	•	0	-
6C	CVTBD	Convert byte to double	src.rb, dst.wd	•	•	•	0
4C	CVTBF	Convert byte to floating	src.rb, dst.wf	•	•	•	0
98	CVTBL	Convert byte to long	src.rb, dst.wl	•	•	•	0
99	CVTBW	Convert byte to word	src.rb, dst.ww	•	•	•	0
68	CVTDB	Convert double to byte	src.rd, dst.wb	•	•	•	0
76	CVTDF	Convert double to floating	src.rd, dst.wf	•	•	•	0
6A	CVTDL	Convert double to long	src.rd, dst.wl	•	•	•	0
69	CVTDW	Convert double to word	src.rd, dst.ww	•	•	•	0
48	CVTFB	Convert floating to byte	src.rf, dst.wb	•	•	•	0
56	CVTFD	Convert floating to double	src.rf, dst.wd	•	•	•	0
4A	CVTFL	Convert floating to long	src.rf, dst.wl	•	•	•	0
49	CVTFW	Convert floating to word	src.rf, dst.ww	•	•	•	0
F6	CVTLB	Convert long to byte	src.rl, dst.wb	•	•	•	0
6E	CVTLD	Convert long to double	src.rl, dst.wd	•	•	•	0
4E	CVTLF	Convert long to floating	src.rl, dst.wf	•	•	•	0
F9	CVTLP	Convert long to packed	src.rl, dstlen.rw, dstaddr.ab, [R0-3.wl]	•	•	•	0
F7	CVTLW	Convert long to word	src.rl, dst.ww	•	•	•	0
36	CVTPL	Convert packed to long	srclen.rw, srcaddr.ab, [R0-3.wl], dst.wl	•	•	•	0
08	CVTPS	Convert packed to leading separate	srclen.rw, srcaddr.ab, dstlen.rw, dstaddr.ab, [R0-3.wl]	•	•	•	0
24	CVTPT	Convert packed to trailing	srclen.rw, srcaddr.ab, tbladdr.ab, dstlen.rw, dstaddr.ab, [R0-3.wl]	•	•	•	0
6B	CVTRDL	Convert rounded double to long	src.rd, dst.wl	•	•	•	0
4B	CVTRFL	Convert rounded floating to long	src.rf, dst.wl	•	•	•	0
09	CVTSP	Convert leading separate to packed	srclen.rw, srcaddr.ab, dstlen.rw, dstaddr.ab, [R0-3.wl]	•	•	•	0

OP	MNEMONIC	DESCRIPTION	ARGUMENTS	N	Z	V	C
				COND. CODES			
26	CVTTP	Convert trailing to packed	srclen.rw, srcaddr.ab, tbladdr.ab, dstlen.rw, dstaddr.ab, [R0-3.wl]	•	•	•	0
33	CVTWB	Convert word to byte	src.rw, dst.wb	•	•	•	0
6D	CVTWD	Convert word to double	src.rw, dst.wd	•	•	•	0
4D	CVTWF	Convert word to floating	src.rw, dst.wf	•	•	•	0
32	CVTWL	Convert word to long	src.rw, dst.wl	•	•	•	0
97	DECB	Decrement byte	dif.mb	•	•	•	•
D7	DECL	Decrement long	dif.ml	•	•	•	•
B7	DECW	Decrement word	dif.mw	•	•	•	•
86	DIVB2	Divide byte 2-operand	divr.rb, quo.mb	•	•	•	0
87	DIVB3	Divide byte 3-operand	divr.rb, divd.rb, quo.wb	•	•	•	0
66	DIVD2	Divide double 2-operand	divr.rd, quo.md	•	•	•	0
67	DIVD3	Divide double 3-operand	divr.rd, divd.rd, quo.wd	•	•	•	0
46	DIVF2	Divide floating 2-operand	divr.rf, quo.mf	•	•	•	0
47	DIVF3	Divide floating 3-operand	divr.rf, divd.rf, quo.wf	•	•	•	0
C6	DIVL2	Divide long 2-operand	divr.rl, quo.ml	•	•	•	0
C7	DIVL3	Divide long 3-operand	divr.rl, divd.rl, quo.wl	•	•	•	0
27	DIVP	Divide packed	divrlen.rw, divraddr.ab, divdlen.rw, divdaddr.ab, quolen.rw, quoaddr.ab, [R0-5.wl, −16(SP):−1(SP).wb]	•	•	•	0
A6	DIVW2	Divide word 2-operand	divr.rw, quo.mw	•	•	•	0
A7	DIVW3	Divide word 3-operand	divr.rw, divd.rw, quo.ww	•	•	•	0
38	EDITPC	Edit packed to character string	srclen.rw, srcaddr.ab, pattern.ab, dstaddr.ab, [R0-5.wl]	•	•	•	•
7B	EDIV	Extended divide	divr.rl, divd.rq, quo.wl, rem.wl	•	•	•	0
74	EMODD	Extended modulus double	mulr.rd, mulrx.rb, muld.rd, int.wl, fract.wd	•	•	•	0
54	EMODF	Extended modulus floating	mulr.rf, mulrx.rb, muld.rf, int.wl, fract.wf	•	•	•	0
7A	EMUL	Extended multiply	mulr.rl, muld.rl, add.rl, prod.wq	•	•	0	0
EE	EXTV	Extract field	pos.rl, size.rb, base.vb, [field.rv], dst.wl	•	•	0	-
EF	EXTZV	Extract zero-extended field	pos.rl, size.rb, base.vb, [field.rv], dst.wl	•	•	0	-
EB	FFC	Find first clear bit	startpos.rl, size.rb, base.vb, [field.rv], findpos.wl	0	•	0	0
EA	FFS	Find first set bit	startpos.rl, size.rb, base.vb, [field.rv], findpos.wl	0	•	0	0
00	HALT	Halt (Kernel Mode only)	[−(KSP).w*]	•	•	•	•
96	INCB	Increment byte	sum.mb	•	•	•	•
D6	INCL	Increment long	sum.ml	•	•	•	•
B6	INCW	Increment word	sum.mw	•	•	•	•
0A	INDEX	Index calculation	subscript.rl, low.rl, high.rl, size.rl, entry.rl, addr.wl	•	•	0	0
0E	INSQUE	Insert into queue	entry.ab, addr.wl	•	•	0	•
F0	INSV	Insert field	src.rl, pos.rl, size.rb, base.vb, [field.wv]	0	0	0	-
17	JMP	Jump	dst.ab	-	-	-	-
16	JSB	Jump to subroutine	dst.ab, [−(SP)+.wl]	-	-	-	-
06	LDPCTX	Load process context (only legal on interrupt stack)	[PCB.r*, −(KSP).w*]	-	-	-	-

OP	MNEMONIC	DESCRIPTION	ARGUMENTS	N	Z	V	C
			COND. CODES				
3A	LOCC	Locate character	char.rb, len.rw, addr.ab, [R0-1.wl]	0	•	0	0
39	MATCHC	Match characters	len1.rw, addr1.ab, len2.rw, addr2.ab, [R0-3.wl]	0	•	0	0
92	MCOMB	Move complemented byte	src.rb, dst.wb	•	•	0	–
D2	MCOML	Move complemented long	src.rl, dst.wl	•	•	0	–
B2	MCOMW	Move complemented word	src.rw, dst.ww	•	•	0	–
DB	MFPR	Move from processor register (Kernel Mode only)	procreg.rl, dst.wl	•	•	0	–
8E	MNEGB	Move negated byte	src.rb, dst.wb	•	•	•	•
72	MNEGD	Move negated double	src.rd, dst.wd	•	•	0	0
52	MNEGF	Move negated floating	src.rf, dst.wf	•	•	0	0
CE	MNEGL	Move negated long	src.rl, dst.wl	•	•	•	•
AE	MNEGW	Move negated word	src.rw, dst.ww	•	•	•	•
9E	MOVAB	Move address of byte	src.ab, dst.wl	•	•	0	–
7E	MOVAD	Move address of double	src.aq, dst.wl	•	•	0	–
DE	MOVAF	Move address of floating	src.al, dst.wl	•	•	0	–
DE	MOVAL	Move address of long	src.al, dst.wl	•	•	0	–
7E	MOVAQ	Move address of quad	src.aq, dst.wl	•	•	0	–
3E	MOVAW	Move address of word	src.aw, dst.wl	•	•	0	–
90	MOVB	Move byte	src.rb, dst.wb	•	•	0	–
28	MOVC3	Move character 3-operand	len.rw, srcaddr.ab, dstaddr.ab, [R0-5.wl]	0	1	0	0
2C	MOVC5	Move character 5-operand	srclen.rw, srcaddr.ab, fill.rb, dstlen.rw, dstaddr.ab, [R0-5.wl]	•	•	0	•
70	MOVD	Move double	src.rd, dst.wd	•	•	0	–
50	MOVF	Move floating	src.rf, dst.wf	•	•	0	–
D0	MOVL	Move long	src.rl, dst.wl	•	•	0	–
34	MOVP	Move packed	len.rw, srcaddr.ab, dstaddr.ab, [R0-3.wl]	•	•	0	–
DC	MOVPSL	Move processor status longword	dst.wl	–	–	–	–
7D	MOVQ	Move quad	src.rq, dst.wq	•	•	0	–
2E	MOVTC	Move translated characters	srclen.rw, srcaddr.ab, fill.rb, tbladdr.ab, dstlen.rw, dstaddr.ab, [R0-5.wl]	•	•	0	•
2F	MOVTUC	Move translated until character	srclen.rw, srcaddr.ab, escape.rb, tbladdr.ab, dstlen.rw, dstaddr.ab, [R0-5.wl]	•	•	•	•
B0	MOVW	Move word	src.rw, dst.ww	•	•	0	–
9A	MOVZBL	Move zero-extended byte to long	src.rb, dst.wl	0	•	0	–
9B	MOVZBW	Move zero-extended byte to word	src.rb, dst.ww	0	•	0	–
3C	MOVZWL	Move zero-extended word to long	src.rw, dst.wl	0	•	0	–
DA	MTPR	Move to processor register (Kernel Mode only)	src.rl, procreg.rl	•	•	0	–
84	MULB2	Multiply byte 2-operand	mulr.rb, prod.mb	•	•	•	0
85	MULB3	Multiply byte 3-operand	mulr.rb, muld.rb, prod.wb	•	•	•	0
64	MULD2	Multiply double 2-operand	mulr.rd, prod.md	•	•	•	0
65	MULD3	Multiply double 3-operand	mulr.rd, muld.rd, prod.wd	•	•	•	0
44	MULF2	Multiply floating 2-operand	mulr.rf, prod.mf	•	•	•	0
45	MULF3	Multiply floating 3-operand	mulr.rf, muld.rf, prod.wf	•	•	•	0
C4	MULL2	Multiply long 2-operand	mulr.rl, prod.ml	•	•	•	0

OP	MNEMONIC	DESCRIPTION	ARGUMENTS	N	Z	V	C
			COND. CODES				
C5	MULL3	Multiply long 3-operand	mulr.rl, muld.rl, prod.wl	•	•	•	0
25	MULP	Multiply packed	mulrlen.rw, mulradr.ab, muldlen.rw, muldadr.ab, prodlen.rw, prodadr.ab, [R0-5.wl]	•	•	•	0
A4	MULW2	Multiply word 2-operand	mulr.rw, prod.mw	•	•	•	0
A5	MULW3	Multiply word 3-operand	mulr.rw, muld.rw, prod.ww	•	•	•	0
01	NOP	No operation		-	-	-	-
75	POLYD	Evaluate polynomial double	arg.rd, degree.rw, tbladdr.ab, [R0-5.wl]	•	•	•	0
55	POLYF	Evaluate polynomial floating	arg.rf, degree.rw, tbladdr.ab, [R0-3.wl]	•	•	•	0
BA	POPR	Pop registers	mask.rw, [(SP)+.r*]	-	-	-	-
0C	PROBER	Probe read access	mode.rb, len.rw, base.ab	0	•	0	-
0D	PROBEW	Probe write access	mode.rb, len.rw, base.ab	0	•	0	-
9F	PUSHAB	Push address of byte	src.ab, [-(SP).wl]	•	•	0	
7F	PUSHAD	Push address of double	src.aq, [-(SP).wl]	•	•	0	
DF	PUSHAF	Push address of floating	src.al, [-(SP).wl]	•	•	0	
DF	PUSHAL	Push address of long	src.al, [-(SP).wl]	•	•	0	
7F	PUSHAQ	Push address of quad	src.aq, [-(SP).wl]	•	•	0	
3F	PUSHAW	Push address of word	src.aw, [-(SP).wl]	•	•	0	
DD	PUSHL	Push long	src.rl, [-(SP).wl]	•	•	0	
BB	PUSHR	Push registers	mask.rw, [-(SP).w*]	-	-	-	-
02	REI	Return from exception or interrupt	[(SP)+.r*]	•	•	•	•
0F	REMQUE	Remove from queue	entry.ab, addr.wl	•	•	•	•
04	RET	Return from procedure	[(SP)+.r*]	•	•	•	•
9C	ROTL	Rotate long	count.rb, src.rl, dst.wl	•	•	0	
05	RSB	Return from subroutine	[(SP)+.rl]	-	-	-	-
D9	SBWC	Subtract with carry	sub.rl, dif.ml	•	•	•	•
2A	SCANC	Scan for character	len.rw, addr.ab, tbladdr.ab, mask.rb, [R0-3.wl]	0	•	0	0
3B	SKPC	Skip character	char.rb, len.rw, addr.ab, [R0-1.wl]	0	•	0	0
F4	SOBGEQ	Subtract one and branch on greater or equal	index.ml, displ.bb	•	•	•	-
F5	SOBGTR	Subtract one and branch on greater	index.ml, displ.bb	•	•	•	-
2B	SPANC	Span characters	len.rw, addr.ab, tbladdr.ab, mask.rb, [R0-3.wl]	0	•	0	0
82	SUBB2	Subtract byte 2-operand	sub.rb, dif.mb	•	•	•	•
83	SUBB3	Subtract byte 3-operand	sub.rb, min.rb, dif.wb	•	•	•	0
62	SUBD2	Subtract double 2-operand	sub.rd, dif.md	•	•	•	0
63	SUBD3	Subtract double 3-operand	sub.rd, min.rd, dif.wd	•	•	•	0
42	SUBF2	Subtract floating 2-operand	sub.rf, dif.mf	•	•	•	0
43	SUBF3	Subtract floating 3-operand	sub.rf, min.rf, dif.wf	•	•	•	0
C2	SUBL2	Subtract long 2-operand	sub.rl, dif.ml	•	•	•	•
C3	SUBL3	Subtract long 3-operand	sub.rl, min.rl, dif.wl	•	•	V	0
22	SUBP4	Subtract packed 4-operand	sublen.rw, subaddr.ab, diflen.rw, difaddr.ab, [R0-3.wl]	•	•	•	0
23	SUBP6	Subtract packed 6 operand	sublen.rw, subaddr.ab, minlen.rw, minaddr.ab, diflen.rw, difaddr.ab, [R0-5.wl]	•	•	•	0
A2	SUBW2	Subtract word 2-operand	sub.rw, dif.mw	•	•	•	•

OP	MNEMONIC	DESCRIPTION	ARGUMENTS	COND. CODES			
				N	Z	V	C
A3	SUBW3	Subtract word 3-operand	sub.rw, min.rw, dif.ww	•	•	•	0
07	SVPCTX	Save process context (Kernel Mode only)	[(SP)+.r*, −(KSP).w*]	−	−	−	−
95	TSTB	Test byte	src.rb	•	•	0	0
73	TSTD	Test double	src.rd	•	•	0	0
53	TSTF	Test floating	src.rf	•	•	0	0
D5	TSTL	Test long	src.rl	•	•	0	0
B5	TSTW	Test word	src.rw	•	•	0	0
FC	XFC	Extended function call	user defined operands	0	0	0	0
8C	XORB2	Exclusive OR byte 2-operand	mask.rb, dst.mb	•	•	0	−
8D	XORB3	Exclusive OR byte 3-operand	mask.rb, src.rb, dst.wb	•	•	0	−
CC	XORL2	Exclusive OR long 2-operand	mask.rl, dst.ml	•	•	0	−
CD	XORL3	Exclusive OR long 3-operand	mask.rl, src.rl, dst.wl	•	•	0	−
AC	XORW2	Exclusive OR word 2-operand	mask.rw, dst.mw	•	•	0	−
AD	XORW3	Exclusive OR word 3-operand	mask.rw, src.rw, dst.ww	•	•	0	−

CALL INSTRUCTION ARGUMENT LIST FORMAT

The format of an argument list is a sequence of longwords:

```
+-----------------------+--------+
|           0           |    n   |  :ARGLIST
+-----------------------+--------+
|         ARG 1                  |
|         ARG 2                  |
|           •                    |
|           •                    |
|           •                    |
|         ARG n                  |
+--------------------------------+
```

The argument count n is an unsigned byte contained in the first byte of the list. The high order 24 bits of the first longword are reserved for future use and must be zero. To access the argument count, the called procedure must ignore the reserved bits and pick up the count with the equivalent of a MOVZBL instruction.

INSTRUCTIONS

NUMERIC ORDER

00	HALT	40	ADDF2	80	ADDB2	C0	ADDL2
01	NOP	41	ADDF3	81	ADDB3	C1	ADDL3
02	REI	42	SUBF2	82	SUBB2	C2	SUBL2
03	BPT	43	SUBF3	83	SUBB3	C3	SUBL3
04	RET	44	MULF2	84	MULB2	C4	MULL2
05	RSB	45	MULF3	85	MULB3	C5	MULL3
06	LDPCTX	46	DIVF2	86	DIVB2	C6	DIVL2
07	SVPCTX	47	DIVF3	87	DIVB3	C7	DIVL3
08	CVTPS	48	CVTFB	88	BISB2	C8	BISL2
09	CVTSP	49	CVTFW	89	BISB3	C9	BISL3
0A	INDEX	4A	CVTFL	8A	BICB2	CA	BICL2
0B	CRC	4B	CVTRFL	8B	BICB3	CB	BICL3
0C	PROBER	4C	CVTBF	8C	XORB2	CC	XORL2
0D	PROBEW	4D	CVTWF	8D	XORB3	CD	XORL3
0E	INSQUE	4E	CVTLF	8E	MNEGB	CE	MNEGL
0F	REMQUE	4F	ACBF	8F	CASEB	CF	CASEL
10	BSBB	50	MOVF	90	MOVB	D0	MOVL
11	BRB	51	CMPF	91	CMPB	D1	CMPL
12	BNEQ, BNEQU	52	MNEGF	92	MCOMB	D2	MCOML
13	BEQL, BEQLU	53	TSTF	93	BITB	D3	BITL
14	BGTR	54	EMODF	94	CLRB	D4	CLRF, CLRL
15	BLEQ	55	POLYF	95	TSTB	D5	TSTL
16	JSB	56	CVTFD	96	INCB	D6	INCL
17	JMP	57	reserved	97	DECB	D7	DECL
18	BGEQ	58	ADAWI	98	CVTBL	D8	ADWC
19	BLSS	59	reserved	99	CVTBW	D9	SBWC
1A	BGTRU	5A	reserved	9A	MOVZBL	DA	MTPR
1B	BLEQU	5B	reserved	9B	MOVZBW	DB	MFPR
1C	BVC	5C	reserved	9C	ROTL	DC	MOVPSL
1D	BVS	5D	reserved	9D	ACBB	DD	PUSHL
1E	BCC, BGEQU	5E	reserved	9E	MOVAB	DE	MOVAF, MOVAL
1F	BCS, BLSSU	5F	reserved	9F	PUSHAB	DF	PUSHAF, PUSHA
20	ADDP4	60	ADDD2	A0	ADDW2	E0	BBS
21	ADDP6	61	ADDD3	A1	ADDW3	E1	BBC
22	SUBP4	62	SUBD2	A2	SUBW2	E2	BBSS
23	SUBP6	63	SUBD3	A3	SUBW3	E3	BBCS
24	CVTPT	64	MULD2	A4	MULW2	E4	BBSC
25	MULP	65	MULD3	A5	MULW3	E5	BBCC
26	CVTTP	66	DIVD2	A6	DIVW2	E6	BBSSI
27	DIVP	67	DIVD3	A7	DIVW3	E7	BBCCI
28	MOVC3	68	CVTDB	A8	BISW2	E8	BLBS
29	CMPC3	69	CVTDW	A9	BISW3	E9	BLBC
2A	SCANC	6A	CVTDL	AA	BICW2	EA	FFS
2B	SPANC	6B	CVTRDL	AB	BICW3	EB	FFC
2C	MOVC5	6C	CVTBD	AC	XORW2	EC	CMPV
2D	CMPC5	6D	CVTWD	AD	XORW3	ED	CMPZV
2E	MOVTC	6E	CVTLD	AE	MNEGW	EE	EXTV
2F	MOVTUC	6F	ACBD	AF	CASEW	EF	EXTZV
30	BSBW	70	MOVD	B0	MOVW	F0	INSV
31	BRW	71	CMPD	B1	CMPW	F1	ACBL
32	CVTWL	72	MNEGD	B2	MCOMW	F2	AOBLSS
33	CVTWB	73	TSTD	B3	BITW	F3	AOBLEQ
34	MOVP	74	EMODD	B4	CLRW	F4	SOBGEQ
35	CMPP3	75	POLYD	B5	TSTW	F5	SOBGTR
36	CVTPL	76	CVTDF	B6	INCW	F6	CVTLB
37	CMPP4	77	reserved	B7	DECW	F7	CVTLW
38	EDITPC	78	ASHL	B8	BISPSW	F8	ASHP
39	MATCHC	79	ASHQ	B9	BICPSW	F9	CVTLP
3A	LOCC	7A	EMUL	BA	POPR	FA	CALLG
3B	SKPC	7B	EDIV	BB	PUSHR	FB	CALLS
3C	MOVZWL	7C	CLRD, CLRQ	BC	CHMK	FC	XFC
3D	ACBW	7D	MOVQ	BD	CHME	FD	reserved
3E	MOVAW	7E	MOVAD, MOVAQ	BE	CHMS	FE	reserved
3F	PUSHAW	7F	PUSHAD, PUSHAQ	BF	CHMU	FF	reserved

GENERAL REGISTER ADDRESSING MODES:

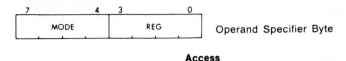

Hex	Dec	Mode	Assembler	r	m	w	a	v	PC	SP	Indexable?
0-3	0-3	literal	S^literal	y	f	f	f	f	—	—	f
4	4	indexed	i[Rx]	y	y	y	y	y	f	y	f
5	5	register	Rn	y	y	y	f	y	u	ug	f
6	6	register deferred	(Rn)	y	y	y	y	y	u	y	y
7	7	autodecrement	−(Rn)	y	y	y	y	y	u	y	ux
8	8	autoincrement	(Rn)+	y	y	y	y	y	p	y	ux
9	9	autoincr deferred	@(R)+	y	y	y	y	y	p	y	ux
A	10	byte displacement	B^D(Rn)	y	y	y	y	y	p	y	y
B	11	byte displ deferred	@B^D(Rn)	y	y	y	y	y	p	y	y
C	12	word displacement	W^D(Rn)	y	y	y	y	y	p	y	y
D	13	word displ deferred	@W^D(Rn)	y	y	y	y	y	p	y	y
E	14	longword displacement	L^D(Rn)	y	y	y	y	y	p	y	y
F	15	longword displ deferred	@L^D(Rn)	y	y	y	y	y	p	y	y

PROGRAM COUNTER ADDRESSING (reg = 15)

Hex	Dec	Mode	Assembler	r	m	w	a	v	PC	SP	Indexable?
8	8	immediate	I^constant	y	u	u	y	y	—	—	y
9	9	absolute	@address	y	y	y	y	y	—	—	y
A	10	byte relative	B^address	y	y	y	y	y	—	—	y
B	11	byte rel deferred	@B^address	y	y	y	y	y	—	—	y
C	12	word relative	W^address	y	y	y	y	y	—	—	y
D	13	word rel deferred	@W^address	y	y	y	y	y	—	—	y
E	14	longword relative	L^address	y	y	y	y	y	—	—	y
F	15	longword rel deferred	@L^address	y	y	y	y	y	—	—	y

ADDRESSING LEGEND

Access	Syntax	Result
r = read	i = any indexable addr mode	y = yes, always valid addr mode
m = modify	D = displacement	f = reserved addr mode fault
w = write	Rn = general register, n = 0-15	— = logically impossible
a = address	Rx = general register, n = 0-14	P = Program Counter addressing
v = field		u = unpredictable
		uq = unpredictable for quad and double (and field if position + size > 32)
		ux = unpredictable for index register same as base register

OPERAND SPECIFIER NOTATION LEGEND

The standard notation for operand specifiers is:

    <name>.<access type><data type>

where:

1. Name is a suggestive name for the operand in the context of the instruction. It is the capitalized name of a register or block for implied operands.

2. Access type is a letter denoting the operand specifier access type.

      a— Calculate the effective address of the specified operand. Address is returned in a pointer which is the actual instruction operand. Context of address calculation is given by data type given by <data type>.

      b— No operand reference. Operand specifier is branch displacement. Size of branch displacement is given by <data type>.

      m— operand is modified (both read and written)

      r— operand is read only

      v— if not "Rn", same as a. If "RN", R[n + 1]'R[n].

      w— operand is written only

3. Data type is a letter denoting the data type of the operand

      b— byte

      d— double

      f— floating

      l— longword

      q— quadword

      v— field (used only on implied operands)

      w— word

      x— first data type specified by instruction

      y— second data type specified by instruction

      *— multiple longwords (used only on implied operands)

4. Implied operands, that is, locations that are accessed by the instruction, but not specified in an operand, are denoted in enclosing brackets, [ ].

CONDITION CODES LEGEND

      * = conditionally cleared/set
      — = not affected
      0 = cleared
      1 = set

ASSEMBLER NOTATION FOR ADDRESSING MODES

S^#5	forced short literal
#5	optimized short literal
R10	register
(R10)	register deferred
−(R10)	autodecrement
(R10)+	autoincrement
#START	immediate
I^#1	forced immediate
@(R10)+	autoincrement deferred
@#START	absolute
1(R10)	optimized byte displacement
0(R10)	optimized register deferred
@1(R10)	optimized byte displacement deferred
@(R10)	implied byte displacement deferred
START	optimized pc relative
@START	optimized pc relative deferred
1234(R10)	optimized word displacement
@1234(R10)	optimized word displacement deferred
12345678(R10)	longword displacement
@12345678(R10)	longword displacement deferred
B^12(R10)	forced byte displacement
B^START	forced byte pc relative
@B^12(R10)	forced byte displacement deferred
@B^START	forced byte pc relative deferred
W^12(R10)	forced word displacement
W^START	forced word pc relative
@W^12(R10)	forced word displacement deferred
@W^START	forced word pc relative deferred
L^12(R10)	forced longword displacement
L^START	forced longword pc relative
@L^12(R10)	forced longword displacement deferred
@L^START	forced longword pc relative deferred
(R10)[R11]	register deferred indexed
−(R10)[R11]	autodecrement indexed
(R10)+[R11]	autoincrement indexed
@(R10)+[R11]	autoincrement deferred indexed
@#START[R11]	absolute indexed
1(R10)[R11]	optimized byte displacement indexed
0(R10)[R11]	optimized register deferred indexed
@1(R10)[R11]	optimized byte displacement deferred indexed
@(R10)[R11]	implied byte displacement deferred indexed
1234(R10)[R11]	optimized word displacement indexed
@1234(R10)[R11]	optimized word displacement deferred indexed
12345678(R10)[R11]	longword displacement indexed
@12345678(R10)[R11]	longword displacement deferred indexed
START[R11]	optimized pc relative indexed
@START[R11]	optimized pc relative deferred indexed
B^12(R10)[R11]	forced byte displacement indexed
B^START[R11]	forced byte pc relative indexed
@B^12(R10)[R11]	forced byte displacement deferred indexed
@B^START[R11]	forced byte pc relative deferred indexed
W^12(R10)[R11]	forced word displacement indexed
W^START[R11]	forced word pc relative indexed
@W^12(R10)[R11]	forced word displacement deferred indexed
@W^START[R11]	forced word pc relative deferred indexed
L^12(R10)[R11]	forced longword displacement indexed
L^START[R11]	forced longword pc relative indexed
@L^12(R10)[R11]	forced longword displacement deferred indexed
@L^START[R11]	forced longword pc relative deferred

PROCESSOR STATUS LONGWORD

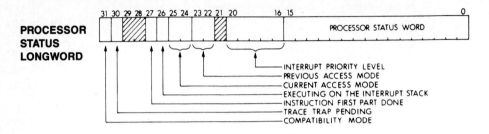

- INTERRUPT PRIORITY LEVEL
- PREVIOUS ACCESS MODE
- CURRENT ACCESS MODE
- EXECUTING ON THE INTERRUPT STACK
- INSTRUCTION FIRST PART DONE
- TRACE TRAP PENDING
- COMPATIBILITY MODE

PROCESSOR STATUS WORD

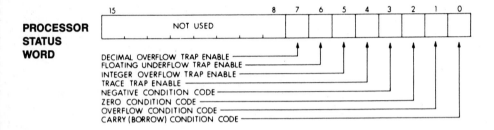

- DECIMAL OVERFLOW TRAP ENABLE
- FLOATING UNDERFLOW TRAP ENABLE
- INTEGER OVERFLOW TRAP ENABLE
- TRACE TRAP ENABLE
- NEGATIVE CONDITION CODE
- ZERO CONDITION CODE
- OVERFLOW CONDITION CODE
- CARRY (BORROW) CONDITION CODE

POWERS OF 2		POWERS OF 16	
2^n	n	16^n	n
256	8	1	0
512	9	16	1
1024	10	256	2
2048	11	4096	3
4096	12	65536	4
8192	13	1048576	5
16384	14	16777216	6
32768	15	268435456	7
65536	16	4294967296	8
131072	17	68719476736	9
262144	18	1099511627776	10
524288	19	17592186044416	11
1048576	20	281474976710656	12
2097152	21	4503599627370496	13
4194304	22	72057594037927936	14
8388608	23	1152921504606846976	15
16777216	24		

DATA TYPES

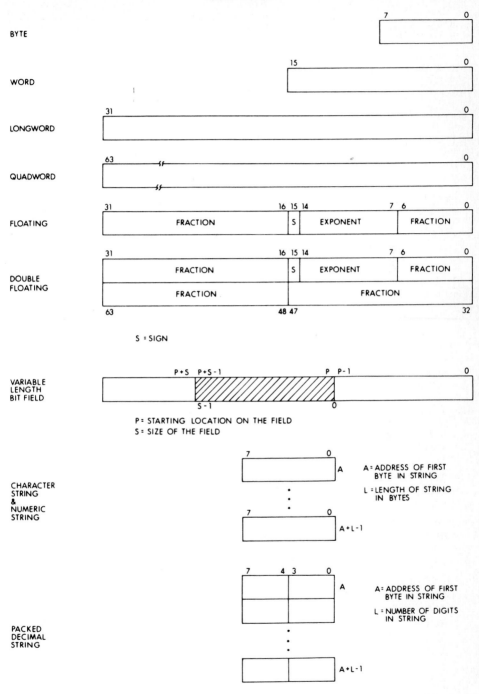

Index